History

for the IB Diploma

Communism in Crisis 1976–89

Author and series editor: Allan Todd

Cambridge University Press's mission is to advance learning, knowledge and research worldwide.

Our IB Diploma resources aim to:
- encourage learners to explore concepts, ideas and topics that have local and global significance
- help students develop a positive attitude to learning in preparation for higher education
- assist students in approaching complex questions, applying critical-thinking skills and forming reasoned answers.

CAMBRIDGE UNIVERSITY PRESS

CAMBRIDGE
UNIVERSITY PRESS

University Printing House, Cambridge CB2 8BS, United Kingdom

Cambridge University Press is part of the University of Cambridge.

It furthers the University's mission by disseminating knowledge in the pursuit of education, learning and research at the highest international levels of excellence.

www.cambridge.org
Information on this title: www.cambridge.org/9781107649279

© Cambridge University Press 2012

This publication is in copyright. Subject to statutory exception and to the provisions of relevant collective licensing agreements, no reproduction of any part may take place without the written permission of Cambridge University Press.

First published 2012
Reprinted 2014

Printed in the United Kingdom by Cambrian Printers Ltd

A catalogue record for this publication is available from the British Library

ISBN 978-1-107-64927-9 Paperback

Cambridge University Press has no responsibility for the persistence or accuracy of URLs for external or third-party internet websites referred to in this publication, and does not guarantee that any content on such websites is, or will remain, accurate or appropriate.

This material has been developed independently by the publisher and the content is in no way connected with nor endorsed by the International Baccalaureate Organization.

Dedication
For our daughters,
Megan and Vanessa

Contents

1 Introduction	**5**
2 The Soviet economy 1976–85	**18**
• How did Brezhnev's early rule contribute to the crisis after 1976?	20
• What were the main features of the Soviet economy under Brezhnev from 1976 to 1982?	27
• What economic reforms were attempted in the period 1982–85?	33
• What impact did the Cold War have on the Soviet economy?	37
3 Political developments in the USSR 1976–85	**42**
• How did Brezhnev's early consolidation of power contribute to the political crisis after 1976?	44
• What were the main signs of political stagnation between 1976 and 1982?	48
• How did Brezhnev's foreign policy contribute to the crisis of Soviet communism?	54
• How did Andropov and Chernenko deal with political developments between 1982 and 1985?	62
4 The Soviet economy under Gorbachev	**67**
• What was 'Gorbachevism' and what were Gorbachev's early actions?	69
• What was *perestroika* and what were its main policies between 1986 and 1989?	76
• What problems did Gorbachev's economic reforms encounter in 1990–91?	82
5 Political developments in the USSR under Gorbachev	**90**
• What were Gorbachev's early political aims?	92
• What were Gorbachev's main political reforms between 1986 and 1990?	97
• Why did the Soviet Union collapse in 1991?	108
6 Gorbachev, the Cold War and Eastern Europe	**114**
• What were Gorbachev's foreign policy aims?	116
• What were the main developments in Eastern Europe during the 1980s?	122
• What were the main steps in Czechoslovakia's 'Velvet Revolution'?	131
• What were the results of the changes in Eastern Europe?	138
7 China and the struggle for power after 1976	**143**
• What was the significance of events before 1971?	144
• Why was there another power struggle after the Cultural Revolution?	151
• What were the main stages of the power struggle between 1976 and 1981?	155

8 The Chinese economy under Deng Xiaoping 163
- What economic policies were followed by Hua in the period from 1976 to 1978? 165
- What were the main features of Deng's 'Revolution' between 1979 and 1989? 169
- How successful have Deng's economic reforms been? 177

9 Political developments in China under Deng 186
- What was Deng's political approach in the period from 1976 to 1979? 188
- Why did political unrest re-emerge in the period from 1980 from 1988? 192
- What led to the Tiananmen Square Massacre of June 1989? 199

10 Conclusion: Communism – from crisis to collapse 210
- What caused the collapse of communism? 210
- The end of history? 211
- The idea of communism 213

11 Exam practice 214
- Paper 1 exam practice 214
- Paper 2 exam practice 232

Further information 236
Index 237
Acknowledgements 240

1 Introduction

This book is designed to prepare students for the Paper 1 topic *Communism in Crisis 1976–89* (Prescribed Subject 3) in the IB History examination. It examines the major internal and external economic, political and social challenges facing the main communist states in the period from 1976 to 1989. The book also looks at the way the communist regimes responded to the various challenges. In the case of the Soviet Union, the government's unwillingness or inability to respond, and its slowness to make reforms, led to the collapse of the Soviet Union and the East European satellite states. In China, on the other hand, the regime used a combination of economic reform and political repression to contain the challenges. This strategy has enabled the Chinese Communist Party to remain in power.

Events that occurred after 1989 are briefly covered, in order to complete the overall 'story' and provide additional context. However, students should note that these events are, strictly speaking, outside the focus of this option, which is 1976–89. Thus, detailed knowledge of events before 1976, and after 1989, is not required for this paper.

People standing on top of the Berlin Wall, in front of the Brandenburg Gate, on 10 November 1989

Communism in Crisis

An unknown Democracy Movement protester, known as 'Tankman', confronts People's Liberation Army (PLA) tanks in Tiananmen Square, June 1989; his fate remains uncertain

Themes

To help you prepare for your IB History exams, this book will cover the main themes relating to *Communism in Crisis*, as set out in the IB *History Guide*. It will examine the Union of Soviet Socialist Republics (USSR), Eastern Europe and China in the late 20th century, in terms of:

- the economic problems of the Brezhnev era
- the political and foreign policy problems of the Brezhnev era
- the economic and political developments in the Soviet Union under Gorbachev
- the impact of Gorbachev's policies on Eastern Europe
- the struggle for power in communist China after the death of Mao Zedong
- the Chinese economy under Deng Xiaoping
- political developments in China under Deng Xiaoping.

Each chapter will help you to focus on the main issues and to compare the main developments, problems faced, and the roles of individual leaders and parties in the respective states.

Theory of knowledge

In addition to the broad key themes, the chapters contain Theory of knowledge (ToK) links to get you thinking about aspects of Theory of knowledge that relate to history, which is a Group 3 subject in the IB Diploma. At times, historians writing about communist states and their leaders have been influenced by the highly political issues covered in this book. Thus, questions relating to selection of sources, and to differing interpretations of these sources by historians, have clear links to the IB Theory of knowledge course.

For example, historians have to try to explain certain aspects of policies implemented by leaders. When exploring these leaders' motives, and their success or failure, historians must choose which evidence to use to make their case – and which evidence to leave out. But to what extent do the historians' personal political views influence them when selecting what they consider to be the most relevant sources? Is there such a thing as objective 'historical truth'? Or is there just a range of subjective historical opinions and interpretations about the past, which vary according to the political interests of individual historians?

You are therefore encouraged to read a range of books offering different interpretations of the situations, events, policies and leaders of the states covered by this book, in order to gain a clear understanding of the relevant historiographies (see Further information, page 236). It is also important to be aware that since 1985 – and especially since 1991 – many more archives from the former Soviet Union have been opened up. The records in these archives were not available to historians writing in earlier periods.

IB History and Paper 1 questions

Paper 1 and sources

Unlike Papers 2 and 3, which require you to write essays using just your own knowledge, Paper 1 questions are source-based. Whether you are taking Standard or Higher Level, the sources and the questions, and the markschemes applied by your examiners, are the same.

To answer these questions successfully, you need to be able to combine your own knowledge with the ability to assess and *use* a range of sources in a variety of ways. Each Paper 1 examination question is based on five sources – usually four written and one visual. The visual source might be a photograph, a cartoon, a poster, a painting or a table of statistics.

Captions and attributions

Before looking at the types of sources you will need to assess, it is important to establish one principle from the beginning. This is the issue of *captions and attributions* – the pieces of information about each source provided by the Chief Examiner.

Captions and attributions are there for a very good reason, as they give you vital information about the source. For instance, they tell you who wrote it and when, or what it was intended to do. Chief Examiners spend a lot of time deciding what information to give you about each source, because they know it will help you give a full answer, so they expect you to make good use of it! Yet, every year, candidates throw away easy marks because they do not read – or do not use – this valuable information.

Essentially, you are being asked to approach the various sources in the same way as a historian. This means not just looking carefully at what a source says or shows, but also asking yourself questions about how reliable, useful and/or typical it may be. Many of the answers to these questions will come from the information provided in the captions and attributions.

Types of source

Most of the sources you will have to assess are written ones, and these are sometimes referred to as 'textual sources'. They might be extracts from books, official documents, speeches, newspapers, diaries or letters. Whatever type of source you are reading, the general questions you need to ask are the same.

> As an example of the relative value of a source, if you want to find out about a particular event ask yourself, is a recent history book *more* valuable than a speech?

These questions concern the content (the information the source provides); its origin (who wrote or produced the source, when and why); and its possible limitations and relative value, as a result of the answers to those questions.

Although visual (or non-textual) sources are clearly different from written sources in some respects, the same questions are relevant when looking at them.

Approaching sources as a set

As well as developing the ability to analyse individual sources, it is important to look at the five sources provided *as a set*. This means looking at them *all*, and asking yourself to what extent they agree or disagree with each other.

This ability to look at the five sources together is particularly important when it comes to the last question in the exam paper. This is the question where you need to use the sources *and* your own knowledge to assess the validity of a statement or assertion, or to analyse the significance of a particular factor. Here, you need to build an answer (a 'mini-essay') that combines precise knowledge with specific comments about the sources. Try to avoid falling into the trap of dealing with all the sources first, and then giving some own knowledge (as an afterthought) that is not linked to the sources.

Exam skills

If all this sounds a bit scary, don't worry! Throughout the main chapters of this book, there are activities and questions to help you develop the understanding and exam skills necessary for success. Before attempting the specific exam practice questions at the end of each main chapter, you might find it useful to refer *first* to Chapter 11, the final exam practice chapter. This suggestion is based on the idea that, if you know where you are supposed to be going (in this instance, gaining a good grade), and how to get there, you stand a better chance of reaching your destination!

Questions and markschemes

To ensure that you develop the necessary understanding and skills, each chapter contains questions in the margins. In addition, Chapter 11 is devoted to exam practice. It provides help and advice for all Paper 1 questions and for Paper 2 essay questions, and sets out worked examples for Paper 1 judgement questions and for Paper 2 essays. Worked examples for the remaining three Paper 1-type questions (comprehension, value/limitations and cross-referencing) can be found at the end of Chapters 2 to 9.

In addition, simplified markschemes have been provided, to make it easier for you to understand what examiners are looking for in your answers. The actual IB History markschemes can be found on the IB website.

Finally, you will find activities, along with examiners' tips and comments, to help you focus on the important aspects of the questions. These examples will also help you avoid simple mistakes and oversights that, every year, result in some otherwise good students failing to gain the highest marks.

Background to the period

A brief background history of the states studied in this book will help put in context the developments that took place after 1976. Before the 20th century,

Introduction

Russia and China were ruled by emperors, and both countries were extremely undemocratic. They were essentially underdeveloped agricultural economies, where most of the population were poor peasants. There were frequent famines, in which millions died. Both countries also often found themselves at the mercy of stronger, more advanced states, such as Britain, the US and Japan, and they were frequently exploited by foreign companies. This was especially true of China.

As a result of all these problems, groups of would-be political reformers emerged in both countries during the 19th century. These groups tried to push for reforms to modernise and democratise their societies, but they were usually crushed by their brutal governments. Their lack of success eventually led some reformers to believe that revolution – violent, if necessary – was the only way things could be improved.

However, those wanting reform (or revolution) often found it hard to agree on which strategy offered the best way forward. At first, in both Russia and China, groups wanting radical change adopted liberal and nationalist ideologies. Soon, though, Marxism (see page 15) began to appeal to an increasing number of reformers and revolutionaries.

Some industrialisation had begun to take place in Russia by the end of the 19th century (though many of the factories were owned by British, French and Belgian firms and banks). Perhaps partly because of this growing industrialisation, the first signs of a Marxist revolutionary movement came in Russia, in 1905.

Although there was a nationalist revolution in China in 1911, Marxism did not become significant there until the late 1920s. Both Russia and China eventually had communist governments (based to some extent on Marxism), but it should be remembered that these governments were often opposed to each other.

The USSR

Communism in the 20th century really began with the Bolshevik Revolution in Russia, in November 1917. The Bolsheviks were the more revolutionary element of the Russian Social Democratic Labour Party (RSDLP), a Marxist party founded in 1898. In March 1917, the tsar (emperor of Russia) gave up his throne following a revolution. The Bolsheviks then agitated for another revolution to end the First World War and to begin a socialist transformation of Europe. They came to power in this November 1917 revolution and, in 1918, they changed their name to the Russian Communist Party. Later, they changed their name again, to the Communist Party of the Soviet Union. The Communist Party remained in power until the collapse of the USSR in 1991.

The Bolshevik Revolution was led by **Vladimir Ilyich Lenin**, who continued as leader of the Bolsheviks until he died, on 21 January 1924. After the November Revolution, Lenin became the chairman of the Council of People's Commissars, the equivalent of prime minister. Under his leadership, in 1921, other political parties (including factions within the Russian Communist Party itself) were banned. This was supposed to be a temporary ban, lasting a few years until the economy recovered. But it stayed in place, and **Joseph Stalin** later took advantage of it to increase his power.

After the Bolshevik Revolution, Lenin oversaw the formation of the Russian Socialist Federal Soviet Republic (RSFSR) in 1918. The RSFSR was a loose federation of Russia and the other parts of the old tsarist empire.

Vladimir Ilyich Lenin (1870–1924) Lenin's real name was Vladimir Ilyich Ulyanov. He joined the RSDLP in 1898 and provoked a split in the party – his faction became known as the Bolsheviks. He remained abroad, in exile, until April 1917, when he returned to Russia. Lenin then pushed for the Bolsheviks to overthrow the Provisional Government. He was the leader of the Bolsheviks until his death in 1924, following a series of strokes.

Joseph Stalin (1880–1953) Stalin's real name was Joseph Djugashvili. When the RSDLP split in 1903, he sided with Lenin and the Bolsheviks. In 1922, he took on the post of general-secretary of the Communist Party. Lenin later tried to get Stalin removed. Once he had won the power struggle, Stalin got rid of his main rivals during the 1930s, and ruled the USSR until his death in 1953.

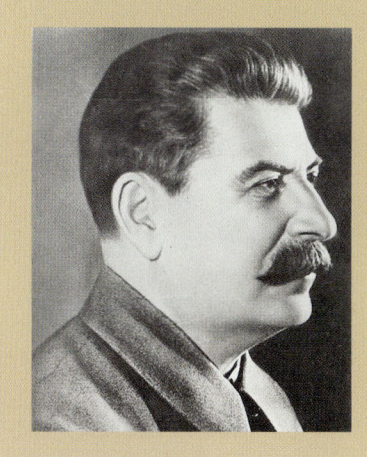

Communism in Crisis

In 1922–23, as commissar for nationalities, Stalin supervised the drafting of a constitution for a new Union of Soviet Socialist Republics (USSR). The new Union contained 15 republics, each governed by a system of *soviets* (or councils), according to the principles of communism. The USSR was therefore a much more centralised, federal state than the RSFSR.

Lenin was very ill at this time, and he was worried that what he saw as 'Great Russian chauvinism' (nationalism) was dominating the other Soviet republics. However, his attempts to reduce central control of the republics failed, and the new constitution came into effect in July 1923. Towards the end of his life, Lenin tried to halt Stalin's growing power within the Communist Party and the government. But when Lenin died, there was a power struggle, which Stalin eventually won. The new constitution of the USSR was formally adopted on 31 January 1924 – ten days after Lenin's death. Thus, it was under Stalin that the Soviet Union became a permanent one-party state.

In the late 1920s and the 1930s, Stalin pushed through rapid industrialisation of the USSR. This industrialisation was implemented through a series of Five-Year Plans, designed to make the USSR a modern industrial nation that would be able to withstand attack from any enemy. In many respects, it was this economic transformation that enabled the Soviet Union to resist – and eventually defeat – Nazi Germany's invasion in 1941.

After the Soviet Union's victory in the Second World War, the leading communists (and many ordinary Russians) who had survived were reluctant to make many changes to the regime. Many of the features of the USSR therefore continued largely unchanged after Stalin's death. This was especially true of the political structure and system, and the economic policy.

This attitude became increasingly entrenched as tensions with the USA and its allies developed following the Second World War. In fact, much of what happened in the Soviet Union and Eastern Europe after 1976 was linked to what one historian called the **'Great Contest'**.

The Cold War

The **Cold War** began towards the end of the Second World War, when the Grand Alliance between Britain, the USSR and the USA (united in the struggle against Nazi Germany) became increasingly strained. Tensions between the allies grew over issues such as the US nuclear weapons monopoly, and how to treat Germany after the war. The term 'Cold War' (originally used in the 14th century, about the conflict between Christian and Islamic states) is used to describe the rivalry between the USA and the USSR in the period 1945–91.

The Cold War lasted almost 50 years, and went through different phases. While historians disagree about the precise dates of some of these phases, they generally agree that a 'First Cold War' began in the period 1946–53, as a result of US foreign policy and the Soviet Union's takeover of Eastern Europe (see page 12). After that, from 1954 to 1968, relations fluctuated between antagonism and improved relations (the latter often known as 'The Thaw'). There was then a phase, from 1969 to 1979, in which the two superpowers reached various agreements, especially over nuclear weapons. This period of improved relations is known as *détente* (a French word meaning 'relaxation') and marked a lessening of tensions and an increase in co-operation.

The Japanese city of Hiroshima after it was devastated on 6 August 1945 by the first atomic bomb to be used in warfare; the bomb, which was dropped by the USA, killed over 75,000 people

'Great Contest' This was the term used by the historian Isaac Deutscher to describe the global conflict between the two rival political systems of capitalism and socialism. According to Deutscher, this contest began as soon as the Bolsheviks came to power after the November 1917 revolution. Several other historians had similar views. Howard Roffman said that the Cold War proceeded 'from the very moment the Bolsheviks triumphed in Russia in 1917' and began to establish the world's first workers' state. The struggle between the US and the Soviet Union therefore began long before the Cold War.

Cold War This phrase refers to hostile relations that do not build up into a 'hot war' (direct military conflict). The term was popularised in 1946–47 by the US journalist Walter Lippmann and the US politician and businessman Bernard Baruch.

Communism in Crisis

SDI ('Star Wars') The Strategic Defense Initiative (SDI), popularly known as 'Star Wars', involved developing satellites that could shoot down all missiles. The US government was aware that the ailing and stagnating Soviet economy could not afford to develop this kind of sophisticated technology. If the SDI was successfully developed, the US would be safe from Soviet missiles, while the USSR would have no effective nuclear defence. US development of SDI was announced by President Ronald Reagan in March 1983.

satellite states This term means countries that are allied or connected to another more powerful state, and it generally implies an unequal relationship. The satellite states are either *puppet* states (in practice, controlled by the more powerful country) or *client* states (which receive economic or political support in return for backing the more dominant state).

Fact
The Sovietisation of Eastern Europe is often seen as a factor in the start of the Cold War, yet this is rather a 'chicken and egg' situation. One could also argue that US actions under President Harry S. Truman pushed the USSR into taking firmer control of these Eastern European countries, in order to establish a 'security belt' in case of another war. Once established, this security belt was seen as fundamental to Soviet security. Consequently, any developments that appeared to threaten Soviet control were quickly crushed. One fear was that the USA would interfere in these Eastern European countries and try to bring about governments that would be hostile to the USSR and would become US allies.

However, détente came to an end in 1979. A Second Cold War now began, which lasted until 1985. Some historians think this Second Cold War was the result of the Soviet Union's military intervention in Afghanistan, while others believe it was caused by changes in US foreign-policy strategies. These US policies included stepping up the nuclear arms race – in particular, by announcing and developing the **SDI ('Star Wars')** project.

The Second Cold War was followed by a new period of improved relations and co-operation. This was largely due to the 'New Thinking' on foreign policy pursued by Mikhail Gorbachev, who became the USSR's new leader in 1985. Improved relations lasted until the collapse of the USSR at the end of 1991, when the USA was left as the only superpower.

The Cold War and Eastern Europe

Following the Second World War, Stalin was painfully aware of the death and destruction that the German invasion had caused in the Soviet Union, and fearful of the US nuclear weapons monopoly. He decided that the USSR, which had been invaded through Poland three times since 1900, needed a security zone on its western borders. Stalin insisted on having 'friendly' governments in the countries of Eastern Europe, such as East Germany, Hungary, Poland and Czechoslovakia. These countries formed a buffer zone to guard against invasion from the West. As the Cold War developed, they effectively became **satellite states** of the USSR, as Stalin brought about the 'Sovietisation' of Eastern Europe during the period 1945–53.

This policy of maintaining control over the East European countries was followed by Stalin's successors. For example, in Hungary, the reform communist Imre Nagy attempted to liberalise the political and economic system in 1956. It also looked as if he was likely to take Hungary out of the Warsaw Pact (see page 13). In response, the Soviet Red Army was sent in to crush the revolt, and Nagy, along with other reform communists, was executed.

Similarly, in 1968, when Alexander Dubček in Czechoslovakia tried to establish 'socialism with a human face' in his 'Prague Spring' (see Chapter 6), the Soviet leader Leonid Brezhnev oversaw an invasion by Warsaw Pact troops. He then issued what became known as the 'Brezhnev Doctrine'. This essentially said that the USSR and other Eastern European states had the right to intervene in any Eastern European state where political developments threatened Soviet security. In both cases, the USSR then imposed new rulers (seen as more reliable Soviet allies) on these countries: János Kádár in Hungary and Gustáv Husák in Czechoslovakia.

Not surprisingly, the threat of Soviet military intervention mostly kept these satellite states quiet. However, once Gorbachev made it clear, as early as 1985, that he would not enforce the 'Brezhnev Doctrine', the situation in many of these countries began to change. By 1989, all the communist regimes in Eastern Europe had fallen in the face of mass popular protests.

Government of the USSR

Ever since the 1921 'temporary' ban on other parties, the USSR had been a one-party state. This meant that just one party, the Communist Party of the Soviet Union (CPSU), held political power. The CPSU had congresses – and, sometimes, special conferences, which were called to deal with specific issues.

However, ever since Stalin's rule, it was not the whole party that ruled the country, but the leaders at the top of the party.

Although in theory the party congress was the most powerful party body, in practice the Politburo (Political Bureau) was the most important group. After this, there was the Central Committee (CC). The full membership (or 'plenum') of the CC met to make the most important decisions; less serious issues were usually decided just by the leading members of the CC.

The most important party post was that of general-secretary of the CPSU. The first person to have this role was Stalin, appointed in 1922. In effect, the general-secretary was the real ruler of the Soviet Union – but there were always powerful rivals who were keen to take his place.

The Politburo and the Central Committee made all the significant decisions in the USSR. However, there was also a separate government (the Council of Ministers), headed by a prime minister, and a sort of parliament (known as the Congress of Soviets). The Congress of Soviets only met for a short period, but it elected a Supreme Soviet, which was, in theory, the most important political body within the USSR (deciding, for example, on any changes to the constitution). The executive committee of the Supreme Soviet was known as the Presidium. In theory, the Presidium supervised the work of the Council of Ministers; the president of the Presidium was like a presidential head of state.

For most of its existence (until Gorbachev's reforms), the Supreme Soviet had little real power, as the one-party system ensured that only members or loyal supporters of the CPSU were 'elected'. The Supreme Soviet therefore mainly acted as a 'rubber stamp', approving decisions taken by the Politburo and the government. Apart from controlling defence and foreign policy, the government also oversaw the direction and management of the centralised, planned Soviet economy.

To ensure that there was no serious dissent – and to counter the Cold War activities of US spies and agents – the USSR (like all countries) had its secret police. For the period under study, the secret police force was the *Komitet gosudarstvennoy bezopasnosti* (KGB), meaning 'Committee for State Security'. In previous periods, it had been known as the Cheka, the NKVD and MGB.

China

At first, communism in China was heavily influenced by what had happened in the Soviet Union. Marxist ideas first began to spread in China in the early 20th century and, in 1921, the Chinese Communist Party (CCP) was formed. One of its founder members was **Mao Zedong**.

In fact, the formation of the CCP had been encouraged by the communist leaders in Soviet Russia. At the time, most Soviet leaders believed the CCP was too small to play an independent role in Chinese politics. Instead, the Chinese communists were instructed to join the Chinese Nationalist Party (the *Guomindang*, or GMD), which was attempting to free China from foreign control and influence. However, in 1925, the GMD leadership was taken over by **Jiang Jieshi**, who was strongly anti-communist. In 1927, Jiang Jieshi began a massacre of communists in areas controlled by his armies. Soon a civil war was raging between the GMD and the CCP. During this war, Mao became the new leader of the Chinese communists.

Fact
The Warsaw Pact was the military alliance set up by the USSR in 1955, as a response to the West's North Atlantic Treaty Organisation (NATO), established in 1949.

Mao Zedong (1893–1976)
Mao came from a relatively prosperous peasant family. In 1918, he helped establish a 'Society for the Study of Marxism', which then formed the Chinese Communist Party (CCP). Mao became its leader in 1935, and held this position until his death in 1976.

Jiang Jieshi (1887–1975)
Jiang Jieshi became leader of the *Guomindang* (GMD) in 1925. Later, from 1928 to 1948, he was the president of the government of Nationalist China. Some textbooks may use the older version of his name: Chiang Kai Shek. Jiang Jieshi was determined to destroy the CCP.

Stalin put pressure on the CCP to seek a new alliance with the GMD during the civil war, and this made Mao even more suspicious of Soviet communists. After the end of the Second World War, Stalin (as part of his agreements with the US and the West) wanted the CCP to form a coalition government in China with the GMD. The two parties signed a truce in 1945, but civil war broke out again in China in 1946. This war was eventually won by the CCP, which proclaimed the formation of the People's Republic of China (PRC) in October 1949. Further tensions with Stalin followed, in particular over the GMD presence in Taiwan, and events in the Korean War. When Stalin died in 1953, tensions between China and Stalin's successors increased. Eventually, the Chinese Communist Party put itself forward as a rival to the Soviet Communist Party. The Chinese Communist Party now wished to lead the communist bloc.

Government in China

Like the USSR, Communist China – still officially known as the People's Republic of China (PRC) – is a one-party state, run by the Chinese Communist Party (CCP). In theory, power is shared between the CCP, the People's Government, and the People's Liberation Army (PLA). While the names of many of the political posts and bodies are different from those used by the Soviet Union while it existed, the relationships are essentially the same.

Although the CCP did have a general-secretary, at first the most important party post in practice was that of chairman. The first chairman was Mao Zedong, who held the position until his death in 1976. This post, however, was later abolished under Deng Xiaoping, and the role of general-secretary became more important. The CCP also has a Politburo, which contains the top leaders of the CCP, and a Central Committee. The Politburo's smaller Standing Committee meets almost continually and includes the most powerful and influential leaders. The government, known as the State Council, is headed by a premier (prime minister). There is also a president (head of state) of the National People's Congress, which is the equivalent of a parliament.

Terminology and definitions

When studying these communist states, you may face difficulties with some of the terminology. Some of the terms can have different meanings, according to who is using them and what beliefs they hold. This is true of the six main terms you will encounter: communism, Marxism, Leninism, Marxism–Leninism, Stalinism and Maoism.

Communism

This term refers to a social and economic system in which all significant aspects of a country's economy are socially owned and managed – either by the state or by local communities or co-operatives. Unlike in capitalist countries, where land, industries and banks are privately owned, social ownership is intended to result in a classless society.

Before a classless society can be achieved, a socialist stage is needed. During this socialist stage, the majority of the population are supposed to become the ruling class. Such ideas came to prominence with the writings of Karl Marx and Friedrich Engels. The first attempt to put them into practice was made in Russia, following the Bolshevik Revolution in 1917. However, practice turned out to be very different from theory – and many have argued that communism has never yet been truly implemented anywhere.

The title page of the Communist Manifesto, *with a photograph of Karl Marx*

Marxism

Marxism refers to the political and economic writings of one man, Karl Marx (1818–83), or two men, if Marx's close collaborator, Friedrich Engels (1820–95), is included. Marx's writings were based on his theory that human history was largely determined by the struggle between the ruling class and the oppressed class, which had conflicting interests. Marx believed that if the workers succeeded in overthrowing capitalism, they would then be able to build a socialist society. This society would still contain social classes, but – for the first time in human history – the ruling class would be the majority of the population.

From this new form of human society, Marx believed it would be possible to move eventually to an even better one: communism. This would be a classless society. As it would be based on the economic advances of industrial capitalism, it would be a society of plenty, not of scarcity.

Marx did not write much about the political forms that would be adopted under socialism and communism. He merely said that, as the majority of the population would be in control, this society would be more democratic and less repressive than previous societies. After the **Paris Commune** in 1871, Marx argued that measures should be adopted from day one, after the workers' revolution, to bring about the eventual 'withering away' of the state.

Marx did not believe that this 'progression' through the stages of society (from capitalism to socialism to communism) was inevitable. He also said that, in special circumstances, a relatively backward society could 'jump' a stage – but only if that state was then aided by sympathetic advanced societies. He certainly did not believe that a poor agricultural society could move to socialism on its own, as socialism would require an advanced industrial base.

Leninism

Marx did not refer to himself as a 'Marxist'. He preferred the term 'communist', as in the title of the book he and Engels wrote in 1847, *The Communist Manifesto*. However, many of Marx's followers preferred to call themselves 'Marxists' as well as communists. In this way they distinguished themselves from other groups that claimed to be 'communist', and also emphasised that Marxism and its methods formed a distinct philosophy.

One such Marxist was the Russian revolutionary Vladimir Ilyich Lenin (see page 9). Lenin developed some of Marx's economic ideas, but his main contribution to Marxist theory related to political organisation. His ideas, partly based on the extremely undemocratic political system operating in tsarist Russia, became known as **democratic centralism**. He believed that that there was a need for a small 'vanguard' party (a leading group) of fully committed revolutionaries.

Leon Trotsky (1879–1940), a leading Russian Marxist, disagreed with Lenin. Between 1903 and 1917, Trotsky argued that democratic centralism would allow an unscrupulous leader to become a dictator over the party. Nevertheless, both Lenin and Trotsky believed in the possibility of moving quickly to the socialist phase. This idea was similar to Marx's theory of 'permanent revolution', which argued that, as soon as one revolutionary stage had been achieved, the struggle for the next would begin almost immediately.

Paris Commune This refers to the revolutionary provisional government that took over Paris from April to May 1871, following the Franco–Prussian War of 1870–71. Its democratic organisation inspired Marx to add to his views on the nature of the state and politics after a workers' revolution. He argued that measures should be adopted immediately to bring about the eventual 'withering away' of the state. Marx shared this aim with many anarchists, who wished to do away with government completely and let people govern themselves. These ideals, of democracy and self-government, were a long way from the communist regime that actually came into existence in the Soviet Union.

democratic centralism This was one of Lenin's main adaptations of Marx's ideas. Lenin believed that all members of the party should be able to form factions ('platforms') to argue their points of view. This was the 'democratic' part of democratic centralism. However, the repressive nature of tsarist Russia meant the party could only operate effectively in a centralised way. Once the party had made a decision, Lenin argued that all party members (even those who had voted against it) should fully support that decision. He said they should support it, even if the decision had won by only one vote (the 'centralism' part). Under Lenin, freedom of debate amongst members of the Communist Party continued at least until 1921–22.

Communism in Crisis

Fact
Lenin introduced the New Economic Policy (NEP) in 1921, to deal with the economic and political crisis resulting from the Russian Civil War (1918–21). This war was fought between the Reds (the Bolsheviks and their supporters), and the Whites (all those opposed to the Bolsheviks, ranging from liberals to monarchists, landowners and would-be military dictators). The Whites were supported by foreign states, including the US and Britain. The NEP involved allowing small, privately owned firms and trading companies to operate. It also allowed peasants to sell some of their surplus produce in private markets. Though the state retained control of the main industrial enterprises and foreign trade, it was a partial return to capitalism.

socialism in one country
This is an aspect of Stalinist ideology, based on the belief that even an economically backward country could construct socialism without any outside help – contrary to the view held by Marx and Lenin. 'Socialism in one country' contributed to the rapid industrialisation of the USSR because it stimulated national pride in what the Soviet people could achieve through their own efforts.

purges
This term refers to the massive purges Stalin initiated in the 1930s, during which most of the communist leaders were executed. They were accompanied by 'show trials', in which the accused 'confessed' to their 'crimes', such as plotting against Stalin. These confessions were often extracted after sleep deprivation, beatings and threats to family members. The purges were far more brutal than previous 'cleansings', which had merely expelled members for such things as drunkenness or political inactivity.

Like Marx, both Lenin and Trotsky believed that Russia could not succeed in carrying through any 'uninterrupted revolution' without outside economic and technical assistance. This assistance failed to materialise, despite their earlier hopes of successful workers' revolutions in other European states after 1918. However, Lenin proved to be an extremely pragmatic ruler, who was quite prepared to adopt policies that seemed to conflict with communist goals, and even with those of the 'lower' socialist stage. The clearest examples of his pragmatism were the New Economic Policy (NEP) and the ban on factions and other parties. Lenin argued that these were just adaptations to the prevailing circumstances and that, as soon as conditions allowed, there would be a return to 'socialist norms'.

Marxism–Leninism

The term Marxism–Leninism, invented by Stalin, was not used until after Lenin's death in 1924. It soon came to be used in Stalin's Soviet Union to refer to what he described as 'orthodox Marxism'. This increasingly came to mean what Stalin himself had to say about political and economic issues. Essentially, Marxism–Leninism was the 'official' ideology of the Soviet state and all communist parties loyal to Stalin and his successors – up to 1976 and beyond.

However, many Marxists (even members of the Communist Party itself) believed that Stalin's ideas and practices (such as **socialism in one country** and the **purges**) were almost total distortions of what Marx and Lenin had said. The Chinese Communist Party also followed the 'socialism in one country' ideology – until it adopted its own version, which became known as 'Maoism'.

Stalinism

The term Stalinism is used by historians, and by those politically opposed to Stalin, to describe practices associated with Stalin and his supporters – and with the Chinese communists. Historians and political scientists use the word to mean a deeply undemocratic (and even dictatorial) set of beliefs and type of rule.

Marxist opponents of Stalin and post-Stalin rulers (and Mao and post-Mao rulers) used the term in some of the same ways. However, they were also determined to show that Stalinism was not just an adaptation of Marxism. On the contrary, they saw it as being completely different from both Leninism and Marxism, and from revolutionary communism in general. In particular, opponents stressed the way in which Stalin and his supporters – and later Mao and his successors in China – rejected the goal of **socialist democracy** (see page 17) in favour of a permanent one-party state. They also emphasised the way Stalinism placed the national interests of the Soviet Union and China above the struggle to achieve world revolution.

Maoism

Maoism is a particular form of Stalinism that originated with Mao in China and was given a more definite form during the 1950s and 1960s. It was the official ideology of the Chinese Communist Party (CCP) until Deng Xiaoping took over in the late 1970s. It differed from official 'Marxism–Leninism' in that it placed the peasantry at the head of the revolutionary movement, rather than the industrial working class (known as the proletariat). Maoism also based its strategy on guerrilla warfare. According to Maoist theory, the 'revolutionary countryside' was supposed to encircle and capture the 'bourgeois/capitalist towns', and then carry out a socialist revolution.

Although Maoism seemed to contain a greater democratic element, in practice the CCP was just as authoritarian as Stalin's party. The CCP also often resorted to purges of those who had different ideas. During the late 1950s and early 1960s, it accused the Soviet Union of being **revisionist**. Under Nikita Khrushchev, the USSR was carrying out limited de-Stalinisation, as well as seeking 'peaceful co-existence' with the West. This led the Chinese Communist Party to believe that the Soviet Union was departing from orthodox Marxism, especially regarding foreign policy, and doing deals with capitalist states. These arguments split the international communist movement into pro-Moscow and pro-Beijing parties. However, in the early 1970s, Mao was also prepared to do deals with the 'imperialist' USA, thus showing Maoism's strong nationalist aspect. Just like Stalin, the Maoist CCP often put national interests before ideology.

Summary

By the time you have worked through this book, you should be able to:

- understand and explain the economic situation, problems and policies of the Union of Soviet Socialist Republics (USSR) and Eastern Europe, and of the People's Republic of China (PRC), in the period 1976–89
- understand the political and power structures that existed in both the USSR and the PRC in this period, and the challenges to them
- understand and explain the influence of the respective Communist Parties, and the various reforms they attempted in order to deal with changing circumstances
- compare and contrast, and evaluate, the various explanations and interpretations of these issues and developments put forward by different historians
- use and assess – as historical evidence – a range of different types of sources relating to the histories of these two states, by considering aspects such as comparison and contrast, and value and limitations
- combine evaluation of sources with relevant knowledge of your own in order to develop supported arguments, explanations and judgements about the crises facing these communist states in this period.

socialist democracy This term refers to a form of democracy advocated by revolutionary socialists and Marxists. In this type of democracy, government is in the hands of the people, who have the right to dismiss any elected representatives who break their promises. In this system, all parties that accept the goal of ending capitalist exploitation should be allowed to exist. The state also makes newspaper facilities available to all groups that have sufficient popular support. A limited version of this system operated in the Soviet Union from 1917 to 1921, but under Stalin the USSR became a one-party state in both practice and theory. This one-party state continued until Gorbachev began to introduce democratic reforms after 1985.

revisionist This term means that the revolutionary aspects of Marxism were being 'revised' (or abandoned), in favour of a more moderate, less revolutionary policy. The term 'revisionist' was first used in the late 19th century, about the leaders of the Social Democratic Party of Germany, who argued that a country could become socialist without having to overthrow the capitalist classes.

2 The Soviet economy 1976–85

Timeline

1964 **Oct:** Brezhnev replaces Khrushchev as first secretary of the CPSU; Kosygin becomes prime minister

1965 **Sept:** start of Kosygin's reforms

1971 9th Five-Year Plan

1973 **Oct:** start of world oil crisis

1976 10th Five-Year Plan

1977 **Oct:** new ('Brezhnev') constitution

1980 **Dec:** Kosygin dies

1981 11th Five-Year Plan

1982 **Nov:** Brezhnev dies; replaced by Andropov

1984 **Feb:** Andropov dies; Chernenko takes over

1985 **Mar:** Chernenko dies; Gorbachev takes over

Introduction

This chapter and Chapter 3 deal with the final six years of Leonid Brezhnev's leadership of the Soviet Union (1976–82), and the following three years (under Yuri Andropov and Konstantin Chernenko), until Mikhail Gorbachev took over in 1985. Brezhnev came to power in 1964, after the overthrow of Nikita Khrushchev, and remained as leader until his death in 1982.

By 1976 (nearly 60 years after the 1917 Bolshevik Revolution), the Soviet model of state planning was already showing signs of an impending crisis. On the surface, the Soviet Communist Party's control over political life in the USSR seemed secure, and the Soviet economy appeared strong. The reality was actually very different but this was not apparent to most people until the 1980s, when serious signs of 'communism in crisis' began to appear.

Over the previous decades, the Soviet Union had sent Sputnik, the world's first satellite, into space; sent the first man into orbit; provided large amounts of aid to allies such as Cuba; and spent huge sums on developing and producing high-tech weaponry. In view of all these achievements, many people assumed that the Soviet Union would carry on more or less as it had done since the massive and rapid industrialisation begun by Stalin in the late 1920s.

Key questions

- How did Brezhnev's early rule contribute to the crisis after 1976?
- What were the main features of the Soviet economy under Brezhnev from 1976 to 1982?
- What economic reforms were attempted in the period 1982–85?
- What impact did the Cold War have on the Soviet economy?

2 The Soviet economy 1976–85

Overview

- In 1964, Khrushchev was overthrown and replaced by Brezhnev as head of the Communist Party of the Soviet Union (CPSU).
- Khrushchev had tried various reforms to make the Soviet economy more efficient. At first, his changes were put on hold, but in September Prime Minister Kosygin got approval to introduce some similar economic reforms.
- However, many Soviet leaders (including Brezhnev) were not very supportive. By 1970, Kosygin's reforms had largely stalled.
- As a result, the Soviet economy began to stagnate. Despite overall production increases, there was little progress in improving efficiency and productivity in order to match such developments in the West.
- The impending economic crisis became even more apparent under Brezhnev, after 1976 – even though some aspects of the economy improved.
- As Cold War defence spending continued to increase, less government money was available to invest in modernising industrial machinery.
- When Brezhnev died in 1982, some limited reforms were introduced by Andropov. But, when Andropov died in 1984, there was another period of 'drift' before Gorbachev took over in 1985.

A map of the USSR and Eastern Europe in 1985, showing the Trans-Siberian Railway (in blue) and the Baikal-Amur Mainline (in red)

Communism in Crisis

How did Brezhnev's early rule contribute to the crisis after 1976?

Before considering the economic crisis that emerged under **Leonid Brezhnev**, it is necessary to examine the system that existed when he came to power. This provides a context for the main problems faced by Soviet leaders, and why particular reforms were (or were not) attempted.

The planned economy

Following the Bolshevik Revolution of 1917, there were attempts to end all capitalist ownership, and so create a socialist and eventually a communist society. A system of state planning began, with the main means of production taken into state ownership, and the state directing the economy.

The economy under Stalin

Under Stalin, this central control and direction was developed further. In 1928, he launched the USSR's first Five-Year Plan, in a bid to create 'socialism in one country' (see page 16). This plan was supposed to make the Soviet Union self-sufficient in both agricultural and industrial production.

The desire for **autarchy** was partly due to the fact that no successful workers' revolution had come to the aid of the USSR. In the late 1920s, the Soviet Union was isolated. It was also surrounded by hostile, powerful capitalist states that had already tried to overthrow the world's first workers' state. Stalin claimed that the Soviet Union had ten years to catch up with the West in order to be able to withstand the next attack. (This attack was widely expected, and finally came in 1941.) The massive push to expand and modernise the Soviet economy would be achieved by central control of the economy and state planning.

Leonid Brezhnev (1906–82)
Brezhnev was the son of a steelworker and joined the Young Communists (Komsomol) in 1923. During the late 1920s, he was involved in the push for collectivisation of agriculture. Later, in 1931, he became a full party member, supported by Khrushchev. He was appointed as a political commissar during the Second World War. In 1952, he was appointed to the Politburo, but lost his new position after Stalin's death. Though reinstated by Krushchev in 1956, Brezhnev eventually helped to overthrow him.

autarchy Sometimes spelled 'autarky', this term means 'self-sufficiency'. It is usually applied to countries or regimes that try to exist without having to import particular foods, fuels, raw materials or industrial goods. It can also refer to the attempt to be totally self-sufficient in all important areas. Invariably, such attempts have had limited success.

Gosplan This was the State General Planning Commission, based in Moscow and first created in 1921. Although each of the 15 Soviet republics had its own Gosplan, they were all subordinate to Moscow. Gosplan was ultimately responsible for co-ordinating all economic planning – in both the short and long term.

SOURCE A

Under state socialism, ministries and local authorities manage production enterprises. Prices and output of individual firms are largely determined by central or regional boards. Industries and their sub-units (enterprises) operate like ministries in Western countries. Profits and losses accrue to the state exchequer. [...]

The Soviet economy is an 'administered' or 'command' economy in which the influence of individual consumers and producers is replaced by administrative bodies, which make decisions for the whole economy. These determine what and how much is to be produced and the price at which things must be sold. This entails decisions by the central planners about which goods are to be produced. In industry, all prices (of goods and labour) are fixed by the planners.

Lane, D. 1985. *Soviet Economy and Society*. Oxford, UK. Basil Blackwell. pp. 3–4.

2 The Soviet economy 1976–85

Under the centrally planned Soviet economy (also known as a 'command economy'), the planning departments decided what economic activity should be carried out by the production enterprises (industries and state farms). The planning departments therefore made decisions on matters such as the rate of growth, and the prices and amounts of materials, energy, labour and goods to be used.

The Soviet government (largely under the control of the Communist Party) directed the economy via a number of economic planning committees and bodies. The various government and republican ministries supervised the implementation of the economic plans drawn up by these bodies. Of these planning organisations, the most important was **Gosplan** (see page 20). Gosplan was responsible for preparing the various types of plans. The most common of these were the Five-Year Plans, which were first used under Stalin.

This system of central planning led to a number of economic problems, which in turn affected political developments. These would eventually result in the collapse of the Soviet Union in 1991.

Khrushchev's reforms

The Soviet Union achieved major economic growth under Stalin, through his Five-Year Plans. The USSR also played a major role in the defeat of Nazi Germany in the Second World War, and established a series of satellite states on its eastern borders. After Stalin died in 1953, there was a brief period of collective rule but, by 1955, **Nikita Khrushchev** had become the dominant leader. Despite the achievements made under Stalin's regime, Khrushchev soon realised that the country's rigid command economy needed to be modernised. If it was reformed, he was convinced that the USSR could overtake the capitalist West and demonstrate the superiority of a planned socialist economy.

In order to succeed, Khrushchev's modernisation programme required various economic reforms. Khrushchev and his supporters made bold claims that the USSR's economic growth would enable it to rapidly overtake the Western capitalist economy. However, they knew that agricultural production (always the weakest part of the Soviet economy) was actually declining, and that Soviet machinery needed updating.

Khrushchev's plans were sometimes contradictory, and frequently subject to change. The plans centred on relaxing central control of the economy, by giving factory managers more autonomy (control over their own enterprises). The belief was that this would allow them to manage more efficiently and so increase their workers' productivity rate. To encourage people to work harder, Khrushchev wanted to increase standards of living and provide more consumer goods.

However, many older members of the Communist Party did not fully support him. Various failures in Khrushchev's economic reforms – as well as certain problematic developments in politics and foreign affairs – led party members to overthrow Khrushchev in 1964.

The Soviet economy 1964–70

Leonid Brezhnev came to power in October 1964, when leading members of the Soviet Communist Party decided it was time to replace Khrushchev. Brezhnev became first secretary of the CPSU, while **Alexei Kosygin** became prime minister.

Nikita Khrushchev (1894–1971) Khrushchev supported Stalin before the Second World War, and was put in charge of agriculture in Ukraine. On Stalin's death, he became first secretary of the CPSU and, in 1958, premier (chairman) of the Council of Ministers. He then began a limited process of de-Stalinisation. This was one cause of the Hungarian Revolt in 1956, which he crushed. Khrushchev oversaw the USSR's successful space programme, but was toppled in 1964 by Brezhnev and Kosygin.

Alexei Kosygin (1904–80) Born into a working-class family, Kosygin became an industrial manager in Siberia in 1921. During the Second World War, he became a member of the State Defence Committee. Once Khrushchev took over as leader, Kosygin was appointed in 1959 as chairman of Gosplan, before becoming first deputy of the Council of Ministers. One of the more reformist Soviet leaders, he favoured a more liberal solution to the events that took place in Czechoslovakia in 1968 (see Chapter 6).

Left to right: Nikolai Podgorny, Leonid Brezhnev and Alexei Kosygin in 1976

Industry and the Kosygin reforms

Brezhnev's period of rule was characterised by what has been called **entropy or 'stagnation'**. Although Brezhnev had some interest in agriculture, he was mainly focused on party matters. Eventually, Khrushchev's economic reforms were either abandoned or slowed down and, in many ways, the old methods of management continued.

At the beginning of Brezhnev's rule, there were some attempts at industrial reform. The main person responsible for these efforts was Alexei Kosygin. As prime minister, Kosygin pushed hard for increased investment and real economic reforms. He tried to make the economy more efficient and dynamic, especially through increased production of consumer goods. In September 1965, he revived Khrushchev's 1962 plans to give factory managers greater control over certain decisions. However, many managers were too afraid of failure.

Kosygin stressed that the framework of the established planning system would remain – with the addition of some 'market' elements. However, the desire to give extra powers to managers (and so reduce the influence of Gosplan) had political consequences. In particular, it reduced the authority of the various economic ministries and of the CPSU itself. Many of Kosygin's colleagues therefore opposed this shift from centralised planning to a system partly based on profit-making and managerial initiative.

Although Kosygin was given formal approval by the Central Committee to press ahead with his plans, Brezhnev decided not to support Kosygin against his party critics. Significantly for future economic developments in the USSR, Brezhnev then did what he could, behind the scenes, to obstruct Kosygin's plans.

There were some successes and improvements during the 8th Five-Year Plan (1965–70). By 1970, the output of factories and mines had risen 138%, compared to 1960. However, these increases in production were not maintained, and plan targets were frequently not met. By 1970, there were signs of a move back towards greater central control.

> **entropy or 'stagnation'** The term 'entropy' is normally used in physics when discussing transfer of heat or energy. When applied to a system or a society, entropy means 'inevitable and steady deterioration' of that system or society. 'Stagnation' means a failure to grow or develop.

SOURCE B

Industrial output, 8th and 9th Five-Year Plans, 1965–75

	8th Five-Year Plan, 1965–70			9th Five-Year Plan, 1971–75	
	(1965 = 100)			(1970 = 100)	
	1965	1970 plan	1970 actual	1975 plan	1975 actual
A. Index numbers					
National income (utilised)	100	139.5	141	138.6	128
Industrial production	100	148.5	150	147.0	143
Producers' goods	100	150.5	151	146.3	146
Consumer goods	100	144.5	149	148.6	137
B. Quantities					
Electricity (milliard kilowatt/hours)	507	840	740	1065	1039
Oil (million tons)	243	350	353	505	491
Gas (milliard cubic metres)	129	233	200	320	289
Coal (million tons)	578	670	624	694.9	701
Steel (million tons)	91	126	116	146.4	141
Fertiliser (million tons)	31	63.5	55	90	90.2
Motor vehicles (thousands)	616	1385	916	2100	1964
Tractors (thousands)	355	612	458	575	550

Note: Some plan figures are midpoints of ranges. The figures of '100' for 1965 and 1970 are the baselines (starting points) against which later economic performances have been measured.

Adapted from Nove, A. 1989. *An Economic History of the USSR*. London, UK. Penguin. p. 370.

Agriculture

As early as March 1965, Brezhnev used his increasing political strength to insist on a bigger allocation of agricultural funding, to pay for more chemical fertilisers and advanced mechanical equipment, in order to overcome grain shortages. This took resources away from Kosygin's industrial plans. However, increased state investment in agriculture (combined with the effects of industrial reforms begun by Khrushchev and Kosygin) led to improved agricultural production. From 1960 to 1970, Soviet agricultural output increased at an annual average of 3%.

Communism in Crisis

Brezhnev's policies 1970–76

By the end of the 1960s, most Politburo members believed they had established the best methods of maintaining both political rule and economic growth – ways that avoided the brutalities of Stalin and the erratic approach of Khrushchev. They believed this approach would successfully and safely stabilise the Soviet Union.

In fact, in the early 1970s the Soviet Union seemed to be strong and secure. In addition to its military strength (almost equal to that of the US), it was the world's second-largest industrial economy, producing more steel, oil, pig-iron, cement and tractors than any other country in the world. There were even some people in the West (not supporters of the USSR) who thought that the centrally planned economy might succeed in out-producing advanced capitalist states in many other economic areas.

SOURCE C

Accounting for its work in this very important direction of activity, the Central Committee of the Party has every justification to say that the Soviet people, having worthily completed the Eighth Five-Year Plan, has taken a new great step forward in the creation of the material-technical base of communism, in the reinforcement of the country's might and in the raising of the standard of living of the people.

Brezhnev's report at the 24th Party Congress, 1971. Quoted in Service, R. 1997. *A History of Twentieth-Century Russia*. London, UK. Allen Lane/Penguin. p. 406.

Agriculture and industry

After 1970, Brezhnev maintained the established system of organising the collective farms or **kolkhozy**. Output quotas were still set centrally, along with instructions on what crops to plant – and even *when* to plant them. Brezhnev shared Khrushchev's belief that combining farms to form bigger *kolkhozy* would raise productivity. He also still insisted on massive increases in government financial support for agriculture. During the 1970s, collective farms received 27% of all state investment, and this figure did not include the sums spent on chemical fertilisers, tractors and other farm equipment.

Despite the need to be more flexible, the USSR continued with Five-Year Plans. The 9th Five-Year Plan ran from 1971 to 1975. This projected a slight increase in the production of consumer goods from light industry, such as furniture and radios. However, as before, the bulk of the money was made available for medium and heavy industry. As a consequence, by 1975, the production of consumer goods had expanded at a rate that was 9% lower than the rate of increase in industrial goods.

The oil crisis, 1973

The USSR was a major oil and natural gas producer, so it benefited at first from high oil prices after the 1973 world oil crisis. The oil crisis also coincided with a boom in raw materials. As the prices of raw materials rose faster than prices for manufactured goods, the USSR could afford to import grain and technology from the West.

---

kolkhozy These collective farms were first set up under Stalin. Stalin's rural policies had done considerable damage to the agricultural system, which was then further devastated by the Nazi occupation during the Second World War. There were also state farms, known as *sovkhozy* (singular *sovkhoz*). These were run as state enterprises, farmed by paid workers.

2 The Soviet economy 1976–85

Fact
The 1973 oil crisis occurred because many Arab oil-producing states imposed an oil embargo (stopped exporting oil) in October 1973. The Arab states did this in retaliation for the US decision to re-supply Israel with weapons during the Yom Kippur War in 1973. The embargo lasted until 1974, and caused problems for many oil-dependent economies.

Oil drilling platforms, near Baku, on the Black Sea

Even though its coal production declined slightly, the leadership was not worried, as the Soviet Union had plenty of oil. Consequently, the USSR did not respond to the crisis by making more efficient use of oil to reduce consumption. Nor did it push through economic reforms to modernise its economic structures and machinery by increasing efficiency and productivity in the way that Western capitalist economies did. Thus, Brezhnev and his colleagues missed an excellent opportunity to seriously reform the Soviet economy. They did not seem to realise that, without such reforms, there would be both economic and political trouble in the decades ahead.

Fact
The USSR later decided to increase the oil prices they charged their allies in the Soviet bloc. From 1980, these allies found themselves having to pay almost full world-market prices, rather than the five-year averages they had previously paid. Some countries, such as the German Democratic Republic (East Germany), were particularly badly hit, and this worsened their economic problems. These regimes then had to take measures that contributed to growing political unrest in the region. The unrest ultimately ended with mass protests and the collapse of communist regimes across the whole of Eastern Europe in 1989–90.

SOURCE D

Since the 1930s the Soviet Union had rapidly industrialised, captured Hitler's Berlin, launched Sputnik ... and boasted it would bury capitalism. But by winning the Second World War, and therefore having no necessity or feeling no desire, to change fundamentally, to compete in the transformed post-war international context, the Soviet Union, in a way, doomed itself ... right in the midst of its great 1970s oil boom, the socialist revolution entered a decrepit old age.

Kotkin, S. 2001. Armageddon Averted. Oxford, UK. Oxford University Press.

SOURCE E

Unwittingly the oil-producing Arab states had rescued the Soviet budget in 1973 by increasing the world-market prices for oil. The USSR was a major exporter of oil, petrol and gas. The reality was that the country, so far from catching up with the advanced capitalist West, was as reliant upon the sales abroad of its natural resources as it had been before 1917; and, in contrast with the Tsarist period, it could no longer find a grain surplus for shipment to the rest of Europe. There can as yet be no exact statement of the percentage of industrial growth achieved. The sceptics suggest that no growth at all occurred. Be that as it may, nobody denies that by the end of the 1970s chronic absolute decline was in prospect.

Service, R. 1997. A History of Twentieth-Century Russia. London, UK. Allen Lane/Penguin. p. 408.

Activities

1. Carry out some research on the economic reforms Khrushchev attempted to implement. Then draw a chart, entitled 'Economic Reforms', with the following headings: Khrushchev | Brezhnev & Kosygin | Gorbachev.

   Start to fill in the chart by listing the various attempted reforms described in this chapter. You will be able to add more reforms as you read the following chapters.

2. Find out what you can about Kosygin's reforms, and why there was opposition to them.

3. Write two speeches to be delivered by Brezhnev: one in favour of Kosygin's reforms and one against.

4. 'The USSR missed an excellent opportunity to solve its economic problems by failing to take advantage of the oil crisis that followed after 1973.' Split into two groups: one to support the statement and the other to argue that it was already too late to carry out any significant reform of the Soviet economy.

What were the main features of the Soviet economy under Brezhnev from 1976 to 1982?

The 10th Five-Year Plan

This period witnessed the 10th Five-Year Plan (1976–80). For the first time, the Soviet economy showed signs of slowing down. However, as the world's second-largest producer of gold, the USSR benefited from the sharp rise in the price of gold, which went up by 75% in 1979. Although its foreign debt was about $17,000 million, the USSR could comfortably service this debt, as long as prices remained high for its natural resources – gold, oil and gas.

The situation under Brezhnev seemed likely to continue in the same way. The building of the Baikal-Amur Mainline (BAM) railway would link Siberia to the Pacific (see map on page 19). This was important for the future, as Siberia was rich in coal, iron, copper, timber and especially oil and natural gas. Though no fundamental changes took place, there were limited attempts at reform.

> **Fact**
> There was also an 11th Five-Year Plan, for 1981–85, but it had only just begun when Brezhnev died in 1982.

SOURCE F

Industrial output, 10th Five-Year Plan, 1976–80

	10th Five-Year Plan, 1976–80 (1975 = 100)	
	1980 plan	1980 actual
A. Index numbers		
National income (utilised)	120	120
Industrial production	137	124
Producers' goods	140	126
Consumers' goods	131	121
B. Quantities		
Electricity (milliard kilowatt/hours)	1380	1290
Oil (million tons)	640	604
Gas (milliard cubic metres)	435	435
Coal (million tons)	800	719
Steel (million tons)	168	155
Fertiliser (million tons)	143	104
Motor vehicles (thousands)	2296	2199
Tractors (thousands)	590	(562)

Note: The figure of '100' for 1975 is the baseline (starting point) against which later economic performances have been measured. Adapted from Nove, A. 1989. *An Economic History of the USSR*. London, UK. Penguin. p. 370.

Agricultural reform

By the late 1970s, collective farms received 27% of all state investment, not including farm machinery and chemical fertilisers. Around 40% of the Soviet population still worked on the land.

Like Khrushchev, Brezhnev believed that increasing the size of the *kolkhozy* would lead to more efficient farming and thus increased production. In 1976, the Politburo therefore issued a resolution calling for several *kolkhozy* to be combined, in an attempt to increase production. However, despite the massive state subsidy for food and agriculture, many *kolkhozy* operated at a loss. This was partly because charges for fuel and machinery went up. These expenses wiped out any advantage from the higher prices paid by the state for farming produce. For example, oil costs in 1977 were almost twice those of the late 1960s, while the price of some agricultural equipment more than doubled.

Generally, the government did not press for reform – though Brezhnev did authorise decrees in 1977 (and again in 1981) that allowed peasants to have private plots that were up to 0.5 hectares (1.2 acres). As some people feared that such changes might lead to total de-collectivisation, publication of the 1977 decree was delayed until 1978.

To keep *kolkhozy* workers happy, Brezhnev decided to increase the prices paid to them for their produce. Meanwhile, subsidised food prices for consumers were kept low, thus satisfying industrial workers. At the same time, life for workers on collectives improved, as they were paid a regular wage instead of having to wait to see what profit there was to share out at the end of the year. Also, for the first time, they each received a pension and an internal passport that allowed them to travel to the cities.

However, these changes did nothing to solve the underlying problems affecting agriculture. These were:

- a shortage of skilled labour
- the payment of farm workers by quantity rather than quality of output
- the difficulties of transporting produce
- the central imposition of quotas
- machinery that was often too large for use on some farms.

Although there was a record grain harvest in 1978 (235 million tonnes), the following year produced only 179 million tonnes – about 47 million tonnes short of the target. This led to the embarrassing spectacle of the Soviet Union having to buy 20 million tonnes of grain from Canada and the US. Though gross agricultural output by 1980 was 21% higher than the average for 1966–70 (with cereal production rising by 18%), these figures masked significant weaknesses. Output in most other areas of agriculture also declined. For example, sugar-beet production decreased by 2% in the period 1970–80.

This situation had arisen despite the fact that, by 1981, state support for agriculture and food already amounted to $33,000 million. Brezhnev's response was simply to increase state investment and subsidies – though he did also support plans for land reclamation and improved irrigation. Because of the cult of personality that was growing up around him (see page 47), there were few who dared point out that this increased state investment would not solve the problems in the long term.

Those who favoured significant reform tended to remain silent. They knew they would risk demotion if they argued for the introduction of material incentives,

Fact
Peasants preferred to work on private plots, rather than the collective's land. By the 1970s, over 30% of agricultural produce was grown on these private plots, although the plots made up only 4% of arable land.

Fact
Subsidised food prices made a big difference to Soviet citizens. For instance, the state subsidy for meat meant that it was sold to consumers at half of cost-price. This was fine while the Soviet Union was benefiting from increased oil and commodity prices, but it was not a long-term solution.

Fact
There was a continuing shortage of skilled labour, even though conditions on the *kolkhozy* were improving. Many skilled male workers decided to move to the urban areas to find better-paid work in the factories. This meant that the labour force on the collectives became mainly female and either late middle-aged or even elderly. This ageing workforce made it increasingly difficult to raise agricultural production to the levels required to feed a modern and expanding industrial society.

and changes to the way work was allocated on the farms, as ways of increasing production. However, some reform-minded local party officials (such as Mikhail Gorbachev) did introduce some of these changes.

Industrial reform

It was during the 10th Five-Year Plan that signs of a real slow-down in industrial growth became apparent. The planned increase in industrial production for 1979 was 5.7%, but the actual increase was 3.4%. Meanwhile, coal production actually declined.

In 1979, a decree on industry was issued. This decree called for scientific planning and, once again, the avoidance of running deficits in the annual accounts. But this did not result in much improvement, and economic trends continued to be disappointing. The official statistics insisted that industrial output rose by 4.4% a year in the period 1976–80. In reality, it showed a steady *decrease* in the rate of expansion: in 1966–70, official statistics had claimed that the annual rise was 8.5%. However, it should be remembered that official statistics – especially from one-party states – are not always reliable.

Question

What does this photograph tell us about the problems of the Soviet Union in the period 1976–85? When trying to discover what a photograph or cartoon can tell us, always read the caption and see what information is relevant to the question.

This photograph shows Brezhnev and other ageing Soviet leaders during a visit to Ukraine in 1981; Brezhnev and his team were increasingly referred to as a 'gerontocracy' – or a government of old men

SOURCE G

Annual production of Soviet industry 1965–81
These figures (based on Soviet statistics) were originally published in the US magazine *Time* on 22 November 1982. They were then reprinted in Halliday, F. 1986. *The Making of the Second Cold War*. London, UK. Verso.

	1965	1981
Figures in millions of metric tonnes except where noted		
Electricity (millions of kilowatt hours)	507	1325
Crude oil	243	609
Natural gas (billions of cubic metres)	127.7	465
Iron ore	153.4	242
Steel	91	149
Grain	121.1	160 (est.)
Milk	72.6	88.5
Meat	9.9	15.2
Passenger cars (thousands)	201.2	1324

Though the manufacturing industry was performing less well than the extractive industries, such as gas, oil and coal, there was little fresh thinking in the Politburo about the economy. Their increasingly unfounded belief was that the USSR could make steady economic advances without any major reforms.

One area where reform *was* seen concerned the creation of 'associations' (*ob'edineniya*), where factories with complementary activities could join forces to help each other. In fact, the first ones had been formed before 1976. By 1980, there were over 4000 such associations, which were responsible for more than half of total annual industrial production. Such associations could be formed without prior permission from Gosplan and the various economic ministries in Moscow. They were expected to operate on a self-financing basis – thus regular deficits were no longer acceptable. However, even this reform was undermined by the fact that central authorities still retained much control over investment, prices, wages, and hiring and firing of workers.

In addition, old problems continued. In order to fulfil the quotas set by the Five-Year Plans, factory managers had to 'bend' the rules: skilled workers had to be paid more than the figure set by the central authorities. Managers found it difficult to deal with unskilled workers who were late, lazy or even drunk. Often, because of the shortage of labour (made worse by a slow-down in the rate of population growth), workers held more than one job, and would split their time between them. Many tended to put more effort into protecting and extending their perks than their actual work. Some people stayed away from their official employment in order to work on their own plots or did 'unofficial' jobs. Some even stole equipment from factories, which was then exchanged for other items that were in short supply.

SOURCE A

For the factory worker, the centralised planning system means, on the whole, a poorly paid, but secure and fairly undemanding life. It is difficult for management to dismiss workers for laziness, incompetence, absenteeism or even drunkenness.

Hosking, G. 1985. A History of the Soviet Union. Quoted in Ingram, P. 1997. Russia and the USSR 1905–1991. Cambridge, UK. Cambridge University Press. p. 59.

Consumer goods

Khrushchev had aimed to increase the supply of consumer goods. This policy was continued by Brezhnev and Kosygin, partly in order to avoid any dissatisfaction and protest, which might arise if workers did not see improvements in their living standards. A workers' protest movement was developing in Poland with the rise of the (initially illegal) trade union Solidarity (see Chapter 3). The Soviet Communist Party wished to avoid anything similar happening in the USSR. For this reason, there was a temptation to make concessions *before* trouble appeared – even if this actually hindered fundamental economic reform. Brezhnev therefore tried to reduce wage differentials. In particular, he ensured that industrial and other blue-collar workers were better-paid than various professional groups. For example, in the 1970s, a bus driver received 230 roubles a month, compared to a secondary school teacher's 150 roubles.

Under Brezhnev's rule, the numbers of families owning electrical goods increased significantly in the period 1970–80. For instance, ownership of refrigerators increased from 32% to 86%, and televisions from 51% to 86%. Even though investment in the industrial consumer goods sector fell behind plan projections, the situation did improve.

There was, however, a slow-down in the production of some consumer goods after 1976. People (usually women) often had to queue for considerable amounts of time when certain items were in short supply. Nevertheless, Brezhnev repeated his promises about increasing and improving the quality of consumer goods at both the 25th Party Congress in February 1976 and the 26th Congress in February 1981 – just a year before he died.

Social developments

For ordinary Soviet citizens, many aspects of life improved under Brezhnev. In addition to state-subsidised prices for the main foodstuffs (such as bread, potatoes and meat), the Soviet people's **social wage** included cheap prices for clothing, electricity, gas and coal, and subsidised rents and public transport. Incredibly, the prices paid by people in the USSR for such items were not much higher than those paid during Stalin's First Five-Year Plan of 1928–32.

In addition, trade unions opened more holiday centres for their members on the Baltic and Black Sea coasts. Some (those who could be trusted) were treated to officially organised trips to Eastern and even to Western European countries.

social wage This term refers to measures of economic and social well-being other than wages – and includes job security. Brezhnev and his colleagues felt it was important to maintain the large state subsidy of this social wage. Though social wages can be very important, they are not usually taken into account when considering the efficiency of an economic system. Yet people took all these advantages for granted – along with free sanitation, health care and education. Brezhnev's successes in the 1970s (compared with the situation he had inherited in 1964) were not acknowledged, but he and the Politburo were blamed for the relatively slow rate of progress.

SOURCE I

Soviet living standards 1965–78
These figures (based on Soviet statistics) were originally published in the *Guardian* newspaper on 17 August 1981. They were then reprinted in Halliday, F. 1986. *The Making of the Second Cold War*. London, UK. Verso.

	1965	1978
Monthly wage	96.5 roubles	159.9 roubles
Number of doctors	554,000	929,000
Families with TV sets	24%	82%
Families with refrigerators	11%	78%
Living space per person: urban areas	10 sq metres	12.7 sq metres
Consumption of meat and meat products per person	41 kg	57 kg
Consumption of vegetables per person	72 kg	90 kg
Consumption of potatoes per person	142 kg	120 kg
Consumption of bread and grain per person	156 kg	140 kg

Communism in Crisis

Fact
The slow-down in upward social mobility also affected the performance of the economy, as those in management posts tried hard to hang on to them. If they had the right connections, even incompetent managers were usually able to avoid losing their jobs.

However, there was a slow-down in upward social mobility, as the expansion of management posts began to slow, thus reducing opportunities for promotion. In fact, this slow-down first started in the 1950s, and it increasingly became a source of dissatisfaction. There were also other social problems linked with the slowing down and stagnation of the economy – these included rising rates of alcoholism, divorce and suicide.

SOURCE J

Rates of alcoholism, mental illness, divorce and suicide went on rising inexorably. The deterioration of the physical environment continued: diseases were on the increase and hospital services worsened. The living space accorded to the normal urban family remained cramped: just 13.4 square metres per person in 1980. Thousands of Moscow inhabitants had no resident permits, and many of them inhabited shacks, doorways and parked trams. The diet of most citizens, furthermore, ceased to improve in the late 1970s. Rationing of staple food products returned to Sverdlovsk ... and several other large cities.

Service, R. 1997. *A History of Twentieth-Century Russia*. London, UK. Allen Lane/Penguin. pp. 417–18.

Theory of knowledge

History, bias and propaganda
According to many historians, the USSR's economic inefficiencies demonstrate the superiority of a capitalist economy to a socialised economy. But do such comparisons take into account the different histories of these economic systems, such as the devastation of the Soviet economy during the Second World War? In addition, what about the different levels of social welfare provision in capitalist and communist economies? And what of the economic depressions (with high unemployment and idle factories) that periodically affect capitalist economies? Does the failure to make such comparisons reflect individual political bias, or the general influence of Cold War propaganda in the West?

Developed socialism

Despite these social problems, as early as 1966 the Soviet leaders felt confident enough about their system to describe it as 'developed socialism'. As a result of such achievements as the 1917 Bolshevik Revolution, the Five-Year Plans and the defeat of Nazi Germany, the Soviet Union had moved into a new and higher period of development. The phrase 'developed socialism' was later included in the 1977 constitution.

SOURCE K

The maturity of the system posed a further problem for Brezhnev and his colleagues: by the late 1980s much of the industrial capital stock was very old; most of it was technically out of date, and much of it was physically worn out as well. This was just one aspect of a larger problem, which also grew worse over time: the Soviet economy was an economy without an exit. Plants were rarely closed, the service lives of machinery and equipment were far too long, and too little attention was paid to obsolescence.

Tompson, W. 2003. *The Soviet Union Under Brezhnev*. Harlow, UK. Longman.

Activities

1. Draw a spider diagram to identify and illustrate the economic problems and policies in both industry and agriculture during the period 1976–82.
2. Carry out some brief research to see what economic problems affected the US and other Western capitalist countries during this period.
3. Imagine you are an economic adviser. Write a report for Brezhnev to (a) point out what you think is wrong with the Soviet economy and (b) suggest what reforms you think are needed.
4. Continue to add to your chart on 'Economic Reforms' (see page 26).

What economic reforms were attempted in the period 1982–85?

When Brezhnev died in November 1982, he had been in power for 18 years – the longest period of office held by any Soviet leader after Stalin. There was considerable stability and continuity during his rule, and consequently the reality of economic stagnation had been hidden from many observers. However, even Brezhnev had been prepared to admit the existence of economic problems. At the 28th Party Congress in 1981, he spoke of the impact of a difficult world economic situation. But he also drew attention to domestic economic weaknesses, such as shortages of food and consumer goods. This turned out to be Brezhnev's last attendance at a Party Congress. In fact, as early as 1980, his declining health was apparent. Other Soviet leaders thus began to think about who should succeed him.

In his final years as leader, Brezhnev considered attempts to move closer to Communist China and so reduce military expenditure, thus releasing money for economic improvements. But this had led to grumblings from the Soviet High Command. In response to these criticisms, in October 1982 Brezhnev made a speech attacking the 'political, ideological and economic offensive against socialism' being waged by the US.

As Brezhnev's health declined, it became clear that the person manoeuvring to take his place was **Yuri Andropov**. When Brezhnev finally died in November 1982, the announcement of his death was delayed, to allow time for the succession to be worked out. The Politburo met before the Central Committee and Andropov was immediately appointed as general-secretary. Although Prime Minister Tikhanov nominated Konstantin Chernenko, Andropov was backed by minister of defence Marshal Ustinov, in what appeared to be almost a coup by the military and the KGB.

Andropov and reform

Andropov's time in Hungary meant he saw at first hand Hungarian attempts to introduce more liberal economic reforms and policies by reducing the influence of central planning agencies. Significantly, it was he who recommended that János Kádár should be the one to replace Nagy (see page 12). His attitude to reform was also influenced by his career in the KGB, as he had received accurate reports about economic situations both in the USSR and abroad. This meant that Andropov knew before he became leader of the USSR what the main problems were, even though official propaganda tried to gloss over some of them. He also maintained contacts with Soviet personnel in various foreign countries. This gave him a broader knowledge and perspective on economic and political issues than many of the other leading Soviet figures.

Fact
The USSR needed to reduce its military expenditure, and improving its relationship with China seemed to offer a possible solution. By 1981, the USSR had large (and apparently superior) conventional forces compared to the US. However, 44 Red Army divisions were deployed along the border with China, compared to only 31 facing NATO in the west. Thus, if warm relations with China could be re-established, the Soviet Union would be able to divert money from defence to economic development. At the same time, the balance of forces in the Cold War would be altered. The US would lose its alliance with China, and the USSR would gain as an ally a country that was becoming increasingly important.

Yuri Andropov (1914–84)
Andropov was Soviet ambassador to Hungary when Soviet troops suppressed the Hungarian Rising of 1956. By 1957, he had been promoted to the Central Committee and, in May 1967, he became head of the KGB. However, Andropov did not favour total repression of dissent. Instead, he emphasised the need to establish and follow proper legal procedures. Later, when Andropov became secretary of ideology, he used his contacts in the KGB to undermine the position of Chernenko – a possible rival for the post of general-secretary.

Communism in Crisis

Fact
Andropov's time in power was so short because of his ill-health. When he became leader in November 1982, his doctors told him that he would probably only live another five years. Yet he confided to a supporter that he would need ten years to carry through a meaningful reform programme.

Mikhail Gorbachev (b. 1931)
Gorbachev came from a relatively well-off peasant family in the Savropol province, and studied law at Moscow University. After graduating in 1955, he began work in the public prosecutor's office in Stavropol. He was horrified by the corruption he saw and, in 1970, became first party secretary there. It was here that Andropov met him, and decided to support his rise. By 1980, aged only 49, Gorbachev was a full member of the Politburo (the average age of Politburo members at that time was over 70). Though not a liberal, he was like Khrushchev, Kosygin and Andropov – a communist reformer who wanted to make the Soviet system more efficient and democratic.

Consequently, even before he came to power, Andropov made speeches criticising certain failures. However, his main aim was to reform and modernise the Soviet economy. He was not a 'liberal' in the sense that he wished to end the Soviet planned system. He just wanted to make it more efficient and productive. In many ways, his attitudes and policies were similar to Khrushchev's, and also pre-dated the early reforms attempted by Gorbachev after 1985. In any case, Andropov's time for reforming the Soviet economy was to be short – he was only in power for 15 months.

Andropov quickly started his reforms – and his first campaign was against absenteeism from work. A report in 1982 showed that, at any one time, 30% of people of working age were recorded as absent from work for 'personal reasons'. Emphasising the need for efficiency and discipline, he established the 'People's Control' inspectorate. These inspectors went around public areas such as cafés and cinemas, questioning people about why they were not at work. Andropov's speeches warned that improvements in wages, and in working and living conditions, would only come from hard work and greater productivity. One of the main reasons for absenteeism was drunkenness and even alcoholism. This was a growing problem in the Soviet Union, and Andropov launched a campaign against alcohol abuse.

It was relatively easy to launch campaigns, but actually making fundamental changes was more difficult. Many people avoided doing anything that removed their perks and benefits, or disrupted their everyday lives. To help carry through his reforms, Andropov quickly appointed those who supported him and his aims. He also demoted some of those who favoured continuing with Brezhnev's 'drift' (his policy of doing very little and avoiding serious reform). Andropov's team tended to be younger party members – Nikolai Ryzhkov became the Central Committee secretary in charge of the new economic programme, and Grigori Romanov was given control of heavy industry. Another Andropov supporter and protégé was **Mikhail Gorbachev**, the youngest member of the Politburo. He typified those who were frustrated by the conservatism of the party members who had come to power under Brezhnev.

After becoming general-secretary, Andropov used *Pravda*, the newspaper of the CPSU, to identify the abuses that were damaging the Soviet economic system. He also suggested reforms, including setting up smaller enterprises and increasing productivity in different sectors of the economy. For example, transport organisations were told that, if they wanted to continue receiving high levels of state funding, they needed to show higher productivity.

In August 1983, Andropov made another speech in which he drew attention to 'accumulated inertia', which he said the USSR needed to overcome. By eradicating this inertia, the entire massive Soviet economy would be transformed into an efficient and well-functioning one.

The reforms Andropov favoured were influenced by the Hungarian policies implemented under Kádár. In January 1984, steps were taken to give more powers to factory managers in what was called a 'limited industrial experiment', in branches covered by five industrial ministries. In particular, managers were to have more powers over decision-making – including decisions relating to production and use of profits. Wages and bonuses were to be more closely linked to production and sales. Any workers whose jobs 'disappeared' as a result of increased labour productivity would be allocated to other enterprises. However, central planning bodies and structures would remain. In some respects, these reforms were similar to those attempted by Kosygin in 1965 (see page 22).

2 The Soviet economy 1976–85

SOURCE L

Labour productivity is growing at rates that cannot satisfy us. The lack of co-ordination in the development of the raw materials and processing branches remains a problem ... Plans continue to be fulfilled at the cost of large outlays and production expenses. There are still a good many economic managers who, while glibly quoting Leonid Ilyich's [Brezhnev's] maxim that the economy should be economical, are in reality doing little to accomplish this task. Apparently the force of inertia and old habits are still at work ... The main thing is to accelerate work to improve the entire sphere of economic management – administration, planning and the economic mechanism ... Conversely, poor work, sluggishness and irresponsibility should have an immediate and inescapable effect on the remuneration, job status and moral prestige of personnel.

Extract from a speech made by Andropov to the Central Committee on 23 November 1982. Quoted in Laver, J. 1997. Stagnation and Reform: the USSR 1964–91. *London, UK. Hodder & Stoughton. p. 57.*

These early reforms were limited, but seemed to point in a clear direction. However, Andropov's poor health affected his ability to push his reforms through against the opposition and inertia he encountered. He was a realist about such problems. Therefore he did not make optimistic statements and promises, as Khrushchev had done in the 1960s. In fact, in 1983, Andropov contradicted Brezhnev's claim that the USSR had reached the stage of 'developed socialism'. Instead, he said that the Soviet Union was only just beginning to construct such a society.

SOURCE M

It was in 1982–83, when Andropov was General Secretary, that a qualitative shift in the orientation of the top Soviet leadership took place. It was decided to break with the existing system of social relations that prevailed in the USSR and with the political system designed to service them. This decision was necessitated by quantitative difficulties. The economy had not only not been growing fast enough, but as Abel Agenbegyan [sic] informs us [in Aganbegyan, A. 1987. *The Challenge: Economics of Perestroika.* London, UK. Hutchinson] during the 1981–5 plan period, the economy was plunging towards zero growth and eventual regression.

Ali, T. 1988. Revolution From Above: Where is the Soviet Union Going? London, UK. Hutchinson. pp. 65–66.

Fact
Andropov soon realised how deeply inertia was entrenched in the Soviet Union. Just a few days after the speech mentioned in Source L, the head of Gosplan (who had been in post for 20 years) told Andropov that any economic reforms would need to be carried out 'cautiously'.

Historical debate
There has been some debate about whether Andropov's reforms would have worked, had he lived long enough to push them through. Some historians, such as John Laver, argue that the Soviet Union's underlying economic problems could never have been overcome by reforms that merely modernised aspects of the established Soviet economic system. (In many ways, these problems had already been tackled under Stalin.) However, there is also a counter-factual argument that can be made. A counter-factual argument is a form of historiography based on reasoning what might have happened if certain actions had/ had not been taken. According to this argument, if these reforms had been extended and accompanied by political democratisation, a successful economic system could have been created. This system would have been based on retaining social ownership, combined with the application of 'socialist market mechanisms'. How useful, and how valid, do you think counter-factual historical arguments are?

Communism in Crisis

> **Question**
> Do you think that, if Andropov had lived for ten years, he would have been able to put right many of the economic problems faced by the USSR in the 1980s?

By mid 1983, it was obvious that Andropov's health was poor and, in November 1983, he was unable to attend the traditional Red Square parade. Despite being in hospital with serious heart and kidney problems, he still tried to push his reform programme. In December, he issued another call for people to work harder – and, at the same time, removed a few more Brezhnevites from top positions. His health continued to decline and, on 11 February 1984, he died.

Chernenko and 'drift'

Andropov had not had sufficient time to push ahead with his reforms, or to overcome the obstructionism that tried to neutralise their impact. Although his attempts had encouraged others to think in similar ways about reform (and had led to the emergence of reform-minded politicians such as Gorbachev and Ryzhkov), the Soviet Union entered a period of 'drift' after his death. It seems that Andropov hoped that Gorbachev would replace him. Gorbachev had managed the internal party elections in late 1983, which had resulted in the replacement of one in five of the party secretaries.

Despite Gorbachev's efforts, those opposed to reform started planning their moves as soon as it became clear that Andropov's health was failing. The Brezhnevites decided that **Konstantin Chernenko** was their preferred candidate, and Chernenko became the next general-secretary. At 72, Chernenko was the oldest man ever to become Soviet leader. More importantly, he was the candidate favoured by the conservative anti-reform faction. Thus, all reforms were put on hold for the next 13 months – especially as Chernenko's health was also poor, and his leadership skills were limited. These weaknesses perhaps explain why the 'old guard' wanted him to succeed Andropov.

Konstantin Chernenko (1911–85) During the 1930s, Chernenko had become a regional party secretary and, in 1937, he became deputy personnel chief of a local NKVD department. (The NKVD was the secret police force, which later became the KGB.) It was also during the 1930s that he began his association with Brezhnev. In 1948, he had been transferred to Moldavia (where Brezhnev was in charge), and became head of propaganda. When Brezhnev went to Moscow, he got Chernenko appointed to the Central Committee's propaganda section. Chernenko then took charge of Brezhnev's private office and soon became his 'minder'. He often joined Brezhnev in drinking sessions when on holiday.

Although Chernenko gave limited approval to some of Andropov's reforms, his approach was designed to establish 'stability'. He used a phrase that neatly summed up his attitude to reform: 'Look before you leap.' Consequently, he attempted to create a government based on a coalition of Andropov and Brezhnev supporters – only four new ministers were appointed, and there were no changes to the Politburo.

Chernenko did not press ahead with economic reforms. Indeed, although Gorbachev was now arguing for reduced defence spending (so that more could be invested in consumer goods production), the conservative military/anti-reform group managed to get a planned 12% increase in the defence budget announced. Chernenko carried on with Andropov's campaign against corruption and also decided to concentrate on education.

In August 1984, Chernenko became seriously ill. Though he recovered for a time, the government was increasingly run by the defence minister, Dimitri Ustinov (1908–84), and Gorbachev. By then, Gorbachev had become chairman of the Foreign Affairs Committee of the Soviet Union. He then took charge of ideology, and this apparently made him Chernenko's unofficial deputy. Following a series of bad harvests, Gorbachev lost his responsibility for agriculture in the autumn of 1984. However, he soon returned to favour, and his political position was strengthened when Ustinov died in December 1984.

In early 1985, Chernenko's health deteriorated further. Now the two groups became rivals and started to compete with each other. One group favoured Gorbachev and other younger, enthusiastic reformers. The other group favoured stability and more experienced personnel. Significantly, in the Soviet Union's press releases to foreign media Gorbachev was increasingly given a high profile. This indicated that he was likely to be the next leader. Finally, on 10 March 1985, Chernenko died. Supported by the Andropov faction, the KGB and those wanting reform, Gorbachev became the next general-secretary. At 54, he was the youngest member of the Politburo.

Activities

1 Write an obituary for Yuri Andropov that assesses his attempts at reform during the period 1982–84.

2 Work together in pairs to produce arguments for and against reducing Soviet military expenditure.

3 Organise a class debate on the following proposition: 'By 1982, the Soviet Union was past any chance of successful reform.'

4 Continue to complete your 'Economic Reforms' chart, making brief notes on the period up to 1985.

What impact did the Cold War have on the Soviet economy?

It is not possible to fully understand the increasing problems of the Soviet economy without examining the impact of the Cold War. In particular, it is necessary to consider the cost of the arms race. In their attempts to catch up, and then keep up, with US rearmament (both nuclear and conventional), the Soviet leaders placed an increasingly heavy burden on the Soviet economy.

Economic stagnation

As discussed on page 21, the official line was that, because of central state planning, the USSR was able to out-perform capitalism in caring for its citizens. For example, it guaranteed employment, health care, shelter, clothing and pensions, along with subsidised travel and food. However, by 1976, many leaders accepted that the Soviet economy had fallen behind the advanced capitalist countries of the West in civilian technology. They also acknowledged that more needed to be done to increase the availability of consumer goods and improve their quality.

Nevertheless, no significant industrial or agricultural reforms were introduced. This is where the Cold War (especially its accompanying arms race) was a major factor in the crisis and ultimate collapse of the Soviet economy: in addition to massive food subsidies, a huge part of the annual budget was taken up by the nuclear arms race.

Defence spending

After the Second World War, all Soviet leaders (concerned with both defence and deterrence) were determined to develop and maintain a strong military capability. As well as possessing a strong conventional force, the USSR managed to end the USA's nuclear weapons monopoly in 1949. The Soviet Union was then determined to build up its nuclear defences.

However, this policy required massive defence spending. By 1980, Brezhnev's determination to catch up and maintain parity with the US meant that 12% of the USSR's **GNP** went on defence. As the **GDP** of the USSR was about half that of the USA, the Soviet Union had to spend twice as much proportionally – just to keep up.

GNP and GDP The Gross National Product (GNP) refers to the gross market value of all goods and services produced by nationals of a country, wherever that production has taken place (even in another country). Another way of measuring a country's wealth and productivity is its Gross Domestic Product (GDP). This refers to the value of all goods and services produced within the borders of a country, no matter by whom (for instance, by a foreign firm that has invested in that country). Per capita data indicates the relative wealth or poverty of a country. For example, high per capita data generally means better health and longer life expectancy. According to the World Bank, the GNP per capita of the USA in 1979 was $10,630, whereas the GNP per capita for the USSR in the same year was $4,110.

Communism in Crisis

The huge amount of money and resources taken up by defence led to the arms industry being known as the 'steel eaters'. The problem with this was that, as has been seen, the Soviet economy was slowing down. As a result, the production of more and better consumer goods began to decline, and the economy continued to stagnate.

> **Question**
> What is the message conveyed by this cartoon? Remember: you need to do two things with questions like this – look carefully at all the details of the picture and pay close attention to the caption.

Notice how the extra cannons have steadied the ship, comrade?

This cartoon, entitled 'Captain Brezhnev runs aground', appeared in the US Chicago Tribune newspaper, and is about the impact of the nuclear arms race on the Soviet economy

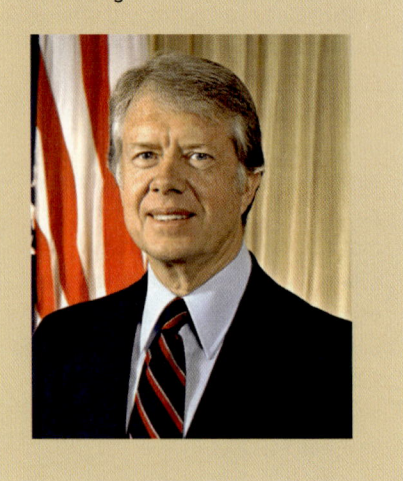

Economic warfare?

In fact, the arms race can be seen as a form of Cold War economic warfare because it forced the Soviet Union to divert proportionately more of its GDP from civilian to military expenditure. This, in turn, restricted the Soviet government's ability to respond to increasing civilian demand for continued improvements in living standards and the availability of newer consumer goods. According to some historians, the US did not end détente and launch a Second Cold War because of the Soviet intervention in Afghanistan. Nor was the US responding to the fact that the USSR had narrowed the nuclear missile gap. Instead, the real US aim was to destabilise the Soviet economy.

Jimmy Carter (b. 1924) Carter served in the US Navy until 1953, and then began to run his family's large peanut farms. He was a Democrat, and acted as a senator, and then governor of Georgia, before becoming US president in 1977. US defence spending was significantly increased under his presidency, while détente was largely abandoned. He was beaten in the 1980 presidential elections by the Republican candidate, Ronald Reagan.

After 1977, when **Jimmy Carter** became US president, this approach was stepped up. Zbigniew Brzezinski, Carter's national security adviser, was very influential – and he believed that a new arms race would ruin the Soviet economy. Indeed, CIA experts reported that the Soviet economy was extremely weak. They claimed that increased defence spending could also cause serious problems for the Soviet Union and its control of Eastern Europe.

By the early 1980s, the crisis threatening the Soviet economy was clear. Essentially, the gross domestic output of the Soviet economy was needed for two main purposes. One part was needed just to keep the economy at its current level (the necessary product). The other part could then be used to increase living standards, invest in improved industrial production and technology, and spend on the military sector (the surplus product). However, throughout the 1970s, there was a slow-down in the growth of the total gross domestic output, resulting in a relatively smaller surplus. Meanwhile, a growing proportion of the necessary product was being absorbed by state subsidies for food, rents and public transport. In addition, much of what was produced was such poor quality that it was unusable. It seemed that one obvious remedy would be to greatly reduce the defence budget, and so fund increased investment in the civilian economy.

2 The Soviet economy 1976–85

SOURCE N

The drive for [US] superiority and the increases in US defence expenditure make another contribution to the conflict with the USSR, namely the cost which they impose on the Soviet Union itself. Even if not used, weapons cost money, and the expenditure burden which the USSR carries, with a GNP less than half that of the USA, has enormous debilitating consequences for the rest of the economy. The USA has been ahead in almost all areas of military technology since World War II, and, given the Soviet desire to match US capabilities, US advances have imposed new expenditures on the USSR. The development of the MX missile and of Cruise and Pershing in the 1980s will force further expenditure on the USSR and will thereby create new problems for the Soviet economy. Some US officials, such as Secretary of Defense Caspar Weinberger, have been particularly clear about the impact of US military development upon the USSR: without any of the weapons being used, they nonetheless serve to weaken the enemy camp.

Halliday, F. 1983. *The Making of the Second Cold War*. London, UK. Verso Press. p. 51.

Fact
There were two main alternatives to cutting the defence budget. One was to cut the real living standards of the Soviet people, and release funds that way. The other was to borrow heavily from capitalist states abroad. But these two possible solutions, along with the proposed reduction in defence spending, were all seen as unacceptable by many Soviet leaders. In fact, the share of the budget spent on health, education and pensions had already begun to decrease, leading to a serious decline in the Soviet health service and welfare system.

Brezhnev's foreign policy was based on heavy defence spending and not angering the West (see Chapter 3). The assumption was that such strength and reasonableness would result in détente. Then the West would agree to weapons reductions and loans, which would enable the Soviet economy to improve through better funding. However, this policy failed in the late 1970s. At this point, the West began to abandon détente and instead embarked on a Second Cold War, developing and deploying newer and more expensive nuclear weapons. The growing threat from the USA meant that calls to reduce Soviet military expenditure had few supporters before Gorbachev came to power. This form of economic warfare by the US therefore posed an ever-increasing challenge to the USSR.

Activities

1. Carry out further research on the various causes of the Second Cold War. Then list them in order of importance.

2. Visit the website (www.sipri.org/) of the Stockholm International Peace Research Institute (SIPRI). See what information you can gather on Soviet and US military expenditure during the period 1976–85.

3. 'It was external economic pressures, not internal weaknesses, which were the main reason for the declining state of the Soviet economy.' With a partner, produce two discussion papers (or speeches): one of you should support the statement and the other one oppose it. Then swap your work, and assess each other as regards: (a) clear argument and (b) precise supporting evidence.

4. Write a newspaper article on the state of the Soviet economy by 1985. It can either be optimistic or pessimistic.

Communism in Crisis

End of chapter activities

Summary

You should now have a sound understanding of the main problems facing the Soviet economy during the 1970s and the early 1980s. You should also be able to describe the various economic reforms, and their outcomes, attempted by Brezhnev, Andropov and Chernenko during the period up to 1985.

Summary activity

Copy the table below and, using the information in this chapter and from any other available sources, summarise:

- the weaknesses of the Soviet economy 1976–85
- how Soviet leaders tried to deal with them
- what the results were.

The Soviet economy 1976–85			
	Weaknesses	Attempted reforms	Results
Industry			
Agriculture			

SOURCE A

The innovations announced by Alexei Kosygin in September 1965 which enhanced the role of management and encouraged the application of mathematical techniques among other things produced good results, especially where labour productivity was concerned, in the short term. Enterprises could actually release labour but only on condition that they found the redundant workers jobs elsewhere. However, by 1970 the trend towards more administrative direction from the centre was again reasserting itself ... The net result, if industrial output is the criterion of success, has not been encouraging.

The eighth FYP [Five Year Plan] (1965–70) saw a healthy increase in national income of 41% and industrial output up 50% ... The ninth FYP (1971–75) was quite a different story. Industry and agriculture both failed to live up to expectations ... The ninth FYP was the first in which the growth of consumer goods output was planned to keep ahead of capital goods production but this never materialised and the consumer was relegated to second position as usual.

McCauley, M. 1981. *The Soviet Union Since 1917*. London, UK. Longman. pp. 220–21.

Paper 1 exam practice

Question

According to Source A (left), how successful were the economic reforms under Brezhnev in the period before 1976?
[2 marks]

Skill

Comprehension of a source

2 The Soviet economy 1976–85

Before you start

Comprehension questions are the most straightforward questions you will face in Paper 1. They simply require you to understand a source *and* extract two or three relevant points that relate to the particular question.

Before you attempt this question, refer to page 215 for advice on how to tackle comprehension questions, and a simplified markscheme.

Student answer

According to Source A, Brezhnev's various economic reforms before 1976 were not very successful, as the ninth FYP did not reach its targets.

Examiner comments

The candidate has selected **one** relevant and explicit piece of information from the source that clearly identifies an outcome. This is enough to gain 1 mark. However, as no other result of the reforms from 1964 to 1976 has been identified, this candidate fails to get the other mark available.

Activity

Look again at the source, and the student answer above. Now try to identify **one** other comment in the source about the success or failure of reforms, and try to make an overall comment about the source's message. This will enable you to obtain the other mark available for this question.

Paper 2 practice questions

1. What were the main problems facing the Soviet economy in the late 1970s?
2. Analyse the successes and failures of the reforms attempted by Brezhnev in the period 1976–82.
3. Examine the main economic reforms attempted by Soviet leaders in the period 1982–85.
4. 'The main reason for the weaknesses of the Soviet economy after 1976 was the impact of Cold War defence spending.' To what extent do you agree with this assertion?

3 Political developments in the USSR 1976–85

Timeline

1964 Oct: Brezhnev replaces Khrushchev as first secretary of the CPSU; Kosygin becomes prime minister

1968 Aug: Warsaw Pact invasion of Czechoslovakia

1975 Aug: Helsinki Final Act

1976 Feb: 25th Congress CPSU

May: first Helsinki monitoring group established in USSR

1977 Jun: Brezhnev replaces Podgorny as head of state

Nov: New ('Brezhnev') Constitution

1979 Dec: Soviet Union intervenes in Afghanistan; start of Second Cold War

1980 Jan: Sakharov placed under house arrest

Jul–Aug: Moscow Olympic Games

Sep: Solidarity formed in Poland

Dec: Kosygin dies

1981 Jan: 26th Congress, CPSU

Dec: martial law declared in Poland

1982 Jun: SALT II signed

Sep: Helsinki groups in USSR disbanded

Nov: Brezhnev dies; replaced by Yuri Andropov

1984 Feb: Andropov dies; Chernenko takes over

1985 Mar: Chernenko dies; Gorbachev takes over

Introduction

This chapter deals with the main political and foreign policy developments in the period 1976–85. As discussed in Chapter 2, there was mixed evidence regarding the growing economic crisis facing the Soviet Union. Some of the apparent contradictions may be due to the fact that production statistics vary according to their source. However, it is true that, just as the signs of a serious slow-down in economic growth were emerging in the late 1970s, many Soviet citizens had relatively good living conditions. In fact, they were enjoying a higher standard of living than they had before Brezhnev – and much higher than they would experience after the Soviet Union collapsed in 1991.

In many ways, the 'crisis of communism' facing both the USSR and China in 1976 came about because they were neither capitalist nor fully socialist, but were in transition, and could therefore go in either direction. Many of the policies needed to increase economic growth required greater economic freedom from central control. Yet, at the same time, granting increased economic freedom often led to growing demands for greater freedom from party and state control.

To a large extent, Brezhnev's regime failed to respond effectively to these problems, and this lack of response played a significant role in the eventual collapse of the USSR. In particular, especially during Brezhnev's later rule, the reluctance of the Soviet leaders to openly acknowledge the growing economic and social problems brought the CPSU into increasing disrepute. This created a sense of alienation in the people, and so contributed to a growing political crisis.

Key questions

- How did Brezhnev's early consolidation of power contribute to the political crisis after 1976?
- What were the main signs of political stagnation between 1976 and 1982?
- How did Brezhnev's foreign policy contribute to the crisis of Soviet communism?
- How did Andropov and Chernenko deal with political developments between 1982 and 1985?

3 Political developments in the USSR 1976–85

Overview

- As well as a growing economic crisis in the years 1976–85, the Soviet Union also experienced a political crisis – possibly more important than the economic one.
- Under Brezhnev, who became increasingly dominant after 1964, the top party and state leadership were controlled by ageing conservatives, who were reluctant to make radical changes to the system.
- A new constitution in 1977 continued the dominance of the CPSU, and a one-party system. By then, a cult of personality was developing around Brezhnev.
- One sign of the emerging crisis was a growth in the amount of dissidence (artistic and national), though only from a small proportion of the population. Brezhnev's regime responded with tighter controls, and by confining dissidents to psychiatric hospitals.
- There were also political problems related to foreign policy in both Eastern Europe and the continuing Cold War. Reform in Czechoslovakia was stopped in 1968 but, by 1980, unrest was affecting Poland.
- After initial successes, détente gave way to a Second Cold War, especially after the Soviet Union sent troops into Afghanistan in 1979.
- Although Brezhnev died in 1982, political 'drift' continued under his successors, Andropov and Chernenko.

The main institutions of the Soviet political system 1976–85

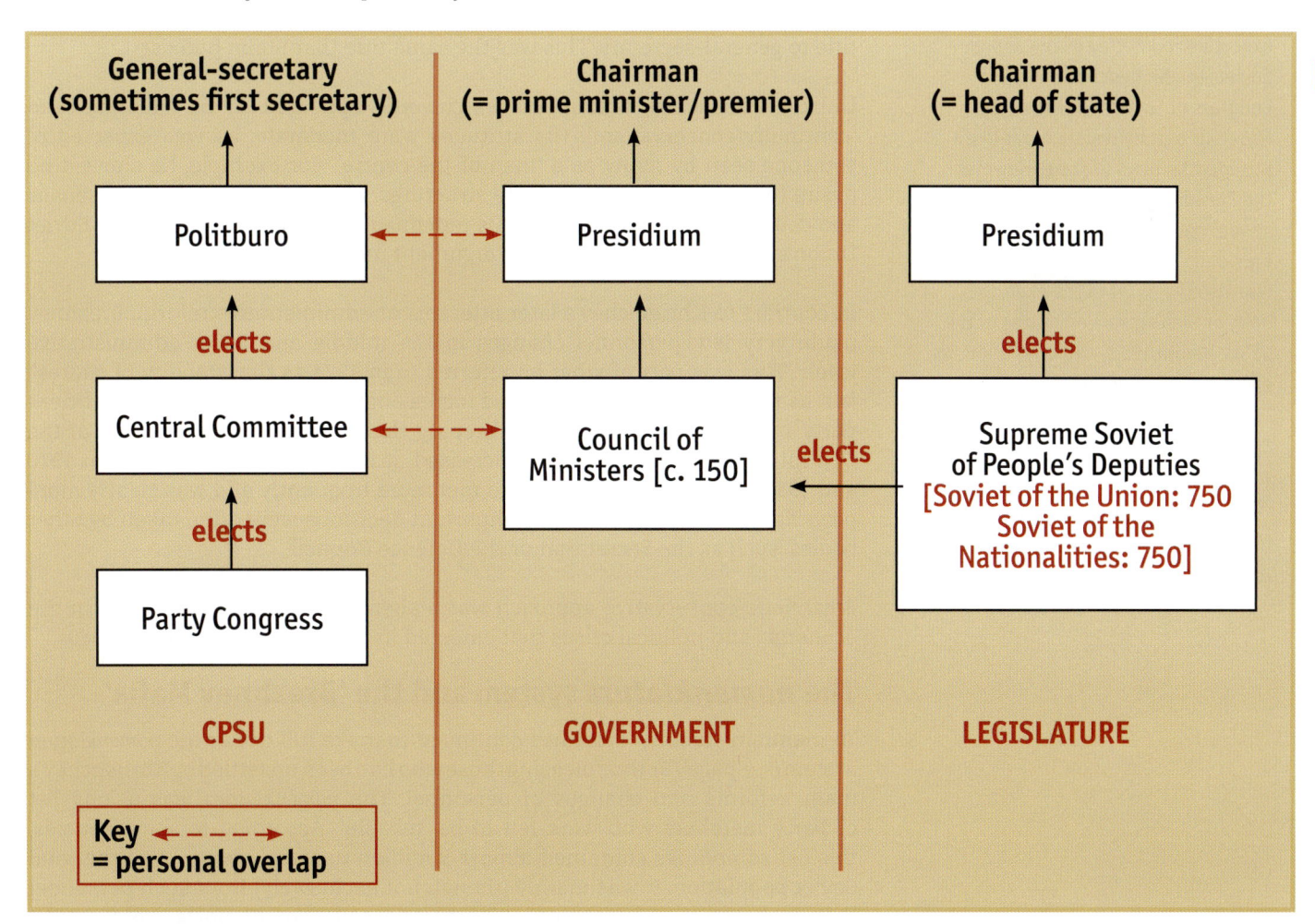

CPSU

- General-secretary (sometimes first secretary)
  - Politburo
  - ↑ elects
  - Central Committee
  - ↑ elects
  - Party Congress

GOVERNMENT

- Chairman (= prime minister/premier)
  - Presidium
  - ↑
  - Council of Ministers [c. 150]

LEGISLATURE

- Chairman (= head of state)
  - Presidium
  - ↑ elects
  - Supreme Soviet of People's Deputies [Soviet of the Union: 750 Soviet of the Nationalities: 750]
  - elects → Council of Ministers

Key ←---→ = personal overlap

Communism in Crisis

How did Brezhnev's early consolidation of power contribute to the political crisis after 1976?

After Khrushchev's fall in 1964, the political leadership of the CPSU decided to try to prevent anyone ever again being able to hold so many posts and thus concentrate power in their own hands. In future, no one would be able to become both prime minister (officially titled Chair of the Council of Ministers) and leader of the CPSU. Instead there would be a broader *collective* leadership, with a triumvirate (three leaders) at the very top. Brezhnev was given the post of first secretary of the CPSU, Kosygin became prime minister, while **Nikolai Podgorny** became chair of the **Presidium** of the Supreme Soviet and thus head of state.

One of the leadership's main early tasks was to reassure military leaders, government administrators and economic managers that the instability and unpredictability that had characterised much of Khrushchev's time in office would end. As a first step, Khrushchev's party reforms were reversed in November 1964. This meant that local party leaders once again had control at all territorial levels.

In theory, first secretary and prime minister were posts of equal importance, but Brezhnev soon began to assert his dominance. At the 1966 Party Congress, the strength of Brezhnev's position was made clear, when the Congress changed his title to general-secretary. This was the same title that Stalin had used.

Unlike Khrushchev, Brezhnev's watchwords appeared to be 'stability' and 'continuity/conservatism'. His attitudes were moderate, as was expected of someone seen by many as a 'man of the centre'. For example, he showed no desire to reform the party or state structures, and clearly preferred consensus and compromise to argument. (This remained the case even though the Soviet Union's emerging problems made argument increasingly necessary.)

In contrast to Khrushchev's later attempts at administrative reform, Brezhnev made very few personnel changes in the middle and lower administrative levels. This was part of what he referred to in 1974 as the 'stability of cadres'. Just as poor factory workers proved increasingly difficult to sack, so inefficient party members could be sure of keeping their jobs. Although the size of the Central Committee was greatly increased, it met only 12 times between 1970 and 1985. Meanwhile, the Politburo met more frequently and was clearly more powerful, yet some of the really important decisions were often taken by other bodies, such as the Secretariat or the Defence Council.

Brezhnev's conservative approach was a significant contributory factor in the economic and political crises that emerged in the late 1970s and early 1980s.

The *nomenklatura* system and the 'Brezhnev Mafia'

To maintain stability, Brezhnev continued to make full use of the *nomenklatura* system (see page 73), thus pleasing those who had been unsettled by Khrushchev's many reforms and changes of personnel. The *nomenklatura* was a long list of party members who were felt to be 'reliable'. According to some sources, this list sometimes contained almost 5 million names – about 2% of the total Soviet population. It was mainly (though not exclusively) from such personnel that appointments to important party and government posts were drawn.

Nikolai Podgorny (1903–83)
Podgorny was Ukrainian and worked as an industries minister before joining the Politburo in 1960. He played an important role in bringing down Khrushchev in 1964. However, as early as December 1965, he was effectively sidelined by being given the relatively unimportant post of chair of the Presidium of the Supreme Soviet. Like Kosygin, he was more liberal-minded than Brezhnev. After Kosygin's loss of influence, he became Brezhnev's second-in-command, before being ousted in 1977.

Presidium The Presidium was the executive committee of the Supreme Soviet, the highest body of the Congress of Soviets (parliament). The chair of the Presidium was like a presidential head of state. However, the Presidium of the Supreme Soviet should not be confused with 'the Presidium'. From 1952 to 1966, this was also the name of the executive body of the Central Committee of the CPSU. Before 1952, and after 1966, its name was 'the Politburo'.

Fact
The 1966 Party Congress also changed the name of the CPSU Presidium back to the Politburo.

3 Political developments in the USSR 1976–85

Reliability and a 'safe' record were often the main criteria when considering someone for promotion. However, it also helped to have a 'sponsor' at a higher level. People on the list benefited from this system of promotion because they gained the special privileges available to those who reached the higher levels of the party.

At the very top, Brezhnev did his best to promote his supporters, with the top positions dominated by ageing hardliners. By 1971, the Politburo was largely made up of his supporters, and by 1981 a total of 8 of the 14 full Politburo members were his protégés. Four of these men were members of the group unofficially known as the 'Brezhnev Mafia' (the men who had worked with him since the 1940s).

As part of his attempts to establish and maintain political stability, Brezhnev tended to replace retiring or dying officials with other elderly appointees – and particularly with his supporters. Thus, by 1978, the average age of Politburo members was 68 (ten years higher than it had been in 1960). By 1982, members of the Central Committee were aged 63 on average, and the average age of the Council of Ministers was 65.

SOURCE A

The central political leadership had turned into a gerontocracy. By 1980 the average age of the Politburo was sixty-nine years. Each member, surrounded with toadying assistants, wanted an old age upholstered by material comfort and unimpeded power. The idea of preparing a younger generation of politicians to take over the state leadership was distasteful to them … Brezhnev's Politburo was composed mainly of Stalin's ageing promotees. Their fundamental attitudes to politics and economics had been formed before 1953. They were proud of the Soviet order and present achievements. Change was anathema to them.

Service, R. 1997. *A History of Twentieth-Century Russia*. London, UK. Allen Lane/Penguin. pp. 404–5.

These appointees usually favoured the continuation of existing methods. Their conservatism increasingly undermined efforts, by would-be reformers such as Kosygin, to make political and economic changes. In fact, many of the party secretaries and ministers appointed in October 1964 were still in post when Brezhnev died in 1982.

Though Brezhnev avoided purges of possible political rivals, he quietly removed people he saw as possible threats. He did this by taking away their posts, or moving them to less important positions. For instance, Nikolai Podgorny was removed from the Politburo in June 1977. He was then effectively forced into political retirement, as he thus lost his position as president of the Supreme Soviet. Brezhnev took over this position as head of state, while retaining his post as general-secretary. Another potential rival, Alexander Shelepin (probably the main organiser of Khrushchev's fall), was also demoted.

Fact
The upper layers of Soviet bureaucracy had numerous special privileges. They earned four or five times the average salary, and had many additional advantages, such as better shops, reserved rooms in hospitals and privileged access to élite schools for their children. Leading academics and writers often earned ten times the average wage. In 1956, Khrushchev had tried to reduce both wage differentials and special privileges, but had then re-introduced some of them. These privileges created two problems. Firstly, they caused growing resentment among ordinary people; and, secondly, they led to corruption. This corruption caused further resentment, and also helped undermine attempts at economic and political reform.

Question
According to Source A, what were the main problems relating to Brezhnev and his Politburo?

Communism in Crisis

Fact

By the time Brezhnev celebrated his 74th birthday, he already had four Orders of Lenin, a Victory Medal, the title of Hero of the Soviet Union, and the Lenin Peace Prize. In fact, the announcement of Kosygin's death was delayed so as not to spoil Brezhnev's birthday celebrations. When his memoirs were published, he was awarded the Lenin Prize – even though they were written by someone else! On his 75th birthday, he awarded himself more medals. As a result, he had 114 in all – more than Stalin and Khrushchev combined. He also had more military decorations than Marshal Zhukov, the hero of Leningrad and Stalingrad, and the man who had taken Berlin in 1945.

Combining the posts of president and general-secretary gave Brezhnev control of both the party and the state bureaucracy. By 1977, he was even able to sideline or block many of Kosygin's attempts at economic reform. These proposed economic changes angered the conservative bureaucrats who wanted to maintain old ways. Although he remained in his post, Kosygin was increasingly ignored.

The leadership was still portrayed as being collective in theory, but in reality Brezhnev was becoming increasingly dominant. This dominance continued for 18 years, until his death in 1982. His ability to consolidate his position rested on his quiet but continuous re-appointments, and his support for consensus, order and stability. This was, of course, appreciated by those who had survived the ruthless purges of Stalin's regime, and then experienced the unpredictability that often marked Khrushchev's rule. Brezhnev's excessive power was revealed by the fact that there was no obvious deputy or heir. It was only when he became increasingly and obviously ill that other leading party members began to plot about who would succeed him.

This photograph, from a British history of the USSR, shows Brezhnev being helped to his seat; by 1979, his health was already visibly declining

Question

What message is conveyed by this picture? Remember to look at the information provided about the photograph, as well as the photograph itself.

Cult of personality

From the mid 1970s, a **cult of personality** was built around Brezhnev – even though he had very little 'personality' or charisma. At the 25th Party Congress in February 1976, he was proclaimed as the 'universally acclaimed leader', and was made a marshal. In December 1980, on his 74th birthday, he awarded himself the Second Order of the October Revolution. At the 26th Congress in February 1981, he was called the 'outstanding political leader and statesman', the 'true continuer of Lenin's great cause' and an 'ardent fighter for peace and communism'.

As an indication of the 'stability of cadres', just before Brezhnev's death in 1982, the entire Politburo and Secretariat of the party were re-elected without any changes. This had never happened before. At the same time, Brezhnev's son and his son-in-law were given high positions, and other members of his family, along with many of his friends, were also promoted. This **nepotism** was something that Andropov was later determined to end.

SOURCE B

Leonid Brezhnev ... became increasingly the central element in the political leadership ... Originally, in 1964, a 'collective leadership', it had become a leadership 'headed by comrade L. I. Brezhnev' by the early 1970s. The Politburo had been listed in alphabetical order after 1964 to emphasise its collective character, but in 1973, after the KGB chairman Yuri Andropov had joined it, Brezhnev's name continued to be listed first although this was a violation of strictly alphabetical principles ... At the 26th Party Congress in 1981 ... Brezhnev's son, Yuri, a first deputy minister of foreign trade ... became a candidate member of the Central Committee ... and so too did his son-in-law Yuri Churbanov, a first deputy minister of internal affairs.

White, S. 1993. *After Gorbachev.* Cambridge, UK. Cambridge University Press. p. 2.

Party stagnation and corruption

The increasing conservatism of the Brezhnev era had an impact on the CPSU itself. Under Khrushchev, there had been a period of continuous growth in membership. However, after 1964, Brezhnev imposed stricter admission requirements. As a result, the annual growth rate in party membership declined from 7% in 1965 to less than 2% by 1973. This lower rate continued for the next ten years.

There were also worrying signs that the 'stability of cadres' was leading to growing corruption, as increasingly noted in KGB reports. Not surprisingly (given the involvement of members of his own family), Brezhnev did nothing to stamp it out. Some younger party members, such as Gorbachev, were appalled by this corruption and complacency. Meanwhile, the general public's growing awareness of these practices undermined respect for the party and the system it enforced. Increasing numbers of people no longer bothered to vote in the one-party elections.

---

cult of personality The personality cult had also been an aspect of Stalin's rule. Increasingly, photographs and posters of Brezhnev appeared in public places, and he was frequently mentioned in the media – much more so than other Soviet leaders. Films were made about his life, and his war experiences were exaggerated. As under Stalin, cities and factories were named after him.

nepotism This term means showing favouritism towards close relatives by appointing them to official positions. Originally, the term referred to 'nephews'. It first arose when popes and other church leaders found posts for their illegitimate children. Brezhnev's daughter Galina and her husband soon became notorious for nepotism and corruption.

Fact
Group 68–80, a dissident organisation, reported on voting figures for three different types of Soviet elections (national, republican and regional) between 1979 and 1982. According to these figures, 50% of voters either had their names removed from the register, asked others to vote for them, or simply refused to vote. However, this is similar to the numbers of US voters who have not bothered to vote in presidential elections in some years.

Communism in Crisis

Discussion point

Historians have often emphasised the extent of corruption under Brezhnev. Many of them have seen it as a contributing factor to the crisis that was building up in the Soviet Union. Working in pairs, develop two arguments about corruption:
(i) that it was inevitable under such a centralised political/economic system
(ii) that it exists in all societies, and was only a serious problem when combined with other problems, which could have been tackled.

SOURCE C

Underlying the stagnation – but also constituting its main symptom – was a deadlocked Politburo around a brain-dead Brezhnev … The other aspect of the picture, which was blatant enough to be widely known throughout Russia, was the spread of a tentacular corruption. Members of Brezhnev's family were ostentatiously involved in it – a subject poor Leonid did not like to hear spoken about. Mushrooming mafia networks, with which many highly placed party officials were associated, were something else the country (if not certain leaders) was aware of. Nothing on such a scale had been known before.

Lewin, M. 2005. *The Soviet Century*. London, UK. Verso. p. 261.

Activities

1. Write a report for the CPSU, pointing out how Brezhnev's policy of maintaining the 'stability of cadres' was leading to political stagnation within the party. Then add something to show how this was linked to economic stagnation.
2. Carry out some additional research on the *nomenklatura* system.
3. Find out more about the extent of the corruption that began to flourish under Brezhnev, including the involvement of members of his own family. To what extent do you think this was linked to the *nomenklatura* system?
4. Draw a chart, entitled 'Political Reforms', with the following headings:
Khrushchev | Brezhnev | Gorbachev
Begin to fill in the chart, giving brief details of both party and state reforms. As you go through other chapters, you will be able to add more details to your chart.

What were the main signs of political stagnation between 1976 and 1982?

'Developed socialism'

Because Khrushchev wanted to widen political participation, he announced that the **'dictatorship of the proletariat'** had been replaced by 'the state of the whole people'. He said this change had come about as a result of economic advances. His aim was to extend political participation from the top party élites, to include everyone in the project of building a communist society. He believed this would make people more involved, and so more supportive of and committed to the system. Khrushchev actually predicted that, by 1980, a classless communist society of plenty would be built in the Soviet Union.

'dictatorship of the proletariat' This is a Marxist term. The 'proletariat' is the industrial working class; while 'dictatorship' here means 'dominance' (*not* harsh and repressive rule). According to Marxist theory, in any class-divided society, the dominant ideas are always those of the dominant classes (such as the people who own the factories, land and banks). Thus Marx described the parliamentary democracy of late 19th-century Britain as a 'dictatorship of the bourgeoisie' (the capitalist class), even though ordinary British people had the right to vote.

Question

What was meant by the term 'developed socialism'?

Khrushchev even said that other regimes might be able to achieve developed socialism via different political systems – including a multi-party parliamentary system. This acceptance of 'differing roads to socialism' alarmed many of the more conservative members of the CPSU, and eventually played a part in Khrushchev's downfall.

Brezhnev spoke for these conservative party members, and during 1966–67, steps were taken to partially rehabilitate Stalin's record. In 1967, Stalinism was referred to as a time of 'unfortunate and temporary errors'. Brezhnev made it clear that there would be no return to Stalin's methods. However, it was also obvious that mass political involvement (let alone significant dissent) would not be tolerated. As the Soviet system produced more and more better-educated people, these citizens became increasingly frustrated. Some of them just became alienated from the system and opted out; others turned to protest and dissent.

As early as 1971, Brezhnev claimed that the USSR had succeeded in building 'developed socialism'. By this, he meant that the socialist stage of construction had been completed. In 1977, this claim was repeated, and Brezhnev spoke about the further great economic advances that would be achieved in the move towards communism. However, many party members thought Brezhnev's promises were unrealistic. As the Soviet Union's economic problems (see Chapter 2) became increasingly obvious to those at the top, 'developed socialism' was spoken of less and less.

The Brezhnev Constitution

In 1977, as part of the 60th anniversary celebrations of the Bolshevik Revolution, a new constitution was brought in to replace the Stalin Constitution of 1936. This became known as the Brezhnev Constitution. The 1936 Constitution had 'guaranteed' several civil rights, though Stalin's methods of rule meant that most of these rights were totally ignored. It also said that the USSR was 'on the road to socialism'. Now, because 'developed socialism' had been reached (according to the preamble of the 1977 Constitution), the Soviet parliament's name was changed from the 'Soviet of the Working People's Deputies' to 'The Soviet of People's Deputies'.

As well as declaring that the USSR was now a developed socialist state, the new constitution confirmed that the CPSU was the 'leading and guiding force in Soviet society and the nucleus of the political system, of all state and public organisations'. Furthermore, the party would continue to determine 'the general perspectives of the development of society and the line of the domestic and foreign policy of the USSR'.

In December 1977, Brezhnev claimed that this constitution was intended to deliver a form of 'socialist democracy' (see page 17). However, there was clearly no intention of allowing a multi-party system, so it was far removed from the usual meaning of the term. It was not until 1985, under Gorbachev, that any attempt was made to introduce aspects of real democracy into the USSR.

Fact

In 1956, Khrushchev made a speech to the 20th Party Congress, which attacked Stalin's record, including some of his policies and his style of rule. This repressive style of rule had helped to provoke several protests and revolts in some of the Eastern European states, particularly in Hungary. The desire for greater political freedom continued, and in 1968 the events known as the 'Prague Spring' took place in Czechoslovakia (see Chapter 6).

Historical debate

Although most history books stress the stagnation and conservatism of the Soviet Union in the 1970s and early 1980s, some political commentators think such judgements are overly simplistic. For instance, Mandel saw the Soviet Union experiencing contradictory developments during this period, due to a combination of 'dynamism and immobility'. The dynamism resulted from impressive long-term social and economic growth, despite an increasing slow-down. The immobility resulted from the bureaucratic stranglehold on the state. So were political, rather than economic, factors the main reason for the growing crisis of Soviet communism?

Communism in Crisis

> **SOURCE D**
>
> 1. Principles of the Social Structure and Policy of the USSR
> Chapter 1
> The Political System
>
> Article 1. The Union of Soviet Socialist Republics is a socialist state of the whole people, expressing the will and interests of the workers, peasants, and intelligentsia, the working people of all the nations and nationalities of the country.
>
> Article 2. All power in the USSR belongs to the people. The people exercise state power through Soviets of People's Deputies, which constitute the political foundation of the USSR.
> All other state bodies are under the control of, and accountable to, the Soviets of People's Deputies.
>
> Article 4. The state and all its bodies function on the basis of socialist law, ensure the maintenance of law and order, and safeguard the interests of society and the rights and freedoms of citizens.
> State organizations, public organizations and officials shall observe the Constitution of the USSR and Soviet laws.
>
> Article 6. The leading and guiding force of Soviet society and the nucleus of its political system, of all state and public organizations, is the Communist Party of the Soviet Union. The CPSU exists for the people and serves the people.
>
> *Extracts from the* Constitution (Fundamental Law) of the USSR, 1977. Quoted in Lane, D. 1985. State and Politics in the USSR. Oxford, UK. Basil Blackwell. p. 348.

This new constitution contained guarantees of various freedoms, including speech, assembly and conscience. But citizens could only exercise these freedoms as long as they did not 'injure the interests of society and the state, and the rights of other citizens'. In practice, many of these freedoms were significantly limited, because the CPSU decided what 'the interests of society and the state' actually were.

Dissidents

Some people *were* prepared to push their rights as citizens to the limits, and beyond: these were the dissidents. Increasingly, certain **intellectuals** and artists became confident that they could assert their civil rights, as it was clear that Soviet leaders had no wish to go back to the harshness and brutality of the Stalin era. This relatively more relaxed atmosphere also saw the beginnings of rebellious underground youth movements. One example was the Independent Song Club. Although it was closed down by the authorities in 1975, many of its members continued their activities elsewhere.

---

intellectuals This term refers to writers, artists, philosophers and academics. Lenin, in line with Marxism, believed the forces of modern historical progress lay in the cities. From the cities, he thought intellectuals would help spread a cultural revolution to the countryside. Both Lenin and Marx also said that a socialist society would inherit and build on earlier culture. Lenin deplored the low level of culture of the Russian people. Indeed, at the end of his life, he felt that this lack of culture was partly why the Russian Revolution seemed to be degenerating.

3 Political developments in the USSR 1976–85

SOURCE E

Although less developed than in Western Europe, the United States and China, the expression of cultural rebellion among young people began to be seen in the Soviet Union towards the end of the 1970s. They were particularly concerned with popular music, jazz and pop songs. Some of these demonstrations had ... a quasi-political character, insofar as they involved a constant clash with the censorship if not its open rejection ...

The most typical case of this youth cultural rebelliousness was the poet-singer Vladimir Vysotsky, who died in 1980 at the age of 42. He had become an idol of Russian youth. His songs played a similar role to that of the protest songs of the Beatles, Joan Baez, and Bob Dylan in the USA and Britain in the 1960s ... On the day of his funeral tens of thousands of people gathered ... This was the biggest spontaneous demonstration ... since 1927.

Mandel, E. 1989. Beyond Perestroika. London, UK. Verso. p. 23.

However, under Brezhnev, some aspects of state control were strengthened: the legal code was tightened, police powers were increased, and the death penalty was re-introduced for several offences. At the same time, Brezhnev ended the 'people's courts' and 'comrades' courts' (which had been set up before 1964 to encourage more popular participation in justice). Increasingly, the Soviet Union under Brezhnev began to treat all serious critics of the regime either as traitors in the pay of the West, or as psychologically disturbed.

This photograph of the Troizkoje Psychiatric Clinic was taken without official permission, and was then smuggled out of Russia, to be published abroad

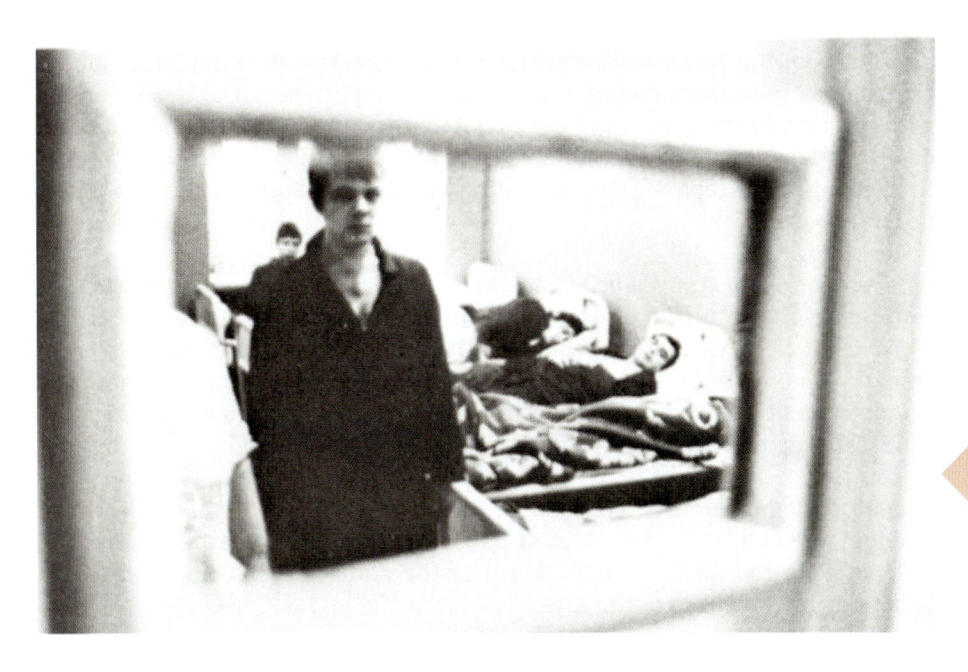

Fact
The authorities frequently claimed that dissidents were psychologically disturbed, and placed them in psychiatric hospitals or wards. This method of controlling dissidents allowed the authorities to avoid any trials. For instance, Vladimir Bukovsky was arrested in 1963 for circulating 'anti-Soviet literature'. He spent several years confined in psychiatric hospitals, before being expelled from the Soviet Union in 1976. Other victims included left-wing dissidents, such as Pyotr Grigorenko and Leonid Plyushch. Alexei Nikitin, a miner who tried to obtain overtime payments for 22 fellow miners in the Ukrainian city of Donetsk, was also sent to a psychiatric hospital.

Questions
What value does this photograph have for historians studying the treatment of dissidents in the USSR in the 1970s? What are its limitations? As well as looking at the source, remember to think about the 'W' questions (see page 214) and don't forget to look at the attribution information provided.

Communism in Crisis

> **Andrei Sakharov (1921–89)**
> Sakharov was a nuclear physicist. He first became politically active in the 1960s, when he spoke out against the nuclear arms race. He then became an activist for human rights. As a result, he was not allowed to leave the USSR to receive the Nobel Prize he had won. After speaking against the Soviet intervention in Afghanistan, he was sentenced to internal exile and house arrest. In 1986, Gorbachev allowed Sakharov to return to Moscow.

Yet, although the evidence is limited, there were few signs of really determined, open political opposition to the Soviet regime under Brezhnev. For many people (though not in all regions), standards of living were higher than they had been in 1964. There was a shorter working week, and education had improved. Despite signs of developing social problems (such as in housing, and in health – largely due to growing alcohol abuse), most Soviet citizens seemed reasonably content. This sense of contentment is often borne out by KGB reports, so political acceptance of the system was not just the result of propaganda.

In fact, the early dissidents rarely put forward any coherent political programme. This was partly because they often had quite different views and aims, focused on various specific grievances. They were therefore rarely united. This situation began to change as early as December 1965. At this time, a group of artists and scientists demonstrated in Red Square in Moscow, calling for the individual freedoms promised in the 1936 Constitution to be honoured. Though they were detained and questioned, the dissidents were then released. They included **Andrei Sakharov** and Alexander Ginsburg.

In 1966, the Brezhnev regime tightened the criminal code to make it illegal to circulate 'false information'. It was soon made clear that dissidents who (in their opinion) undermined the Soviet system, would not be tolerated. For example, in February 1966, the authorities were quick to move against Andrei Sinyavsky and Yuri Daniel. Sinyavsky and Daniel were found guilty of 'anti-Soviet propaganda', although they had both been tolerated by Khrushchev during the time of his 'de-Stalinisation' policy. As their trial was conducted in open court, the criticisms made by these dissidents received some publicity. Soon, several other intellectuals began to state their support. After the 'Prague Spring' in 1968 (see Chapter 6), attitudes to dissent amongst the top leadership hardened. This was especially true when some Soviet citizens demonstrated against the Warsaw Pact intervention.

> **Alexander Solzhenitsyn (1918–2008)** Solzhenitsyn was the author of *One Day in the Life of Ivan Denisovitch*, published under Khrushchev, and other books such as *Cancer Ward*. Many in the West later felt that he had 'lost the plot' when, after being expelled from the USSR in 1974, he called for the US to launch a nuclear war against the Soviet Union. His reactionary form of Russian patriotism, and his adherence to the Russian Orthodox religion, also increasingly lost him supporters both inside and outside the USSR.

For a brief time, there was a softening of attitudes towards the arts, and the magazine *Novy Mir* argued for a more liberal approach to artistic expression. However, this was followed by another crackdown. Some of the more famous dissidents affected included Andrei Sinyavsky in 1973, and **Alexander Solzhenitsyn** in 1974, after his book *The Gulag Archipelago* (about his experiences in the Soviet labour camps) was published abroad. Many other dissidents began to make contact with Western journalists to get their books and pamphlets published in other countries. Meanwhile, the CIA-funded radio station Radio Liberty broadcast into the USSR from Europe – giving a reading of dissident Boris Pasternak's novel, *Doctor Zhivago*.

As a way of overcoming official censorship, critics of the regime increasingly resorted to circulating 'unofficial' literature. This type of literature was known as *samizdat* if it was from within the USS and *tamizdat* if it came in from abroad. Some of these journals were published in their thousands, and had a wide circulation. Every so often, the security forces would make arrests and confiscate copies of journals, but this underground form of protest continued.

Despite its policy of strict censorship, the state did allow a greater degree of freedom for some of the arts, such as painting. However, if an artist was judged to have gone too far in their criticism of the state, the exhibition would be broken up by the police or the KGB.

Dissidents gained something of a boost during the period of détente between the West and the USSR. In August 1975, the Soviet Union actually endorsed the **Helsinki Accord**. As a consequence, several 'Helsinki groups' were established in the USSR in 1976, and in theory Brezhnev allowed them to monitor the Soviet record on human rights. However, in practice, their leading members were often hounded by the authorities. These members included Dr Andrei Sakarov and Yuri Orlov.

After 1977, Brezhnev's regime cracked down harder. Orlov spent seven years in a labour camp for 'anti-Soviet activities', followed by five years' internal exile. By 1980, over 20 members of such groups were in prison. Sakharov was placed under house arrest in Gorky in January 1980. Further arrests followed and, in September 1982, the Helsinki monitoring groups were disbanded. By then, over 60 of their 80 members had been put on trial or in prison, while the rest had been deported or gone into exile. However, while most citizens avoided the risks of open dissent, there were many who sympathised with some of the dissidents. For example, many managers and technicians were beginning to see that the system was holding back progress.

Nationalism

Much of the dissent in the USSR during this period was based on demanding greater political and artistic freedoms, but there was also some nationalist dissent beginning to emerge. At first, during the early 1970s, nationalist dissent was most obvious in the Baltic republics such as Estonia and Latvia. Here, it was a combination of Catholic religious sentiments and unofficial trade union activities. During the late 1970s and early 1980s, developments in both these republics were increasingly influenced by events in Poland (see pages 56–57).

As well as protests in Estonia and Latvia, there were demonstrations in Ukraine and Georgia over religion and 'Russification'. For example, nationalists began to protest about the numbers of Russians migrating to their republics – and even against their incorporation within the USSR. There were also some protests, especially in Georgia, over the 1977 Constitution. The main contentious point was that the new constitution gave the impression that the Soviet government might be thinking of making Russian the only official language in the USSR. These nationalist demonstrations resulted in speedy promises that different national languages would still be recognised as official.

There were also signs of growing unrest in the Muslim Central Asian republics that bordered on Afghanistan. Such nationalist protests were a sign of a significant political crisis that was beginning to emerge in the Soviet Union. Under Gorbachev, the failure to deal early enough with such nationalist sentiments played a big part in the eventual collapse of communism in the USSR.

Under Brezhnev, though, all forms of dissent were essentially controlled, and did not appear to pose much of a threat to the continuation of Soviet rule. Given their control of the media, it was easy for the authorities to show dissidents in a bad light. They either portrayed them as ungrateful beneficiaries of all that the Soviet state had given them, or as traitors in the pay of Western powers and their secret services. Consequently, such people received only limited support from ordinary citizens.

Helsinki Accord Also known as the Helsinki Final Act, this was part of the Conference on European Security and Co-operation (CESC) that first met in 1973. The countries of Europe were represented, along with Canada and the USA. It dealt with issues including trade, borders and human rights. In theory, the Helsinki Accord committed the USSR to upholding free speech and freedom of assembly and conscience.

Theory of knowledge

History and 'truth'
During the Brezhnev period, many Soviet citizens undoubtedly realised that the Soviet media did not usually give the full picture regarding the state of the Soviet economy and the West. How different is this from the situation in the West, where most newspapers and TV channels are owned and controlled by wealthy individuals or companies, such as the Italian ex-prime minister Silvio Berlusconi, or Rupert Murdoch's News International?

Fact
Nationalist dissent included demands from many Soviet Jews to be allowed to emigrate to Israel or the US, for either religious or financial reasons. During the Brezhnev era, over 250,000 Jews left the Soviet Union. The peak year was 1979, when 51,000 were allowed to leave. However, by 1982, restrictions had been imposed.

Fact
Before the USSR sent troops into Afghanistan in December 1979, there is evidence that the CIA was fostering fundamentalist religious unrest in the Muslim Central Asian republics of the USSR, which shared borders with Afghanistan (see page 58).

Communism in Crisis

Activities

1 Imagine you are a journalist. Write a brief article on why Brezhnev's policy of trying to partially rehabilitate Stalin's record will lead to political stagnation, and prevent any chance of increasing political democracy within the Soviet Union.

2 Look again at the extracts from the 1977 Brezhnev Constitution on page 50. Then, in pairs, discuss any recent examples of certain states (including democracies) that have ignored some of the 'rights' set down in their written constitutions. Do such examples mean that written constitutions are worthless?

3 Carry out some additional research on dissent in the Soviet Union under Brezhnev. Then write a newspaper article about some of the main dissidents, their criticisms and their activities.

4 Continue completing your chart on 'Political Reforms'.

How did Brezhnev's foreign policy contribute to the crisis of Soviet communism?

The main external issues contributing to the crisis of Soviet communism in the period 1976–89 were: developments within Eastern Europe; the ongoing attempt to maintain satisfactory relations with the West; and the Soviet intervention in Afghanistan. In practice, these factors were closely linked. They all contributed to a breakdown of international relations, which led the USA to launch a Second Cold War. In addition, they all had a significant impact on the Soviet Union's ability (or inability) to address its economic problems. Before looking at events in Eastern Europe, we need to establish the wider international context of the Cold War.

Détente

Détente before 1976

At the start of his leadership, Brezhnev was keen to improve relations with the West, and this concern was primarily driven by economic pressures. Firstly, there was the cost of maintaining parity with the US in the 'arms race' (see page 37). Secondly, the USSR was suffering from the impact of the worsening rift with China that had developed under Khrushchev between 1960 and 1963. China's rise made it a rival for the leadership of the communist world. The Soviet Union was also burdened with greater military expense, as it had to defend its long border with China.

This made détente with the West an attractive proposition. The invasion of Czechoslovakia in 1968 initially prevented better East–West relations. However, from around 1969, Brezhnev's attitude was an important factor in the development of a period of détente.

Kosygin, in particular, worked hard to improve East–West relations, as he hoped the Soviet economy could benefit from increased access to Western technology. He formed an especially close working relationship with Willi Brandt, the Social Democratic chancellor of West Germany, who followed *Ostpolitik* (a new 'eastern policy') after winning power in 1969. This policy aimed at improving West Germany's diplomatic and trading relations with East Germany and the USSR.

Fact
When Khrushchev was in power, he had talked of 'peaceful coexistence'. He believed that the USSR only needed a minimum of nuclear weaponry to act as a deterrent – just enough to do significant damage, thus making any attack on the USSR too costly. Brezhnev broke with this attitude and instead favoured attempting to catch up with the US in as many areas as possible (at great cost to the Soviet economy). However, Brezhnev did build on Khrushchev's policy of trying to reach agreements on nuclear weapons. Before he was toppled, Khrushchev had signed a Nuclear Test Ban Treaty in 1963.

Question
Why was Kosygin keen to develop closer relations with Western states?

3 Political developments in the USSR 1976–85

Brezhnev with Brandt, the West German chancellor

Although Brezhnev abandoned Khrushchev's 'minimum' nuclear policy, he eventually became aware that his attempt to keep pace with the US was causing serious problems for the Soviet economy. In 1969, President Nixon launched a US programme to develop both **MIRV** and anti-ballistic missiles – as well as being the first to put a human on the moon in July of that year. At this point, even Brezhnev realised that matching all aspects of the US programme would put a massive burden on the Soviet economy. But he reasoned that, if the USSR *tried* to match the US, then, from this position of strength, he could negotiate a reduction in nuclear weapons. He believed he could also import Western technology (though not, as he reassured the conservatives, Western liberalism).

This policy of negotiating with the West for weapons reductions really got underway in 1969–70, with the beginning of the **SALT 1 talks**. The talks attempted to slow down the nuclear arms race. In 1972, further agreements were made. At the same time, the USSR signed several trade deals with the US and its Western allies, including West Germany.

Relations improved further when, in 1973, the US was finally forced to withdraw its forces from Vietnam. In August 1973, the Helsinki Act of the European Security Conference was signed. This recognised existing borders in Europe, and also (in theory) guaranteed human rights. Brezhnev had high hopes of a second SALT agreement. But, although a second agreement was reached in principle in June 1982, it was never ratified by the US. By then, the **Second Cold War** had begun.

MIRV This stands for Multiple Independently Targeted Re-entry Vehicles. Essentially, this means vehicles with multiple warheads, each of which could be directed to a different target.

SALT 1 talks These were the Strategic Arms Limitations Talks, which dealt with different types of strategic weapons (missiles capable of delivering nuclear warheads). They were intended to limit the number of ballistic and anti-ballistic missiles each side could produce. However, these first rounds of talks did not cover the newer MIRV weapons – and the USSR wanted all nuclear missiles that could reach the Soviet Union to be included. Brezhnev's eagerness to set these limitations was due to the fact that Soviet relations with China were worsening. In 1969, there were even armed border clashes.

Second Cold War Some in the US had argued for several years that the Soviet Union had been exporting revolution under cover of détente. Certainly, in the period 1975–79, the US saw several of its client regimes (many of them dictatorships) fall as a result of revolutions or coups. These included the dictatorships of Nicaragua (1975) and Iran (1979). However, such claims were simplistic at best, while accusations that the USSR was trying to develop a first strike capability were simply untrue. (A first strike capability meant the ability to launch a massive surprise nuclear attack that would completely overwhelm the enemy, leaving it too weak to respond.) In fact, under President Reagan in the early 1980s, this was actually the aim of the US.

Communism in Crisis

> **'socialism with a human face'**
> Dubček tried to introduce this new brand of socialism during the period sometimes known as the 'Prague Spring' (see Chapter 6). Soviet leaders initially supported Dubček's appointment, and were prepared to tolerate some of his early reforms. However, they later became afraid that demands for similar reforms would spread into their other satellite states.

> **Comecon** This is short for the Council for Mutual Economic Assistance, set up by the USSR in 1949. Comecon's role was to co-ordinate industrial development and trade between the USSR and the Eastern European satellite states.

> **Fact**
> Agriculture was not collectivised in Poland, as in other Eastern European states, and food shortages could arise.

> **Fact**
> Since the end of the Cold War, it has been proved that the CIA was involved in helping Solidarity (formed in September 1980). According to Robert Gates, a former senior CIA chief, the CIA provided Solidarity with printing materials, communications equipment and other supplies.

> **Fact**
> Some historians argue that martial law was declared in order to prevent the USSR from applying the Brezhnev Doctrine and intervening militarily. Many in the Soviet Union and Eastern Europe worried about the growth of an independent trade union. However, as the Soviet Union was already involved in Afghanistan, it probably would not have risked another military intervention in Poland. Thus, Jarulzelski and the Polish communists seem to have acted largely alone.

1976–79 – the end of détente

Until the mid-1970s, Brezhnev's policies put a strain on the Soviet economy, but also brought some benefits as a result of reasonably stable East–West relations. However, by 1976, powerful sections of the establishment in the US decided to abandon détente. Many of the US political figures who came to be known as the 'New Right' (or 'Neo-Cons') had been unhappy about it from the start. President Carter therefore began a new arms race. In December 1978, there was a big increase in US defence spending, and the beginning of 1979 marked the start of the Second Cold War.

Eastern Europe

Developments in Eastern Europe were crucial to the Soviet Union. Brezhnev's main aim was to maintain the USSR's buffer zone of Eastern European satellite states, established by Stalin after the end of the Second World War. Most of the Soviet leaders since Stalin had been through the horrors of the Nazi invasion and occupation of the Soviet Union during the Second World War. They therefore felt it was vital to maintain this buffer zone. This belief was strengthened by the fact that the USSR faced a militarily and economically more powerful US-dominated alliance. It was the desire to maintain a buffer zone that motivated Khrushchev to put down the Hungarian Revolt in 1956. It was also the reason why Brezhnev finally ordered Warsaw Pact forces into Czechoslovakia in August 1968, to end Dubček's attempt to introduce **'socialism with a human face'** in the 'Prague Spring'.

A few months later, in November 1968, Brezhnev made a declaration known as the Brezhnev Doctrine. This claimed the right to interfere in the internal affairs of its **Comecon** allies if Soviet security or the gains of the people's republics were under threat. In effect, this was a statement of intent – the Soviet Union would intervene, if necessary, to prop up the existing regimes in Eastern Europe.

Poland

Once the Second Cold War began, in 1979, the USSR was faced with growing problems in Poland, which, like Czechoslovakia, were seen as potentially undermining Soviet defences. Nationalism (especially anti-Russian sentiments) remained strong in Poland throughout the communist era, partly because of the influence of the Catholic Church. More seriously, there were economic problems in Poland. In the 1970s, in an attempt to modernise industry and improve the economy without granting political reforms, the Polish government (like many in Eastern Europe) borrowed heavily from Western banks. These banks were happy to lend, on the assumption that the Soviet Union would ultimately be able to guarantee the loans. However, by 1980, Poland's debt had risen to the equivalent of $25 billion.

During the late 1970s, food prices rose as a result of shortages. When the government tried to pass these increases on to the workers, there were strikes and demonstrations – in 1976 and especially in 1980. Against this background of unrest, the independent trade union Solidarity was formed in September 1980, led by **Lech Wałęsa** (see page 57). The Soviet leadership reluctantly accepted the concessions the Polish government was forced to make to Solidarity. These included: recognising a trade union; increasing wages; reducing censorship; and allowing the Catholic Church to broadcast its services. By January 1981, Solidarity claimed to have 8 million members.

3 Political developments in the USSR 1976–85

The Polish government tried to push through economic reforms, but Solidarity wanted political reforms, too. In October 1981, General **Wojciech Jarulzelski** became prime minister and formed the Military Committee for National Salvation, but the crisis continued to develop. In December 1981, martial law was declared, and Solidarity's leaders were arrested.

Although it pushed the Polish government to eventually declare martial law and ban Solidarity in December 1981, the Soviet Union (by then heavily involved in Afghanistan) did not seriously consider invading.

Polish soldiers in Gdansk, photographed on 31 August 1982, during the period of martial law imposed to crush the Solidarity movement

Other developments in Eastern Europe

During Brezhnev's time in office, some Eastern European countries, such as Hungary and Romania, were increasingly taking financial, trade and diplomatic actions independently of Moscow. This was partly because, during détente, many had made trade and finance deals with Western states. Again, this trade and financial relationship continued after Brezhnev's death in 1982, and was one cause of the crisis that unfolded in the late 1980s.

Afghanistan

Of all Brezhnev's foreign policy decisions between 1976 and 1982, perhaps the one that had the greatest impact on international relations was when the Soviet Union sent troops into Afghanistan in December 1979. The Western powers chose to take this as a serious act of aggression by the USSR. It was not, in fact, the main cause of the end of détente. However, it was the final act that officially brought détente to a close.

> **Question**
> What were the main points of the Brezhnev Doctrine?

Lech Wałęsa (b. 1943) Wałęsa was an electrician in the Gdansk shipyards, and a union activist; he was also a committed Catholic. During the mass protests against food price increases in 1980, he co-founded an unofficial trade union *Solidarnosc* (Solidarity). This was the first unofficial trade union to be legalised in the Soviet bloc. Wałęsa was president of Poland from 1990 to 1995, when he forced through rapid privatisation of the economy, known as the 'big bang'.

Wojciech Jarulzelski (b. 1923) Jarulzelski was minister of defence in 1968, and sent Polish troops to join in the Warsaw Pact suppression of the Prague Spring reforms in Czechoslovakia. In 1981, he became prime minister and also the chair of the Polish Communist Party (PUWP). From 1985 to 1989, he was president. He resigned after the democratic elections in 1989.

Communism in Crisis

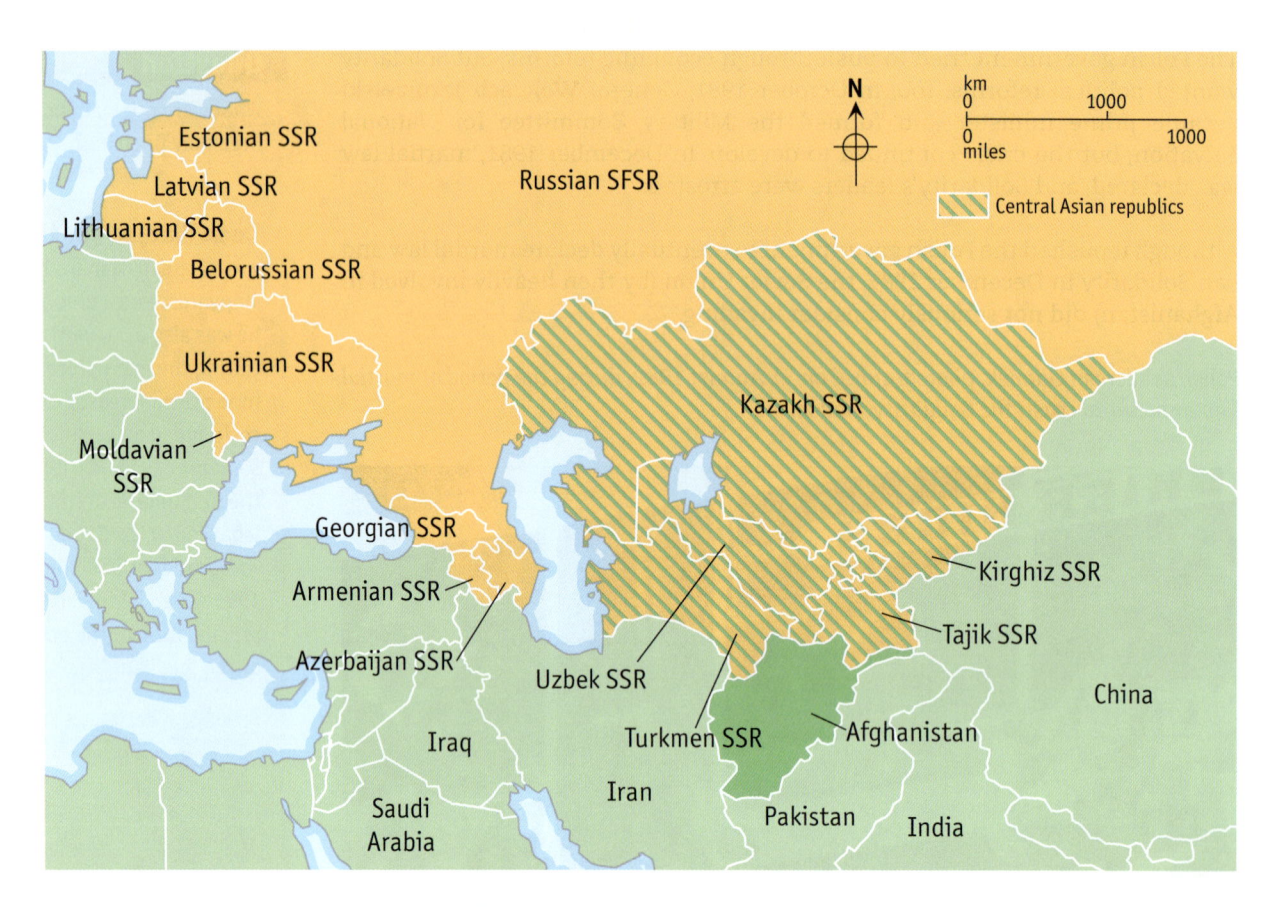

A map showing Afghanistan and the Soviet Central Asian republics; three of these Soviet republics had common borders with Afghanistan

Background to the invasion

In April 1978, a military coup took place in Afghanistan, establishing the Democratic Republic of Afghanistan. The People's Democratic Party of Afghanistan (PDPA) formed the new communist government, led by Nur Muhammad Taraki (a hardline faction leader). In December 1978, the USSR signed an agreement with the new Afghan government, giving economic aid, sending advisers and promising to send military assistance if requested.

This pro-Soviet PDPA government soon came under attack. It was opposed by conservative feudal landowners and religious fundamentalists, who were against government reforms (such as land redistribution, equal rights for women, and secular education for both boys and girls), and the sometimes brutal way these reforms were put into effect. In March 1979, those resisting the reforms killed a large number of Soviet advisers and their families in Herat. There was also opposition from a more moderate PDPA faction, led by Babrak Karmal. In September 1979, Hafizullah Amin, another hardline faction leader, overthrew Taraki, who was then executed.

A full-scale civil war began, in which Islamist fundamentalists set up the *Mujahideen* and declared a *jihad* (holy war) against Amin's government. At first, Amin was supported by Brezhnev's government. However, the USSR became worried about the possibility of a 'blood bath' on its borders, as well as Amin's apparently growing links with the CIA and the US, and his shift to an anti-Soviet position. The USSR was also extremely concerned about the threat spilling across the borders into their Central Asian republics. There was mounting evidence that Pakistan (with US support) and Iran were both already involved on the side of the *Mujahideen*.

Mujahideen This was the name applied to the various groups of rebels fighting against the PDPA government and then against Soviet armed forces. The alliance between these rebel groups was very loose. After the Soviet withdrawal, they soon began fighting amongst themselves. These groups included the Taliban and al-Qaeda. As part of the Second Cold War, the US had already been backing and arming such groups. After the Soviet invasion, this activity was stepped up. Funds and weapons were provided (via Pakistan, a US ally) in a secret CIA programme called Operation Cyclone.

3 Political developments in the USSR 1976–85

SOURCE F

Long reliant on the USSR for most of its military aid, and for much of its trade and economic assistance, Afghanistan had remained a poor and largely undeveloped country until in April 1978 the local communist party, the PDPA, took power in a military coup. There is no evidence of Soviet encouragement for this coup – it was not like communist actions in eastern Europe after the war – and it appears that it was the PDPA who decided to act when faced with the choice of suppression by the then government or taking power itself. Once established, the PDPA government was recognised by both east and west.

What altered the situation was the increase in rural opposition to the regime ... encouraged from outside, by Pakistan and China.

Halliday, F. 1986. *The Making of the Second Cold War*. London, UK. Verso. p. 155.

SOURCE G

Brezhnev – Not a day goes by when Washington has not tried to revive the spirit of the 'Cold War' to heat up militarist passions. Any grounds are used for this, real or imagined. One example of this is Afghanistan. The ruling circles of the US and of China as well, stop at nothing, including armed aggression, in trying to keep the Afghanis from building a new life in accord with the ideals of the revolution of liberation of April 1978. And when we helped our neighbour Afghanistan, at the request of its government ... to beat back the attacks of bandit formations which operate primarily from the territory of Pakistan, then Washington and Beijing raised an unprecedented racket ... We had no choice other than the sending of troops.

Extract from the plenum meeting of the Central Committee of the CPSU, 23 June 1980. From http://www.wilsoncenter.org

The Soviet leadership was split. The KGB favoured a quick intervention to help restore stability, while the military advocated overthrowing Amin, in case Afghanistan was invaded by Pakistan, with US support. Brezhnev, in particular, was concerned that failure to intervene in this Soviet 'sphere of influence' might send the wrong signal, leading the communist states in Eastern Europe to think that the USSR was no longer willing to act on the Brezhnev Doctrine to maintain Soviet control there, or to resist US power. Initially, the Soviet leadership therefore backed a pro-Soviet faction in the PDPA, led by Karmal, which overthrew Amin in December 1979.

Question

Source F and Source G are both about the background to the Soviet military intervention in Afghanistan in December 1979. What are the points of similarity and difference between the two sources? Remember: when you make your comments, you should discuss the two sources *together*, pointing out the similarities and then the differences. If you discuss one source and then the other, you may end up just describing/paraphrasing what they say, and not making *clear* and *explicit* points of comparison/contrast.

Historical debate

According to the official Soviet line, Karmal (who had been in exile in the USSR) had returned to Kabul and carried out the coup. He had then supposedly murdered Amin, without any Soviet involvement. However, according to several experts (including the Russian historian Vladimir Boukovsky), there is evidence that the Soviet leadership had decided *before* the coup that Amin and his closest supporters should be killed. On the other hand, Fred Halliday points out that it was Amin who initially asked for Soviet assistance. He also mentions that Karmal issued an invitation *after* Soviet troops had already crossed the borders.

Communism in Crisis

Fact

Afghanistan had long been an area of Russian interest, even before 1917. More recently, given its common borders with the USSR's Central Asian republics, it had been generally accepted by the West that Afghanistan lay within the USSR's 'sphere of influence'. This explains the West's acceptance of the internal military coup that took place in April 1978, establishing the PDPA as the new communist government. It was only when the USSR actually launched an invasion that the US attitude changed dramatically.

The USSR sends in troops

Eventually, in late December 1979, acting on an appeal from the new communist government in Kabul, the Soviet Union sent in troops to assist. By April 1980, there were over 100,000 Soviet soldiers in Afghanistan.

The strength of the US response to the Soviet invasion of Afghanistan surprised the Soviet leaders, who had not expected any serious consequences. President Carter, on advice from his national security adviser Zbigniew Brzezinski, described it as 'the greatest threat to world peace since the Second World War', and demanded an immediate Soviet withdrawal. His 'Carter Doctrine' soon followed. This policy stated that there was an 'arc of crisis' stretching from Iran to the Persian Gulf, and that the US would intervene if its interests there were threatened. By 1985, the US was supplying the *Mujahideen* with anti-aircraft missiles capable of bringing down Soviet helicopters.

Mujahideen fighters carrying Stinger missiles; estimates of the numbers of portable Stinger missiles supplied by the US to the Mujahideen vary from 500 to 2000

Question

What does this photo tell us about the nature of the war in Afghanistan, and US involvement in it?

The Soviet decision turned out to be ill-judged, and the adventure was to play a big part in the unfolding crisis. The invasion of Afghanistan did nothing for the Soviet Union's image abroad (in particular, it upset many of its Middle Eastern allies), and the intervention soon became a massive drain on Soviet manpower and its already-struggling economy. Apart from the actual costs involved, the US imposed a boycott on exports of grain and technology to the USSR, and other countries followed suit. These actions led to some shortages in the USSR, and affected public opinion.

There was also a large organised boycott of the Olympics, which were held in Moscow from July to August 1980. In addition, although the Soviet media carefully controlled what news was reported to the Soviet people, there was rising dissatisfaction at the human and financial costs of this war. In all, over 15,000 Soviet troops died and 50,000 were wounded. There were even anti-war demonstrations in the USSR. By the time Brezhnev died, it was clear that this had become the USSR's 'Vietnam' – a war it could not win. In fact, the war in Afghanistan was one of the most important factors behind Gorbachev's push for 'new thinking' after 1985.

Conclusion

The general crisis facing Soviet communism under Brezhnev was the result of many different factors. These included concerns about developments in Eastern Europe – especially Poland. There was also the impact of defence spending (on the arms race with the US, and on maintaining Soviet defences against China) on the Soviet economy.

In fact, events in Afghanistan illustrated the wider impact of Brezhnev's desire to maintain Soviet defences at levels comparable to the USA's. The Soviet military was pleased about his continued commitment to invest in the latest weaponry. However, investing so much in defence put an increasingly heavy burden on the Soviet economy. At this point, the economy was showing signs of slowdown and stagnation, partly because of this heavy defence spending. Although Brezhnev had achieved parity with the US in many areas, the domestic effect was an increasing shortage of certain consumer goods. This, not surprisingly, contributed to growing dissatisfaction and thus a developing domestic and foreign political crisis. His successors then had to try to deal with the crisis.

Activities

1 'The Soviet Union should never have attempted to achieve military parity with the US in the period 1976–82.' The class should divide into two groups to prepare a class debate: one group to develop arguments to support the statement; the other to oppose it. Make sure you back up your arguments with precise information.

2 Draw a table, entitled 'Arms reductions, 1976–91', with two headings:

Nuclear | Conventional

Under these headings, give dates and brief details of agreements made during the period 1976–85. You can complete this chart for the remaining years as you read through later chapters.

3 Carry out some further research, then draw a mind map to explain the various reasons why the Soviet Union was concerned about developments in Poland from 1980 to 1982. Make sure you include some *brief* references to: (a) reasons for the Soviet takeover in Eastern Europe after 1945; and (b) how the USSR responded to events in Hungary (1956) and Czechoslovakia (1968). Were there any similarities between these two events and the rise of Solidarity in Poland?

4 Using the information in this chapter, and any other sources available to you, prepare a brief for a court case. First, argue that the Soviet intervention in Afghanistan was essentially defensive – and partly a reaction to earlier actions by the US. Then develop a counter-argument.

Communism in Crisis

How did Andropov and Chernenko deal with political developments between 1982 and 1985?

After Brezhnev's death, the 'drift' that took place in economic reform was largely repeated in confronting the growing political problems that had emerged before 1982.

Andropov

Political reform

Andropov's brief rule saw a number of significant economic reforms (see Chapter 2). On becoming general-secretary, Andropov made several personnel changes at intermediate and lower levels in the economic and party structure, to help push through his reforms. Though he was only in power for 15 months, he replaced 205 of the regional party secretaries, 20% of ministers and 30% of the departmental heads of the Central Committee secretariat. He also decided to take a much tougher line on corruption. This was an attempt to weaken the positions of Brezhnev appointees, who were dragging their feet on implementing reforms, and also to make corruption seem less attractive.

Nevertheless, although Andropov put his own team in place as far as possible, the number of Brezhnevites in post (at both senior and intermediate levels) meant that he had to act cautiously. Moreover, although he avoided any personality cult and recognised the need to reform both the party and the Soviet bureaucracy, Andropov was not a liberal. Like Brezhnev and previous Soviet leaders, he was fully conscious of the continued US–Western ideological onslaught against the USSR. His main focus was on economic reform – and he clearly had no plans for any fundamental political changes. In fact, when a group of young Marxist intellectuals formed the 'Russian New Left' and claimed that a new ruling class had emerged since the Revolution in 1917, they were quickly arrested.

Dissent

Other dissenters were also firmly repressed. Andropov was in charge of the KGB before 1982, and was responsible for the suppression of dissent in all its forms. For instance, he took the decision to send Sakharov into exile in Gorky in 1980. After Andropov came to power, Sakharov and his wife were continually harassed, while **Roy Medvedev** was warned to stop his 'anti-Soviet activities'. In addition, the Soviet authorities continued to be concerned about 'decadent' and 'alien' trends in the arts.

Nevertheless, when Andropov came to power his response was not a simple one of increasing repression. He encouraged ordinary citizens to voice complaints to officials, and he took a more sympathetic attitude to nationalist unrest. For example, he accepted that 'mistakes' had been made in the past. He was also aware that not all regions had benefited from the improvements in living standards under Brezhnev, and promised that benefits would be spread more equally. He even tried to persuade certain dissidents that their criticisms were harming the country.

Under Andropov, mass arbitrary arrests became a thing of the past. According to Moshe Lewin, fear of the secret police had mostly faded by the 1980s. (In fact, fear of the secret police had been gradually decreasing since the 1960s.)

Fact
Andropov took such a tough line on corruption that several of Brezhnev's associates were executed for being corrupt.

Roy Medvedev (b. 1925)
Medvedev was a dissident Marxist historian. He was expelled from the CPSU in 1969 for writing a book called *Let History Judge*, which was highly critical of Stalin. He campaigned for a return to Leninism, and a reformed, democratic socialism. In 1970, Medvedev, Sakharov and other dissidents signed an Open Letter to the Soviet leadership, calling for reform. Medvedev supported Gorbachev's reforms, and rejoined the CPSU in 1989.

3 Political developments in the USSR 1976–85

> **SOURCE A**
>
> For Andropov, a policy of repression had to be conceived as a way of resolving a problem. Faced with Solzhenitsyn, Sakharov, Medvedev and other dissidents, the approach he adopted aimed to limit the political damage they could cause – and not to destroy the persons themselves, as a Stalinist ... would have done. Andropov was an analyst, not an executioner. Whereas the hardliners wanted to isolate Solzhenitsyn by despatching him to Siberia, he opted to exile him abroad. I do not know what their preference was in the case of Sakharov, but Andropov's solution – exile to Gorky – threatened neither his health nor his pursuit of his intellectual work.
>
> Lewin, M. 2005. *The Soviet Century*. London, UK. Verso. p. 256.

This change made dissidence and other forms of political activity easier. However, ironically, it also helped undermine Andropov's regime, which was responsible for relaxing controls and repression, and allowing people more freedom to express themselves.

Foreign policy

Andropov never seriously considered withdrawing troops from Afghanistan, even though this had become a major source of discontent within the USSR. He took an essentially conservative approach to foreign policy.

However, he did suggest further arms controls in November 1982, and in 1983 he reduced the Soviet space programme in an attempt to save money – though President Reagan's insistence on the Star Wars project made this difficult. In 1983, Andropov again called for arms controls. He even offered to suspend work on anti-ballistic missiles, and to reduce Soviet missiles in Europe. But the US and its allies refused to make similar concessions, so the offer fell through. There was another attempt to reach agreement at Geneva at the end of November 1983, but this failed. By that time Andropov's health had got worse and he was seriously ill.

Chernenko

Just before Andropov died, he removed some more Brezhnevite officials from top positions. However, they were still strong enough to ensure that their preferred candidate, Chernenko, succeeded, in preference to Andropov's favourite, Gorbachev.

Those favouring reform now had to wait, as Chernenko maintained Brezhnev's policies of caution and conservatism. During his brief time in office, he continued with the previous coalition of factions. Only four new ministers were appointed, and there were no changes to the Politburo. Although he continued Andropov's anti-corruption policies, Chernenko dropped plans to reduce the scale of bureaucracy. Party officials could once again look forward to jobs for life. He also presided over the drawing up of a new Party Programme, tightened censorship, and took a hard line on dissent; though he did try to address some of the nationalities' issues (see page 104).

Fact
Andropov was actually one of the leaders who had strongly advised Brezhnev to send troops into Afghanistan in the first place.

Communism in Crisis

Chernenko tried to resume good relations with the US and the West, despite some Soviet military leaders who wished to drop détente. However, Reagan's Star Wars programme and the continued Soviet presence in Afghanistan made this almost impossible. As a result, and in retaliation for the 1980 Olympics boycott, the Soviet bloc boycotted the 1984 Los Angeles Olympics.

During 1984, Chernenko grew increasingly ill. At this point, a struggle began between some sections of the military (who wanted the USSR to invest in new high-tech weaponry and take a hard line against the West) and some of the political leadership. Gorbachev let it be known that he was strongly in favour of reducing military expenditure and securing arms reductions by means of negotiations with the West. Eventually, when Chernenko died in March 1985, those favouring reform were able to secure Gorbachev's succession.

Activities

1 Draw a spider diagram giving brief details of how dissenters were treated in the period 1982–85.

2 Carry out further research on Soviet dissidents in this period. Then compose short biographies of any *two* who you think were particularly significant.

3 Jokes were often an important way of expressing dissatisfaction and even opposition in the Soviet Union, as in this parody of an official state obituary for an important leader:

'Today, due to bad health and without regaining consciousness, Comrade Chernenko took up the duties of secretary-general'.

See what other jokes you can find relating to the period 1976–85.

4 Continue completing your table on 'Political Reforms'.

3 Political developments in the USSR 1976–85

End of chapter activities

Summary

You should now have a sound understanding of the main Soviet political and foreign policy developments under Brezhnev, and the reasons for them. You should also be able to comment on the emergence of political, artistic and nationalist dissidence, and its significance during this period.

Your study of Chapters 2 and 3 should enable you to make balanced assessments of the reasons for, and extent of, the economic and political crises facing the post-1985 Soviet government.

Summary activity

Copy the diagram on the right. Then, using the information in this chapter and from any other available sources, make brief notes under all the headings and sub-headings shown. Remember to include information on historical debate/interpretations, including the names of historians.

The emerging political crisis 1976–85

1 The Soviet political system 1976–85
- Brezhnev's rule
- Andropov and Chernenko

2 Dissent
- Extent and significance
- How Soviet leaders tried to deal with it

3 Foreign policy
- Détente
- Eastern Europe
- Afghanistan

Paper 1 exam practice

Question

With reference to their origin and purpose, assess the value and limitations of Source A (right) and Source B (on page 66) for historians studying relations between the Soviet Union and the USA in the period 1976–85.
[6 marks]

Skill

Value and limitations (utility/reliability) of sources

SOURCE A

This Cold War cartoon, which relates to US threats against Nicaragua in the early 1980s, shows the Soviet view of US foreign policy in general.

Communism in Crisis

SOURCE B

The struggle to consolidate the principles of peaceful coexistence, to assure lasting peace, and to reduce and in the long term to eliminate the danger of world war remains the main element of our policy towards the capitalist states. Considerable progress has been achieved in the past five years. The passage from the cold war to détente was primarily connected with changes in the correlation of world forces. Though world peace is by no means guaranteed yet, we have every reason to declare that the improvement of the international climate is convincing evidence that lasting peace is not merely a good intention but an entirely realistic objective.

Extract from Brezhnev's report to the 25th Congress of the CPSU, Feb–Mar 1976. Quoted in Roberts, G. 1999. *The Soviet Union in World Politics: Co-existence, Revolution and Cold War, 1945–1991.* London, UK. Routledge. p. 61.

Before you start

Value and limitations (utility/reliability) questions require you to assess **two** sources over a range of possible issues – and to comment on their value to historians studying a particular event or period of history. You need to consider both the **origin and purpose** and also the **value and limitations** of the sources. You should link these in your answer, showing how origin/purpose relate to value/limitations.

Before you attempt this question, refer to pages 216–17 for advice on how to tackle these questions and a simplified markscheme.

Student answer

These sources have little value, as they are both from the Soviet Union – and they show different attitudes. Source A shows that the USSR was frightened of the US, while Source B says they are getting on OK. Also, there aren't any US sources.

Examiner comments

The response here has only basic/limited comments on the origins of the two sources, and thus on their value/limitations. In addition, there is nothing on possible purpose, and no really **explicit** reference to the question. Instead, the focus is mainly on content. The candidate has only done enough to get into Band 3, and so be awarded 1 or 2 marks at most.

Activity

Look again at the two sources, the simplified markscheme, and the student answer above. Now try to write a paragraph or two to push the answer up into Band 1, and so obtain the full 6 marks. As well as assessing origin and possible purpose, try to assess value as well as limitations for **both** sources. You should also make a linking comment to show value in relation to the question.

Paper 2 practice questions

1. How did Brezhnev's style of rule contribute to the developing political crisis of the Soviet Union up to 1982?
2. 'The Brezhnev regime's methods of dealing with dissent were largely successful.' To what extent do you agree with this assertion?
3. Compare and contrast the treatment of corruption and dissent by Brezhnev and Andropov.
4. For what reasons, and with what results, did the USSR intervene in Afghanistan?

4 The Soviet economy under Gorbachev

Introduction

When Gorbachev came to power in March 1985, his main stated aims were to establish and maintain a reformed socialist system. He also intended to revitalise the CPSU – by means of economic reforms, combined with greater freedoms and democracy. Essentially, he wanted to maintain the broad structures of the non-capitalist Soviet system but to remove its economic and political failings. He thus began as a communist reformer – not someone who wanted to replace socialism and instead create a capitalist state.

Indeed, Gorbachev said on several occasions that he wanted to return to the early ideals of the Bolshevik Revolution, when Lenin was in charge. In other words, he hoped to combine aspects of Lenin's economic policies with political democracy. He wanted to avoid the excesses of both the Stalinist past and Western capitalism, in order to create a 'self-managing socialism', in which there would be less state domination of the economy.

In fact, many of Gorbachev's ideas were close to those advocated by Leon Trotsky in the late 1920s and the 1930s, before and after his expulsion from the Soviet Union. For example, Gorbachev established a new form of Lenin's New Economic Policy (NEP), returned parts of farming to family production, and set up genuine co-operatives in the service sectors of the economy. All these strategies had also been proposed by Trotsky. He, like Gorbachev, argued for a reformed, efficient and properly planned state sector to oversee all these changes.

In 1986, Gorbachev announced that his aims were to be achieved via three main policies: *perestroika*, *glasnost* and *demokratizatsiya*. These three terms mean, respectively: restructuring, openness and democratisation. *Perestroika* is normally associated with his economic reforms, which were meant to make the Soviet economic system more modern and so increase productivity. However, the term also soon came to be applied to aspects of political reform, all of which were intended to modernise the USSR. In fact, Gorbachev often spoke of *perestroika* in this wider sense – to apply to the entire Soviet system. The associated policies of *glasnost* and *demokratizatsiya* will be discussed in the next chapter.

Timeline

1985 Mar: Gorbachev becomes general-secretary of the CPSU; Ryzhkov becomes prime minister

Jun: Gorbachev informs Central Committee about economic problems

Jul: Romanov sacked

Dec: Grishin replaced by Yeltsin as party boss of Moscow

1986 Feb–Mar: 27th Congress of CPSU; official launch of *perestroika*; 12th Five-Year Plan launched

Nov: Law on Individual Labour Activity

Dec: Law on Joint Enterprises

1987 May: Law on State Enterprises

1988 Jan: Law on State Enterprises comes into effect

May: Law on Co-operatives

Jun: 19th Party Conference

1989 Jul: strikes by miners in Kuzbass region

Dec: Congress of People's Deputies votes for Abalkin Programme of economic reforms

1990 Aug: Shatalin Plan presented

Sep: Shatalin Plan rejected

1991 Jan: Russian Supreme Soviet legalises ownership of private property

Dec: collapse of USSR

Communism in Crisis

Gorbachev was aware that opportunities for fundamental reform had been missed both during the Brezhnev era and in 1982–85, despite attempts by Andropov to get things moving. Ironically, though, after only six years in power, Gorbachev turned out to be the apparent 'grave digger' of the system he was trying to reform. He presided over the total collapse of the Soviet Union in 1991, and went down in history as its last leader.

Key questions

- What was 'Gorbachevism' and what were Gorbachev's early actions?
- What was *perestroika* and what were its main policies between 1986 and 1989?
- What problems did Gorbachev's economic reforms encounter in 1990–91?

Overview

- By the time Gorbachev came to power in March 1985, the signs of a stagnating economy had become too serious to ignore. By then, he had already reached the conclusion that reform was necessary.
- First, in order to ensure that he would be able to see his reforms through, he made changes to the membership of the Politburo and the Central Committee, promoting those he knew also favoured reform.
- His first attempt to increase productivity was through an approach that became known as *uskorenie*, meaning 'acceleration' or 'accelerated growth'.
- This was essentially an attempt to make the existing system more efficient by putting pressure on managers to increase productivity, and having campaigns against problems such as alcoholism and corruption.
- However, by 1986, it was clear that these measures were not having the desired results, so he officially launched his new economic reform policy. This was *perestroika*, or restructuring. The aim was to reduce, but not end, state control of local enterprises, and give managers more power to make decisions. Gorbachev hoped this would lead to increased efficiency and production.
- He also introduced reforms that allowed a certain amount of private economic activity in the agricultural and services sectors. However, the results were mixed, while signs of economic decline and political opposition continued.
- By 1988–89, the developing crisis led to more far-reaching reforms being suggested. These included moving to an essentially market-dominated economy. Such plans were too much for Gorbachev and his supporters, while conservative hardliners increasingly feared that capitalism would soon be restored.
- During 1990–91, the economic (and political) crisis deepened, with individual republics such as Russia increasingly taking their own economic decisions. Eventually, in December 1991, the Soviet Union collapsed.

French president François Mitterrand (left) visits Moscow to offer his condolences to the new Russian president Mikhail Gorbachev (right) in March 1985, following the death of Chernenko, the former general-secretary of the Communist Party

4 The Soviet economy under Gorbachev

What was 'Gorbachevism' and what were Gorbachev's early actions?

By the mid 1980s, the centralised economy had largely managed to deliver full employment; cheap housing, fuel and transport; and subsidised food prices. In many ways, given that only 70 years (many of which had seen political turmoil and wartime destruction) had passed since 1917, this was perhaps no mean achievement.

SOURCE A

We ought, perhaps, to remind ourselves that these fifty years [1917–67] have not been a single uninterrupted period of growth and development. Seven or eight of the fifty years were taken up by armed hostilities which resulted in severe setbacks and widespread destruction, unparalleled in any other belligerent country. Another twelve or thirteen years were spent on replacing the losses. The actual periods of growth cover the years from 1928 to 1941 and from 1950 onwards, about thirty years in all. And in these years an unusually high proportion of Soviet resources, about one-quarter of the national income on the average, was absorbed in the arms race that preceded and followed the Second World War. If one could calculate the advance in ideal units of truly peaceful years, one would conclude that the Soviet Union achieved its progress within twenty or, at the most, twenty-five years. This has to be kept in mind when one tries to assess the performance.

Deutscher, I. 1967. *The Unfinished Revolution: Russia 1917–1967*. Oxford, UK. Oxford University Press. p. 42.

The Soviet economy in 1985

Consumer demands and expectations were rising at a time when it was clear that the Soviet economy was showing serious signs of stagnation. Some of these signs were labour shortages and low productivity, along with poor-quality goods in certain areas. In fact, it was, and still remains, difficult to get a true picture of the Soviet economy. This is partly because different economists and historians have used different indicators (such as productivity, Gross Domestic Product or Gross National Product). In addition, there is the problem of reliability when using Soviet statistics. However, according to most sources, the growth rates of the Soviet economy had been falling since the late 1960s.

For example, it was claimed that the average annual growth in Soviet national income dropped to as low as 3.5% by 1981–85, compared to 7.75% in the period 1966–70. In addition, despite a rising agricultural output overall, the USSR was increasingly dependent on importing fodder grain from Western states – including its Cold War enemy, the US.

Communism in Crisis

This decline was mirrored across a range of other economic indicators, as shown by the data given in Source C, which were based on official Soviet statistics.

SOURCE B

Average growth in Soviet national income, 1951–85

1951–55	11.2
1956–60	9.2
1961–65	6.6
1966–70	7.75
1971–75	5.75
1976–80	4.75
1981–85	3.5

Mandel, E. 1989. *Beyond Perestroika*. London, UK. Verso. p. 3.

SOURCE C

Soviet economic growth, 1951–85

	Produced national income	Gross industrial production	Gross agricultural production	Labour productivity in industry
1951–55	11.4	13.2	4.2	8.2
1956–60	9.2	10.4	6.0	6.5
1961–65	6.5	8.6	7.2	4.6
1966–70	7.8	8.5	3.9	5.8
1971–75	5.7	7.4	2.5	6.8
1976–80	4.3	4.4	1.7	4.4
1981–85	3.6	3.7	1.0	3.4

White, S. 1993. *After Gorbachev*. Cambridge, UK. Cambridge University Press. p. 104.

By 1985, according to some estimates, the average annual growth rate of the Soviet Gross National Product (GNP) was down to 2% a year. This was by no means enough to do all that was necessary or expected by consumers. In fact, this figure marked a continuous decline in the average annual growth rate: from 5% by 1965, to 3.75% in 1975 and 2.5% in 1980. Yet it was estimated that a rate of growth of 4% or 4.5% (or 3%, according to some) was the *minimum* needed to ensure that the Soviet economy could fulfil its three main objectives. These objectives were investment to improve industrialisation and modernisation; military spending to maintain 'parity' with the West; and improving living standards for the general population. Any drop below these figures meant that the USSR would no longer be able to meet these three targets, which had been more or less achieved following the death of Stalin in 1953.

Several historians have argued that even these worrying figures understated the real decline. For instance, according to Jacques Sapir, the true average percentage of annual growth rates was much lower – thus the official Soviet statistics needed to be revised downwards.

SOURCE D

Annual rate of growth (average percentage)

	1975–79	1980–84
Gross social product	2.64	1.74
Industrial production	2.24	1.74
Industrial productivity	0.47	–0.07

Sapir, J. 1986. 'Crises et mutations de l'économie sóvietique', in *La Nouvelle Alternative*. Paris, France. No. 4.

4 The Soviet economy under Gorbachev

These (more pessimistic) figures were largely confirmed by those published in the *Observer* newspaper in 1980. The *Observer* figures shown in Source E were based on CIA estimates submitted to the US Congress.

SOURCE E

Rate of growth 1951–85 (average percentage)

	1951–56	1956–60	1961–65	1966–70	1971–75	1976–79	1981–85
National income							
Official sources	11.4	9.1	6.5	7.7	5.7	4.2	4.0
CIA estimates	6.0	5.8	5.0	5.5	3.7	3.0	1.5–2.5
Industrial output							
Official sources	13.1	10.4	8.6	8.5	7.4	4.7	
CIA estimates	11.3	8.7	7.0	6.8	6.0	3.5	

Frankland, M. Observer, 7 December 1980.

However, according to **Abel Aganbegyan**, who became Gorbachev's main economic adviser, even these figures underestimated the signs of economic decline in the Soviet economy. During the course of the 11th Five-Year Plan (1980–85), Aganbegyan calculated that the annual growth rate of the Soviet economy was actually zero.

SOURCE F

Graph showing rate of growth (%) across Five-Year Plans:
- 1966–70: 41
- 1971–75: 28
- 1976–80: 21
- 1981–85: 16.5
- 1986–90: 22
- 1991–95: 28

Key: —— national revenue   – – – national revenue adjusted

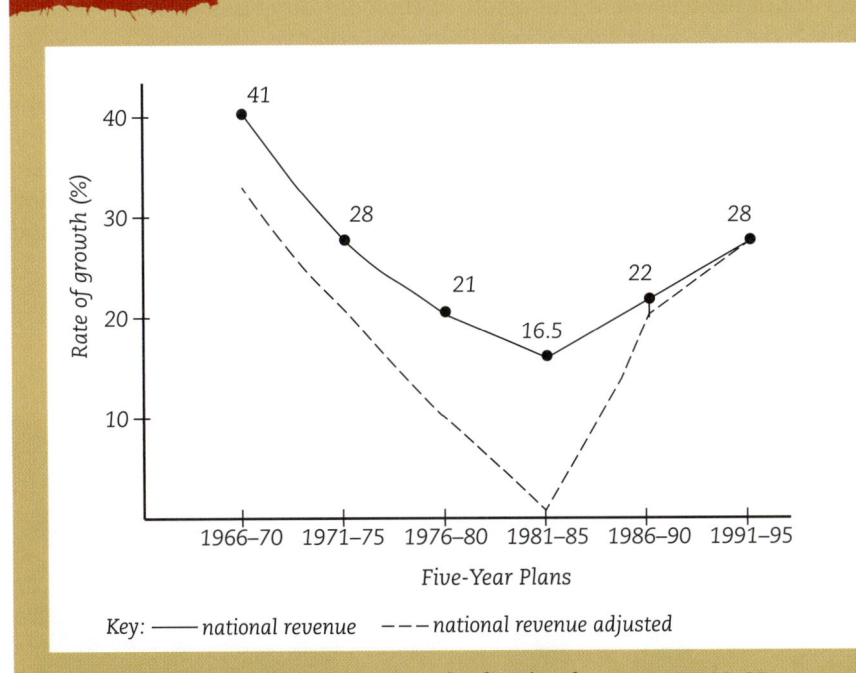

Abel Aganbegyan's statistics on growth of national revenue, 1966–85. Quoted in Mandel, E. 1989. Beyond Perestroika. London, UK. Verso. p. 3.

Later, in 1988, on a visit to Britain, Aganbegyan argued that there needed to be a fundamental shift in Soviet priorities, in relation to three areas: social provision (housing food supplies, health and education); improved industrial technology and efficiency; and reforms in the way large enterprises were managed.

Question
For historians trying to find out about the state of the Soviet economy in 1985, what are the limitations of Sources C and E, as regards their origins?

Abel Aganbegyan (b. 1932)
Aganbegyan was a member of the Soviet Academy of Sciences, and became Gorbachev's main economic adviser. Before that, he was one of the principal economic advisers at the time of the Kosygin reforms. He played a key role amongst the young technocrats who favoured radical reform of the Soviet economy. However, because of the failure of the Khrushchev and Kosygin reforms of the 1960s and early 1970s, Aganbegyan and others tended to be rather cautious about making practical proposals.

Communism in Crisis

SOURCE G

It would be truer, therefore, to name the present Soviet regime [1937] in all its contradictoriness, not as a socialist regime, but a preparatory regime transitional from capitalism to socialism ... To define the Soviet regime as transitional, or intermediate, means to abandon such finished categories as capitalism (and therewith "state capitalism") and also socialism. But besides being totally inadequate, in itself, such a definition is capable of producing the mistaken idea that from the present Soviet regime only a transition to socialism is possible. In reality a backslide to capitalism is wholly possible ... Without a planned economy the Soviet Union would be thrown back for decades. In that sense, the [Soviet] bureaucracy continues to fulfil a necessary function. But it fulfils it in such a way as to prepare an explosion of the whole system which may completely sweep out the results of the [1917] revolution.

Trotsky, L. 1972. *The Revolution Betrayed: What is the Soviet Union and Where is it Going?* New York, USA. Pathfinder Press. pp. 47, 254 and 285–86.

Discussion point

Try to find out more about the concept of the Soviet Union being a 'transitional society'. Do you think this concept was still applicable to the USSR in 1985? Was the eventual collapse of the Soviet Union in 1991, and the restoration of capitalism, the most likely result of Gorbachev's attempts at reform?

Despite the depressing figures, very few people predicted the sudden collapse of one of the two superpowers just six years after Gorbachev came to power. However, as Source E shows, some in the Western security services were well informed about the growing economic, financial and political weaknesses of the Soviet Union.

Nevertheless, a small number of contemporary political commentators echoed the warnings made by Trotsky in the 1930s. They viewed the Soviet Union as a transitional society (i.e. halfway between capitalism and socialism), and argued that it could not remain in that state for ever. Instead, it would have to either return to private enterprise or forge a stronger drive to socialism (based on a more efficient economy), and then move on to communism.

Gorbachevism

The developments that began in 1985 can perhaps best be explained as the product of all the contradictions and problems that had characterised the Soviet Union since 1976 (and perhaps even since Stalin's death in 1953). Gorbachev's role as an individual, and his various initiatives, were probably less important. Essentially, Gorbachevism and its consequences were the result of the contradictions arising from the dynamic forces of Soviet society and all its conservative structures.

As the tables on pages 70–71 show, the disastrous results of these contradictions had been apparent for decades, in the falling economic growth rates and growing social problems (such as shortages) for millions of Soviet citizens. Gorbachevism was the response of the reformist wing of the Soviet bureaucracy. This faction wished to overcome the growing problems of economic stagnation and technological decline (in both domestic and national defence spheres) by modernising the system.

Shoppers wait in line to buy imported shoes in Moscow in 1989

The reformist section of the party enjoyed a certain amount of support. Since the final days of Brezhnev, Abel Aganbegyan and **Tatiana Zaslavskaya** had both been arguing that there was a fundamental problem in the Soviet economy, which went beyond the problem of shortages of consumer goods. They claimed that the Soviet economy was approaching a state in which it would begin to break down.

There were also many scientists, technical specialists and intellectuals who supported Gorbachev's attempts – though some wanted to go further than he did. They were not dissidents but people who were interested in having greater contact with the West and who wanted opportunities to make more money. This meant they were not so concerned about keeping the basic underlying philosophy and ideology of socialism operating.

Despite this support, Gorbachev faced enormous resistance to his reforms. The conservative layers of the bureaucracy, especially the ***nomenklatura***, did not grasp the depth of the economic and political crisis facing the USSR by the mid 1980s. They were therefore reluctant to support radical changes that undermined their power and privileges – even though their privileges did not equal those enjoyed by wealthy capitalists in the West.

Gorbachev therefore faced much greater problems than the ones President Roosevelt faced in the USA in the 1930s, when Roosevelt was trying to persuade those opposed to his New Deal reforms of the vital need for change. This was because, in the US, despite the impact of the Great Depression, the owners of banks and factories still had sufficient wealth to make some reluctant concessions to the ordinary people. The Soviet economy in 1985 did not have such resources for Gorbachev and his supporters to call on. Thus, in order to benefit the mass of the Soviet population, he needed to radically change both the system of economic management and the system of political power. *Perestroika* (Gorbachev's attempts to deal with the economic crisis) will be examined in this chapter. His responses to the political crisis are dealt with in the next chapter.

Consolidation of Gorbachev's position

Gorbachev was sponsored by Andropov when it was already clear that Brezhnev would not live much longer, in the hope that he would support and carry out the reforms that Andropov believed were needed. After Andropov's death, Konstantin Chernenko was installed by those who were reluctant to press ahead with significant reforms. However, because of Chernenko's growing illness, Gorbachev had been unofficially running the USSR for three months before he actually came to power in March 1985.

After 1985 – being aware of what had happened to Khrushchev and Kosygin and their plans for reform – one of Gorbachev's first priorities was to strengthen his position. In particular, he faced opposition from people such as Grigori Romanov (a leading Politburo member, and a strong supporter of Andropov's reforms) and Victor Grishin (party boss of Moscow). Both these men had previously been seen as Gorbachev's rivals for the post of general-secretary. However, Gorbachev was supported by people such as Andrei Gromyko, the long-serving foreign minister and an important member of the Politburo.

Tatiana Zaslavskaya (b. 1927) Zaslavskaya is an economic sociologist working at the Novosibirsk Institute, specialising in agriculture. In 1968, she was elected to the Soviet Academy of Sciences. In 1983, a report she had written on the structural problems of the Soviet economy – especially in agriculture – was leaked. This report became known as the Novosibirsk Report. It emphasised the need to strengthen both central planning and the powers of the directors of enterprises, and reduce the intermediate layers of the bureaucracy. However, like the earlier suggestions put forward under Khrushchev and Kosygin, most of her reform proposals were limited and vague.

nomenklatura This privileged Soviet élite held the most important positions in party and state, at both central and local levels. They were on a list of 'reliable people' who could safely be promoted to high-ranking posts (see page 44). They were not a ruling *class*, but only a ruling administrative *group* – they did not own the economic resources of the USSR. This meant their position depended on the bulk of the Soviet population remaining passive. Hence Gorbachev's policies, which seemed to encourage greater popular participation, threatened the status and power of the *nomenklatura*.

Communism in Crisis

Yegor Ligachev (b. 1920)
Ligachev was originally a supporter of Andropov and then Gorbachev – and he tried to get Gorbachev appointed as general-secretary in 1984. Ligachev held several posts, including the important post of secretary for ideology, under Gorbachev. However, in 1987, he was sacked as ideology secretary; by 1988, he had become a leading conservative critic of Gorbachev – and Boris Yeltsin.

Nikolai Ryzhkov (b. 1929)
Ryzhkov was from Ukraine, and gained his early experience in industry, becoming first deputy chairman of Gosplan in 1979. He supported Gorbachev's economic reforms, and was the last prime minister of the USSR, from 1985 to 1991.

Alexander Yakovlev (1923–2005)
Yakovlev was ambassador to Canada and was another supporter of reform. He was arguably the most liberal member of Gorbachev's Politburo. Some historians and political observers have seen him as the main theorist behind *perestroika*, *glasnost* and *demokratizatsiya*.

Gorbachev began by moving some of his supporters into the Politburo in April 1985, including **Yegor Ligachev**, **Nikolai Ryzhkov** (who became prime minister) and Victor Chebrikov (head of the KGB). When Ligachev started to oppose Gorbachev, he was sacked in 1987 and replaced by **Alexander Yakovlev**.

Gorbachev then started making changes at local party levels, where some officials were accused of inefficiency and even corruption. Next, he moved his attention back to the senior levels. In July 1985, his rival Romanov was sacked and, at the end of the year, Grishin was replaced as head of the Moscow party by Boris Yeltsin. Finally, after 30 years as foreign minister, Gromyko retired, and his place was taken by **Eduard Shevardnadze** (see page 75).

Gorbachev quickly added five of his own supporters of reform to the Politburo. But in 1985 over half the Central Committee was still composed of those appointed by Brezhnev, and many of them had grave misgivings about Gorbachev's intended reforms. He thus began to make more new appointments, and carried out some sackings, both at the top and at lower levels. By 1987, he had the support of 75% of the Politburo and 52% of his Central Committee were new. Between 1986 and 1989, all the party first secretaries of the republics were replaced, along with two-thirds of secretaries of local party organisations below republican level. In addition, 70% of party officials at district and city level were replaced. By 1991, most of the party leaders were considerably younger and better educated than those in power under Brezhnev's regime.

Gorbachev also made changes at government level, appointing 42 new ministers. However, these changes did cause some protests. For example, in 1986 there were riots in Kazakhstan, when the local leader was replaced by a Russian.

Economic reform, 1985–86
There were significant political problems to address, such as opposition to Gorbachev's reforms in the CPSU, and rising nationalist unrest in several of the Soviet republics. However, the main problem at first seemed to be the economy. Even before he came to power, Gorbachev (like Andropov) was convinced of the need for economic modernisation. If the Soviet Union was going to meet the rising expectations of Soviet citizens, and compete with the USA and China, he believed it would have to modernise.

Plenum of the Central Committee, June 1985
Gorbachev pointed out the various problems of the Soviet economy in his report to the Plenum of the Central Committee on 11 June 1985. In particular, he mentioned technological backwardness, the poor quality of many industrial goods, unbalanced planning, and wastage of energy and raw materials. In addition, labour productivity was hampered by factors such as poor management, alcoholism and corruption. Indeed, according to Andropov, a third of the paid work hours in the USSR were 'wasted', due to workers' 'laziness' or 'lack of drive' and because of bureaucratic mismanagement and inefficiency. Gorbachev also wanted to tackle the 'black economy'. One aspect of this was employees who reported for work, but who then left their workplaces to work unofficially, for example as plumbers, electricians or carpenters.

Gorbachev warned that there was very little time in which to act, as the rate of growth of industrial production had fallen again (after a brief increase under Andropov). Official figures showed it had grown by only 3.1% between January and June 1985, compared to 4.5% in the same period in 1984 (it had been 4.15% in 1983). The emphasis was now to be on 'discipline', and on modernisation to ensure more rational use of investments (particularly reducing the number of new factories to be constructed and, instead, modernising existing factories and machinery).

4 The Soviet economy under Gorbachev

Uskorenie, 1985–86

During the first year of Gorbachev's leadership, from 1985 to 1986, he followed an approach known as *uskorenie* – meaning 'acceleration' or 'accelerated growth'. This approach was first tried by Andropov from 1983. Andropov was influenced by the ideas of Tatiana Zaslavskaya (see page 73), and her reports were an important influence on Gorbachev's reform project too. It essentially involved exerting increased pressure from the top to achieve increased production, by making the existing unreformed system work more efficiently.

To achieve a rapid increase in the quantity and quality of consumer goods produced, Gorbachev called for greater administrative efficiency from managers responsible for delivering the targets set for the 12th Five-Year Plan for 1986–90. These targets were much higher than those set for the 11th Five-Year Plan of 1980–85, even though many of these earlier targets had not been met. In fact, Gorbachev personally intervened to raise the targets, and pushed for the doubling of national income by 2000. Most of this was to come from massive new investment, mainly in European Russia.

These administrative measures included the use of repression. Gorbachev's first public campaign was, in fact, a drive against alcohol abuse – and the absenteeism and poor work that accompanied it. This was discussed in the Politburo as early as April 1985, and the campaign earned Gorbachev the nickname 'Lemonade Joe'. Prices for alcoholic drinks were increased, and the police were instructed to arrest those found drunk at work or in public places. His target was to reduce vodka production by 10% over a five-year period. Although this target was achieved within one year, it did not have the effects he had hoped for. It cost the state almost 100 billion roubles in lost tax revenue, while many state vineyards and distilleries were closed down. In addition, continuing illegal production and the black market meant that alcohol was still widely available.

Gorbachev also launched a campaign against corruption – again following in Andropov's footsteps. This resulted in many corrupt officials losing their posts. However, it also led to increased nationalist resentment against Moscow and the centre when local bosses were dismissed and prosecuted. These local bosses were sometimes replaced by those from different republics in an attempt to break up local 'mafias'.

Consequently, Gorbachev's reforms did not earn him much popularity within the CPSU, and they had little positive effect on the economic problems. In addition, most workers did not like the idea of having to work harder for no extra pay. Meanwhile, the rising prices and declining value of real wages caused much resentment.

Activities

1. Carry out some additional research on the reformers that Gorbachev brought into the Politburo in 1985.
2. Make a list of the main initiatives associated with *uskorenie*. Then write down brief explanations of how successful they were.
3. Imagine you are a factory worker and a member of the CPSU, and that you have to convince your workmates to support Gorbachev's initiatives. Using the information in this book, and any other sources available to you, compose a short speech to persuade your workmates to give Gorbachev their support.
4. Continue completing your chart on 'Economic Reforms'.

Eduard Shevardnadze (b. 1928) Shevardnadze was from Georgia, where he opposed corruption in the local party. He was another strong supporter of reform. However, when he was appointed as Gromyko's replacement, he had no experience of foreign affairs or diplomacy. He remained a loyal supporter of Gorbachev until the break-up of the USSR. He then became the president of an independent Georgia.

Fact
Most of the planned investment (see page 74) went into the energy industries and agriculture, not machine-building as originally intended. This was largely because the energy industries and agriculture were run by powerful bureaucrats who used their influence to secure large funds for their own industries.

Fact
Andropov had also campaigned against alcohol abuse and corruption (see pages 34 and 35).

Question
What was *uskorenie*, and why did Gorbachev adopt this approach?

Communism in Crisis

What was *perestroika* and what were its main policies between 1986 and 1989?

In 1986, Gorbachev officially launched his *perestroika* programme of economic reforms. This called for a great reduction in centralised planning, with more self-management at local enterprise levels. It also meant the end of subsidised prices, which meant 'restructuring' the economy. In many ways, it was a continuation of earlier attempts to reform the Soviet economy, by Khrushchev in the 1960s and by Kosygin in the 1970s.

By 1986, it was clear that, almost 70 years after the Bolshevik Revolution of November 1917, the system of state planning was in crisis. There was an urgent need to address the question of industrial productivity. Gorbachev and his supporters recognised that they had to fundamentally rethink the Soviet political economy. However, they did not seem to have very clearly agreed ideas on the way forward.

Soviet leader Mikhail Gorbachev explains his reforms to factory workers near Moscow in 1987

The 27th Congress of the CPSU, 1986

In February 1986, at the 27th Congress of the CPSU, Gorbachev said that administrators who adopted a 'wait and see' approach to implementing the new changes would not keep their jobs. He also announced further moves against corruption and the black market. In many ways, *perestroika* at this stage was very similar to earlier reforms in the 1960s and 1970s – and in some ways less far-reaching. Precise details of Gorbachev's *perestroika* plans were lacking but his intention was clear. He wanted to give more initiative to factory managers, with the central planners focusing on long-term strategic planning and investment rather than the day-to-day decisions.

SOURCE A

A little later [after the 27th Party Congress], the academician Abel Aganbegyan, the principal economic adviser to Gorbachev, gave a complete account of the poor use of equipment in the Soviet Union and stressed the fact that the Soviet Union produced less grain than the United States but used four times as many tractors. He might also have added that the Soviet Union had nine times as many people employed in the agricultural sector. In other words, the productivity of labour in the Soviet agricultural sector is 10 per cent of what it is in the United States … Soviet agriculture continues to stagnate. The shortage of animal fodder leads to a reduction in meat production, which has levelled off at about 60 kilos per head of population. The comparable figure in France is 100 kilos and in East Germany 92.

Mandel, E. 1989. Beyond Perestroika. *London, UK. Verso.* pp. 58–59.

4 The Soviet economy under Gorbachev

Following this Congress, factory and farm managers were given a greater say in what they produced and whom they employed. Eventually, from 1987 to 1989, self-financing was phased in, with enterprises paying for their operating costs out of their profits. In 1987, a quality inspection agency was created, to improve the standards of goods produced. Also in 1987, steps were taken to widen opportunities for private enterprise – but only on a small scale, and private employment was still not allowed. In order to prevent private employers exploiting workers, only the state was allowed to employ people.

In the face of growing conservative opposition, Gorbachev justified these policies by comparing them to Lenin's NEP (see page 16). He also stated that, if Lenin had lived, he would have restored the early form of Soviet democracy, with different parties being legal once more. However, there were more serious problems than the signs of growing opposition. In April 1987, Ryhzkov reported a *decline* in economic growth, while a drop in world oil prices *increased* the Soviet Union's foreign debt. In fact, figures for 1986–87 showed that the USSR's position in world trade was also declining. The result was that, by 1986–87, the Soviet Union's external trade was more like that of an underdeveloped country than that of the second-most industrialised country in the world. This decline in the Soviet Union's economy was shown in figures relating to the overall world economy. Even according to Soviet statistics, there had been an even greater decrease in trade with capitalist states during 1985–86, with exports down by 19.5%, and imports down by 23%.

Fact
Around 62% of Soviet exports were made up of natural resources such as oil, natural gas, minerals, wood and gold. More than 35% of Soviet imports were items of equipment and transport, more than 20% food products, and around 12% industrial consumer goods. Because of the fall in oil and gas prices in 1986, the value of Soviet exports fell by 8% in that year, and by a further 4% in the first quarter of 1987.

SOURCE 1

Share in world gross national production (percentages)

	1960	1980	2000 (projection)
Japan	3	10	12
USA	33	22	20
Rest of OECD* countries	26	31	26
USSR	15	13	12
China	5	4	5
Third World	14	15	20

* Organisation for Economic Co-operation and Development

Figures provided by the Economic Planning Agency, Japan. Originally published in Neue Züricher Zeitung, 12 May 1987.

In addition, the Soviet fuel extraction industries (coal, gas and oil) were running at a loss. In consequence, the USSR was becoming more and more reliant on foreign loans and grain imports. The result was a large and increasing budget deficit. In 1985, it was 3% of national income, but by 1989 it had grown to 14%. It was therefore clear that Gorbachev's early top-down policy of 'acceleration' had been limited and ineffective.

Agriculture and services

Gorbachev had become aware that one obstacle to his planned reforms was large sections of the CPSU. He soon realised he would need to change the political system, in order to undermine the positions of his opponents in the party, so that he could carry through economic reforms. As a first step, Gorbachev began to make some far-reaching reforms in agriculture and in the service industries.

Communism in Crisis

Fact
Gorbachev's agricultural reforms were very similar to the reforms implemented by Deng Xiaoping in China (see Chapter 7).

In these areas, *perestroika* turned into a partial re-privatisation. It effectively legalised the black market in goods and labour, which Gorbachev had earlier wanted to eliminate. Gorbachev now wanted to stimulate private production by both *kolkhoz* and *sovkhoz* workers (see page 24), on private plots and in co-operatives. This private activity soon came to represent 25% of all agricultural production in the Soviet Union. By 1987–88, around 30% of the agricultural produce of both *kolkhozy* and *sovkhozy* could be sold on the private market. Those who worked most efficiently could increase their average monthly earnings of 200 roubles by 30%, by working two days a week on their own initiative.

SOURCE J

Private agricultural production as a percentage of gross production

	1940	1965	1982
Grain	11	2	2
Potatoes	65	63	63
Vegetables	48	41	31
Fruit	70	54	41
Meat	72	40	30
Milk	77	39	30
Eggs	94	67	31
Wool	39	21	24

Mandel, E. 1989. *Beyond Perestroika.* London, UK. Verso. pp. 58–59.

In November 1986, the Law on Individual Labour Activity allowed individuals in the service sector to start private enterprise concerns, such as private taxi services. According to an article published in 1985 in *Izvestia* (the official newspaper of the Soviet government), the service industries were among the sectors that gave least satisfaction to Soviet consumers. The most far-reaching experiments took place in Estonia. Here, waiting lists for repairs of radios and television sets were reduced and bribes disappeared, while the quality of repairs improved. Further legislation allowing small-scale private enterprises in the service sector came in May 1987. There were also some private doctors and clinics.

These moves were obstructed by those who saw them as undermining the idea that 'unearned income' (in other words, private profit) was an anti-social capitalist evil, which resulted from exploitation. According to *Business Week* on 7 December 1987, the reforms were still relatively small-scale, involving only about 200,000 people and 8000 new co-operatives with 80,000 members.

Central planning

When it came to heavy industry and the planning system, the aim of the often vague proposals was to retain a socialist economy. Gorbachev repeatedly stated that his intention was to push these reforms through in order to create a modern and efficient socialist economy – not to restore capitalism. His approach was therefore designed to make significant use of market mechanisms in an economy dominated by central planning (i.e. a 'socialist market'). He did not intend to adopt 'market socialism', where market regulation is dominant. However, a number of Soviet economists and reformers saw a socialist market as merely a transition to market socialism.

Fact
The firm Elektron rented one of its sections to a brigade of technicians who each had to pay 650 roubles a month to cover costs, including use of machinery. The technicians had to pay for materials, electricity and heating, but could then charge their customers what they considered fair prices. The state enterprise took 30% of the income; the rest was kept by the technicians. Waiting lists dropped from two weeks (lower than in Moscow or Leningrad) to two days. It was the success of this experiment that led to the 1987 Law on Private Labour.

Conservative hardliners and bureaucrats had so far managed to stop or blunt Gorbachev's attempts. Their reasons had mainly been two-fold. They worried that his reforms would disrupt their normal working patterns and end many of their privileges. They also feared that too much economic liberalisation would (in the context of the 'Great Contest' and the Cold War) result in the re-emergence of capitalism.

In the end, this is exactly what happened – capitalism did re-emerge. However, whether this was ultimately the result of Gorbachev's economic policies, or of his opponents' obstruction of them, is a much-debated point. Gorbachev often described himself as a Leninist, and seems to have been genuinely convinced that he could establish a reformed, liberal, socialist society.

4 The Soviet economy under Gorbachev

Despite opposition, Gorbachev began to implement changes in the central industrial organisation, by attempting to reduce the 60 or more industrial ministries and state committees to six or seven 'super-ministries'. The first one to be set up was Gosagroprom (State Committee for the Agro-Industrial Complex), in late 1985. In many ways, however, this was just a new version of centralised control. It was burdened with bureaucracy, and in the end did not lead to increased efficiency. Similar problems emerged with the super-ministries that were established for energy and machine-building.

During 1986, Gorbachev became increasingly aware that little was changing or improving, so he toured the country. He discovered that many middle-ranking bureaucrats were still obstructing reform, while ordinary people were complaining about shortages and higher prices. He also found that a law that had set up elections for managers of enterprises was causing confusion and inefficiencies.

In December 1986, Gorbachev pushed through the Law on Joint Enterprises. This was meant to encourage foreign companies to invest in joint schemes in the USSR. But there were significant problems, including confusion and corruption. In addition, the new law gave rise to fears about growing capitalist interference in the Soviet economy. This led to increased opposition to Gorbachev from some quarters.

Fact
The fear of the re-emergence of capitalism was quite well founded. In the 1920s, when Lenin's NEP was introduced in order to get the economy going again, this threat was pointed out, and it explained the ban on factions and other parties that accompanied the NEP. The New Economic Policy had in fact led to the rise of wealthy peasants (*kulaks*) and speculators (*Nepmen*), who were seen as threatening the socialist state.

SOURCE K

The monopoly of foreign trade is a vitally necessary instrument for socialist construction, under the circumstances of a higher technological level in the capitalist countries. But the socialist economy now under construction can be defended by this monopoly only if it continually comes closer to the prevailing levels of technology, production costs, quality, and price in the world economy. The aim of economic management ought to be not a closed-off, self-sufficient economy, for which we would pay the price of an inevitably lower level and rate of advance, but just the opposite – an all-sided increase of our relative weight in the world economy, to be achieved by increasing our rate of development to the utmost.

Extract from *The Platform of the Left Opposition, 1927, Moscow.* Quoted in Trotsky, L. (ed.) Allen, N. and Saunders, G. 1980. *The Challenge of the Left Opposition (1926–27)*. New York, USA. Pathfinder Press. p. 335.

Though state ownership of the main parts of the economy was to be retained, such moves caused widespread concern and even opposition. This was because any move away from strict central control had political implications, in view of how closely state and party were connected. Again, there were fears that this would lead to the re-emergence of capitalism. Moreover, it was evident that the removal of price controls would hit Soviet citizens hard. As has been seen, citizens benefited from a significant social wage, including low food and fuel prices (often below the cost of production), and cheap public transport. Yet this was expensive from the government's point of view, as it was on top of the economic aid and subsidies it was giving to foreign states in its 'sphere of influence'.

Communism in Crisis

By the end of 1987, Gorbachev and those supporting his reforms came to realise that 'acceleration' and small-scale adaptations were not going to achieve the improvements they wanted. More extensive reforms were needed.

Further reforms, 1988–89

However, even the reformers were uncertain about what to do, so initially Gorbachev decided that more political changes were needed. His aim was to have more openness about the problems, to identify those obstructing reform, and to loosen central political controls over managers of enterprises. This meant further reducing the power of the CPSU and the Soviet state industrial ministries in Moscow over the economy. It also meant transferring some additional powers from the centre to the republics, and from planners to factories and farms.

In January 1988, the Law on State Enterprises came into effect. In total, 60% of state enterprises were shifted from tight central control to control by their managements. This meant that they could set their own prices, and negotiate and trade with other firms for the products they needed. Workers were given more incentives to increase production, as well as the right to elect managers. However, there were still state quotas that had to be met. The ministries retained final control, though any surplus could be sold for profit. In 1989, the remaining 40% of state enterprises were similarly released from central control.

In May 1988, there was a new Law on Co-operatives. This took the 1986 Law on Individual Activity a little further, by allowing small and medium-sized private co-operative enterprises to operate not only in the service sector (as before), but also now in manufacturing and even foreign trade. In addition, workers' co-operatives and small private businesses could be set up to trade (though there were limits on the numbers they could hire, as there was still the principle that workers should not be exploited for profit). However, as with the 1986 law, there was both bureaucratic obstruction and lack of funds, as these businesses were not entitled to state subsidies. They also faced tight employment restrictions (to avoid exploitation) and heavy taxes, though these were later reduced.

In agriculture, from 1988, Gorbachev continued with moves to carry out a kind of privatisation – by extending the private plots that peasants already had. Peasants and farmers were now allowed to take out long-term leases on land belonging to the collectives. The state would thus still retain ownership of land. It was hoped that this would lead to increased productivity. Farmers would pay for the leases, and be taxed on their profits (this was similar to Lenin's NEP). At first, though, many collective farm managers were reluctant to agree to lease land out.

SOURCE L

To overcome the 'braking mechanism' and the forces of inertia which have accumulated during the course of many years in all spheres of social life; to conquer the social apathy which affects a large section of our workers; to create solid guarantees for the irreversible character of this reorganisation [greater managerial independence from ministries]: all of this today demands of the party, as it did seventy years ago, a firm political will, iron discipline and actions which are practical, daring, creative and full of initiative … Communists have to set an example, by working according to new principles; they should be the first to fight the forces of inertia. At this stage these forces are particularly resistant. Don't believe that these forces are external to us; they are among us.

Extract from Gorbachev's speech made in Leningrad on 13 October 1987, celebrating the 70th anniversary of the November 1917 Revolution. Published in Pravda, 14 October 1987.

Fact

The NEP (which involved a partial return to capitalism after the period of war communism and the civil war) was seen by Lenin and his supporters as running the risk of a full restoration of capitalism. For this reason, a ban on opposition parties was introduced in 1921. Communists opposed to NEP, for this very reason, called it 'the new exploitation of the proletariat' (see page 16).

4 The Soviet economy under Gorbachev

In January 1987, Gorbachev made a speech appealing (over the heads of the Communist Party and government) to the people. In this speech, he called for economic reform and democratisation. Similarly, he used the occasion of the 19th Party Conference in June 1988 to attack those who were slow to implement the reforms.

SOURCE M

We have got to be self-critical; we must see clearly that despite all the positive effects, the state of affairs in the economy is changing too slowly. Some advances are on hand. But they cannot satisfy us ... And those who are holding up the process, who are creating hindrances, have got to be put out of the way. Difficulties arose largely due to the tenacity of managerial stereotypes, to a striving to conserve familiar command methods of economic management, to a resistance of a part of the managerial cadre. Indeed, we are running into undisguised attempts at perverting the essence of the reform, at filling the new managerial forms with the old content ... To put it plainly, the reform will not work, will not yield the results we expect ...

Extracts from Gorbachev's Address to the 19th Party Conference, Moscow, June 1988.

Gorbachev (centre, front) speaking at the 19th Party Conference in June 1988

By 1989, it was possible to detect three main economic strategies:

1. a 'conservative' approach, i.e. one that aimed to keep things as they had been, with strong central planning and no concessions to capitalism
2. a strategy put forward by those radical socialists who wanted to preserve a mix, i.e. a system that would keep state ownership, but under workers' self-management; people would be able to lease state property but not own it
3. a strategy that aimed to introduce more market-based reforms (and even full capitalism); confusingly its proponents were often called 'radicals' too.

Fact
Professor Marcel Drach said there were three possible 'models' for the reform of the Soviet economy: a decentralised model, as in Hungary; a dual model (a rationalised state sector and a limited private sector), as in East Germany; and a 'coercive' model, as in Czechoslovakia. He believed that Gorbachev, after trying the second model, had eventually decided on the Hungarian approach. This gave businesses greater autonomy and also made them self-financing.

Communism in Crisis

SOURCE N

Gorbachev and the party leadership as a whole distanced themselves both from the more extreme 'monetarist' and from the more radical 'workerist' perspectives. For Gorbachev personally, there could be no talk of a transition to full-scale private ownership – did they really want to be employed by capitalists, he asked a group of Leningrad workers? – and price increases, where they were allowed to occur, must be discussed widely and introduced in such a way that living standards were not affected. Gorbachev was equally severe, however, on the 'ultra-left', who imagined that their objectives could be accomplished in a 'single stroke', and he gave no encouragement to the radicals within the new Supreme Soviet or the wave of working-class activism that developed in the summer of 1989 and again in 1991.

White, S. 1993. After Gorbachev, Cambridge, UK. Cambridge University Press. pp. 141–42.

However, to many observers (both supporters and opponents), it seemed as if Gorbachev had no real plan in mind. They thought he just swung pragmatically from one option to another, adjusting his position according to circumstances.

Activities

1. Make a list of the main problems faced by Gorbachev in this period in trying to get his reforms implemented. Then try to rank them in order of importance.

2. 'Gorbachev's economic reforms were very similar to Lenin's New Economic Policy (NEP) of 1921'. Briefly investigate the main points in Lenin's NEP. Then write two short newspaper articles – one agreeing with the statement, and one disagreeing. Make sure your arguments are backed up with precise details.

3. Do further research on the three main economic options that were being put forward during 1988–89. Which, if any, do you think was the most realistic?

4. Continue completing your chart on 'Economic Reforms'. Try to ensure that you give precise dates and brief details.

What problems did Gorbachev's economic reforms encounter in 1990–91?

As the substance of Gorbachev's reforms became clearer, they increasingly ran into obstacles that raised doubts about their successful implementation.

Unemployment and living standards

One of these obstacles was the great difficulty posed by introducing changes that would lead to unemployment. Though the great bulk of the economy was under public ownership in the USSR, its political leaders could not do exactly what they wanted. Gorbachev and his supporters wanted to speed up economic growth, improve economic efficiency, and modernise the country on every level, but there were enormous socio-structural constraints.

For example, creating unemployment and ending state-subsidised prices for food, housing, gas, electricity and transport were likely to cause mass unrest (as in Hungary in 1956, Czechoslovakia in 1968 and Poland in 1981). Any attempt to remove the economic security of Soviet workers risked provoking a serious political crisis, just as any attempt to undermine the economic security of private capitalists would risk causing an economic crisis in the West.

Impact of the economic reforms

Despite his positive aims, most of Gorbachev's changes actually led to more, rather than fewer, problems. For one thing, the 'market' elements did indeed lead to increased prices and unemployment – both a real shock to most Soviet citizens. By 1990, though wages for some had increased, 25% of citizens were living below the poverty line.

Fact

At the time Gorbachev was in power, unemployment was a huge problem in the seven most important states in the West, where there were about 20 million people out of work. Opinion polls in countries such as Britain regularly showed that most people regarded unemployment as a serious problem. Yet no major British party, whether on the right or the left, ever promised a statutory right to work. This was mainly because a legal right to employment is unrealistic under capitalism. Guaranteed jobs are incompatible with the idea of a 'free' market. Such socio-economic factors place limits on what politicians can achieve in any system.

In addition, factories had increasing problems obtaining the supplies and materials they needed from the state, so shortages often worsened. Soon, shops were left with empty shelves. In fact, by the end of 1988, rationing had to be brought in for certain foods in some parts of the USSR.

In July 1989, miners in the Kuzbass region went on strike in protest over the lack of soap. Soon, over 500,000 were on strike – along with over 150,000 other workers. Before long, they started demanding better working conditions – and even a 'free' trade union like Solidarity in Poland (see Chapters 3 and 6). Significant signs of labour unrest (for example, by railway workers) also occurred in the last two years of the USSR's existence.

Although progress was made in some other areas (for example, improvements in medical care reduced infant mortality by 10% in the late 1980s), these received little publicity. Instead, most workers just felt that their living conditions had got worse. Old people, too, were increasingly affected by rising prices, which used up much of their pensions, while the previously subsidised services now cost more.

The earliest result of many of Gorbachev's economic reforms was therefore austerity for many workers, who saw their living standards decline. Not surprisingly, this did not encourage them to make greater efforts to increase productivity. For many ordinary people, it seemed that the system that had worked for them before 1985 was now being destroyed by *perestroika*.

Such unrest and instability led to an economic slow-down and then a decline. In 1990 there was a 4% fall in production, and in 1991 a fall of 15%.

> **Fact**
> This unhappiness about the way things were going was felt not just by ordinary people, but also by some intellectuals. One example was Gavril Popov, a professor of management at Moscow University. He argued against bureaucratic, top-down initiatives, in favour of political reform that would allow those 'below' to push for economic reform. He was one of many who believed the political problems needed solving more urgently than the economic issues.

SOURCE O

Soviet economic growth, 1986–91 (official data, %)

	1986–90	1986	1987	1988	1989	1990	1991
Average (plan)							
National income produced	4.2	2.3	1.6	4.4	2.4	−4.0	−15.0
Industrial output	4.6	4.4	3.8	3.9	1.7	−1.2	−7.8
Agricultural output	2.7	5.3	−0.6	1.7	1.3	−2.3	−7.0

White, S. 1993. *After Gorbachev*. Cambridge, UK. Cambridge University Press. p. 121.

All this was the exact opposite of what Gorbachev wanted. Nevertheless, the prospect of working-class discontent was increasingly used by Gorbachev's conservative opponents to frustrate his reforms.

Other factors

Political factors also contributed to the growing economic collapse. For example, the CPSU lost much of its power to force enterprises to implement the reforms that Gorbachev had decided on. This enabled managers to ignore any reforms that they did not like, or to wait for state help when they found the new rules difficult.

These political factors will be discussed in Chapter 5. The main point is that Gorbachev's political reforms had reduced and undermined party and state control of the economy. This meant that the state was increasingly unable to take strong action to solve the problems.

> **Fact**
> Another factor identified by many historians was Gorbachev's indecision at times, and the fact that he and his team were not trained economists. However, the 2008 banking crisis in the capitalist world suggests that they might not have done any better even if they *had* been!

Communism in Crisis

Events in the various Soviet republics caused additional problems. Many of these republics began to introduce customs barriers to protect their own economies. This disrupted trade and led to unemployment and worker unrest in both Russia and the republics, which only added to the existing problems. Enterprises also continued to lie about production figures – and even switched to other goods, which they thought might be more profitable. Thus the government had no accurate picture of what was happening in the economy. Furthermore, the collapse of the Eastern European regimes during 1988–89 (see Chapter 6) meant the loss of the former Comecon trading partners. On top of all this was the rising cost of trying to maintain military parity with the US. (The US was deliberately 'upping the game' at a time when the Soviet economy could least afford it.) By 1991, the revenue of the **All-Union government** was only 15% of what it had planned for.

> **All-Union government**
> This means the government of the USSR as a whole, as opposed to the governments of the individual republics that made up the Soviet Union.

A market economy?

In December 1989, the Congress of People's Deputies voted for the Abalkin Programme. This was named after Leonid Abalkin who headed the committee, set up by Gorbachev, which drafted the report. The programme called for the gradual de-nationalisation of state property, which would then be sold off and privatised, to create a market economy. The state would only retain control of raw materials, fuel and defence. However, Gorbachev and his government did not want to go down this route.

Yet, by 1990, it was clear that the Soviet economy was experiencing a major crisis. In May 1990, Ryzhkov presented a new economic plan to the Supreme Soviet. This plan called for transition to a state-regulated 'market' economy, in three stages, to be achieved by 1995. Central planning would be gradually reduced. The plan also claimed that the fall in living standards would be reversed by 1993.

One group of reformers, including Boris Yeltsin (see page 100), began to press for an end to these compromises by pushing ahead with the introduction of a total market economy. With Gorbachev's approval, a team of economists was assembled, under Stanislav Shatalin. In August 1990, the Shatalin Plan recommended moving to a full market economy in 500 days. It also proposed giving most economic powers to the Soviet republics, as well as the full legalisation of the unofficial black (or second) economy. However, this was a step too far for Gorbachev and Ryzhkov.

The end of Soviet socialism

Gorbachev and his supporters rejected the Shatalin Plan on 1 September 1990. The problem was that, to carry out any meaningful reforms, a strong state with popular support was needed; this did not exist. Instead, Gorbachev got the Supreme Soviet's approval for a compromise package the following month. This proposed four main steps:

> **Question**
> Why was the Shatalin Plan so radical, and why did Gorbachev reject it?

1. the commercialisation of state enterprises
2. relaxation of state price controls (though with social security measures to help those workers 'adversely affected' – i.e. made unemployed)
3. changes to the housing market
4. the rouble to be fully convertible with foreign currencies (to allow trade with other countries).

Even this compromise caused much dissent and argument. More importantly, as will be seen in Chapter 5, the political situation was becoming increasingly difficult. Thus, even where it was accepted that more far-reaching reforms were necessary, there was the problem of actually being able to deliver them.

4 The Soviet economy under Gorbachev

Two significant events occurred in January 1991. Firstly, ongoing difficulties with the money supply came to a head. Inflation had been a growing problem as some price controls were removed, while the government controlled the supply of money. The rouble collapsed. Then, in January 1991, all high-denomination banknotes were withdrawn at short notice so that the government could issue new ones, in an attempt to stop inflation. This gave people little time to exchange their banknotes for lower-value ones. Many citizens kept all their money in cash and consequently lost all their savings.

Also in January 1991, the Supreme Soviet of the Russian Federation (the biggest and wealthiest of the 15 republics that made up the USSR) passed a law legalising private property ownership. This effectively ended the legal basis of the planned and socially owned economy, since private enterprises could now be set up. Meanwhile, the Russian Federation also began to take over all the oil, mining and gas enterprises in the republic, which were technically All-Union property. This seriously undermined the entire Soviet economy, and was a major contributory factor to the collapse of the Soviet Union less than 12 months later. To many Russians, it seemed that *perestroika* was pushing a reasonably functioning economy to the point of crisis and even collapse.

1991 and after – a perspective

Much of what happened in the former Soviet republics after December 1991 shows the extent of the economic problems Gorbachev was attempting to overcome. The economic experience of these republics has similarities to the **economic 'shock therapy'** applied in the former Eastern European satellite states after 1989. However, several commentators have described the application of these economic policies in Russia and the other former Soviet republics as 'All shock, no therapy'. Such commentators include the economist J. K. Galbraith, who wrote about the impact of these 'neo-liberal' economic policies in an article entitled 'Shock without therapy', published on 25 August 2002 in the monthly US journal *The American Prospect*.

These economic policies led to the rapid emergence of several billionaire Russian oligarchs (often referred to as 'the Chicago boys'). Meanwhile, an estimated 140 million Russians were falling below the official poverty line.

This cartoon, published in 1996, was by an American cartoonist, and was commenting on life in Yeltsin's post-Soviet Russia, after the implementation of his economic 'shock therapy' programme

Historical debate
Some historians have argued that Gorbachev's plan – to have a modern and efficient economy, operating many market aspects yet still under party-state control – was impossible. For instance, Dmitri Volkogonov has said that Gorbachev was attempting to change a system that could not be changed. Instead of *perestroika* (restructuring), *novostroika* (a new structure) was needed. This is precisely what the Chinese Communist Party seems to have done since 1976, as Chapters 7–9 will discuss.

economic 'shock therapy'
This term refers to the ideas of Friedrich Hayek and Milton Friedman. From the 1960s onwards, Hayek and Friedman advocated economic policies (such as monetarism and 'rolling back' the welfare state) for 'free-market' or unrestrained capitalism. They were members of the 'Chicago School', whose ideas were first applied in the military dictatorships of Chile and Argentina in the 1970s. The same ideas were later adopted by the Reagan government in the US and the Thatcher government in the UK.

Question
What is the message of this cartoon?

Examiner's tip
Look carefully both at what is drawn, and the words that appear in the cartoon. Also, don't forget to look at the attribution information.

Communism in Crisis

Several commentators have seen such developments as suggesting that no single economic system has all the right answers, and that there were no easy solutions to the particular economic problems that Gorbachev attempted to tackle. For instance, according to expert on Soviet society David Lane, the under-utilisation of industrial capital in the US during the 1970s was about 20%. Similarly, in the US in early 1980s, there were over 8 million unemployed and a further 5 million under-employed. Such views have been more widely voiced since the 2008 banking crisis and its worldwide impact.

SOURCE P

The most common explanation [of the problems of the Soviet economy] in the West today is a very simple one: planning does not work and you must have a market. This simple thesis is then given an ideological colouring: the market equals capitalism and it works; the plan equals socialism and it does not work. This is an entirely worthless argument at the level of general principles. Perfect markets would be fine and perfect planning would be fine, but neither are feasible in the present world. The neo-liberal case is based on an obvious double-standard. It compares a non-existent perfect market with the actually-existing Soviet planning mechanism. As the Polish economist W. Brus has often pointed out, in the East people exaggerate the qualities of markets because they haven't experienced it. The fact is that both planning and markets possess benefits and deficiencies. What is clearly required is to practically combine the advantages of each while minimising their costs.

Ali, T. 1988. Revolution From Above: Where is the Soviet Union Going? London, UK. Hutchinson. pp. 70–71.

Theory of knowledge

History and bias

History is often seen as being more prone to bias than the natural sciences, especially when it involves consideration of political and economic theories and systems. Is it possible, for instance, for Western historians and economists to make objective judgements about whether Gorbachev had any realistic chance of reforming the Soviet Union's economy? Or are they likely just to look for evidence that supports the cultural, economic and political values of their own societies?

Activities

1. 'The right to employment is more important than the right to choose between different political parties in elections.' Split into two groups: one to argue in support of the statement, the other to oppose it. Use information from this book, and any other sources available to you, to support your arguments.

2. Write a short newspaper article explaining why, by 1991, many workers were opposing Gorbachev's economic reforms.

3. Draw a spider diagram to show all the obstructions and problems Gorbachev faced when trying to implement his economic reforms. Give dates and brief details. Then try to list the problems in order of importance. Finally, write a short paragraph justifying the order in which you have placed the problems. For example, explain why you think the one at the top of the list is the most important.

4. 'Too much, too quickly' or 'Too hesitant and too uncertain'. Write a couple of paragraphs, in the style of an obituary, to say which of these two comments best describes Gorbachev and his attempts at reforming the Soviet economy.

4 The Soviet economy under Gorbachev

End of chapter activities

Summary

You should now have a sound understanding of the state of the Soviet economy in 1985, and of the main economic policies attempted by Gorbachev in the period from 1985 to 1991. You should also be able to comment on the relative success of his reforms – and the reasons why they ultimately failed.

Summary activity

Using the information in this chapter and from any other available sources, copy the chart shown below, and try to explain why Gorbachev's attempts at reforming the Soviet economy had failed by 1991. Remember to include information on historical debate/interpretations, including names of historians.

Factors affecting Gorbachev's *perestroika* reforms 1985–91					
Economic	Political	Social	International	Bad luck

Use your chart to assess which factor you think was the most important reason for his failure.

Paper 1 exam practice

Question

Compare and contrast the views expressed in Source A (right) and Source B (on page 88) about the Soviet economy and its problems. [6 marks]

Skill

Cross-referencing

SOURCE A

In the long struggle between two irreconcilably hostile social systems – capitalism and socialism – the outcome will be determined in the last analysis by the relative productivity of labour under each system. And this, under market conditions, is measured by the relation between domestic prices and world prices. It was this fundamental fact that Lenin had in mind when in one of his last speeches he warned the party of the 'test' that would be 'imposed by the Russian and international market, to which we are subordinated, with which we are connected, and from which we cannot isolate ourselves' [Collected Works, vol. 33, pp. 276–77]. For that reason, Bukharin's notion that we proceed toward socialism at any pace, even a 'snail's pace,' is a banal and vapid petty-bourgeois fantasy. We cannot escape from capitalist encirclement by retreating into a nationally exclusive economy. Just because of its exclusiveness, such an economy would be compelled to advance at an extremely slow pace, and in consequence would encounter not weaker, but stronger pressure, not only from the capitalist armies and navies ('intervention'), but above all from cheap capitalist commodities.

Extract from The Platform of the Left Opposition, 1927, Moscow. Quoted in Trotsky, L. (ed.) Allen, N. and Saunders, G. 1980. The Challenge of the Left Opposition (1926–27). New York, USA. Pathfinder Press. pp. 334–35.

Communism in Crisis

SOURCE B

Seventy years after the October Revolution [1917] the model of autarchic state planning is in a crisis. A country which sent the first Sputnik into space and which regularly orbits its space-people in the stratosphere is incapable of providing toothpaste in sufficient quantity to its citizens. An economy which can produce high-grade weaponry has to import its grain for livestock. A state which provides massive aid to Cuba and Nicaragua suffers a permanent shortage of sugar and coffee. The crisis of consumer goods has, of course, a long pedigree in the USSR, but almost five decades since the Second World War the problem remains unresolved. The fact that this is now publicly admitted has made possible an open debate on the changes needed to increase labour productivity and introduce a mechanism which reflects consumer needs outside the rigid constraints of 'the plan'.

Ali, T. 1988. Revolution From Above: Where is the Soviet Union Going? London, UK. Hutchinson. p. 65.

Before you start

Cross-referencing questions require you to compare **and** contrast the information/content/nature of **two** sources.

Before you attempt this question, refer to page 216 for advice on how to tackle these questions and a simplified markscheme.

Student answer

Sources A and B are quite similar in their views about the problems of the Soviet economy. Source A, written in 1927, refers to the fundamental importance of the 'relative productivity of labour' between the USSR and capitalist countries. This is also touched on towards the end of Source B, written in 1988, which refers to 'labour productivity' as still being something that needs to be addressed by Gorbachev 60 years later.

Sources A and B also agree about the problems caused by trying to develop a socialist economy in isolation (Stalin's idea of 'Socialism in One Country'). Source A stresses how the USSR 'cannot isolate ourselves' and how it 'cannot escape … by retreating into a nationally exclusive economy'. This is also referred to in Source B, which says that, 70 years after the Bolshevik Revolution of 1917, the 'model of autarchic state planning is in a crisis'. 'Autarchic' here means 'self-sufficient' – and this was what Stalin tried to achieve in the 1930s and 1940s: this is the 'nationally exclusive' economy mentioned in Source A.

Examiner comments

There are several clear/precise references to both the sources, and several similarities/comparisons are identified. Also, the sources are clearly linked throughout, rather than being dealt with separately. The candidate has thus done enough to get into Band 2, and so be awarded 4 or 5 marks. However, as no differences/contrasts are made, this answer fails to get into Band 1.

Activity

Look again at the two sources, the simplified markscheme, and the student answer above. Now try to write a paragraph or two to push the answer up into Band 1, and so obtain the full 6 marks.

Paper 2 practice questions

1 Compare and contrast the economic policies of Andropov and Gorbachev.

2 For what reasons, and with what results, did Gorbachev attempt to reform the Soviet economy?

3 To what extent did Gorbachev's policy of *perestroika* succeed in reforming the Soviet economy?

4 'Too little, too late.' To what extent do you agree with this description of Gorbachev's economic reforms in the period 1985–91?

5 Political developments in the USSR under Gorbachev

Timeline

1985 Mar: Gorbachev becomes general-secretary

1986 Feb–Mar: 27th Congress of CPSU

Apr: Chernobyl disaster

1987 Jan: Central Committee agree on limited competitive elections

Apr: 18th Congress of Soviet Trade Unions

Jun: first competitive elections

1988 Jan: Central Committee extend competitive elections to all soviets

Jun: 19th Party Conference

Dec: Electoral Law

1989 Mar–Apr: elections for new Congress of People's Deputies

Apr: nationalist unrest in Georgia

May: first meeting of new CPD and Supreme Soviet

1990 Feb: Article 6 amended

Mar: contested elections in all republics; Gorbachev becomes executive president

May: Russian Supreme Soviet votes for sovereignty

Jun–Jul: 28th Congress of CPSU

1991 Mar: referendum on new Union Treaty

Jun: Yeltsin elected president of Russia

Aug: attempted coup; Gorbachev resigns as general-secretary

Dec: formation of CIS; Gorbachev resigns as Soviet president; end of the USSR

Introduction

With hindsight, it is clear that the future of the Soviet Union, as a transitional state, was decided on three closely inter-related levels. These were: modernisation of the economy; democratisation of Soviet society; and a solution to the national question. Gorbachev saw his main political policies as necessary pre-conditions for the successful implementation of his economic reforms. This would be achieved partly by stimulating some pressure from below to help him overcome his conservative opponents in the bureaucracy.

The upper layers of bureaucracy comprised about 400,000 people. Their monopolisation of political power gave them additional privileges, including holiday homes and foreign travel. Top academics, writers and artists often had even higher incomes. Many ordinary citizens were aware of these privileges. After Gorbachev's economic and political initiatives, some even noted in letters to *Pravda* how such high-level bureaucrats were opposed to change.

Gorbachev realised that Khrushchev's reforms had failed partly because Khrushchev's opponents in the bureaucratic apparatus had been able to 'absorb' and neutralise his reforms, before reversing them and then overthrowing him. At first, Gorbachev's reforms were limited and gradual so as not to upset the party apparatus. This was what some observers called 'bureaucratic self-reform under bureaucratic control'. Then, from 1986 (when it became increasingly clear that *perestroika* would not benefit the mass of Soviet workers in the short run), he began to push for more far-reaching political reforms. He hoped these would 'sweeten' the economic 'medicine'.

This approach became more marked with the 19th Party Conference, held in June 1988. As well as attempting to alter the internal system in the USSR, Gorbachev tried to make fundamental changes in Soviet foreign policy – largely so that money could be diverted into economic modernisation. His political reforms were built on the twin policies of **glasnost** and **demokratizatsiya** (see page 91).

At first, several commentators saw Gorbachev as a progressive, reformist element within the Soviet élite. In his attempts to preserve the Soviet Union, they believed he would trigger a political revolution that would end the whole *nomenklatura* system of privileges on which the power of the Soviet bureaucracy rested. However, for Gorbachev, much of his political reform programme was carried out as a way of pushing through the economic reforms

5 Political developments in the USSR under Gorbachev

he believed were essential. Nonetheless, he did eventually come to realise that the nationalist tensions emerging in some of the Soviet republics would also have to be addressed politically.

All this would entail reforming the Communist Party to make it a popular and progressive force. This would in turn require some form of political pluralism in both party and state. Gorbachev and his supporters eventually concluded that reform of the economic system would not succeed without significant democratisation. However, they also realised that disrupting the upper levels of Soviet society by encouraging a partial re-politicisation and mobilisation of the lower levels would be a very risky enterprise. It could possibly lead to events that would escape their control, as in the 'Prague Spring' (see Chapter 6). In fact, it turned out to be even riskier than what happened in Czechoslovakia. Just six years after Gorbachev began his reforms, the Soviet Union collapsed. Thus, its collapse can be seen as being ultimately due to political, rather than economic, factors.

Key questions
- What were Gorbachev's early political aims?
- What were Gorbachev's main political reforms between 1986 and 1990?
- Why did the Soviet Union collapse in 1991?

Overview

- From 1986, in order to push through his economic reforms, Gorbachev began to implement two political programmes – *glasnost* and *demokratizatsiya*.
- *Glasnost* concentrated on more government openness, and giving people more freedom to criticise. However, the nuclear accident that occurred at Chernobyl in April 1986 was not handled well.
- *Demokratizatsiya* involved various reforms that were designed to develop greater democracy – in both state and party.
- The first multi-candidate elections to local soviets took place in some areas in 1987. This was extended to all areas in 1988.
- Then, in March/April 1989, semi-free elections took place across the USSR for a new Congress of People's Deputies, which elected a new Supreme Soviet.
- At the same time, Gorbachev tried to separate party and state bodies, and began to introduce more democracy into the CPSU. However, his conservative opponents in the party became increasingly concerned that these reforms would lead to the break-up of the Soviet Union, as well as reducing their own powers and privileges.
- By 1989, there was growing nationalist unrest in many of the Soviet republics. In 1990, following contested elections in all the republics, Lithuania became the first to vote to secede from the USSR.
- Attempts to draw up a new Union Treaty for a looser federation of republics met with little success. However, a referendum in nine republics in March 1991 saw almost 75% vote in favour of keeping some federation.
- In June 1991, Boris Yeltsin became president of Russia and began negotiations with the leaders of other republics. In August, conservative hardliners attempted a coup against Gorbachev, but this collapsed in days. Gorbachev resigned as general-secretary.
- The USSR finally collapsed in December 1991, when Russia, Belorussia and Ukraine formed the Commonwealth of Independent States (CIS). Gorbachev then resigned as president.

glasnost *Glasnost* was a policy of 'openness'. Initially this referred to government policy, but Gorbachev soon wanted past mistakes and current problems to be voiced, including criticism of the CPSU leadership and government policies.

demokratizatsiya *Demokratizatsiya* was the attempt to make the Soviet system more democratic. Elections were reformed, to give greater choice to voters; and political clubs and organisations were allowed to operate outside party control. Gorbachev also tried to make the state more independent of party control.

Communism in Crisis

This poster, designed by Kanstantsin Khatsyanouski, shows the difficulty Gorbachev faced in trying to get his reforms through party officials and bureaucrats; the slogan means 'Just try to rebuild, and you will fail'

What were Gorbachev's early political aims?

Gorbachev was a lawyer before becoming a member of the CPSU, and this may have contributed to his desire to rule within the law. When Chernenko died, Gorbachev was nominated by the foreign minister, Andrei Gromyko, for the post of general-secretary of the CPSU. Once elected, he immediately announced that the posts of president and head of the party would not be combined, as they had been under Brezhnev. He used his position as general-secretary of the CPSU to concentrate on party and economic reform. He and his team of reformers eventually drew up a political strategy involving three elements: liberalisation of the media and the citizens' right to criticise (*glasnost*); a political purging and modernisation of all branches of the bureaucracy; and greater freedom and flexibility for the political institutions that exercised power.

Domestic politics

When Gorbachev came to power in March 1985, there was no obvious sign of any political crisis, either amongst the leadership or in the Soviet Union itself. There was no significant internal opposition. The dissident movement had been isolated and defeated by 1980, and many of its leaders were in exile. Nor were there any signs of serious discontent within the working class. Though often in despair, the intelligentsia were not voicing any dissent. Despite increasing signs of stagnation, the Soviet economy was still growing, albeit much more slowly than in previous decades.

However, there was a crisis in the Soviet Union, though it was not very visible at first. It was in fact located within the leadership of the CPSU itself, and was the result of fundamental differences over how things should continue.

Fact
Ironically, given all the calls from the West, and within the USSR, for the introduction of a market economy in the Soviet Union, many Western capitalist states had major economic problems themselves in the early 1980s. Declining industries and high unemployment were common problems in the West, affecting millions.

5 Political developments in the USSR under Gorbachev

Several sections – including the one headed by Gorbachev – were convinced that the old framework was bankrupt, and that change was necessary in order to avert a catastrophe.

Gorbachev was just one of several younger, reformist, modern leaders who had emerged during the Brezhnev era, and who had been helped into positions of power by Andropov. Those wanting to maintain the status quo had managed to put Chernenko in power following Andropov's death, but this had only been a temporary delaying tactic.

There were strong links between economic and political reforms in the USSR. Because it was a planned economy, politics was of central importance in the planning mechanisms. In particular, because Soviet workers had no fear of unemployment to 'motivate' them, the planning system had to come up with some *positive* motivations. This involved more than just financial incentives. It also involved respect for the party leaders, and faith in their ability to keep the economy growing. Thus, there was no market or profit motive in the socialised Soviet economy (unlike in capitalist economies). The absence of economic and political democracy held back the development of the full potential of total planning. Realising there would be some negative economic effects with *perestroika*, Gorbachev felt he needed to improve the political situation for Soviet citizens.

What was not always clear at the start was that Gorbachev and his supporters intended to challenge the ideological basis of the party and the state. Indeed, these moves ultimately split the superstructure of the state itself. Yet, as early as the 27th Congress of the CPSU in February 1986, the new general-secretary made his intentions clear. At this point, Gorbachev made a speech that included references to Lenin's struggle (at a crucial time in Bolshevik history) for acceptance of his **April Theses** – against almost the entire leadership of the Russian Bolsheviks.

SOURCE A

These facts [about the fight over the April Theses] were not written about in the Soviet Union, in the decades that followed Lenin's death in 1924, but they were talked about a great deal. So Gorbachev's listeners in February 1986 would have understood (and many did, especially his opponents) that this particular reference to Lenin implied that what was at stake was nothing less than an assault on the entire tradition of the present CPSU (a tradition, it should be pointed out, that dates back to the Thirties). Gorbachev was calling into question the entire programmatic orientation of the Party … So we note that everything – the entire future of the Soviet state and of the Communist Party – is at stake in the current turn. If it fails, everything could fail … What is being stated is that a crucial section of the Soviet leadership considers that the state and the party are facing one of the most serious crises in its history. Gorbachev is arguing that the Party is not politically prepared for confronting and overcoming this crisis.

Ali, T. 1988. *Revolution From Above: Where is the Soviet Union Going?* London, UK. Hutchinson. pp. 5–6.

Fact
The Brezhnev era was not (as is often claimed by some Western 'Kremlinologists') monolithic. Nor were people afraid to voice their real views. There were two sides to the Brezhnev regime. While he eased out radical democratisers, he also curbed the Stalinist wing of the CPSU. Between these two extremes, various figures amongst the élite were able to suggest reforms. Andropov had no real desire to democratise the Soviet Union. However, he did see the need for economic reform – hence his sponsorship of Gorbachev.

Fact
The absence of economic and political democracy does not necessarily hold back capitalist economies. For instance, the profit motive proved completely compatible with reactionary regimes such as Hitler's Germany and Pinochet's Chile.

Question
Why might Gorbachev's mention of the debates over Lenin's April Theses in 1917 have worried some leading members of the CPSU?

April Theses On his return from exile in April 1917, Lenin had been shocked to find that the Bolshevik leadership in Russia were giving critical support to the Provisional Government. Since the March Revolution, this Provisional Government had kept Russia in the First World War. At that time, only Lenin in exile (and Trotsky, who was not as yet a member of the Bolsheviks) had argued that Russia was approaching the stage for another revolution that, this time, would be socialist. The April Theses called for a revolution that would give power to the people and their soviets.

Communism in Crisis

> **Theory of knowledge**
>
> **History, language and meaning**
> When historians write about political change, they often use terms such as 'conservative', 'radical', 'reformer' and 'reactionary'. However, do these words always have the same meaning? Or does their meaning depend, to some extent, on the historical context (the particular time or society being studied)? Are such problems of meaning greater in one-party states like the USSR?

Only a few Western observers noted at the time the potential seriousness of the changes Gorbachev was attempting to make. Ultimately, if the economy did not improve sufficiently, the democracy process would be seriously threatened. This was because workers would lose interest, preferring better living standards to greater democracy. And this would leave Gorbachev with no socio-political base outside the ranks of his supporters in the bureaucracy. This was something that many of the hardline conservatives were hoping for.

Glasnost

This was the first of Gorbachev's political reforms, and referred to 'openness', and 'publicity' (meaning that the government should explain their policies to the public). Gorbachev's initial aim was not full freedom of information and expression. What he wanted was a greater willingness to admit to problems, and to allow ordinary people to voice concerns and criticisms. For example, if there was more openness about corruption and incompetence, it would make it easier for him to identify and remove corrupt and incompetent individuals. All of this, he believed, would do two things – make reform easier to achieve, and increase popular support for the system. His more relaxed, frank and open style (very much like Khrushchev's 30 years before) was suited to this approach. On his 'walkabouts', he talked – and listened – to ordinary employees.

Yakovlev, as minister responsible for the media, believed *perestroika* would not be successful without *glasnost* – so the media were given greater freedom to publish criticisms. Television often showed discussions in which people made criticisms to ministers who answered them. Even Western politicians were interviewed on television.

There was not complete freedom, as publishers (rather than the party, as previously) were still supposed to 'vet' new works. Nonetheless, previously forbidden books – for instance, by Boris Pasternak and Vladimir Nabokov, and by foreign writers – were legalised. Meanwhile, the press and films dealt with contemporary social problems such as alcohol and drug abuse, abortion, suicide and crime. This more open atmosphere led some former émigrés, such as the ballet dancer Mikhail Baryshnikov, to return to the Soviet Union.

Chernobyl

Glasnost did not get off to a good start. It seemed that even the new Gorbachev government was reluctant to put it into effect when, on 26 April 1986, a nuclear reactor exploded at the Chernobyl nuclear plant in Ukraine.

This spread high levels of radiation – but it was not reported at first by the plant to the government. Nor was it reported by the media or the Soviet government. There is some evidence that, on 28 April, Gorbachev called for full reporting – but this was blocked by the Politburo. It was only when the Swedish government announced that high levels of radiation had been detected coming from Ukraine that the Soviet authorities admitted an accident had taken place. Even then, the extent of it was not fully revealed.

Gorbachev had previously shown his determination to end the practice of keeping news about the failings of the system from the Soviet people, and Chernobyl was a huge setback. It was also a clear sign of the unaccountability and inefficiency of the Soviet system.

> **Fact**
> The official death toll from Chernobyl was 31, but the real figure was certainly much higher. The refusal to make early public announcements delayed evacuation of the worst-affected areas. For instance, the neighbouring town of Pripyat was not evacuated until the following day. The problems continued until the middle of May. An investigation blamed the top managers of the plant, who were sentenced to hard labour for failing to observe safety procedures.

5 Political developments in the USSR under Gorbachev

The Chernobyl nuclear power plant three days after the explosion in April 1986

Question
Why did the Chernobyl incident make Gorbachev think that his political reforms needed to go further?

Dissent – past and present

Another aspect of *glasnost*, which affected economic reform, was the decision to open the state archives. This gave historians (and, later, the public) access to information in order to re-examine aspects of Soviet history, including the Stalin era. This soon led to an increasingly open debate on past policies, such as forced collectivisation and centralised planning. It also led to revelations about the purges. Gradually, former 'enemies of the state' (especially those who had been executed or assassinated under Stalin) were politically rehabilitated.

This also led to a more liberal attitude to contemporary internal critics and dissidents. For instance, Sakharov, who had been exiled to Gorky in 1980 (see page 52), was released. He was then allowed to travel abroad, making speeches about repression and the Soviet gulags. Though he was widely known and admired in the West, his support within the USSR was more limited.

Fact
High-ranking people who were politically rehabilitated after their deaths included Grigori Zinoviev, Lev Kamenev and Nikolai Bukharin. However, Trotsky was not fully 'cleared' before the collapse of the USSR in 1991. In all, about 1 million sentences handed down under Stalin were eventually annulled.

Intellectuals were of course pleased by the relaxation of policy, but there was a mixed response within the top levels of the party. Conservatives, in particular, objected to the printing of attacks on Stalin – and even on Brezhnev. This was partly because they feared that such openness and freedom would lead to social and political instability, and so undermine the Soviet system. However, Gorbachev continued with his reforms. Even in 1990, when he was beginning to take a firmer attitude towards his critics, his Press Law abolished censorship, and established the rights of freedom of information and free expression.

Demokratizatsiya

To begin with, it seems that Gorbachev saw increasing democracy as a way of sugaring the bitter pill of *perestroika* for Soviet workers (higher prices and temporary unemployment). As part of his programme to increase democracy in the USSR, and to sideline opponents of his economic reform, Gorbachev made various changes. At first, he tried to get the CPSU to accept the need for change, but he met much opposition from the *nomenklatura*, who worried that many of their special privileges would be lost.

Gorbachev's chances of success were not as limited as they might have appeared on the surface. Although this bureaucratic caste wielded more power than any property-owning ruling class in modern times, its position was much weaker than other such classes. It was also divided in itself, with Gorbachev and his supporters making up one wing of it.

Historical debate

The diversity of opinion within the Soviet leadership came as a surprise to those who had described the USSR as a totalitarian state. However, it was less unexpected for those who had seen the USSR as a bureaucratic pluralist regime. The orthodox Cold War theories of totalitarianism, as applied to the USSR, came under attack from revisionist historians in the early 1970s. Such historians included Robert Daniels, Stephen Cohen, and Jerry Hough, who challenged the idea of the Soviet Union as a passive, inert society, dominated by a united and all-powerful élite. Hough believed that pluralism in the USSR and the USA had a number of common features. Daniels did not go this far, but he described the USSR as trying, since Khrushchev's time, to form a 'participatory bureaucracy'.

SOURCE B

[The bureaucracy's] power is exceptional because it is economic, political and cultural at the same time. Yet, paradoxically, each of these elements of power has had its origins in an act of liberation [the November 1917 Revolution] ... Because of the workers' inability to maintain the supremacy they held in 1917, each of these acts of liberation turned into its opposite ... But the conflict between the origins of the power and its character, between the liberating uses for which it was intended and the uses to which it has been put, has perpetually generated high political tensions ... which have again and again demonstrated the lack of social cohesion in the bureaucracy ... They have not eradicated from the popular mind the acts of liberation from which they derive their power; nor have they been able to convince the masses – or even themselves – that they have used the power in a manner compatible with those acts. In other words, [the bureaucracy] has not obtained for itself the sanction of social legitimacy.

Deutscher, I. 1969. *The Unfinished Revolution: Russia 1917–1967*, Oxford, UK. Oxford University Press. pp. 57–8.

In addition, the bureaucracy did not have popular support in the country. Thus, any mass mobilisations (especially if encouraged from the top) would soon expose its weaknesses. This was shown across Eastern Europe during 1988 and 1989, where, with the exception of Romania, popular protests swept away similar ruling bureaucracies (see Chapter 6).

Activities

1 See what else you can find out about the Chernobyl incident. How far-reaching were its effects? How does the Soviet government's response compare to that of the Japanese government, following the damage to nuclear reactors in Fukushima, caused by the March 2011 tsunami?

2 Make a list of the main objections by conservative members to Gorbachev's early policies of *glasnost* and *demokratizatsiya*.

3 Continue adding to your 'Political Reforms' chart.

4 Imagine you are a journalist interviewing Gorbachev about his *glasnost* policies. Try to draw up a list of questions that challenge his commitment to real freedom of speech and information. Then compile some responses he might have made about such freedoms in your country.

What were Gorbachev's main political reforms between 1986 and 1990?

27th Congress of the CPSU

Gorbachev's first attempt to change things took place at the 27th Congress of the CPSU, February–March 1986, when the Central Committee Secretariat was given a larger role. The Congress gave a top job to Alexandra Biryukova, who was put in charge of light industry, food and consumer services – the first woman to have such a high-level job since Khrushchev's administration. It also approved a new Party Programme, which for the first time modified the one drawn up under Khrushchev in 1961. This programme publicly stated that progress to communism would be difficult, and there was also criticism of the years of 'inertness'.

This Congress confirmed Gorbachev in his position of general-secretary. However, the bureaucracy also attempted to keep some control over him and his reforms. Yegor Ligachev, a senior member of the Politburo, was put in charge of party ideology, to ensure party stability. Ligachev supported economic reform, but he was not in favour of democracy. It was also made clear that Ryzhkov, as prime minister, would be in charge of implementing policy. In addition, the majority of the old Central Committee initially stayed in place.

Despite this, Gorbachev intended to push ahead with party reform. After making some changes to the leadership bodies, he insisted on calling a Party Conference in order to gain approval for a new set of guidelines to supersede those made at the 27th Congress. Among other things, he wished to avoid the fate of Khrushchev, in 1964.

Gorbachev hoped that he would be able to prevent any serious splits in the party over his political and economic reforms. In January 1987, at a Central Committee meeting, he announced that the Soviet economy and society were in crisis. He said that to solve these problems, the party and state political systems needed to be democratised. To start with, there were to be competitive elections, with a choice of candidates, for members of some local soviets, which would in future be directly elected by the people. There were also to be direct elections to other important soviet posts. In this way, Gorbachev hoped to weaken party control over the state and to increase the number of supporters of reform.

Fact

In 1964, Khrushchev was overthrown – to prevent him implementing plans to totally reorganise the leading bodies of the Communist Party. While Khrushchev was away on holiday, the KGB broke into his private safe, where they found his plans. Copies were made and circulated to members of the plenum of the Central Committee. At the same time, the KGB cut him off from all contact, so his supporters in Moscow could not warn him. In many ways, this was similar to the attempted coup against Gorbachev in August 1991.

Communism in Crisis

At the 18th Congress of Soviet Trade Unions in April 1987, Gorbachev made a strong speech in favour of democratisation, which was now under heavy criticism from sections of the bureaucracy. He made it clear that the USSR was facing a crucial test. If it failed, it might not get the opportunity again. In particular, he stressed the need for workplace democracy to ensure that *perestroika* was a success. The speech also advised union officials to stop 'dancing cheek to cheek with economic managers' and, instead, to protect the interests of their members.

SOURCE C

We possess [the] necessary political experience and theoretical potential to resolve the tasks facing society. One thing is clear: we should advance without fail along the path of reorganisation. If the reorganisation peters out the consequences will be far more serious for society as a whole and for every Soviet citizen in particular …

I will put it bluntly: those who have doubts about the expediency of further democratisation apparently suffer from one serious drawback which is of great political significance and meaning – they do not believe in our people. They claim that democracy will be used by our people to disorganise society and undermine discipline, to undermine the strength of the system … Democracy is not the opposite of order. It is the order of a greater degree, based not on implicit obedience, mindless execution of instructions, but on fully-fledged, active participation by all the community in all society's affairs … Democracy means self-control by society, confidence in civic maturity and awareness of social duty in Soviet people. Democracy is unity of rights and duties.

Extracts from Gorbachev's speech to the 18th Congress of Soviet Trade Unions, April 1987. Quoted in Ali, T. 1988. Revolution From Above: Where is the Soviet Union Going? London, UK. Hutchinson. pp. 11–12.

Question

What does Gorbachev say in this speech about democracy and its importance?

SOURCE D

We are obviously not going to change the system of Soviet power or its fundamental principles … [but] we attach priority to political measures, broad and genuine democratization, the resolute truggle against red tape and violations of the law, and the active involvement of the masses in managing the country's affairs. All of this is directly linked to the main question of any revolution, the question of power … The perestroika drive started on the Communist Party's initiative, and the Party leads it … Hence we must – if we want perestroika to succeed – gear all our work to the political tasks and the methods of the exercise of power … When the command-economy system of management was propelled into existence, the soviets were somehow pushed back … This lessened the prestige of the soviets. From that moment the development of socialist democracy began to slow down. Signs appeared that the working people were being alienated from their constitutional right to have a direct involvement in the affairs of state.

Gorbachev, M. 1987. Perestroika: New Thinking for Our Country and the World. London, UK. HarperCollins. pp. 54–55 and p. 111.

In June 1987, multi-candidate elections were held in some constituencies. Then, at a meeting of the Central Committee on 27–28 January 1988, further reforms were proposed. These included a choice of candidates for elections to all local and regional soviets, and this was eventually established by a new Electoral Law in December 1988. There was also agreement on secret ballots for the election of party officials, and on a choice of candidates for the election of trade union delegates within enterprises.

Gorbachev was aware of the contradictions within his policies – especially concerning the exercise of power, political pluralism and the power of the bureaucracy. Some of these were set out in his book, *Perestroika*.

19th Party Conference

On 28 June 1988, at the CPSU's 19th Party Conference, in Moscow, Gorbachev launched radical reforms that were meant to reduce party control of the government apparatus. He successfully proposed a new executive in the form of a presidential system, as well as a new All-Union legislative body, to be called the Congress of People's Deputies. This would have 2250 seats, directly elected by the people. Two-thirds of this Congress was to be elected by universal suffrage, and one-third (750 seats) from 'people's organisations', of which the CPSU (which had 100 seats allocated) was to be only one. The CPSU seats were to be filled by those nominated by the Politburo. Only Congress would be allowed to amend the constitution.

Congress would then elect from amongst its members deputies to sit in a new, permanent, 400-member All-Union Supreme Soviet. The Congress would have the power to ratify or amend any laws coming from the Supreme Soviet. This new Supreme Soviet would sit twice a year for sessions lasting several months. It would make laws – and would ratify (or not) ministerial appointments, including the president's choice of prime minister. It could question ministers, and set up commissions and committees. This two-tier structure was also to be set up in the various republics, where elections would take place in March 1990.

Gorbachev also proposed making all party officials accountable to the law. This would be achieved by making judges and the legal system independent of the CPSU. There would also be a new constitution that would guarantee civil rights, and separate party and state organisations. However, at first, Gorbachev intended to keep the one-party system. A new constitution was not finally drafted until June 1989.

Fact
The 19th Party Conference took place at Gorbachev's insistence. This was the first time since 1941 that a party conference had been held.

Question
What important political changes were made by the 19th Party Conference?

SOURCE E

The main direction of the democratisation of our society and state is the restoration in full of the role and authority of Soviets of People's Deputies as sovereign bodies of popular representation. V. I. Lenin discovered in the Soviets, born of the experience of revolutions in Russia, a political form in accordance with the nature of socialism. At once representative bodies of power and mass organisations of the population, the Soviets organically combine the principles of statehood and self-government ...

At the same time, we see serious shortcomings in the activity of the Soviets and dissatisfaction with their work among the working people. As a result of well-known deformations, the rights and powers of the representative bodies have been curtailed, and Party committees continue to exercise unwarranted tutelage over them. In many instances, ministries and departments resolve questions of economic and social development behind their backs ... It is necessary to change this situation fundamentally and to return real governing powers to the Soviets.

Extracts from the Central Committee Theses, passed by the 19th Party Conference of the CPSU, Moscow, June 1988. Quoted in White, S. 1993. *After Gorbachev*. Cambridge, UK. Cambridge University Press. p. 40.

Communism in Crisis

Fact
These elections were 'semi-free', in that people could vote for non-CPSU candidates. Some 88% of those elected were Communist Party members – but critics and dissidents, such as Sakharov (on the Academy of Sciences list), were also elected. However, the local electoral commissions were often dominated by the Communist Party. This led to much criticism, so the local electoral commissions were not used in the elections that took place in the republics and local districts in 1990. At the 19th Party Conference, it had been decided that local party secretaries should chair the republican soviets and local soviets. This happened in 1990, and again enabled the Communist Party to keep a large amount of control.

Boris Yeltsin (1931–2007)
When Gorbachev appointed Yeltsin as the new head of the Moscow party, replacing the corrupt Victor Grishin (who had links with an 'economic mafia'), it was seen as one of Gorbachev's more imaginative moves. At first, Yeltsin was a supporter of Gorbachev. But it soon became clear that he wished to go further and move more quickly than Gorbachev wanted. When Yeltsin launched a strong attack on Ligachev, he was forced to resign from the Central Committee, and was later removed as party boss of Moscow.

The 1989 elections

Elections to the Congress of People's Deputies were held throughout the Soviet Union in March and April 1989. These were the first semi-free elections in the Soviet Union since 1921. Almost 90% of registered voters turned out. About 50 senior regional party secretaries who did not have reserved seats were defeated, as were many local government officials and military candidates. Despite their limitations, these elections marked a weakening of party control – and this was noted in many of the Eastern European states.

The Congress of People's Deputies met for the first time on 25 May 1989, to elect representatives from Congress to sit on the Supreme Soviet of the Soviet Union. Gorbachev was elected chairman of the Supreme Soviet (or head of state).

Sakharov (front, centre) was one of the dissidents who was elected in 1989; here, he addresses the first session of the Congress of People's Deputies, 25 May 1989

Nonetheless, the Congress posed problems for Gorbachev; its sessions were televised, airing more criticism and encouraging people to expect ever more rapid reform. In the elections, many Communist Party candidates were defeated. Furthermore, **Boris Yeltsin** – who had not been nominated as one of the Communist Party's reserved seats – was elected in Moscow for one of its territorial seats. He then returned to political prominence and became an increasingly vocal critic of Gorbachev.

Other deputies also proved to be critics of the government, the Supreme Soviet and the CPSU. Some of these critics formed the Inter-Regional Deputies' Group, and this increasingly organised opposition encouraged the formation of political clubs outside the Congress. For the first time since the 1921 ban, there were organised factions, if not opposition political parties. However, under Gorbachev's policies, opposition parties would also soon appear.

5 Political developments in the USSR under Gorbachev

> **SOURCE F**
>
> I did not address Baranov [a legal officer involved in the registration of political groups] as comrade, but called him Citizen Baranov. We told him that the Popular Front believes in democratic, self-managing socialism which unites workers, students and artistic groups. We said we wanted to accelerate the process from below and that we would fight every violation of the law, small or big. Citizen Baranov listened carefully and then said: 'We don't allow perestroika from below.' I asked who the 'we' was. He replied, 'the Party!' I asked where is this party registered? How is it that it can exist without being registered? What became very obvious is that the party apparatus is scared of any mobilisation from below.
>
> *Comments made by Mikhail Malyutin, a member of the Popular Front For Perestroika in Moscow, July 1988. Quoted in Ali, T. 1988. Revolution From Above: Where is the Soviet Union Going? London, UK. Hutchinson. p. 141.*

Fact
Several political clubs had emerged since 1987. Such clubs included the Popular Front For Perestroika, formed in Moscow in May 1988. At this time, various clubs that had actively supported Yeltsin decided to merge with several ecology groups. Many of those involved were members of the Communist Party. Some groups also established links with others in various Soviet republics – such as Estonia.

While most of these political groupings were either centre or right-wing, there were also left-wing socialist, green and anarchist groups. These included the Soviet Communist Party of Bolsheviks, and the Moscow People's Front, whose co-ordinator was **Boris Kagarlitsky**.

As agreed in 1988, elections to create similar two-tier systems took place in the republics the following year, in March 1990. In Russia, meanwhile, the success of the Democratic Russia Election Bloc (which, among other things, campaigned against one-party rule) was very important. It was a major factor in the decision of the Soviet parliament in February 1990 to amend Article 6 of the Soviet Constitution by removing the reference to the Communist Party of the Soviet Union (CPSU) as 'the leading and guiding force' of Soviet society. By mid 1991, however, only two parties had registered with the Ministry of Justice, which by then was the requirement. One of these parties was the CPSU. Most of the small groups (there were over 500 such 'parties' at republican level) lacked the resources to be effective in elections.

Executive presidency

As the conflicts between the Congress of People's Deputies, the USSR Supreme Soviet and the USSR Council of Ministers continued, Gorbachev began to implement another of his plans – the creation of an executive presidency. This was established in March 1990. He hoped that a strong executive presidency would be able to push through the reforms *and* keep the USSR together. The president would have the power to veto legislation (though the Supreme Soviet could overrule this) and to appoint the prime minister and other top government posts (though, again, these had to be confirmed by the Supreme Soviet). He would have the power to dismiss the government and dissolve the Supreme Soviet, and to get the Congress to elect a new Soviet. The president could also declare a state of emergency.

Initially, it was proposed that the president should be elected by the whole country, but then it was decided to have this done by the Congress. On 15 March 1990, Gorbachev was elected – unopposed – as the first executive president of the Soviet Union. He also kept his post as general-secretary of the CPSU.

Boris Kagarlitsky (b. 1958)
Kagarlitsky was a left-wing Marxist dissident in the 1970s and 1980s, editing and contributing to various *samizdat* journals. In 1982, he was imprisoned for 'anti-Soviet' activities. After his release, he published his first book, *The Thinking Reed: Intellectuals and the Soviet State From 1917 to the Present*. In 1987, he played a leading role in the establishment of the Federation of Socialist Clubs in Moscow. In 1990, he was elected to the Moscow City Soviet and to the Executive of the Socialist Party of Russia. After the collapse of the Soviet Union in 1991, he co-founded the Party of Labour in October 1992, which was opposed to Yeltsin's programme of market privatisation of state property.

Question
Why was the decision to amend Article 6 of the Soviet Constitution so important?

Communism in Crisis

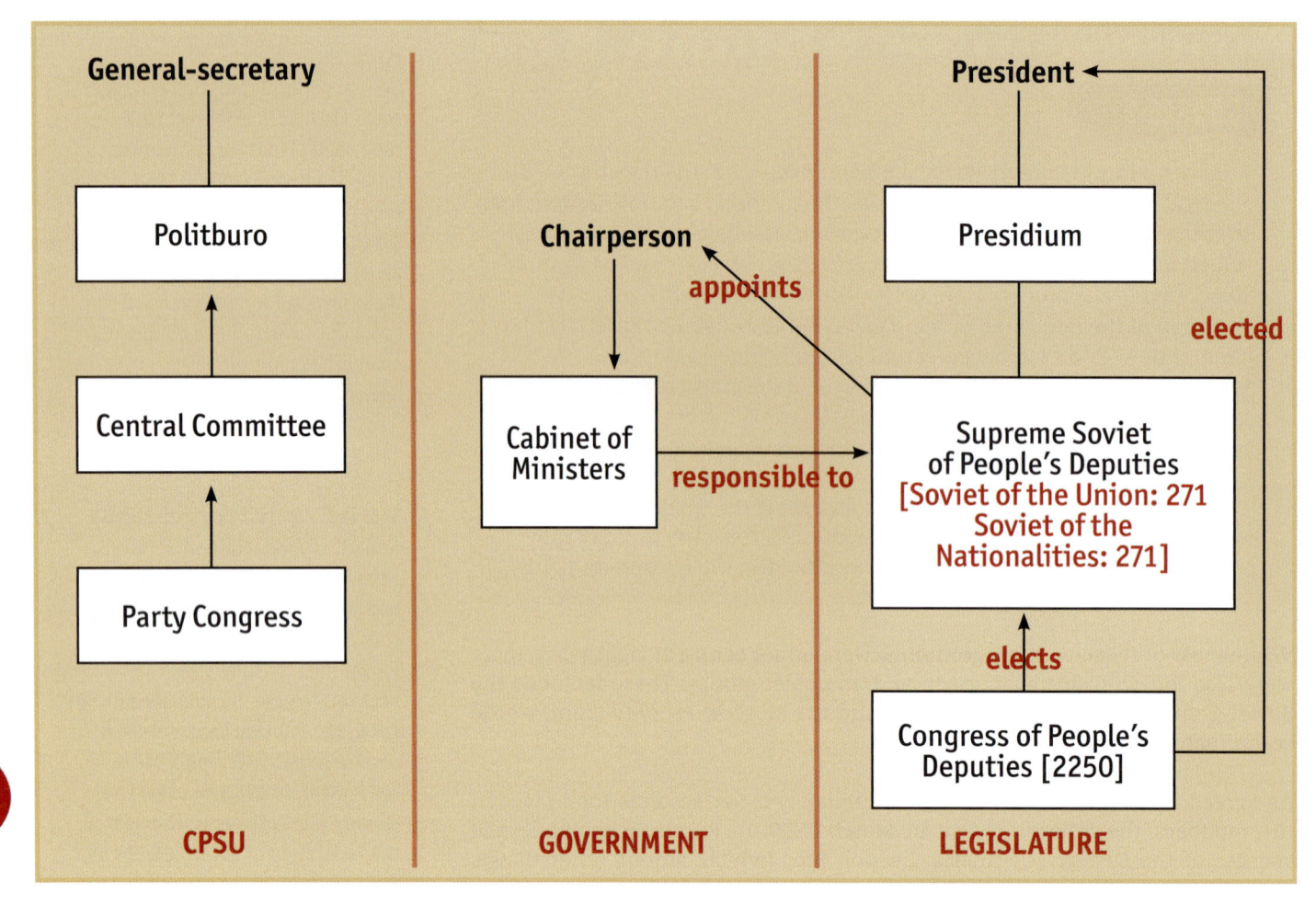

CPSU

- Party Congress → Central Committee → Politburo
- **General-secretary**

GOVERNMENT

- **Chairperson** appoints Cabinet of Ministers
- Cabinet of Ministers responsible to Supreme Soviet of People's Deputies

LEGISLATURE

- **President** ← elected
- Presidium
- Supreme Soviet of People's Deputies [Soviet of the Union: 271, Soviet of the Nationalities: 271]
- Congress of People's Deputies [2250] elects Supreme Soviet

Gorbachev's political structure 1989–91; Gorbachev was elected by the Congress of People's Deputies in 1990 but it was planned that, in future, the president would be directly elected by the people. Adapted from Lane, D. 1992. Soviet Society Under Perestroika. London, UK. Routledge. pp. 58–61.

As part of the new presidency, there were also other bodies: a Council of the Federation, made up of heads of the republics to oversee inter-republican relations; and a Presidential Council responsible for foreign policy. In September 1990, the Council of Ministers became a Cabinet, responsible to the president but headed by a prime minister. There was also a president-appointed Security Council that was responsible for defence and internal security. Gorbachev then abolished the Presidential Council, and used the Council of the Federation to make most of the important state decisions.

Although Gorbachev had great power on paper (even more than Stalin), his position was much weaker in practice. While there is no evidence that most Soviet citizens – as opposed to a few prominent dissidents – were demanding greater democracy before 1985, once Gorbachev began his reforms there were soon calls for a real multi-party system. The longer the reforms continued, the more confident people became in voicing their criticisms.

Reforming the CPSU

At first, Gorbachev wanted the party to retain its leading political role – but he realised it would have to reform itself. He wanted it to be more open, more tolerant of differing viewpoints, and less interfering and autocratic.

Fact
The Democratic Russia Election Bloc was formed in January 1990, and defeated several Communist Party candidates. Other groups included the Democratic Party (wanting a decentralised voluntary union of republics), the Democratic Reform Movement (set up in 1991 by Shevardnadze and Yakovlev, and other Gorbachev supporters), and more right-wing groups such as the Christian Democrats and the Liberal Democratic Party (led by Vladimir Zhirinovsky, an extreme Russian nationalist). Several of these right-wing groups were anti-Semitic.

5 Political developments in the USSR under Gorbachev

As well as reviewing the Five-Year Plan, the party was to have a much more important political role. As early as January 1987, when Gorbachev first proposed holding a party conference, he said that he envisaged this conference coming up with ways 'to further democratize the life of the Party and society as a whole', and that he saw it as 'a serious step toward making our Party life more democratic in practice and developing the activity of communists'. Yet he also made it clear that there would not be multi-party elections. His reforms *within* the party, though, included having genuine elections, with competing candidates, for party officials and conference delegates.

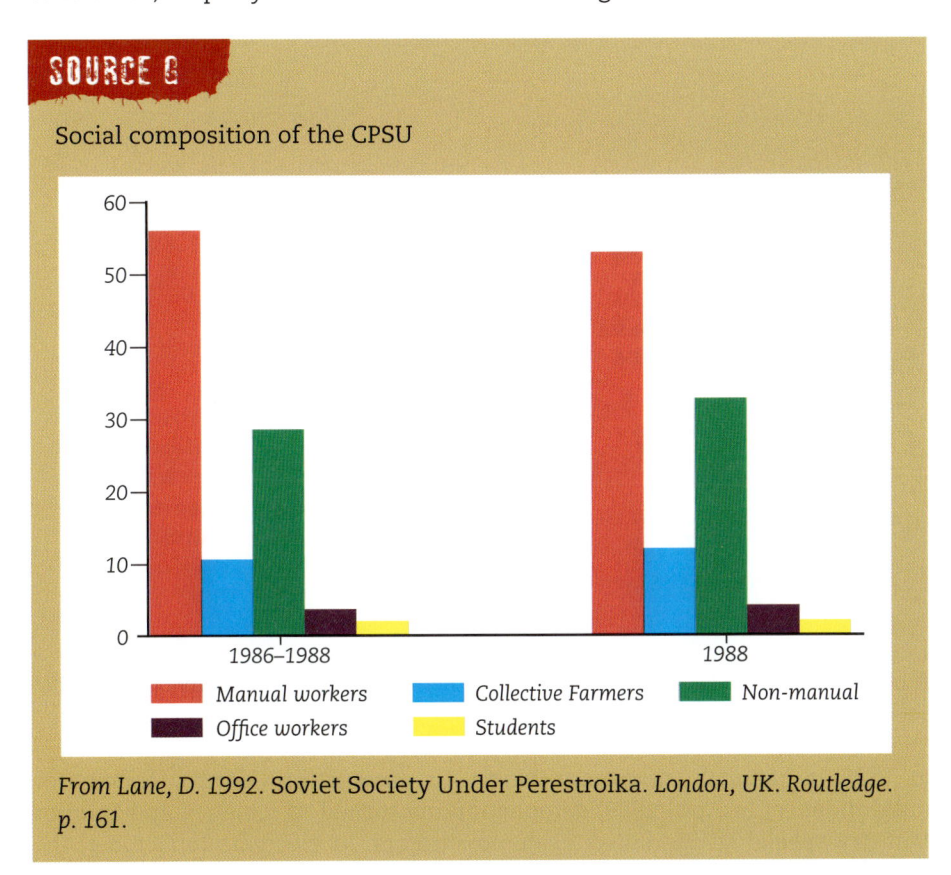

SOURCE G

Social composition of the CPSU

[Bar chart showing social composition of the CPSU in 1986–1988 and 1988, with categories: Manual workers, Collective Farmers, Non-manual, Office workers, Students]

From Lane, D. 1992. *Soviet Society Under Perestroika*. London, UK. Routledge. p. 161.

The 19th Party Conference, in June 1988, decided that party positions could not be held for more than two consecutive terms of five years. The party also lost its control of economic policy, with the Politburo now dealing only with internal party affairs, and no longer with economic policies. However, it retained its leading position in the military and the KGB.

To help separate party and state, it was agreed that nobody could hold both a party and a state position at the top levels. However, Gorbachev did not at first apply this rule to himself. Contrary to Gorbachev's expectations, the introduction of greater democracy led many to leave the party.

In August 1991, a new Programme for the CPSU was drafted, mainly by Gorbachev. This made virtually no mention of communism, and instead talked more about socialism. In many ways it was like a social democratic programme, rather than one for communists. This would be a factor in the attempted coup against him later that month. Though his reforms weakened the party's economic control, the separation of party and state also weakened Gorbachev's own position. Being general-secretary of a weakened CPSU was no longer so important, while the new state structures had yet to establish their authority.

Fact
Members were confused about the significance of the party after these reforms. In 1988, 18,000 left; in 1989, 136,000 left. This was only a small percentage of the CPSU's total membership (which stood at 20 million), but it was a worrying sign. In 1990, 3 million left – mainly as a result of lack of direction, or incomplete democratisation.

Communism in Crisis

The republics and nationalism

Meanwhile, the unrest that had been building in many of the Soviet republics led to calls for greater autonomy and even full independence from 1987 onwards – especially from the Transcaucasian republics like Georgia, and the Central Asian republics such as Kazakhstan. This call for independence was particularly strong in the Baltic republics, as it had been under Brezhnev.

Fact
Though Gorbachev had hoped that freer elections would see more reformers elected, nationalists were elected in many Soviet republics. Many of these republics were extremely right-wing, and often prejudiced against ethnic minorities – several were also anti-Semitic. Previously, the CPSU had usually managed to keep such attitudes under control. Ethnic tensions led to clashes between Azeris and Armenians in 1988–89 in the Nagorno-Karabakh region. A speaker in the Supreme Soviet referred to this crisis as a 'landmine under *perestroika*', while Gorbachev said that, if a solution was not found, it could have 'far-reaching consequences for all *perestroika*'. In 1990–91, violence broke out in Georgia, between Ossetians and Georgians.

Fact
The Baltic republics had been forcibly incorporated into the Soviet Union in 1940, following the Nazi–Soviet Pact of August 1939. They still resented this, and also disliked the number of Russians who migrated there because of their relatively higher standard of living – and their closeness to Western Europe. Popular front organisations (such as the Sajudis in Lithuania) were established during 1988, and these nationalist movements began to demand more sovereignty. Such political groups later contested the March 1990 Republican elections.

Fact
Given the hefty subsidies that many of the Soviet republics received from the centre, it was unlikely that they would be able to escape the economic crisis. Many of these republics, in fact, suffered real economic hardship when the Soviet Union collapsed.

A map showing the Soviet Union's 15 Union Republics and its 20 Autonomous Soviet Socialist Republics, in 1989

In 1988, a popular movement began to emerge in Georgia, calling for independence. In April 1989, demonstrations turned to violence and Interior Ministry special troops killed 23 demonstrators. In elections in October, the Georgian communists did badly, while a coalition of pro-independence groups won 54% of the votes. Then, in November 1989, the new Supreme Soviet of Georgia declared itself sovereign. By the end of 1989, when the USSR had given up its influence over the Eastern European states (see Chapter 6), it seemed to many Soviet republics that independence might be a way of escaping from the growing economic crisis.

Much of the unrest in the republics was long-standing. Under Stalin, the Soviet Union had been set up as a much tighter system than the original federation that had existed under Lenin. Growing awareness of the nature of the new Soviet Constitution, and Stalin's treatment of nationalities, had led Lenin (shortly before he died in 1924) to recommend that Stalin be deprived of his offices, including that of minister for nationalities. Lenin and Trotsky feared that Stalin was resurrecting the old tsarist policy of Russification – trying to make all the states the same, with Russia dominant. During the economic policies and purges of the 1930s, some states (such as Ukraine) had suffered terribly. Furthermore, after the Second World War, Stalin had punished republics such as the Baltic republics and Ukraine, where many had collaborated with the Nazi invaders.

5 Political developments in the USSR under Gorbachev

Lenin, in fact, had said that 'Great Russian' chauvinism was wrong and that the former parts of tsarist Russia should be free to secede – Finland had actually been allowed to do so. However, since 1924, the right to secede had only really existed on paper – and the USSR was not a true union of equals.

In September 1989, the CPSU considered changes to its nationalities policies. It began to consider a looser federation, with more respect for the rights and cultures of the different republics. In March 1990, the 15 republics held free elections for their own congresses and supreme soviets. As well as the communists, there were various electoral blocs and popular fronts. Many of these were quite nationalistic and, in order to compete in these elections, many of the local communist parties also began to use nationalist rhetoric – a complete reversal of what communist ideology was all about. However, it was only the CPSU that could give any coherence to the reality of All-Union institutions, whether party or state. Despite this, the CPSU's leading role was abolished in February 1990. With the weakening of the party under Gorbachev, the eventual break-up of the USSR was always a strong possibility.

In March 1990, the newly elected Lithuanian Supreme Soviet voted to secede from the USSR and issued its own laws. Gorbachev reacted strongly and Soviet troops were sent in, resulting in some deaths. An even more serious threat to the existence of the USSR came in May 1990, when the Russian Supreme Soviet voted for sovereignty. Several other republics soon did the same. Russia also, for the first time, established its own Communist Party and KGB (other republics had always had this, but not Russia). The Russian Supreme Soviet then (narrowly) elected Yeltsin as its president, despite Gorbachev's efforts to prevent this.

A new Union Treaty

Gorbachev accepted the need for reform. However, in April 1990, the Supreme Soviet passed a law saying there ought to be a minimum two-year waiting period before any application for secession could be approved. This would allow time to resolve complex issues such as Soviet enterprises in the republics and the question of nuclear weapons. The situation was further complicated by certain ethnic groups within the various republics also wanting to secede.

In June–July 1990, the 28th Party Congress approved Gorbachev's proposals for a less centralised federal system. A draft of a new **Union Treaty** was approved and published by the Supreme Soviet in November 1990. A drafting committee was set up in January 1991 to make revisions. This led Lithuania to agree to suspend its declaration of independence until the treaty had been amended and ratified. But then the other two Baltic republics, Estonia and Latvia, declared their 1940 annexations illegal. Meanwhile, Moldavia (incorporated into the USSR after the Second World War) was experiencing growing nationalist unrest, spearheaded by the Moldavian Popular Front. In November 1989, this group had forced the resignation of the unpopular Moldavian CPSU secretary.

Six of the 15 Soviet republics (Estonia, Latvia, Lithuania, Moldavia, Georgia and Armenia) refused to participate in the drafting process. A new draft was approved by the Supreme Soviet in March, and Gorbachev then held a referendum on the future of the USSR. All nine republics that had participated in the drafting of the new treaty voted overwhelmingly in favour of maintaining a federal system. The other six republics boycotted the referendum, as they were already moving towards complete independence.

Fact
Brezhnev had in some ways attempted a Stalinist policy of trying to create a 'Soviet' identity, to replace the various national identities. For instance, the Russian language was encouraged, and was needed for promotion anywhere in the USSR. Yet, in 1971, only 54% of the 240 million population was Russian. The CPSU in Moscow was dominant, but each republic had its own party structure. Provided they were loyal to the centre, they were allowed considerable leeway – which often resulted in corruption.

Union Treaty This refers to the treaty that joined the 15 Soviet republics together to form the USSR. This treaty was drawn up by Stalin. It gave prominence to the Russian Federation and was more centralised than Lenin wanted. This had been one of the issues over which, in the last years of his life, Lenin had opposed Stalin. Gorbachev's proposal for a new Union Treaty was for a looser federation, designed to give more power to the Soviet Union's republics.

Communism in Crisis

Gorbachev proposed going ahead with the signing of the treaty with these nine. Yeltsin agreed, but only on condition that Gorbachev agreed to presidential elections in Russia, as in all the other republics.

Russian nationalism

Despite the growing nationalist tensions on the edges of the USSR, it was the events in the Russian Federation under Boris Yeltsin that pushed many republics into wanting to break away completely from central Soviet control. At first, Yeltsin had been a supporter of Gorbachev, but increasingly he moved towards supporting a fully marketised economy. Though sacked as Moscow Party leader in November 1987, he was elected to the Congress of People's Deputies in 1989. In July, he helped create the Inter-Regional Deputies Group. He then managed to get into the new Supreme Soviet, when one of the elected members stood down to let him have the seat. The Democratic Russia group was formed to fight the March 1990 elections to the Russian Congress of People's Deputies.

In May 1990, Yeltsin was elected chairman of the Supreme Soviet of the Russian Federation. At the 28th Congress of the CPSU in June 1990, there were intense arguments between those who wanted a market economy and those who did not. At this point, Yeltsin publicly resigned from the party. While Gorbachev seemed to move away from some of these more extreme calls for a market economy, other reformers resigned their posts – Yakovlev from the Central Committee, and then Shevardnadze from his post of foreign minister. Yeltsin now saw Russia (by far the biggest and wealthiest of the republics) as a useful power base. Before the March 1991 referendum on the new Union Treaty, opponents of Gorbachev in Ukraine and Belorussia formed an alliance with Yeltsin's supporters in Russia to undo the Union. Meanwhile, Gorbachev tried hard to hold it together. Initially, the US supported Gorbachev's approach, as it preferred to deal with one government.

In a further attempt to strengthen his position, Yeltsin called for a Russian presidency. This call was supported by a majority of Russian voters and he was elected in June 1991 as president of Russia. He then increasingly undermined Gorbachev's position. A sort of dual power existed between the Soviet and Russian leaderships. In July, Yeltsin banned members of parties from holding office in state organisations such as the KGB and the army. He also signed an agreement with Lithuania, in which the Russian Federation and Lithuania recognised each other's sovereignty.

Various nationalist groups began to emerge in Russia, often with quite different aims and policies. There were those who thought Russia would do better on its own, while others wanted to impose Russian dominance on the other republics. Soyuz (meaning 'Union'), led by Ligachev and others, wanted to keep the Soviet Union together. Meanwhile, the Russian Orthodox Constitutional Monarchists, founded in May 1990, wanted the traditional Russian empire restored. In July, Yakovlev and Shevardnadze were amongst those forming the New Democratic Movement.

A return to authoritarianism?

The net result of all these moves towards a presidential system was just further confusion. There were also fears that Gorbachev, who previously seemed to be moving towards a parliamentary democracy, was now trying to shift back to a more authoritarian system. One of these critics was Boris Yeltsin, who accused Gorbachev of trying to establish an 'absolutist and authoritarian' regime.

5 Political developments in the USSR under Gorbachev

> **SOURCE A**
>
> There were, in fact, considerable limitations upon the powers of the new President, extensive though they undoubtedly were. He could be impeached by a two-thirds vote of the Congress of People's Deputies; his ministerial nominations required the approval of the Supreme Soviet, which could force the resignation of the Cabinet as a whole if it voted accordingly; and he had himself to report annually to the Congress of People's Deputies upon the exercise of his responsibilities. Explaining his position to a gathering of miners in April 1991, Gorbachev pointed out that he had voluntarily surrendered the extraordinary powers of the General Secretary of the CPSU, powers which at that time were greater than those of any other world leader. Would he have done so if he had been seeking unlimited personal authority?
>
> White, S. 1993. *After Gorbachev.* Cambridge, UK. Cambridge University Press. p. 67.

A further development that supported the argument that Gorbachev was trying to become more authoritarian was the new Law on Press Freedom of June 1990. Thus, Gorbachev's attitude towards *glasnost* seemed at best inconsistent. In many ways, he appeared to be going back on his earlier *glasnost* reforms.

By early 1991, Gorbachev's political reforms had dismantled most of the political system established by Stalin. However, Gorbachev had not managed to replace it with a system based on a combination of Leninism and democracy – in other words, a system of central party control based on the sovereignty of the people. Gorbachev's growing weakness had been revealed in December 1990, when there were calls for him to resign as president. Then, in April 1991, the Central Committee requested that he resign as general-secretary. He survived these calls, but he was increasingly ignored by the republics – especially when they declared that their laws took precedence over those of the USSR.

Activities

1. Draw a chart listing the various changes made to the legislative, executive and party systems of the Soviet Union during the period 1986–90.
2. Carry out further research on the various nationalist conflicts and developments in the different Soviet republics. Then make an assessment of whether these could have been overcome without breaking up the Soviet Union.
3. 'Democrat, or demagogue and buffoon?' Write a couple of paragraphs to explain which description of Yeltsin you think best fits him.
4. Imagine that Gorbachev is on trial for attempting to become a dictator during 1990–91. Prepare two legal arguments: one for the prosecution and one for the defence. Make sure that you use precise information to support your points. You can then be the jury, and write a paragraph to explain your verdict.

Fact
Although the 1990 Law on Press Freedom allowed freedom of information and expression, it insisted that all public media had to be registered with the authorities. In addition, it made it a crime to 'abuse' free speech and to spread information that 'did not correspond with reality' – known as 'unreal' reporting. A month before, in May 1990, a law had been passed giving up to six years in prison for 'insulting the president'. Later on, Gorbachev brought back the State Radio and Television Committee to exert influence on media that were increasingly attacking him and his policies.

Discussion point
Carry out some further research on Gorbachev's actions during 1990–91. What do you think Gorbachev's reasons were for establishing an executive presidency? Was he trying to assume dictatorial powers (as Yeltsin increasingly claimed)? Or was he simply trying to ensure that his economic and political reforms could go through, so that there would be clear divisions between party and state?

Communism in Crisis

Why did the Soviet Union collapse in 1991?

All these political and economic upheavals came to a head in August 1991, when the political and military leaders who were strongly opposed to Gorbachev attempted to stage a coup against him. As well as growing concerns over his foreign policies (see Chapter 6), they were particularly worried about the draft Union Treaty. This would have removed the word 'Socialist' from the country's name, to make it the 'Union of Soviet Sovereign Republics'. It also saw power shift to the republics, and looked as if it would lead to the eventual break-up of the USSR and the end of the Soviet socialist system. In addition, they were opposed to Yeltsin's increasing adoption of policies for a transition to a complete market economy.

From coup to collapse

It soon became apparent that the hardliners were plotting. While on holiday in the Crimea, Gorbachev was placed under house arrest on 18 August by a small group of conservative hardliners, calling themselves the 'State Emergency Committee'.

These hardliners had assumed power in Moscow. However, Gorbachev refused to resign, or to declare a state of emergency, which could lead to the arrest and suppression of 'free' marketeers and those wanting to organise a coup. The plotters therefore declared a state of emergency themselves and issued several decrees. These included cancelling the Union Treaty. Several newspapers, which had strongly supported *glasnost*, were banned, and tanks moved to strategic points in Moscow. When news of this became public, there were protests and demonstrations. These protests grew larger.

Soon Boris Yeltsin took a leading position in the protest in Moscow, and 'protected' the Russian parliament (known as the 'White House') from the plotters. As president of Russia, he then issued a decree, accusing the conspirators of treason. He also called for a general strike – but this did not happen. Some observers dispute the size of the protests, claiming that most citizens did not get involved. As protests, barricades and demonstrations grew in Moscow and especially in Leningrad, the plotters began to waver. In the end, the majority of the army and security forces opted not to back the coup. For this reason, the plotters decided not to use force to crush the protests. Yeltsin now placed himself at the head of the armed forces and, on 21 August, the conspirators gave up and fled. The Supreme Soviet then cancelled the decrees issued by the plotters.

When Gorbachev returned to Moscow, he carried on with discussions about the new Union Treaty. Gorbachev filled the posts previously held by the plotters. Yeltsin was angry, and made strong speeches, forcing Gorbachev to sack the Soviet government. Although most members had not been involved in the coup, they had not opposed it either. On 23 August, Yeltsin banned the Russian Communist Party on 23 August; and Gorbachev was forced to accept that the Russian government had equal status to the Soviet one. On 24 August, Gorbachev resigned as general-secretary of the CPSU, but remained as president of the Soviet Union. On 29 August, the Supreme Soviet banned the CPSU from the entire USSR.

Yeltsin then began moves to establish the power of Russia. This led many republican leaders to fear that he intended to take over all Soviet assets, making Russia the dominant power. It forced many more nationalists to see breaking away from the Soviet Union as the only way to protect their powers.

Fact
The 'State Emergency Committee' consisted of eight Kremlin people, officially led by Gennadi Yanaev (vice-president). It included several who had been appointed by Gorbachev: Vladimir Kryuchkov (chairman of the KGB), Dimitri Yazov (minister of defence), Valentin Pavlov (prime minister), and Boris Pugo (minister of internal affairs).

Fact
The idea of Yeltsin 'protecting' the Russian parliament was somewhat ironic. In 1993, he used military force to stop the criticism and opposition he was facing in the parliament. He actually ruled Russia in a dictatorial way, and was as guilty of nepotism and corruption as the old-style communists of the Soviet Union had been. In fact, there is some debate about whether he led the protests from the beginning – or whether he waited to see how things would turn out first.

5 Political developments in the USSR under Gorbachev

This was especially true when Yeltsin took control of the Soviet budget and promised to defend all Russians living in the various republics. In December, Ukraine voted to leave the Union, thus ending any hopes of a looser federation. The Soviet Union was effectively ended when Russia, Belorussia and Ukraine formed the Commonwealth of Independent States (CIS).

Yeltsin (standing, left, with raised fist) in Moscow in August 1991, opposing the attempted coup, with the Russian 'White House' in the background

> **Activity**
>
> Assess the value and limitations of this photograph in terms of finding out about Yeltsin's role in opposing the August 1991 coup.

The CIS had no parliament or presidency – though it did agree to have unitary control of nuclear weapons, which was something the US wanted. Perhaps significantly, it informed George Bush, the US president, before it contacted Gorbachev. On 25 December 1991, Gorbachev announced his decision to resign as president of the USSR. This marked the formal end of the Soviet Union.

Was Gorbachev's failure inevitable?

Historians are still debating the causes of the crisis and eventual collapse of the Soviet Union. There were clearly many long-standing economic and political weaknesses within the Soviet Union itself, which played important roles in its eventual downfall. These included bureaucratic control of the economy, which resulted in much inefficiency and waste, and rates of productivity that were significantly lower than those achieved in the West. Its undemocratic political system alienated important – if not large – sections of the Soviet society. It has also been argued that Gorbachev's attempts at reform came too late to save a system that was already doomed by 1985.

One analysis – made without the benefit of hindsight – was offered over two years before the collapse of the USSR, by Ernest Mandel. He was a Marxist who, for a time, was an economics lecturer at the Free University of Brussels. In 1989, he saw four possible outcomes for the Gorbachev project:

1. successful reform by 'revolution from above'
2. radicalisation of leading members of the CPSU, leading to a 'Moscow Spring' (similar to developments in Czechoslovakia in 1968)
3. the conservative elements of the *nomenklatura* successfully stopping the democratisation and reform project
4. the possibility of a new working-class political revolution.

Communism in Crisis

However, this optimistic analysis left out a fifth possibility – the total collapse of the Soviet system and of the Soviet Union itself. Arguably, it was Gorbachev's weakening of the CPSU (which was the main element keeping the USSR together and functioning), before there was anything to replace it, which was the biggest cause of the collapse.

Historical debate

Historians are divided on how to assess Gorbachev. Some (such as David Marples and Archie Brown) see him as a genuine – or at least a cautious – reformer. Others (such as Dmitri Volkogonov and Robert Service) see him as essentially a Leninist, whose commitment to reform was limited. Catherine Merridale, however, regards his lack of a coherent reform programme, along with his failure to give wholehearted backing to reform-minded people (both within the CPSU and outside it) as ultimately undermining his chances of success.

SOURCE I

Where is the Soviet Union headed under Gorbachev? What are the possible outcomes of the process that has begun in that country? If pressure from the masses ... is adequate to neutralize the obstruction and sabotage of the more conservative layers of the bureaucracy; if the apparatus is progressively modernized and rejuvenated; if capitalist credits are made available; if Gorbachev's reforms are allowed to continue ... then perestroika will begin to deliver fruits after a period of time and the living standards of the people will improve. In such a case the Gorbachev experience will succeed. Of the four possible scenarios that we outline here, we consider this one the least likely. It underestimates the resistance to reform and the social and political contradictions which are an obstacle to any 'reformist' solution.

Mandel, E. 1989. Beyond Perestroika. London, UK. Verso. pp. xv–xvi.

Fact

Gorbachev was initially told that he would receive much-needed US loans to help solve the USSR's growing economic crisis, if he signed the Conventional Forces in Europe Treaty (which was signed in November 1990). However, he was then told that further aid would not be forthcoming unless the USSR became a capitalist economy. The KGB also claimed to have evidence that the USA was attempting to bring about the disintegration of the USSR. President Bush initially opposed this, and was prepared at first to accept the coup attempt against Gorbachev. However, his administration soon changed tack and made contact with Yeltsin.

However, earlier US policies (especially in maintaining and deepening the nuclear arms race) contributed to the increasing distortion and ultimate collapse of the Soviet Union's economic and political structures. It can therefore be argued that the main reason for the collapse was the much greater strength of the USA. In fact, as early as 1970, Brzezinski (who later became national security adviser to US president Jimmy Carter) had suggested five possible futures for the Soviet Union, given the context of the Cold War. One of those futures was adaptation – in other words, becoming closer to Western economic and political models. Another was disintegration – or collapse and break-up. Both these aims (getting the USSR to adapt to Western models and encouraging its collapse) were pursued by US governments during the Cold War, and especially during the Second Cold War, which began in 1979.

Activities

1 Imagine you are one of those involved in the attempted coup against Gorbachev. Draw up a press release in which you attempt to justify your actions.

2 Carry out some further research on Yeltsin's actions from 1990 to 1991. Do you think he, rather than Gorbachev, was most responsible for the eventual collapse of the Soviet Union? Explain the reasons for your decision in a couple of paragraphs.

3 Complete your chart on 'Political Reforms'.

4 Draw a timeline – giving dates and brief details – of the last year in the existence of the Soviet Union.

End of chapter activities

Summary

You should now have a sound understanding of Gorbachev's main political reforms, and the extent to which they were successful. You should also be able to comment on the new problems they gave rise to.

Your study of this chapter, and of the previous one, should allow you to make balanced assessments of the economic and political crises facing Gorbachev from 1985 to 1991, and the reasons for the collapse of the USSR.

Summary activity

Copy the diagram below and, using the information in this chapter and from any other available sources, make brief notes under the headings and sub-headings shown. Remember to include information on historical debate/interpretations, including names of historians.

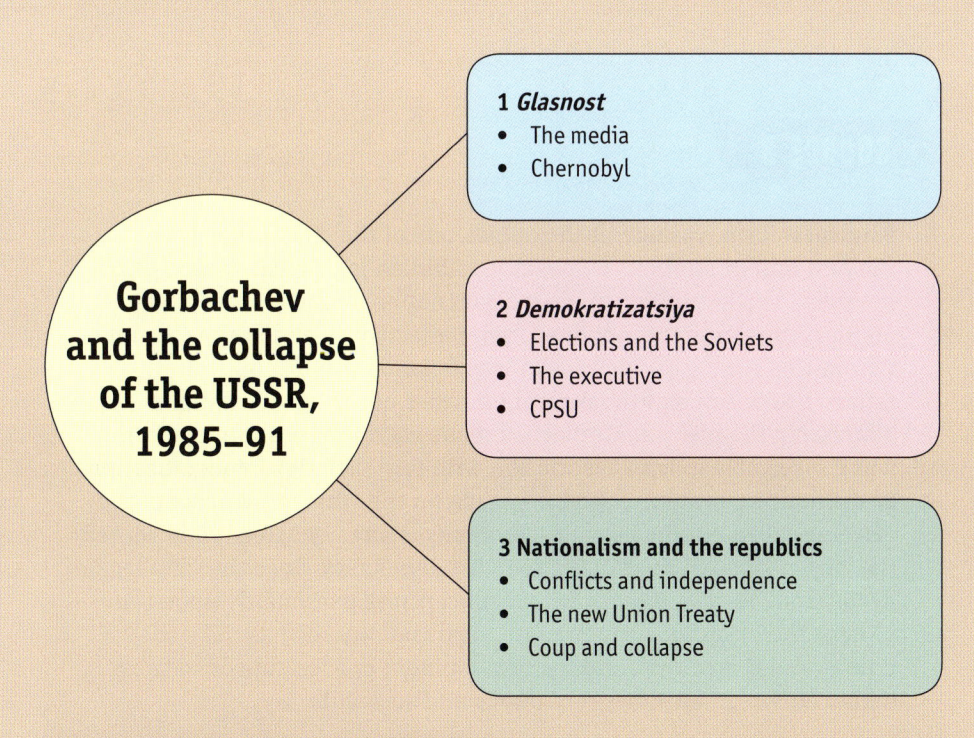

Gorbachev and the collapse of the USSR, 1985–91

1 *Glasnost*
- The media
- Chernobyl

2 *Demokratizatsiya*
- Elections and the Soviets
- The executive
- CPSU

3 Nationalism and the republics
- Conflicts and independence
- The new Union Treaty
- Coup and collapse

Paper 1 exam practice

Question

Compare and contrast the views expressed in Sources A and B (on page 112) about what was needed in the Soviet Union for Gorbachev to successfully carry through his economic and political reforms.
[6 marks]

Skill

Cross-referencing

Communism in Crisis

SOURCE A

The fear of the apparatus [after the 19th Party Conference in June 1988] is that opening up politically could lead to the formation of nationalist parties. Perhaps. The antidote, however, does not lie in bureaucratic repression, but in refounding the CPSU by changing its functions. This, in turn, is tied to the democratisation of the Soviets and a rigid separation of party and state institutions. Now many of the ideas on this level have been initiated from above. Their implementation, however, will depend on a movement from below. It is only when the soviets are multi-party bodies that a real separation between the CPSU and the state can take place.

Ali, T. 1988. Revolution From Above: Where is the Soviet Union Going? London, UK. Hutchinson. p. 217.

SOURCE B

Political reform was not, at the outset, one of the chief priorities of the new administration … Speaking to Indian journalists in late 1986, however, he [Gorbachev] made it clear that he intended to secure a political system that functioned 'more effectively', and at the Central Committee meeting which took place in January 1987 political reform became one of the central priorities of the new leadership … addressing the plenum, Gorbachev made clear that economic reform was conceivable only in association with far-reaching 'democratisation' of the political system … [In his speech on the 70th anniversary of the November Revolution, he said] The changes already agreed represented the 'biggest step in developing socialist democracy since the October Revolution'; further change would concentrate particularly upon the soviets, the electoral system, mass organisations such as the trade unions and Komsomol, and the development of a 'culture of socialist democratism' in all spheres of public and social life.

White, S. 1993. After Gorbachev. Cambridge, UK. Cambridge University Press. pp. 28–29.

Examiner's tips, common mistakes and a simplified markscheme for cross-referencing questions can be found on page 216.

Student answer

> Sources A and B both agree that what is needed is a democratisation of the soviet system – Source A talks about 'the democratisation of the Soviets', while Source B says Gorbachev felt it was necessary to 'concentrate particularly upon the soviets'. However, Source B doesn't actually say they need to be made more democratic, which is what Source A says – so in this sense they are different.

Examiner's comments

There is an explicit identification of a **similarity/comparison** between the two sources (with precise references to both the sources), and also *brief* comments about a contrast/difference (though this difference is rather limited). Also, there is an explicit attempt to link the two sources, rather than dealing with them separately. The candidate has thus done just about enough to get into Band 2, and so be awarded 4 marks. However, there are several other comparisons and, in particular, more obvious contrasts, which could have been made. Consequently, this answer is too short to make the necessary points, and thus fails to get into Band 1.

Activity

Look again at the two sources, the simplified markscheme, and the student answer above. Now try to write a paragraph or two to push the answer up into Band 1, and so obtain the full 6 marks. In particular, look for some clear differences between the two sources.

Paper 2 practice questions

1. For what reasons, and with what results, did Gorbachev attempt to democratise the Soviet Union?
2. In what ways, and with what results, did Gorbachev's conservative opponents resist his political reforms?
3. Analyse the role of nationalism in the break-up of the Soviet Union.
4. 'It was not the conservatism of Brezhnev, but the radicalism of Gorbachev, that destroyed the Soviet Union.' To what extent do you agree with this assertion?

6 Gorbachev, the Cold War and Eastern Europe

Timeline

1968 'Prague Spring' and Warsaw Pact invasion in Czechoslovakia

1986 Mar: First protests in Hungary

1987 Oct: Solidarity re-forms in Poland

1988 Jan: widespread strikes in Poland

Apr: Geneva Conference – USSR and USA end foreign involvement in Afghanistan

May: Moscow Summit; Grósz replaces Kádár in Hungary

Aug: arrest of demonstrators marking 20th anniversary of 'Prague Spring'

1989 Jan: Solidarity legalised in Poland

Feb: Hungarian communists agree to free elections in 1990

May: protests begin in Bulgaria

Jun: Solidarity wins contested seats

Oct: Honecker forced to resign in East Germany (GDR)

Nov: GDR opens Berlin Wall; first protests in Romania; Zhivkov forced to resign in Bulgaria; Communist Party renounces leading role in Czechoslovakia

Dec: Bulgarian communists agree to multi-party elections; Ceaușescus executed in Romania; majority non-communist government formed in Czechoslovakia

1990 Mar: ex-communists out-voted in Hungarian elections; Warsaw Pact dissolved

Jun: free elections in Czechoslovakia

Oct: German reunification

Introduction

When Gorbachev came to power in 1985, he adopted a very different foreign policy from that of his predecessors. This quickly became apparent in his approach to East–West relations and the Cold War; to the ongoing situation in Afghanistan; and in particular to Eastern Europe.

Gorbachev's policies affected the satellite states of Eastern Europe as significantly as they affected the Soviet Union. Ever since the start of the Cold War in 1946–47, the communist-ruled states of Eastern Europe had been politically, economically and militarily bound to the USSR, through the military alliance of the Warsaw Pact.

The Warsaw Pact was the Soviet-led military alliance that dominated Eastern Europe from its creation in 1955 until 1991. It was originally established to counter the West's NATO military alliance, created in 1949. Gorbachev negotiated an extension of the Warsaw Pact Treaty in 1985. However, by 1989, it was clear that he was genuinely committed to giving the countries of Eastern Europe the freedom to carry out reforms without fear of any Soviet or Warsaw Pact intervention. By giving up Soviet influence in Eastern Europe he was effectively marking the end of any Soviet aspirations towards being a superpower, as the USSR had no significant allies outside Eastern Europe.

It should be noted that some Eastern European states – though technically communist – were not members of the Warsaw Pact. Yugoslavia had broken away from Stalin's Soviet Union shortly after the Second World War; while Albania sided with Mao's China during the Sino–Soviet split, which developed under Khrushchev. Thus, in 1985 the Warsaw Pact consisted of seven countries: the USSR, the GDR, Hungary, Poland, Czechoslovakia, Bulgaria and Romania. Like the USSR, these communist regimes were now facing crises due to their economic problems. This was especially true of those states that had borrowed heavily during the 1970s – increasing stagnation led to mounting debts. Attempts to make cuts in order to pay back loans led to protests in several states and, eventually, to demands for political change.

On taking power, Gorbachev was aware that developments within the countries of Eastern Europe, as in the USSR itself, required some changes in policy. His actions regarding these countries were in many ways linked to his attempts to solve the economic problems in the USSR. He hoped that money and resources shifted from aid and armaments could be invested in the Soviet Union's civilian economy.

Several of the developments associated with Gorbachev's 'New Thinking' made him very popular abroad – much more popular than he was in the Soviet Union. Yet his foreign policy also played an important part in the attempted coup against him in August 1991. To some within the USSR, his ending of the Soviet Union's security belt seemed as big a threat as the growing movements for independence in the Soviet republics. Thus, the crises and events in the 'communist' satellite states of Eastern Europe in the 1980s were significant factors in the eventual collapse of the Soviet Union itself.

Key questions

- What were Gorbachev's foreign policy aims?
- What were the main developments in Eastern Europe during the 1980s?
- What were the main steps in Czechoslovakia's 'Velvet Revolution'?
- What were the results of the changes in Eastern Europe?

Overview

- From as early as 1985, Gorbachev made it clear that he intended to adopt a radically different foreign policy, especially in relation to Eastern Europe.
- As well as deciding to end Soviet involvement in Afghanistan, he also pushed hard for agreements to reduce the nuclear arms race. Significant agreements were made at a series of summits with the US.
- As regards Eastern Europe, he publicly announced that the Soviet Union was abandoning the Brezhnev Doctrine. On a series of visits to the Eastern European states, he encouraged communist leaders to adopt economic and political reforms.
- The first significant moves towards reform appeared in Poland in 1987; then, in 1988, changes took place in Hungary.
- The pace of change increased in 1989 in all the Eastern European states. While some initially tried to suppress the growing protests, many leaders who had been in power for decades were soon replaced by reformist communists.
- However, in many countries it soon became clear that revolution (rather than reform) was what the people wanted. In the final months of 1989, most of the governments stepped down in the face of mass protests.
- These 'velvet revolutions' of 1989 (like the one in Czechoslovakia) were thus essentially bloodless. The communist rulers – with the exception of Romania – made no serious attempts to use the armed forces to maintain their regimes. This differs from what happened in China in May 1989.

A Czechoslovakian student, holding a picture of Havel, rings a bell during the 'Velvet Revolution' in Prague in 1989; bells became a symbol of the revolution

Communism in Crisis

What were Gorbachev's foreign policy aims?

Like Deng Xiaoping (see Chapter 8), Gorbachev realised that economic and political changes were necessary in the state he ruled. However, he also saw the need for changes to Soviet foreign policy. This included improving international relations in general, ending the Soviet presence in Afghanistan, and loosening the Soviet Union's control (and economic support) of the states of Eastern Europe.

While Gorbachev, and others, frequently made speeches containing references to Lenin, any attempt to revert to a foreign policy based on **Leninist practices** would clearly not have been realistic. Leaving aside the impact of any attempts to aid revolutions around the world in the context of the Second Cold War, the prospect of a reconciliation between capitalism and the Soviet Union appeared even more unlikely than in the years after 1917. For instance, Alexander Yakovlev (see page 74) was concerned about the close connections between the US government, the military and the largest corporations (which Eisenhower called the 'Military-Industrial Complex'). Yakovlev saw these links as particularly close in President Reagan's Republican administration.

> **Leninist practices** This term refers to the period 1917–24, when the Bolsheviks attempted to encourage socialist revolutions in other countries. They initially did this to help bring about the end of the First World War. Then, after 1918, they continued to help socialist revolutionaries in order to end Soviet Russia's isolation. This strategy was based on Lenin's belief that Russia was too backward to create socialism on its own, without aid from more advanced states such as Germany. This aid would clearly not come from hostile capitalist countries. Once Stalin had risen to power, this policy was replaced by the nationalist policy of 'socialism in one country.'

SOURCE A

The present Washington cabinet is made up of representatives of major corporations, above all, those connected with the military business. Its composition is indicative of the balance of forces in the economic elite … Significantly, Reagan is backed up by a new generation of the rich who have made fortunes by underhand dealings, graft, bribery, Mafia connections and the like … The Reagan administration is often dubbed the 'Bechtel Power Corporation government' because many of its members come from the California construction company specialising in large-scale power and industrial construction projects, some of which are developed in foreign countries.

Yakovlev, A. 1985. *On the Edge of an Abyss: From Truman to Reagan.* Moscow, Russia. Progress. p. 181.

The main aim of Gorbachev's foreign policy was to divert funds from military expenditure in order to overcome the stagnation of the Soviet economy. Gorbachev and his supporters were keenly aware that the Cold War – with its accompanying arms race – was crippling the Soviet economy. They were thus keen to end the Second Cold War, which had begun in 1979 following the USSR's military intervention in Afghanistan (see Chapter 3).

> **Fact**
> Above all, the USSR wanted to avoid the financial costs of a further militarisation of space, which explains Soviet concerns about Reagan's 'Star Wars' Strategic Defence Initiative (SDI) proposals (see page 12). Gorbachev hoped to reduce expenditure on nuclear weapons, and instead try to achieve technological parity with the West in conventional arms.

The cost of the arms race had become unbearable for the USSR. Moreover, the Soviet Union wanted to end the trade and technological blockade that the US had imposed since the Soviet intervention in Afghanistan. Gorbachev also wanted to obtain large-scale credits from the West in order to finance the rapid modernisation of the Soviet economy. This was something that Stalin had not managed to achieve at the end of the Second World War – hence Gorbachev's desire to end the Second Cold War and bring about a new period of détente. This was to be achieved by a radical change in foreign policy, covering the Cold War arms race and Afghanistan, as well as Soviet relations with Eastern Europe.

The Cold War

Gorbachev's new approach included offering to make deep cuts in Soviet armaments. The cuts he offered were largely intended to ease the burden of military attempts to keep up with the much wealthier US. These offers led to a series of summit meetings with US president Reagan at Geneva in November 1985 and in Reykjavik in October 1986. Though the meeting in Reykjavik resulted in no firm agreements, it laid the groundwork for later agreements.

In December 1987, Gorbachev visited Washington, and the conference led to the Intermediate Nuclear Forces (INF) Treaty, which eliminated intermediate-range nuclear weapons from Europe. A further summit in Moscow in May 1988 saw the start of a new Strategic Arms Limitation Treaty (START). Although this treaty was not finalised until 1991, both sides agreed to reduce their respective nuclear stockpiles (the USSR by 25%, the USA by 15%). Overall, though, this was less successful than Gorbachev had hoped, as the US refused to abandon its SDI project.

As a result of all these foreign policy agreements – and the changes in the USSR – there was a period of worldwide 'Gorby mania' (albeit expressed by the people of various countries, rather than by some of their leaders). Gorbachev started speaking about 'our common European home' and the end of the Second Cold War seemed to be in sight at last.

Fact
By 1987, Gorbachev was far less popular in the USSR, not only with conservatives within the CPSU, but also amongst the general public. The Soviet people were beginning to suffer from the ending of state subsidies and rising unemployment – almost unknown in the Soviet Union since the 1930s. Gorbachev's loss of popularity was a turnaround, as when he first became leader he was very well liked by Soviet citizens. Now, in contrast, his economic policies were criticised, while his liberalism towards dissidents was increasingly seen as less important than the 'bread and butter' issues.

'Gorby mania' at its height: President Mikhail Gorbachev and his wife Raisa are greeted by crowds of well-wishers during their 1987 visit to Czechoslovakia

Communism in Crisis

> **Fact**
> An attempt at 'National Reconciliation' in Afghanistan failed, and the fighting continued even after the collapse of the Soviet Union. Najibullah was overthrown in 1992, and the Islamic state of Afghanistan was set up. This marked the end of the various social and economic reforms of the PDPA, but the fighting continued. In 1996, the Taliban, who were backed by Pakistan, took over. They took Najibullah from a United Nations (UN) compound, brutally tortured him and then killed him. Later, in October 2001, the US and Britain launched a war against Afghanistan and their former allies, the Taliban. Though the Taliban government was overthrown, the fighting continues.

> **Fact**
> The Taliban (meaning 'students', from the 'Students of Islamic Knowledge Movement') are a militant fundamentalist Islamist group. They were first active in the *Mujahideen* campaign against the PDPA government and Soviet troops during 1979–89, and at that time were funded by the US, Pakistan and Saudi Arabia. They became increasingly important after 1991, and ruled Afghanistan from 1996 to 2001, when the US–British invasion drove them from power. They continue as an active guerrilla force.

Afghanistan

Though not in Eastern Europe, Afghanistan had long been seen by the USSR – and even by the West until 1979 – as being in the Soviet sphere of influence. Here, Gorbachev made it clear that the Soviet Union was no longer going to maintain the costly intervention, which he referred to as a 'bleeding wound'. In addition to the economic costs, by 1985 the intervention had resulted in many deaths and casualties amongst Soviet troops, and was thus leading to great criticism at home. It was also making any deals with the West (seen as increasingly vital for the Soviet economy) more difficult.

The Soviet Union used the election of a new People's Democratic Party of Afghanistan (PDPA) leader, Mohammed Najibullah, in May 1986, as an opportunity to attempt to stabilise the situation enough to withdraw its troops. The new Afghan leader became president in November 1986 and tried to negotiate a power-sharing deal during 1987, but the *Mujahideen* (see page 58) refused to co-operate.

Nevertheless, from mid 1986 onwards, the Soviet Union began to withdraw troops. In February 1988, Gorbachev publicly announced this withdrawal – without the USSR insisting on any guarantees about what type of government took over in Afghanistan. At the Geneva Conference in April 1988 Gorbachev and Reagan agreed to end all foreign involvement in the Afghan civil war – even though Gorbachev feared the consequences of a fundamentalist Islamic republic on the Soviet borders. By February 1989, after ten years of fighting, the last Soviet troops were withdrawn.

Eastern Europe

Although some of the foreign policies that Gorbachev introduced after 1985 seemed radically different from previous Soviet policy, perhaps the most spectacular changes were in relation to Eastern Europe. By the time Gorbachev came to power, maintaining the post-Second World War 'buffer zone' of Eastern European satellite states was involving an ever-growing cost for the Soviet Union, in terms of aid and subsidies. As the USSR was experiencing serious economic problems, these outgoings were clearly having a very negative impact on the Soviet economy.

Moreover, events in Eastern Europe during the late 1980s showed Gorbachev that at least some reforms were vital if the communist regimes were to hold on to power in these countries. These changes included easing Soviet control, which was fuelling nationalist resentment in several states. In response, Gorbachev attempted to tackle the position of the satellite states, like that of the USSR, with a 'revolution from above'.

He soon began to reduce the Soviet connections to these states, making it clear that he wished to distance the USSR from them. He also encouraged them to follow their own 'paths to socialism', to begin liberalisation reforms, and in particular to be less reliant on Soviet economic assistance.

The end of the Brezhnev Doctrine

Especially important was Gorbachev's public abandonment, in March 1985, of the Brezhnev Doctrine of November 1968. He made it clear that Soviet troops would no longer be sent into any Eastern European state, either to defend an existing regime or to crush reform communists or mass popular movements.

This was reiterated at a Warsaw Pact meeting in April 1985. It later became known as 'The Sinatra Doctrine', in reference to a Frank Sinatra song – 'I Did It My Way'.

This change was reaffirmed in Gorbachev's 1988 speech to the UN, when he stated that the principle of freedom of choice for all nations was a 'universal principle [that] knows no exceptions'. In July 1989, he openly denounced the Brezhnev Doctrine in a speech at the Council of Europe in Strasbourg. In particular, he argued that the people of all countries had a 'sovereign right' to choose a social system they wanted – and that this was an important precondition for normal relations in Europe. Gorbachev also stressed that he believed that any interference in internal affairs, including those of friends and allies, was 'impermissible'.

He later reaffirmed this declaration in Budapest, in November 1989, at what turned out to be the last important meeting of the Warsaw Pact. Here, he made it clear that each member state of the pact had the right to make changes within their own country 'without outside interference'.

Such statements and actions were totally different from those of any previous Soviet leader. They clearly abandoned the old coercive principles on which Soviet foreign policy towards Eastern Europe had been based since 1945.

> **Fact**
> While clearly stating that the USSR would no longer interfere in Eastern Europe, Gorbachev's 1988 speech to the UN expressed the hope that this principle would also apply to US interference in the internal economic and political developments of the Soviet Union and its republics.

Reasons for change

There were multiple reasons for Gorbachev's radical change in policy towards Eastern Europe.

Economic reasons

Economic reasons were the key motivation for Gorbachev's policies towards Eastern Europe. Clearly, the growing cost (in terms of aid and subsidies to the satellite states) was a burden that was proving impossible for the Soviet Union to bear. In addition, given the economic and military strains resulting from Soviet intervention in Afghanistan, he knew the USSR could not really afford to take military action in Eastern Europe to put down any revolt that might arise.

As noted by Shevardnadze, the Soviet foreign minister, a reformed and more prosperous Eastern Europe, with links to Western Europe, would benefit the Soviet Union economically in several ways. Firstly, the USSR could reduce its army if it no longer had to keep troops stationed in Eastern Europe. Secondly, the USSR would be able to stop supplying raw materials, such as natural gas and oil, at cheap subsidised prices to its Warsaw Pact allies. Finally, it would be able to stop paying high prices for the manufactured goods coming from these states, as they would have to charge prices nearer the levels set by the world market.

International relations

Gorbachev also needed to create the right international environment in which to safely implement his economic and political reforms in the Soviet Union, and to reduce Soviet controls over Eastern Europe. In particular, he needed an end to the Second Cold War as soon as possible. His policies in terms of Eastern Europe, like his approach to arms reduction, were therefore consciously aimed at improving relations in Europe as a whole and with the West in general.

Communism in Crisis

SOURCE B

Gorbachev wanted to achieve a relaxation in international tensions in order to create a more stable environment in which to engage in internal reform [in the USSR]. He was aware that the cold war did not just impose material pressures on the Soviet system, it also imposed a psychological fear of war and fear of the 'enemy' on the Soviet people as well as the populations of the Western countries. This is not a good environment in which to impose change. He also wanted to be sure that the United States and NATO would not take advantage of any internal instability that reform might temporarily create in order to destabilise the Soviet system further. He therefore had to transform East-West relations: from being based on fear, mutual distrust, threat and counter-threat, they had to be based on trust, mutual respect and the sincerely held conviction on all sides that interference in another country's affairs was profoundly undesirable.

Walker, R. 1993. *Six Years That Shook the World: Perestroika – The Impossible Project. Manchester, UK. Manchester University Press. p. 212.*

Question

According to Source B, what were Gorbachev's main reasons for changing Soviet foreign policy?

Political and ideological factors

Although Gorbachev's policies in Eastern Europe were largely the result of the Soviet Union's economic problems, it would also have been difficult to push through his political reforms in the Soviet Union without allowing the satellite states to do the same, if they so wished.

In addition, Gorbachev realised that there was a growing number of communist reformers in several of these states – especially in Hungary, where Gorbachev openly supported the changes in leadership and direction.

However, it is necessary to appreciate that these policy changes also resulted from a genuine commitment to end Soviet interference and to make Europe a safer place for all, both East and West. This approach formed the core of his 'common European home' policy, which won him many supporters in Western Europe amongst those who were increasingly anxious about the number of US nuclear weapons deployed in their countries.

A 'Common European Home'

Gorbachev made his new foreign policy principles – as well as his economic and political reforms – explicit in his book, *Perestroika: New Thinking for Our Country and the World*, which appeared in 1987. Part of Gorbachev's 'New Thinking' in foreign policy was based on the idea that the Soviet Union, and Eastern and Western Europe, shared a 'common European home'. He stressed the common history and culture of Europe, and argued that the security of Europe as a whole could only be resolved by pan-European initiatives and bodies. As the European Union in the West grew in size and importance, Gorbachev began attempting to bring about a less divided Europe.

6 Gorbachev, the Cold War and Eastern Europe

> **SOURCE C**
>
> The philosophy behind the concept of a common European home excludes the likelihood of an armed clash and the very possibility of the use or threat of force, above all military force, by one alliance against another, within alliances or anywhere else.
>
> Extract from Gorbachev's speech at Strasbourg, July 1989. Quoted in Laver, J. 1997. *Stagnation and Reform: The USSR 1964–91*. London, UK. Hodder & Stoughton. p. 101.

Questions

Why did comments like these, made by Gorbachev from 1985 onwards, worry some of the communist leaderships in Eastern Europe, but encourage others? What are the value and limitations of this source for historians wishing to identify Soviet foreign policy aims? Remember to focus on the attribution information provided about the source (such as who is speaking, and when; and what type of source it is), as well as looking at the content.

Gorbachev first mentioned the idea of Europe being 'our common home' in February 1986. This idea was raised again in April 1987. Initially, reaction to it was mixed: the British prime minister, Thatcher, remained true to her Cold War mentality, accusing Gorbachev of trying to extend communism worldwide.

Encouraging reform

In addition to ending the Brezhnev Doctrine and emphasising the idea of a 'common European home', Gorbachev encouraged the policies of *perestroika*, *glasnost* and *demokratizatsiya* in the Soviet Union's Eastern European satellite states. During 1986 and 1987, he travelled throughout Eastern Europe, urging the governments of these states to adopt economic and political reforms like the ones he was trying to implement in the Soviet Union.

He stopped short of ordering the various governments to adopt these reforms, but he indicated that the USSR would no longer support governments that wanted to continue with the old party-dominated 'administrative command' system. (This old system had been established in the late 1940s, on Stalin's orders.) At the same time, in private discussions, he made it clear to the party leaders that they could no longer rely on Soviet economic or military help to get them out of any crisis. He also made public speeches that effectively appealed directly to the citizens – often to the annoyance of the political rulers of these states. While many citizens in these countries were keen to enjoy the new freedoms being allowed in the USSR, several East European governments had grave doubts – in particular, the government of the GDR (German Democratic Republic, or East Germany).

Fact

There would be no Soviet or Warsaw Pact intervention, as had happened in Hungary in 1956, or in Czechoslovakia in 1968. Nor would there even be the threat of it (which had hung over East Germany since the protests of 1953, and over Poland since 1980). There would be no more supporting of unpopular regimes against popular protests or communist reformers (such as Dubček in Czechoslovakia in 1968). In the past, Soviet military support had been one of the main instruments 'of last resort' in keeping these regimes in power whenever crises had threatened to break out.

In 1987, Gorbachev launched a serious discussion within the Warsaw Pact alliance on how to reduce Soviet troop levels in the countries of Eastern Europe. These troops were there not only to prop up the regimes, but also to deter any possible US/NATO invasion. Significant withdrawals of Soviet troops began in 1989, and accelerated in 1990–91.

In many ways, Gorbachev's speeches began the process of undermining the authority and position of the hardline Eastern European rulers. Thus, he prepared the way for the events of 1988–89, which resulted in the downfall of the communist regimes in all the Eastern European states.

Fact

One consequence of withdrawing Soviet troops was that thousands of officers and their families, who had enjoyed relatively high living standards in East Germany, Hungary or Czechoslovakia, were suddenly sent back to the USSR. Back in the Soviet Union, little had been done to prepare for their return, and the Soviet economy was already experiencing serious problems.

Communism in Crisis

Activities

1 See what you can find out about: (a) the establishment of Soviet control over Eastern Europe in the three years immediately after the Second World War; and (b) the main causes, events and consequences of the Hungarian Uprising of 1956.

2 Draw a chart to show the summit meetings between Gorbachev and Reagan, giving dates, locations and outcomes.

3 Write a short newspaper article explaining Gorbachev's 'common European home' policy, and describing how people in Eastern and Western Europe responded.

4 Carry out some preliminary research on the main events of 1988–89 in Eastern Europe. Then draw a timeline for these events, using a different colour for each of the five countries that are dealt with in the next section of this chapter.

What were the main developments in Eastern Europe during the 1980s?

The events of 1988–89 took many people by surprise – but, in fact, changes had been taking place in many of the Eastern European states since the start of the 1980s. In many ways, they faced similar problems to those Gorbachev found in the USSR: economic stagnation, indebtedness and a lack of consumer goods. There was also dissidence, from those who continued the struggle to escape Soviet interference in their country's affairs and to challenge the bureaucratic rule of their governments.

The Eastern European regimes might sometimes have resented Soviet interference, but they also relied on the moral and military support of the USSR to ensure their survival in the face of mass opposition. Hence, many of these leaders were unsettled by Gorbachev's rise to power. His rise was shortly followed by his reformist *perestroika*, *glasnost* and *demokratizatsiya* policies, and by his abandonment of the Brezhnev Doctrine. Although the ruling communists in Hungary and Poland welcomed the new opportunities for reform, those of the GDR, Bulgaria, Romania and Czechoslovakia tried hard at first to limit news of Gorbachev's reforms in the Soviet Union.

In contrast, Gorbachev's policies and speeches encouraged dissidents in those states to speak out and become organised. The more Gorbachev spoke of *glasnost* and democracy, the more they were encouraged to act. As the protests grew and spread in 1988–89, the rulers of the Eastern European states (with the exception of the ruler of Romania) were not prepared to use the force of the state to stop the growing opposition movements and protests. Instead, they stood down in the face of mass popular revolt. By the end of 1989, the communist regimes in all the Eastern European states (except Romania) had been overturned in peaceful and bloodless **political revolutions**, which the Soviet Union did nothing to prevent.

The fall of these regimes meant the collapse of communism in Europe, and ultimately contributed to the disintegration of the USSR and the end of the Cold War. Yet, when Gorbachev came to power in 1985, most regimes in the Soviet bloc had seemed reasonably secure and stable. Many of Gorbachev's critics blamed the collapse of these states, in only four years, on Gorbachev's policies.

Fact
The Eastern European reluctance to use force was unlike the communist government in China. There, Deng Xiaoping ordered PLA troops in to suppress the Democracy Movement protests in Tiananmen Square in June 1989 (see page 204).

political revolutions These are revolutions that bring about a change in the ruling political regime, but which make no significant changes to economic and social structures. However, the revolutions in Eastern Europe in 1988–89 soon turned into social revolutions. A social revolution attempts to bring about more fundamental changes – especially transferring economic assets and power from one social group to another. Such revolutions often occur when the existing systems seem stagnated and incapable of further progressive development. After 1989, publicly (or socially) owned property in the Eastern European states was sold to those who were able to buy. It thus became private property, and a return to capitalism was ushered in.

6 Gorbachev, the Cold War and Eastern Europe

SOURCE D

In Poland it took ten years. In East Germany it took ten weeks. In Czechoslovakia it took ten days. And in Romania it took ten hours.

A Central European comment on the comparative speed of the breakdown of the communist regimes in Eastern Europe. Quoted in Almond, M. 1996. *Revolution: 500 Years of Struggle for Change.* London, UK. De Agostini Editions. p. 178.

Fact
At the same time, after some hesitation, Gorbachev also accepted the inevitability of the reunification of Germany. This had been viewed as another huge security issue for the Soviet Union since the First World War, given that Germany had invaded Russia twice in the space of 30 years.

The following section will examine what happened in five of these Eastern European satellites: Poland, Hungary, East Germany, Bulgaria and Romania. A separate 'case study' section will then follow, on events in Czechoslovakia.

A map of Eastern Europe showing the changes that took place in 1988–89

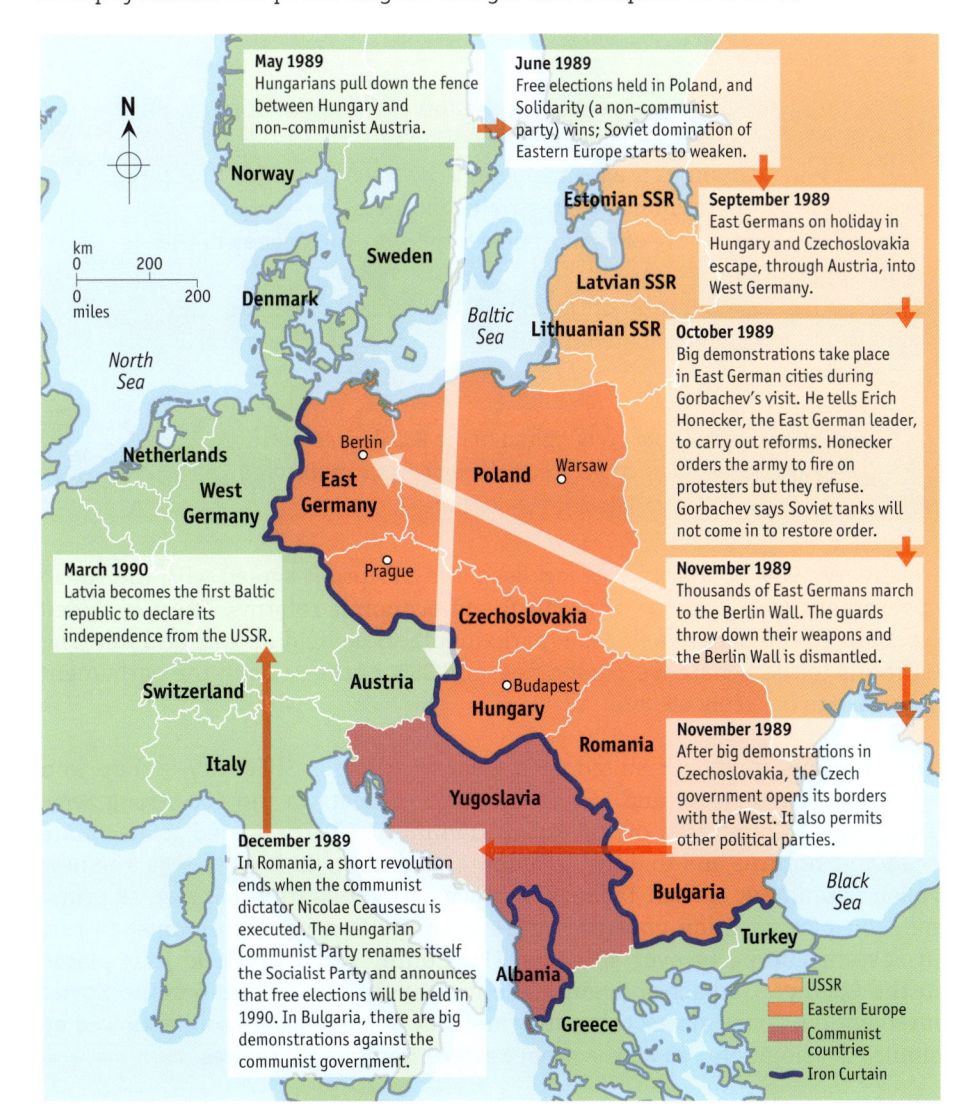

May 1989
Hungarians pull down the fence between Hungary and non-communist Austria.

June 1989
Free elections held in Poland, and Solidarity (a non-communist party) wins; Soviet domination of Eastern Europe starts to weaken.

September 1989
East Germans on holiday in Hungary and Czechoslovakia escape, through Austria, into West Germany.

October 1989
Big demonstrations take place in East German cities during Gorbachev's visit. He tells Erich Honecker, the East German leader, to carry out reforms. Honecker orders the army to fire on protesters but they refuse. Gorbachev says Soviet tanks will not come in to restore order.

November 1989
Thousands of East Germans march to the Berlin Wall. The guards throw down their weapons and the Berlin Wall is dismantled.

November 1989
After big demonstrations in Czechoslovakia, the Czech government opens its borders with the West. It also permits other political parties.

March 1990
Latvia becomes the first Baltic republic to declare its independence from the USSR.

December 1989
In Romania, a short revolution ends when the communist dictator Nicolae Ceausescu is executed. The Hungarian Communist Party renames itself the Socialist Party and announces that free elections will be held in 1990. In Bulgaria, there are big demonstrations against the communist government.

Communism in Crisis

Poland

As noted earlier (page 56), a political crisis broke out in Poland during the early 1980s. This resulted in the creation of an independent trade union, known as Solidarity, and the declaration of martial law by the Polish government.

However, a new economic crisis developed after the introduction of reforms in October 1986. Encouraged by Gorbachev's speeches and reforms, Solidarity re-formed in October 1987. Despite continued harassment by the government, it continued to grow. This was partly because its members were convinced that there would be no Soviet intervention to stop their movement – even if the government requested it. Although the USSR had put pressure on the Polish government to take action against Solidarity in the early 1980s, there had been no Czechoslovakia-type military intervention. In 1988, the economic problems worsened, and the government announced large food price increases. This again led to widespread strikes in January 1988 (often organised independently of the Solidarity leadership), and Solidarity began to demand political reforms.

Fact
In November 1988, Solidarity received support from Margaret Thatcher, the British prime minister, who was visiting Poland to discuss possible further loans. She said that there would only be economic aid for Poland if Solidarity was recognised as an independent trade union. This was seen by some British people as somewhat ironic, in view of the way her government had been dealing with trade unions in Britain. The Thatcher government's tactics included using the police (and even troops disguised as police) to smash the miners' strike of 1985–86, in order to push through her privatisation and economic 'shock therapy' policies.

Fact
Even though Mazowiecki was a non-communist, Poland remained a member of the Warsaw Pact until the alliance was formally dissolved.

Fact
The other Eastern European satellite states did not include Albania, which had not been a member of the Warsaw Pact. Albania had instead been allied to China, because of its differences with the USSR.

SOURCE E

Right now we can begin to discuss the topics for negotiations. I think we should be concerned with two questions:
1) implementation of the promise made by the authorities that there would be no repression toward striking workers.
2) the legalization of Solidarity, consistent with the wishes of the striking workers.
A positive consideration of the above mentioned questions will allow for a broader debate on economic and political reforms in our country.

Extract from a letter from Lech Wałęsa to the Polish government, 4 September 1988. Adapted from http://www.wilsoncenter.org

In January 1989, Solidarity was legalised and in April it agreed with the Polish government on a package of political and economic reforms. These included elections to the Senate and *Sejm* (parliament), to be held in June and July. The elections to the Senate were to be free, and 35% of the seats in the parliament were also to be freely elected.

The elections in June resulted in a clear victory for Solidarity – they won 99 of the Senate seats and 160 of the 161 free seats in the 460-strong *Sejm*. The Central Committee of the Polish Communist Party agreed to negotiate economic reforms and to draw up a new constitution. In August 1989, the new Polish parliament elected Tadeusz Mazowiecki, a Solidarity member, as prime minister of a coalition government. He was the first non-communist to rule in Eastern Europe in over 40 years. The Communist Party held four places in the Cabinet. Gorbachev again made it clear that there would be no Soviet intervention. These moves towards democracy in Poland were soon followed by similar developments in all the other Eastern European satellites.

Hungary

In 1985, when Gorbachev became ruler in the USSR, the ruler of Hungary was **János Kádár**. Even though Kádár had been put in power by the Soviet Union, he actually favoured reform. Under him, Hungary was not just stabilised after the events of 1956, but experienced a degree of liberalisation not seen in any Soviet bloc state until Gorbachev's rise. In fact, under Kádár, reformist communists had been carrying out their own Gorbachev-style policies for some time. As a result, Kádár's regime was relatively popular – both because of its liberal character and because of the higher standard of living its citizens enjoyed. Despite its heavy debt burdens (some of the borrowing was undertaken to maintain living standards), the regime seemed secure. In 1985, Kádár pledged to maintain 'socialist achievements'.

However, trouble began on 15 March 1986, when more than 3000 people demonstrated in Budapest, to celebrate an unofficial independence day (related to the 1848 revolution against Austrian rule). The police kept a low profile while some speakers called for democracy, but took stronger action towards the end of the day.

SOURCE F

The only way to save socialism from the rubbish heap of history is to allow other groups in society, eventually other parties, to compete against the Party. Only if people choose it, of their own free will, is it worth having.

Comments by an official of the Young Communist League (KISZ). Quoted in Hawkes, N. (ed.) 1990. Tearing Down the Curtain: The People's Revolution in Eastern Europe. London, UK. Hodder & Stoughton. p. 38.

At that time, opposition to Kádár's government was either tiny but well organised (such as the Democratic Opposition), or large but unorganised. During the summer of 1986, there were sporadic protests, but the situation changed in October as the anniversary of the 1956 uprising approached. On the actual day (23 October) little happened. Later, though, in the elections to the ruling body of the Writers' Union, all Kádár's supporters lost their places.

In the summer of 1987, Károly Grósz, an authoritarian but pragmatic Politburo member, was appointed as prime minister to tackle the growing economic crisis. He began to reduce party control of the government. On 27 September, **Imre Pozsgay**, a reform communist, called for a new constitution guaranteeing freedom of expression. Following this, the Hungarian Democratic Forum (HDF) was formed. When hardliners began to move against Pozsgay, he found support from Grósz. The anti-reform moves increased in the late 1980s. There were then increasing calls for the government to relax controls and to stop limiting the right to travel – especially to other Eastern European states.

In January 1988, the HDF held a meeting in Budapest and, in March, the New March Front and the Federation of Democratic Youth (FIDESZ) were formed.

János Kádár (1912–89)

Kádár was initially a supporter of Imre Nagy's attempts at reform in 1956 but, at the last moment, he switched sides and was put in power by the USSR. He remained general-secretary of the Hungarian Socialist Workers' Party from 1956 until he was forced to step down in 1988.

Question

According to Source F, why should communists accept a multi-party system?

Imre Pozsgay (b. 1933)

Pozsgay became a member of the Central Committee in 1970 and, in the late 1970s, became minister of culture. Then, in 1982, he was appointed as head of the People's Patriotic Front (PPF). The PPF had been founded by Imre Nagy in 1954 to give non-party members a voice in the country's affairs. Pozsgay used this to provide a forum to discuss reform and the need for greater democracy.

Communism in Crisis

Erich Honecker (1912–94)

Honecker was the general-secretary of the SED from 1971 to 1989, and was also head of state from 1976. He was against serious reform, and was removed from power by the party in 1989. Honecker was a hardliner and, after reunification of the two halves of Germany, for a time, faced the possibility of prosecution for human rights abuses.

Theory of knowledge

History, perceptions and reality

People in East Germany were probably more aware than other citizens of Eastern Europe of what life in the West was like – or, at least, what it appeared to be like. Most people in the states of Eastern Europe were relatively better off in the 1980s than they had been in the past. They enjoyed a range of social and economic benefits as part of their 'social wage', which were not always present in many Western countries. Yet what they saw on their television screens made many feel dissatisfied. It also led many to conclude that their governments had given them a false picture of life in the West. Were their perceptions about life under capitalism, taken from watching Western TV, confirmed or undermined by what happened after 1989?

In April, the FIDESZ was declared illegal. Then, in May 1988, at a special party conference held to discuss the economic crisis, a clear division in the Hungarian Socialist Workers' Party (HSWP) emerged. The split was between Kádár and the hardliners, Grósz and the centrists, and Pozsgay and the reformers. Kádár's proposals were defeated and he was forced to resign – apparently Gorbachev had advised him to do so. Most of the old Politburo and a third of the Central Committee were defeated in secret ballots, and Grósz became the new general-secretary of the party. Meanwhile, Pozsgay was elected to the Politburo.

Press freedom was granted and the HSWP was liberalised, in preparation for multi-party elections, which were accepted by the party's Central Committee on 10 February 1989. Plans for elections in March 1990 were also agreed. It was partly for such reforms that Hungary had been invaded in 1956.

Further, it was agreed to allow the re-burial of the remains of Imre Nagy, the reform communist prime minister of Hungary. Along with many other pro-reform communists, he had been executed following the Soviet suppression of the Hungarian Uprising of 1956. The revolt itself was officially re-designated as a 'popular uprising' instead of an attempted 'counter-revolution'.

On 23 March, the Opposition Round Table was formed. Then, on 2 May 1989, the Hungarian government also removed the fence on its border with the GDR, effectively allowing anyone who wanted to cross to the other country to do so. Later in May, it also opened its border with Austria, thus allowing people (including East Germans) to travel to the West.

Talks between the government and the Round Table on reform and the forthcoming elections began on 13 June. On 7 October, the Hungarian Communist Party became the Hungarian Socialist Party. Then, on 23 October, the anniversary of the 1956 Uprising, a new Hungarian Republic was declared. Meanwhile, the government pushed ahead with plans for a market-based economy. These included a new Company Law, allowing private (and foreign) ownership of firms. In the March 1990 elections, the former communists did badly, despite having pushed through many reforms.

East Germany

It took developments in East Germany (the German Democratic Republic, or GDR) to accelerate the pace of change in the rest of Eastern Europe. The GDR was ruled by the Socialist Unity Party of Germany (SED), as the East German Communist Party was known. Unlike other Eastern European states, citizens in the GDR could watch television programmes from West Germany. They therefore got live coverage of Gorbachev and his reforms and statements, and some idea of life in the West.

The popular revolt here was the most televised of all the events of 1989. In many ways, the GDR was an untypical satellite state. On the one hand, it was the most loyal supporter of the USSR, and was ruled by Stalinist hardliners who relied on their secret police, the Stasi – seen as the toughest of the secret police forces in Eastern Europe. Yet, since Brezhnev and Willy Brandt's *Ostpolitik*, it had also begun to forge economic links with West Germany. The Helsinki Accord (see page 53), which had included recognition of the post-war frontiers of Europe, had seen the GDR accepted as a legitimate regime. In 1984, cultural exchanges were agreed, and the mines along the borders between the GDR and the FRG (Federal Republic of Germany, or West Germany) were removed.

Hence many thought that **Erich Honecker** (see page 126) the East German leader, was secure. He certainly felt able to ignore Gorbachev's economic and political reforms, and refused to make concessions to the growing political unrest in the GDR and elsewhere in Eastern Europe.

In fact, it was Hungary's decision to open its border with Austria that sparked off the crisis in East Germany – as it did in Czechoslovakia. By September 1989, tens of thousands of East Germans were crossing to West Germany via Hungary and Austria, and many then claimed political asylum. This provoked an economic crisis similar to the one that had led to the building of the Berlin Wall in 1961.

However, Honecker, unlike **Walter Ulbricht**, the East German leader in 1961, could not rely on Soviet support. In fact, Gorbachev visited East Germany in October (as part of the 40th anniversary celebrations of the formation of the GDR), and urged him to carry out political and economic reforms. Gorbachev warned Honecker that 'life punishes those who wait too long'.

Honecker (left) meets Gorbachev (right) on his arrival in Germany, to celebrate the 40th anniversary of the GDR, October 1989

When Gorbachev addressed the crowds, he was given much vocal support. However, Honecker refused to follow Gorbachev's example – and even banned Soviet publications that he regarded as too liberal. Demonstrations in support of democracy and reform, and against attempts at repression, spread across the GDR. Unlike other Eastern European leaders, Honecker refused to grant reforms – despite Gorbachev's urgings. Instead, he seemed more inclined to take the path shown by Deng Xiaoping when, in May 1989, he ordered tanks into Tiananmen Square to crush protesters (see page 204).

Walter Ulbricht (1893–1973)
Ulbricht was a German communist, and played a leading role in the creation of the Communist Party of Germany (KPD) in Weimar Germany. Like many communists from Germany and Eastern Europe, he was in exile in the Soviet Union during the years of Nazi rule. From 1950 to 1971, he was first secretary of the Socialist Unity Party (the new party formed after the Second World War by merging the KPD and the SPD in East Germany). Following the West's creation of West Germany, Ulbricht oversaw the establishment of the German Democratic Republic (East Germany). From 1960 to 1973, he was head of state of the GDR. He was a hardliner, and did not favour liberalisation.

Question
Why might this photograph give a false impression of the relationship between Gorbachev and the East German leader in 1989?

Fact
Berlin, like Germany, was divided into four zones after the Second World War, and these divisions became permanent as the Cold War developed. However, Berlin was in East Germany. In 1958, Khrushchev tried to force the West to conclude a formal peace with Germany, and to agree that West Berlin should become an international, demilitarised area. The resulting crisis led to thousands of skilled East Germans migrating to the West. To stop this 'brain drain', and to restrict the infiltration of western spies, the GDR authorities built the Berlin Wall in August 1961. From its building until November 1989, East German soldiers guarded it. Families were divided by the wall, and sometimes those attempting to cross illegally were shot.

Communism in Crisis

Discussion point

Why do you think that the East German regime (and all except one of the other Eastern European communist governments) refused to follow the example of the Chinese communists in violently suppressing the rapidly growing protests of 1988–89? Can you think of other examples in history where such apparently all-powerful regimes gave up power so easily? Do you think capitalist governments would behave in similar ways if faced by mass revolutions wanting socialism?

Egon Krenz (b. 1937) Krenz held various offices in the GDR and, in 1984, he became Honecker's deputy. When Honecker was removed in October 1989, Krenz became leader of the SED and head of state. However, he only lasted three months, being forced to resign after the fall of the Berlin Wall and the collapse of the GDR regime. He was thus the GDR's last communist ruler. After German reunification in 1990, Krenz served a prison sentence for his role in the human rights abuses committed by the regime.

Question

What is the message of this cartoon?

Nevertheless, protests in the GDR grew. In East Berlin and some other cities, such as Leipzig and Dresden, those protesting numbered almost 100,000. This persuaded some party leaders that reforms were necessary if the regime was to survive – given that there would be no help from the Soviet Union. The East German Politburo thus forced Honecker to resign as general-secretary on 18 October, to be replaced by **Egon Krenz**.

Krenz immediately announced that there would be reforms, and stated his support for Gorbachev's policies. However, the demonstrations grew even bigger, culminating in a massive one in East Berlin on 4 November, numbering almost 500,000. Meanwhile, in Leipzig, over 300,000 demonstrated. On the same day, Czechoslovakia opened its borders and 30,000 East Germans left. Offers to relax the travel laws only led to more protests, as they were seen as too little, too late.

Gorbachev then made it clear to the GDR that it should form closer ties with West Germany, pointing out that the USSR could no longer afford to subsidise its economy. On 7 November, the entire GDR Politburo resigned, leaving the government to govern. On 8 November, Krenz decided to open the Berlin Wall, and thousands then travelled to East Berlin and crossed into West Berlin.

In this cartoon, by an American artist, the Soviet Union is portrayed as a dinosaur, with the Berlin Wall as its tail

On 9 November, it was announced that free movement across all the borders with West Germany was permitted. These events in East Germany stimulated mass protests in Czechoslovakia and Bulgaria.

On 1 December, the constitution was changed to remove the dominant 'leading' role of the Communist Party. Then, on 3 December, Krenz and the entire Central Committee resigned. A coalition government was formed, but this was seen as purely provisional, as most citizens wanted reunification with West Germany. Almost immediately, these negotiations began and, on 3 October 1990, the GDR was incorporated into the FRG. Germany was united once more, after 41 years of division.

Bulgaria

In Bulgaria, too, mass demonstrations, over ethnic and economic and political issues, led to a growing crisis. Here, however, this came later than in many of the other East European states. In fact, the first dissident organisation established in Bulgaria, the Independent Society for Human Rights (ISHR), was not formed until January 1988. And the first independent trade union, Podkrepa (Support), was not created until February 1989.

Protests by ethnic Turks in May 1989 were the first signs of unrest. These protests were a reaction to the government reversing earlier policies that had granted some autonomy to ethnic minorities. The way these protests were repressed, and the subsequent mass emigration of ethnic Turks, worried some members of the communist leadership – including **Petar Mladenov**, the foreign minister – and some sections of Bulgarian society. Gorbachev, too, made it clear that he did not support these actions. Though there was no real dissident movement, it did cause divisions within the party. These events began the process that eventually led to the government's resignation and a multi-party democracy, with elections in the spring of 1990.

Unlike the governments of other Eastern European states, the Bulgarian Communist Party had been able to avoid purges such as those that hit Hungary and Czechoslovakia in the 1950s and 1960s, and there had been no mass expulsions of liberals in the 1970s. Also, the party's concentration on maintaining social and economic equality made it reasonably popular. However, by 1977, the economy had begun to slow down, and it rapidly worsened after 1984. Between then and 1989, Bulgaria's debt rose from $3.6 billion to $10.5 billion. This, combined with growing industrial problems, meant that Bulgaria was in a deep crisis by the late 1980s. Attempts at reform failed.

The main turning point came on 10 November 1989, when Petar Mladenov ousted the old hardline leader of Bulgaria, **Todor Zhivkov**, in a political coup carried out by the Central Committee of Bulgaria's Communist Party, known as the Fatherland Front.

Mladenov had come to agree with Gorbachev's reform policies after 1985, though at first he had not argued for these. In October 1989, however, he organised an international Environment Conference in Bulgaria's capital Sofia, under the auspices of the Commission on Security and Co-operation in Europe (CSCE). This organisation had been set up in 1976 by the US to monitor compliance with various agreements, including the Helsinki Final Act on Human Rights. This Environment Conference provided an opportunity for the small dissident movement to emerge.

Ecoglasnost, an official organisation, led by Bulgaria's most popular actor, Petar Slabakov, was particularly important. Mladenov had deliberately included it on the list of participants, and it was able to organise protest demonstrations and launch its 'Ecocharter 89'. At the same time, the ISHR held meetings. When the secret police, the Darzhavna Sigurnost (DS), beat up and arrested 40 environmentalist activists, Mladenov resigned in protest. This precipitated a leadership crisis, which ended with the political ousting of Zhivkov. Shortly afterwards, key hardliners were removed from their posts in the party, while those who had been dismissed for opposition activities were restored.

Petar Mladenov (1936–2000)

Mladenov's father was an anti-fascist partisan, who was killed in action in 1944. He joined the Bulgarian Communist Party soon after graduating in 1963. While a student in Moscow, he made friends with Gorbachev. Mladenov became foreign minister in 1971, and was a close associate of Todor Zhivkov, whom he ousted with Gorbachev's support. He proved to be the last communist ruler of Bulgaria, from 1989 to 1990. Then, briefly, he was the first president of democratic Bulgaria in 1990.

Todor Zhivkov (1911–98)

Zhivkov ruled Bulgaria for 35 years and faithfully followed every development in the Soviet Union – until Gorbachev came to power in 1985. Though Zhivkov supported Gorbachev's reform policies until sometime in 1987, he backtracked when he realised that Gorbachev actually intended to carry out his proposed changes. Zhivkov's control of the country was strengthened by the fact that Bulgaria, unlike Czechoslovakia, had no real democratic traditions. In fact, in the interwar years, a fascist-style government had ruled, until Bulgaria was liberated from Nazi occupation in September 1944 by the Soviet Red Army.

Communism in Crisis

Within a month of this, on 11 December, the party proposed to end its political monopoly and leadership position, in favour of a multi-party system and of separating party and state. Mladenov also held a National Assembly, where he announced an amnesty for political prisoners. The hope was to carry out a top-down reform under the auspices of the Bulgarian Communist Party. Unlike most of the other Eastern European parties, it was able to retain significant popularity once Zhivkov had been removed. These moves also helped weaken the small opposition groups, and ensured a victory for the reformed Communist Party in the 1990 elections.

Romania

The one exception to these peaceful revolutions was Romania, where **Nicolae Ceauşescu**, who had been the country's leader since 1965, used the security forces in an attempt to crush the demonstrators. At first, it seemed as if Romania would be unaffected by the changes taking place in the rest of Eastern Europe, despite signs of a serious economic crisis.

The first signs of serious unrest came in November 1987, when thousands of workers, protesting in Brasov against pay, were suppressed. Then, in the largely ethnic Hungarian village of Timisoara, protests erupted in December 1989 over the dismissal of the local parish priest. A protest march was broken up using force. Soon Romanian students – aware of what was happening elsewhere in Eastern Europe – joined in, and the unrest widened to become a protest against the government in general. Troops were sent in, and hundreds were killed or wounded.

On 21 December, Ceauşescu staged a massive rally in Bucharest, in what is now called Revolution Square, in an attempt to show support for his regime. Yet, when he attempted to speak, the crowd hissed – the first time this had ever happened. Demonstrations then erupted across the country, and were ruthlessly suppressed by the Securitate. On 22 December, Ceauşescu attempted to address the crowds in Bucharest from the balcony of the Communist Party Central Committee headquarters. This time he was shouted down, after which the crowd stormed the building, chanting 'Death! Death!'

While Ceauşescu and his wife attempted to flee the country, the security forces opened fire, and many protesters were killed. However, after several violent clashes across the country, the army changed sides and began to fight the secret police. Ceauşescu and his wife were captured by the army. There was a hasty show trial, which condemned them to death, and they were immediately led out and executed by firing squad on Christmas Day.

The army installed Ion Iliescu as the new president. He had been a member of the Politburo but had argued with Ceauşescu because he favoured some limited Gorbachev-style reforms. Multi-party elections were held in May 1990, and Iliescu was elected president – though there had been intimidation of the opposition. Iliescu summoned thousands of miners to Bucharest to disperse the student demonstrators, who felt that nothing much had changed.

Activities

1 Carry out some further research on Poland in the 1980s. Then try to explain why nationalism remained so strong there.

2 Draw a spider diagram to show developments in Hungary 1985–1990. Give dates, and include brief details of the main individuals, groups and events.

Nicolae Ceauşescu (1918–89)
Ceauşescu tried to resist Soviet influence, and at first had a more open policy towards the West. However, from the late 1970s, he moved to an increasingly repressive and inconsistent leadership, based on a personality cult. He also increasingly gave top party and state jobs to his family, especially to his wife, Elena. When Gorbachev began his reforms in the Soviet Union, Ceauşescu regarded them as a threat to his personal dictatorship. To bolster this, he relied heavily on the secret police, the Securitate.

3 Try to find out about the GDR's secret police, the Stasi. To get started, visit youtube on: http://www.youtube.com/watch?v=fb7B1fHB_0I

How different was this secret police organisation from the ones that exist in your country?

What were the main steps in Czechoslovakia's 'Velvet Revolution'?

Czechoslovakia provides a good case study for understanding the general developments in the Eastern European satellite states. Before 1985, the Czechoslovakian state – like the other Eastern European states – seemed strong. However, the economy showed signs of stagnation, which had begun to affect living standards. The events of 1968 were deeply rooted in the minds of some people, while many more felt alienated from the party. This meant that when change came again, in the later 1980s, the party was seen as an obstacle to reform that had to be removed. Eventually, in 1989, a 'Velvet Revolution' resulted in the resignation of the communist government, and the establishment of a multi-party system.

Czechoslovakia 1968–85

The events of 1968

During 1968, Czechoslovakia experienced what became known as the 'Prague Spring'. This was when the reform communist Alexander Dubček (who became first secretary of the Czech Communist Party in January 1968) launched a series of political and economic reforms in April 1968. This 'Action Programme' was intended to achieve 'socialism with a human face'. Although the programme received much support from the Czech people, the USSR and the Warsaw Pact invaded in August to end these reforms. Many of the leaders of the other Eastern European states were afraid their own citizens would demand the same changes. Shortly after these events Brezhnev formulated his 'Brezhnev Doctrine'.

Czechoslovakia after 1968

After the Warsaw Pact invasion of August 1968, Dubček was replaced as leader by **Gustáv Husák**. Husák began the process of re-establishing communist control known as **'normalisation'**. This lasted for 20 years, and involved the purging of reformers from the party, restoration of censorship, travel restrictions, and centralised economic control.

However, Husák's government had been imposed by Moscow, and therefore struggled to gain popular legitimacy. Intellectuals also suffered: for example, over 900 university lecturers were sacked. The problem was that this created a passive opposition outside the Communist Party – which some now saw very much as a foreign imposition. To 'sweeten the pill' of the invasion and 'normalisation', Husák's government implemented a 'social contract' with the people, to give them basic economic security. This involved the state promising to maintain full employment, free universal health care, subsidised holidays, and pensions. Wages, though lower than those in the West, could buy a range of consumer goods. In fact, by the late 1980s, Czechoslovakia was second in the world for ownership of second homes – with 80% of families having country cottages. This social contract gained the regime some form of consent from most citizens, allowing it to maintain its control with limited opposition. Thus, state repression was usually not needed.

Fact
Czechoslovakia, created following the break-up of the Austro-Hungarian empire after the First World War, had two parts. The eastern half of the country was dominated by Slovaks; the western by Czechs. Before 1992, it existed both as a centralised state (1918–39 and 1945–68) and as a federal state of two equal 'nations' (1969–92). Unlike the other Eastern European states, it had been a democracy before the Second World War, and had had a significant industrial economy. Although the two national groups shared similar languages and ethnic ties, they often did not co-operate with each other. In 1993, it split into two separate countries – the Czech Republic and Slovakia.

Gustáv Husák (1913–91)
Husák joined the Slovak Communist Youth Union when he was 16. In 1933, while studying law at university, he joined the Communist Party of Czechoslovakia (banned during the Nazi occupation and the rule of the Nazi collaborator, Jozef Tiso). He was one of the leaders of the Slovak Uprising against Nazi Germany and Tiso in 1944. He then became *de facto* prime minister of Slovakia from 1946 to 1950. However, he was one of the victims of a Stalinist purge, and was imprisoned from 1954 to 1960. He became party leader in 1969, until he was forced to resign in 1987.

'normalisation' During the 1970s, 327,000 party members – suspected of being radical reformers – were expelled from the party. Another 150,000 voluntarily left. These steps were all designed to undo the reforms associated with Dubček's Prague Spring reforms.

Communism in Crisis

Václav Havel (b. 1936)

Havel came from a wealthy family, and became a playwright, though his plays were banned in 1971. He was involved in the Prague Spring, and spent the 1970s and 1980s agitating for reform. He was imprisoned several times. In 1975, he wrote an 'Open Letter' to Husák, protesting against censorship, and then helped form Charter 77. He became the leader of Civic Forum in 1989. He was the first post-communist president of Czechoslovakia, before it split up into the Czech republic and Slovakia.

Economically, Czechoslovakia did well in the 1970s, with personal disposable income rising and consumerism taking root. Nevertheless, the economic success of the country did not remove some people's enthusiasm for political reform – although those in favour of this were a distinct minority.

Later, Husák hinted at possible economic reform and decentralisation of planning. However, the experiences of 1968 made the party very wary of any action that might weaken its grip on power. Throughout the 1970s, while some economic reforms took place, the regime firmly toed the party line regarding political reform – partly out of fear of another Soviet intervention.

Husák was thus concerned about the continued existence of small dissident groups. For instance, the signing of the Helsinki Accord (see page 53) in 1975 led, in early 1977, to the emergence of a group known as Charter 77. This group called on the Czech government to honour the rights set down in the constitution – and those in the Helsinki Accord and the UN Declaration of Human Rights. Its most famous member was **Václav Havel**. Another group also emerged – VONS (Committee for the Defence of the Unjustly Prosecuted), which publicised the cases of those prosecuted and imprisoned by the regime. Like Charter 77 members, they were often arrested and imprisoned.

Another example of the existence of dissent was The Plastic People of the Universe – a rock band formed shortly after the 1968 Warsaw Pact invasion of Czechoslovakia. Despite censorship, they were able to play at a few venues, and became quite popular. In 1976, they were put on trial and sent to prison. Václav Havel spoke in their defence, and it is claimed that their trial in 1976 helped inspire the formation of Charter 77.

The Plastic People of the Universe, influenced by the Beatles and Frank Zappa

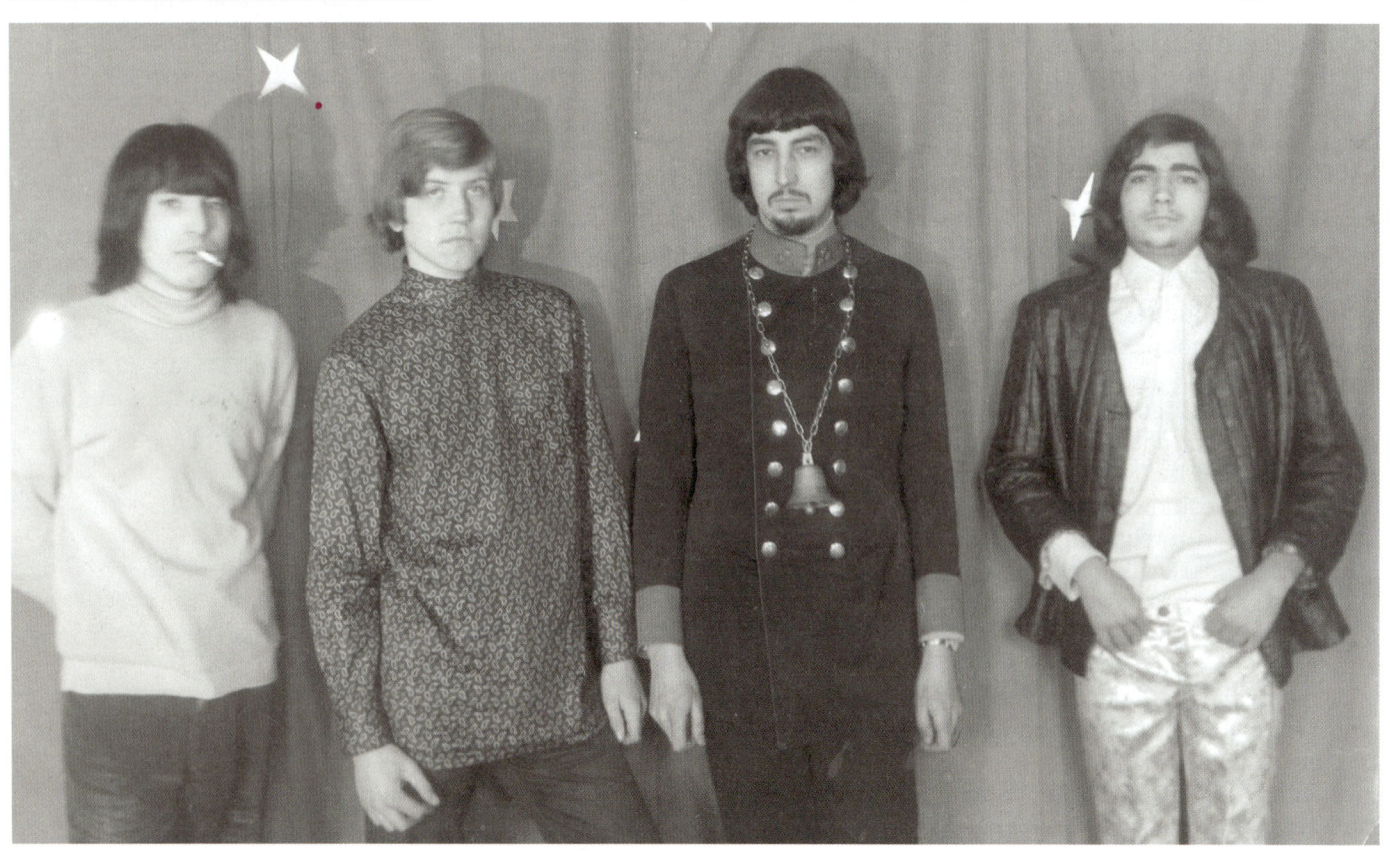

An additional concern for Husák was the fact that, during the late 1970s, Czechoslovakia's economy (like Poland's) began to experience a downturn. This caused growing discontent. By the early 1980s, the economic decline was leading to problems for the workers, and for the continuation of the social contract. This erosion of the social contract removed an important aspect of support for the Husák regime. In addition, by 1987, the country was receiving increasing amounts of Western credit in order to continue functioning.

The impact of Gorbachev from 1985

By the mid 1980s, a crisis had emerged within most of the countries of the Eastern bloc. Gorbachev's calls for reform were very similar to those raised during the Prague Spring of 1968. This made it difficult for Husák's government, which was founded on a rejection of 'socialism with a human face'. Gorbachev also explicitly rejected the Brezhnev Doctrine, which had justified Soviet intervention in Warsaw Pact countries. Though Soviet troops remained in Czechoslovakia until 1990, these developments removed an important external support structure for Husák's government.

> **SOURCE G**
>
> Public dissatisfaction [in Czechoslovakia] remained silent while the Soviet Union pursued a policy of crushing any challenge to Communist rule. But when Gorbachev signalled an end to this policy in the late 1980s, change came quickly. Czech dissidents gathered support and led anti-government demonstrations in 1988 and 1989. The revolution was triggered by a demonstration on 17 November that was violently repressed by the police.
>
> Almond, M. 1996. *Revolution: 500 Years of Struggle for Change.* London, UK. De Agostini Editions. p. 178.

Once Gorbachev introduced his reforms in the USSR, there were mounting calls in Czechoslovakia for the same type of reforms – both economic and political. At first, Husák – who was both first secretary of the Czech Communist Party and president of the state – refused to move. In December 1987, though, he gave up his post of party leader, while still remaining president.

His place was taken by **Miloš Jakeš**. However, Jakeš had no intention of ending communist rule, and it seemed that there would be a continuation of conservative communist policy. He resisted calls to implement reforms like those of Gorbachev. He was apparently hoping that Gorbachev would soon fall from power in the USSR and be replaced by more conservative hardliners. This did not happen – and soon developments in Poland increased the pressure for reforms in Czechoslovakia. Meanwhile, Husák's resignation led to more discussion and growing open opposition to the regime.

In Poland, those campaigning for reform were a mixture of workers, students and even Catholic priests. In contrast, those pushing for reform in Czechoslovakia were mostly intellectuals and students. In the main, workers were not involved – partly since their interests since 1968 had generally been looked after.

Fact
Charter 77 was formed on 1 January 1977, and only had 243 signatures at first. Those who signed the petition were punished. During the next ten years, the number of signatories grew slowly, eventually reaching 1621.

Theory of knowledge

History, the arts, language and emotion
Emotion is one of the four main ways of knowing – and certain forms of art (such as music and drama) use language in order to achieve an emotional response. Consequently, authorities – especially in single-party states – often use harsh methods to suppress aspects of the arts and culture that they feel might undermine their regime by inflaming people's emotions. Why do you think rock groups (such as The Plastic People) or playwrights (such as Havel) posed a *political* threat to the Czechoslovak government in the 1970s?

Miloš Jakeš (b. 1922)
Jakeš was general-secretary of the Czech Communist Party from 1987 until he resigned in November 1989, during the 'Velvet Revolution'. He joined the Communist Party soon after the Second World War. After the Warsaw Pact invasion in August 1968, Jakeš was one of the main people involved in the 'normalisation' process, helping to expel reformers.

Communism in Crisis

> **Fact**
> The Czech student groups included the Czech Children, the John Lennon Peace Club, and the Independent Peace Association–Initiative for the Demilitarisation of Society.

> **Question**
> Why do you think Czech workers were at first not generally in alliance with Czech dissidents?

Those in favour of reform in Czechoslovakia were split into two main sections. One group wanted a more democratic socialism (similar to that attempted under Dubček in the Prague Spring). The other section, made up mainly of non-communist student groups, did not accept the aims of these '68'ers'. In fact, many of them wanted to move towards capitalism. Dubček reappeared on the political scene as the demands for reform increased. However, such groups saw him as someone whose time had already passed.

Encouraged by Gorbachev's statements, many Czechs and Slovaks began to voice their opposition, and single-issue protest groups began to emerge. For example, the Bratislava Aloud group published a report in 1987, criticising the government's lack of an environmental policy. Even some churches – though they were always far less important in Czechoslovakia than in Poland – became centres of opposition, and called for religious freedom. Havel was imprisoned for his involvement in anti-government demonstrations, which only led to even more protests, culminating in his release.

The mounting crisis, 1988–89

At first, the Czech government tried to maintain control. In August 1988, it arrested demonstrators in Prague who were commemorating the Warsaw Pact invasion of 1968. Events in the GDR and Hungary also spurred on protests in Czechoslovakia. During the summer of 1989, large crowds began to demonstrate on the streets of Prague.

In fact, the communist government maintained control right up to the end of 1989, at which point its system rapidly collapsed. From March 1985 onwards, Gorbachev repeatedly announced that the Brezhnev Doctrine was over. This encouraged protests, as Czech demonstrators no longer feared military intervention from the USSR or the other Warsaw Pact countries. This was an important factor in the eventual success of the Velvet Revolution in Czechoslovakia, as in the other Eastern European states.

Many were encouraged by Honecker's forced resignation, on 18 October 1989, in the GDR. Then, on 4 November, the Czech government opened its borders with the GDR and Hungary. More significant still was the effective collapse of the Berlin Wall on 8 November 1989. This event sparked even more protests in Czechoslovakia.

> **Fact**
> The student allegedly killed in the rally was Martin Smid, and the rumours were initially spread by his girlfriend, when she told Petr Uhl, a Trotskyist member of Charter 77. The story was then broadcast by the Voice of America and Radio Free Europe, two US/CIA-funded Cold War radio stations operating from Western Europe.

On 17 November 1989, there was an officially approved International Students' Day rally – to commemorate the anniversary of the funeral of Jan Opletal, a Czech medical student killed during the Nazi occupation in an anti-Nazi demonstration on Czechoslovakia's Independence Day. This rally turned into an anti-government protest, which was violently repressed by the riot police. The police violence triggered even more protests – especially when false rumours began to spread that a student had been killed. On 19 November, Havel and several protest groups used this unrest to form Civic Forum (an 'umbrella' organisation) to put forward the demands of the people. In Slovakia, a similar organisation – called People Against Violence (PAV) – was formed, and held large demonstrations in Bratislava.

Civic Forum and PAV demanded big concessions. The Communist Party, purged of reformers since 1968, could only offer a continuation of 'normalisation'. It therefore failed to follow the examples of the communist governments of either Poland or Hungary. However, the regime also felt unable to order outright suppression of the protests, as had happened in China in Tiananmen Square.

6 Gorbachev, the Cold War and Eastern Europe

In fact, even the loyalty of sections of the police and the military was being eroded in the face of the mass opposition, which soon became known as the Velvet Revolution.

Civic Forum called for a series of demonstrations in Wenceslas Square, Prague, to begin the following day. Even according to the official state-controlled media, the first one – on 20 November – attracted over 200,000 people.

Fact
The fact that both halves of Czechoslovakia formed separate protest reform movements was an early sign that nationalist sentiments and grievances would soon result in a formal division of the country.

SOURCE A

The Prague demonstration [20 November] grew in numbers through the day and by around 4.30pm the square was packed. They swarmed around Wenceslas Square … When the space was filled, the crowd spread upwards: climbing trees, precariously scrambling up scaffolding six storeys high, dancing on top of telephone boxes. The crowd's sense of its power fed on itself, unstoppable.

The chants and banners had real edge now: 'Today Prague, tomorrow the whole country', 'It's the end, Miloš', 'Jakeš out', 'Jakeš in the bin' and, accompanied by the ringing of bells and the jingling of keys, 'Time's up'.

The bells and the keys gave the crowd a fairytale quality. This was literally so, because every Czech children's story – no matter how grim – finishes with a bell ringing and the teller saying 'And that's the end of the story'.

Hawkes, N. (ed.) 1990. *Tearing Down the Curtain: The People's Revolution in Eastern Europe*. London, UK. Hodder & Stoughton. p. 111.

Question
What political point were the demonstrators trying to make by ringing bells and keys?

The following day, a similarly large crowd of demonstrators gathered to demand reform. On 24 November, with large crowds once again gathered in Wenceslas Square, Miloš Jakeš and the entire leadership of the party resigned.

Protesters in Wenceslas Square, Prague, November 1989

Questions
Why do you think the organisers of the protests wanted to encourage as many people as possible to attend? What impact do you think the numbers demonstrating had on: (a) the demonstrators and (b) the authorities?

Communism in Crisis

SOURCE I

The demonstrations reached a climax on Friday, 24 November when Alexander Dubček, the Communist leader during the 'Prague Spring' of 1968, came to Prague. For over twenty years he had been silenced by the regime. Now as he stepped out onto a balcony to speak, a great roar met him. 'Dubček! Dubček!' echoed off the tall houses up and down the narrow square … As the demonstration ended, the people in the square, in a spontaneous gesture, took keys out of their pockets and shook them, 300 000 key-rings producing a sound like massed Chinese bells.

Burke, P. 1995. *Revolution in Europe, 1989. London, UK. Wayland. pp. 31–33.*

Question

To what extent do Source H (page 135) and Source I offer similar views of the November demonstrations in Prague?

Civic Forum, and many union leaders, then called for a general strike to take place on 27 November. This showed that the Velvet Revolution had at last spread from intellectuals and students to the ordinary people and organised workers. (In Poland, this had been the case from the start.) As on 20 November, crowds gathered in Wenceslas Square in Prague, jangling keys and bells, and chanting 'Your time is up.'

The government – while trying to prevent press coverage of the demonstrations – announced that exit visas would not be required to travel to the West. It then renounced its leadership role. On 28 November, parliament voted this through. On 3 December, a new government was announced – but with only five non-communists in a 20-strong cabinet. This did not satisfy the demonstrators and, on 10 December, a new government with a majority of non-communists was elected by the parliament. Husák resigned as president, and plans were made for free elections in 1990. Finally, on 28 December, Dubček was elected speaker of the parliament and on 30 December, Havel was elected president of Czechoslovakia.

SOURCE J

The new government's Foreign Minister was Havel's old cellmate, Jiri Dienstbier; in charge of the Interior Ministry, including, of course, the secret police, was Jan Czarnogursky, who had been their reluctant guest in custody only days before. After some jostling within Civic Forum, a new speaker of the Czech parliament was proposed: Alexander Dubček. He had expressed a desire to become President, and there was much love for the man's simple grace and humanity, but his faithfulness to socialism as an ideal ruled him out as a contender.

Husák's successor, who promised to oversee free elections in the new year, was elected on the last day but one of 1989. His name was Václav Havel.

Hawkes, N. (ed.) 1990. *Tearing Down the Curtain: The People's Revolution in Eastern Europe. London, UK. Hodder & Stoughton. p. 123.*

As with the other regimes, the Soviet Union stood back while Czechoslovakia moved peacefully from authoritarianism to democracy. The Czechoslovakian communist system was finally dismantled in early 1990.

Reasons for the Velvet Revolution's success

One reason for the success of the Velvet Revolution was the relative ages of those in government and those pushing for reform. As in the USSR, many of the leaders in Czechoslovakia in the early 1980s were ageing members (mostly in their seventies) of the old generation of communists. Meanwhile, the younger people who were protesting had not experienced the horrors of the Second World War, but *had* seen the crushing of the Prague Spring in 1968. In addition, many younger Czechs, who saw Western television programmes showing consumer goods, wanted the same for themselves and so were prepared to move towards some form of capitalism. Also, the protesters deliberately avoided the use of violence. Instead, they favoured the use of passive non-violent direct action and peaceful civil disobedience. This type of peaceful protest had been practised by Mahatma Gandhi in India in the 1930s and 1940s, and by the Civil Rights Movement in the US in the 1950s and 1960s, led by Martin Luther King.

The success and speed of the change of regime in Czechoslovakia were also due to its earlier history. In many ways Czechoslovakia was more prepared for the events of 1989–90 than any other state in the Eastern bloc. It was one of the most industrially developed states in the region, with a limited history of democracy. Also, the experience of 1968 had shown that economic reform could not be successful without associated political and social reform. Without the military intervention of the Warsaw Pact, it is possible that Czechoslovakia might have moved to a more democratic system before 1989.

The re-imposition of party dominance in the 1970s did not crush the reformist tendencies of the Czechoslovakian population. Rather, it drove them underground. Furthermore, the pressure for change could not be offset by the rise in living standards experienced by the Czechoslovaks in the 1970s and 1980s. Once Gorbachev had made it clear that he would not repeat the events of 1968, it was arguably only a matter of time before civic unrest toppled the communist government.

Demonstrators marching in Prague carry a photo of Dubček

> **Discussion point**
>
> In view of what happened in Czechoslovakia in 1989 and 1990, do you think the same thing would have happened in 1968, if Warsaw Pact forces had not invaded to end the Prague Spring? Could Dubček and his supporters have succeeded in their aim of building 'socialism with a human face'?

Communism in Crisis

Activities

1. Find out more about Havel and Civic Forum. In particular, try to establish details about the membership of Civic Forum.

2. Carry out more detailed research into the roles of Václav Havel, Miloš Jakeš and Mikhail Gorbachev during the growing crisis in Czechoslovakia. Which person do you think played the most important role? Write a paragraph, giving reasons for your choice.

3. What does the term 'Velvet Revolution' mean? Do you think this applies to all aspects of what happened in Czechoslovakia in 1989?

4. Draw up a list of potential organisational and political weaknesses of the opposition movements in Czechoslovakia that might limit their ability to influence the new post-communist government. Is a spontaneous and unorganised movement the best way to achieve greater democracy?

What were the results of the changes in Eastern Europe?

As protest movements spread across Eastern Europe during 1988–89, Gorbachev's only intervention was to continue to encourage liberal reforms. Though Gorbachev hoped that the new governments would be reform communists or socialists, who would establish democratic socialism in Eastern Europe, the only certainty in 1989 was that the old-style communist governments had gone.

More significantly, the Soviet Union had allowed the disappearance of a 'security belt' that had been the foundation of its foreign policy since 1945. This security belt of satellite states had played a large part in the start of the Cold War – though, in fact, all these East European states had been heavily in debt to the Soviet Union, thus adding to its own economic problems.

This non-interventionist policy was due to Gorbachev's belief in socialist democracy and also his recognition that the Soviet Union was politically and economically *unable* to intervene. The collapse of the Soviet bloc was a clear indication of the serious decline of the USSR itself, both internally and externally, by the end of the 1980s. In March 1990, the Warsaw Pact was dissolved, leaving NATO still in existence, which worried the old-style communists. One of the more significant results of the events in Eastern Europe is that the loss of what had long been seen as an essential security belt hardened the resolve of Gorbachev's opponents in the USSR to stop his reforms – and even overthrow him. In fact, this is what happened in August 1991.

After 1989

Many in the Eastern European states thought that the end of communist rule would usher in a period of freedom and better living standards. However, the reality proved to be quite different in the first years after 1989. In fact, Eric Hobsbawm, a Marxist historian, pointed out that, as a condition for receiving loans from the West, such new governments would be applying neo-capitalist policies in relatively backward economies. This would cause great hardship for the majority of their populations, as both jobs and social services would be cut – although the changes would provide opportunities for a small minority to become very wealthy. Many of these newly liberated states experienced the full effects of what has been described as economic 'shock therapy'.

Historical debate

Some historians – such as Michael McGwire, in his book, *Perestroika and Soviet National Security* (1991) – have argued that Gorbachev and his supporters during 1987–88 deliberately set in motion a set of policies that they knew would lead to the collapse of communist rule throughout Eastern Europe in a matter of a few years. Others argue that the intention was to implement real reforms. They claim that the reform communists were genuinely surprised by the mass demonstrations and by the growing intention, not only to end one-party rule, but to move rapidly towards creating capitalist economies.

Fact

Eric Hobsbawm, though welcoming the moves towards democracy, warned that the collapse of the one-party regimes in Eastern Europe would not necessarily result in tolerant and popular regimes. In particular, he pointed out that before 1945 the governments in that region (with the exception of Czechoslovakia) had been authoritarian and often racist, especially towards their Jewish, and Roma and Sinti, minorities.

Historical debate

The reform communists in the 1980s – including Gorbachev – concentrated on economic reform in order to 'save' communism, but found instead that their attempts ended in political revolutions across Eastern Europe. Yet previous attempts by opponents of these regimes had failed. Different historians account for the success of the 1989 revolutions in a number of different ways: the role of Gorbachev; the 'domino' theory (in which, because of the close connections between these states, protests and changes in one country led to knock-on effects in the others); and the role of the international media and new methods of communication, which made it harder for regimes to restrict the flow of information to and from their citizens.

Activities

1 Imagine that you are a hardline ruler of one of the Eastern European states. Write a letter to Gorbachev, explaining why you oppose his reforms and his public statements. Make sure you support your points with specific and accurate factual details and references.

2 'Economic and social security is more important than political freedom.' Split into two groups: one to present arguments in favour of the statement and one to argue against. As well as making general points, try to make references to specific 20th-century states to back up or illustrate your arguments.

3 Dissident or opposition intellectuals and artists are found in most societies – not just one-party states. Make a list of any artists or groups in your country that criticise aspects of society or government policy. How influential are they? How easy is it for them to gain access to the mainstream media?

Communism in Crisis

End of chapter activities

Summary

You should now have a sound understanding of the main aspects of Gorbachev's 'New Thinking' in relation to foreign policy, and the impact his policies had on Eastern Europe.

You should be able to comment on the course of the different revolutions in these states during the 1980s, and the reasons for the collapse of these regimes.

You should also have a more detailed knowledge of events in Czechoslovakia, and a sound understanding of why its 'Velvet Revolution' was successful.

Summary activity

Copy the diagram below. Then, using the information in this chapter and from any other available sources, make brief notes under the headings and sub-headings shown. Remember to include information on historical debate/interpretations – including names of historians – where relevant.

Gorbachev and Eastern Europe, 1985–1991

1 Gorbachev's 'New Thinking'
- The Cold War
- Eastern Europe

2 The revolutions of 1988–89
- Poland
- Hungary
- East Germany (GDR)
- Bulgaria
- Romania
- Czechoslovakia

Paper 1 exam practice

Question

With reference to their origin and purpose, assess the value and limitations of Sources A and B opposite for historians studying the roles played by Havel and Civic Forum in the 'Velvet Revolution' of 1989.
[6 marks]

Skill

Value and limitations (utility/reliability) of sources

SOURCE A

Members of Civic Forum meet in Prague to discuss strategy during the revolution in Czechoslovakia; this photograph was taken by a British journalist

SOURCE B

Nigel Hawkes and the other contributors to this book were reporters for the Observer *newspaper in Britain. They were the first authors to explain the changes taking place in Eastern Europe.*

In his six years in prison Havel had plenty of time to dream, to plan, to consider how to work once the pack-ice started to break up and now, on the week beginning Sunday 19 November, the moment – his moment – had finally come.

That Sunday evening, Havel, his friends in Charter 77 and the students formed Civic Forum. Its opening declaration stated that it had been brought about 'on behalf of that part of the Czechoslovak public which is increasingly critical of the present Czechoslovak leadership, and which in recent days has been profoundly shaken by the brutal massacre of peacefully protesting students'. The Forum demanded the immediate resignation of 'discredited' Communists, including Jakeş and the Minister of the Interior …

Hawkes, N. (ed.) 1990. Tearing Down the Curtain: The People's Revolution in Eastern Europe. *London, UK. Hodder & Stoughton. p. 110.*

Before you start

Value and limitations (utility/reliability) questions require you to assess two sources over a range of possible issues – and to comment on their value to historians studying a particular event or period of history. You need to consider the both the origin and purpose and also the value and limitations of the sources. You should link these in your answer, showing how origin/purpose relate to value/limitations.

Before you attempt this question, refer to pages 216–217 for advice on how to tackle these questions and a simplified markscheme.

Communism in Crisis

Student answer

Source A, which is just one photograph, was taken by a British journalist. As far as origin is concerned, this could have both value and limitations. However, as the photographer was not a Czech, they are unlikely to be working either for Civic Forum or for the Czech government. As regards purpose, this is difficult to assess – on the one hand, it is possible that the photographer was neutral and was just recording an event. However, it could be that they were biased, and were attempting to give extra publicity for Civic Forum – though the fact that it doesn't show many people suggests this is not the case. These aspects affect the source's value, and point to possible limitations.

Also, while Source A shows a Civic Forum meeting, it does not say who the members were – and, in particular, says nothing about Havel. It also is only one photograph of one meeting, so might not be typical of what Civic Forum did in the revolution of 1989. This would therefore present limitations for a historian trying to get an overall picture of the role of Havel and Civic Forum. Finally, it doesn't tell us when the photograph was taken – it could be of the very start of their activities. However, its value is that it shows Civic Forum was active, and the people shown do seem to be mainly intellectual-types – these were the core of Civic Forum supporters.

Examiner's comments

There is reasonable assessment of Source A, referring clearly to both origin and possible purpose **and** to value and limitations. These comments are also clearly linked to the question – these are not just general comments about a source. The candidate has thus done enough to get into Band 2, and so be awarded 3 or 4 marks. However, as there are no comments about Source B, this answer fails to get into Band 1.

Activity

Look again at the two sources, the simplified markscheme, and the student answer (left). Now try to write a paragraph or two to push the answer up into Band 1, and so obtain the full 6 marks. As well as assessing Source B, try to make a linking comment to show value. For example, do the sources provide similar information?

Paper 2 practice questions

1 'It was the activities of a small number of dissident intellectuals, rather than the discontents of ordinary citizens, which were the main driving force behind the revolutions in Eastern Europe during 1988–89.' To what extent do you agree with this assertion?

2 In what ways, and with what results, did changes in Gorbachev's foreign policy towards Eastern Europe affect developments in two of these states?

3 For what reasons, and with what results, did reform communists in Hungary attempt to respond to demands for change?

4 Analyse the role of nationalism in the events in Poland in the period 1988–89.

5 In what ways, and with what results, did the communist leaders in Czechoslovakia attempt to deal with the growing pressures for reform?

6 Analyse the role of Václav Havel and Civic Forum in the success of the 'Velvet Revolution' in Czechoslovakia.

7 'By 1985, the collapse of communism in Eastern Europe was inevitable.' To what extent do you agree with this assertion?

7 China and the struggle for power after 1976

Introduction

In 1976, Mao Zedong died. He had been in charge of China for most of the time since the communist revolution of 1949. At a time when the Soviet economy was beginning to show signs of stagnation under Brezhnev, Communist China was also facing problems. In the main, these were the same as those arising in the USSR – how to achieve economic growth and modernisation without weakening the political power and control of the party bureaucracy. As this chapter and Chapters 8 and 9 will show, the communists in China (unlike those in the USSR) proved able to achieve rapid economic growth while still maintaining their one-party rule.

Mao's death triggered a struggle for power – and a struggle over what direction China was to take. To understand what happened after his death in 1976, which led to the fall of the Gang of Four (see page 157) and the re-emergence of Deng Xiaoping to political dominance, it is necessary to have some idea of what happened in the previous two decades.

Key questions

- What was the significance of events before 1971?
- Why was there another power struggle after the Cultural Revolution?
- What were the main stages of the power struggle between 1976 and 1981?

Overview

- Mao Zedong led the Chinese Communist Party (CCP) to victory in 1949, and dominated Chinese politics from then on.
- In 1958, he launched the radical Great Leap Forward – but the resulting economic problems reduced his power and influence. Under Liu Shaoqi and Deng Xiaoping, economic policies were introduced that undid many of Mao's initiatives.
- Mao decided to oppose these 'Rightists'. After launching his Socialist Education Movement in 1962, he began the Cultural Revolution in 1966.
- This lasted until 1969, and saw Liu and Deng removed from power.
- Mao was supported in this by Lin Biao, and by what became known as the Gang of Four.

Timeline

1958 Jan: Great Leap Forward announced

1959 Jul: Peng Dehuai's Letter; Lushan Conference

1962 Sep: Socialist Education Movement launched

1964 May: publication of *Quotations from Chairman Mao*

1966 May: start of Cultural Revolution

1969 Apr: Cultural Revolution called off; 9th Congress of Chinese Communist Party (CCP)

1970 Aug: Second Plenum of the 9th Central Committee (CC)

1971 Sep: '571 Affair'; death of Lin Biao

1972 Feb: Nixon's visit to China

1975 Jan: Zhou announces the Four Modernisations

1976 Jan: Zhou dies; replaced by Hua Guofeng

Apr: Qingming Festival protests; Deng dismissed

Sep: Mao dies

Oct: Gang of Four arrested

1977 Jul: Third Plenum of 10th CC; Deng restored to former position

1978 Dec: Third Plenum of 11th CC; Deng attacks Hua and 'Whateverists'

1980 Sep: Hua forced to resign as premier

1981 Jun: Hua resigns as party chairman; Deng left as 'paramount leader'

Communism in Crisis

- However, in 1971, Mao and Lin fell out; after a failed plot, Lin was killed trying to escape. This began another power struggle – between Rightists such as Zhou and Deng, and the Gang of Four.
- Zhou died in January 1976; after protests during the Qingming Festival, leading Rightists were again dismissed.
- In September 1976, Mao died and the struggle intensified. At first, Mao's position was taken by Hua Guofeng, a more moderate Maoist. Hua then arrested the Gang of Four.
- In 1977, Deng and the Rightists were restored to their positions. Slowly, Deng and his supporters sidelined Hua. In 1980 and 1981, Hua was forced to resign from most of his posts, leaving Deng as the 'paramount leader'.

A rally in Beijing, August 1966, at the start of the Cultural Revolution

Zhou Enlai (1898–1976)
Zhou worked closely with Mao, and was premier (prime minister) from 1949 to 1976. Zhou played important roles in the economy (where he supported Deng Xiaoping's ideas) and in foreign policy (until 1958, he was also foreign minister, favouring 'peaceful coexistence' with the West). During the Cultural Revolution, his attempts to moderate the more violent activities of the Red Guards (see page 150) made him a popular and much-respected leader – hence the huge demonstrations following his death.

What was the significance of events before 1971?

Mao Zedong ruled China from October 1949 until his death in September 1976; his closest political ally, **Zhou Enlai**, had been associated with him since the late 1920s. During that time, Mao had consolidated the power of the Chinese Communist Party (CCP). In the early years, Mao had tried various economic and political experiments – in part, in an attempt to assert his and China's independence of the USSR. These experiments had included various land reforms, a five-year plan for industry, the **Hundred Flowers campaign**, and an Anti-Rightist campaign against those holding anti-socialist ideas.

For an understanding of developments in China from 1976 onwards, two main campaigns closely associated with Mao are particularly relevant: the Great Leap Forward (GLF) and the Great Proletarian Cultural Revolution.

Hundred Flowers campaign
During this campaign, which began in early 1957, Mao encouraged people to express their views on what had been achieved since 1949. However, there were growing criticisms of the government and party policies. In June 1957, Mao cracked down on many of these critics. After this repression, Mao launched an Anti-Rightist campaign.

The Great Leap Forward, 1958

Mao's 'Great Leap Forward', announced in January 1958, was his attempt to quickly modernise Chinese agriculture and industry by harnessing the energy of the country's massive population. Most people were grouped in large communes, each comprising several villages. By the end of the year, just over 26,000 communes, covering about 90% of the people, had been established.

However, after some initial successes, things began to go badly wrong. In particular, a crisis in agriculture (partly the result of bad weather) led to food shortages and famine. There was also general economic failure in industry, and the period 1959–61 became known as the 'Three Bitter Years'. This led some to criticise Mao's economic policies. Peng Dehuai, a Long March veteran (see page 197), set these down in a letter to Mao.

SOURCE A

The Great Leap Forward has basically proved the correctness of the General Line for building socialism ... But as we can see now, an excessive number of capital construction projects were hastily started in 1958. With part of the funds being dispersed, completion of some essential projects had to be postponed. This is a shortcoming ... Because we did not have a deep enough understanding, we came to be aware of it too late. So we continued with our Great Leap Forward in 1959 instead of putting on the brakes ... As a result, imbalances were not corrected in time and new temporary difficulties cropped up ...

Extracts from Peng Dehuai's 'Letter of Opinion' of July 1959, pointing out some of the shortcomings of the Great Leap Forward. Quoted in Ebrey, P. (ed.) 1981. *Chinese Civilization: A Source Book.* New York, USA. The Free Press. pp. 436–39.

Although Mao took care to get the Central Committee (CC) to repudiate this letter at a party conference in Lushan in July 1959, the mounting problems caused by the Great Leap Forward led to the loss of some of his influence within the party.

Liu Shaoqi (who had long been seen as Mao's likely successor) took over from Mao as president. Liu believed that the GLF disaster was 70% man-made and 30% due to natural causes. To tackle the serious problems of China's agricultural system, he allowed peasants to have private plots, so that after they had worked on the commune lands they could grow extra food for their families. He also introduced bonuses and other incentives for the hardest workers on the communes, and for factory workers, in order to increase production. With these policy changes, the Chinese economy slowly began to recover.

The Socialist Education Movement and 'Rightist deviations'

However, Mao became increasingly worried about Liu's economic policies. In Mao's view, the party was taking China off the 'revolutionary socialist road', resulting in a tendency towards 'creeping capitalism'.

Question

Why did the Great Leap Forward lead to a loss of influence for Mao?

Fact

At the Lushan conference in 1959, Mao lost some of his influence. He gave up his position as president (head of state); Zhou Enlai remained as prime minister, and Deng Xiaoping became general-secretary of the CCP. Mao, however, remained as chairman of the CCP. Mao then gave up direct supervision of government affairs. Yet, as chairman of the CCP, Mao still retained theoretical precedence over the party, and considerable prestige.

Communism in Crisis

> ### SOURCE B
>
> During the cultural revolution of 1966–1969, the economic policies of the preceding half-decade were condemned for leading China on a retreat from 'socialism' to 'capitalism,' and the Party leaders responsible for implementing those policies were purged as 'capitalist roaders' who allegedly exercised a 'bourgeois dictatorship'. This, in brief, was the Maoist judgment on the early 1960s, or at least the dramatic picture of a 'life-and-death struggle' between capitalism and socialism that Maoists presented to the world.
>
> Yet the differences between what became known as the Maoist and Liuist roads do not appear to be nearly so sharp. It is instructive to compare the economic policies pursued by Liu Shaoqi in the early 1960s with those adopted by Lenin in the Soviet Union forty years earlier … The economic policies adopted by the Chinese leaders … were in some respects similar to Lenin's NEP … Yet, as an alleged 'retreat to capitalism', the Chinese program was but a pale reflection of its earlier Soviet counterpart.
>
> Meisner, M. 1999. *Mao's China and After: A History of the People's Republic.* New York, USA. The Free Press. pp. 260–61.

In order to correct this 'Rightist deviation', he decided that a mass revolutionary campaign was needed amongst Chinese youth. Mao called this the 'Socialist Education Movement'. It involved workers and peasants studying his works, and attending rallies and meetings.

In September 1962, Mao made a speech at a Central Committee meeting, warning that it was still possible for China to move backwards to a 'restoration of the reactionary classes'. He persuaded the Central Committee that the period of transition to communism would be marked by a continuing class struggle between the proletariat and the bourgeoisie. He said it was therefore necessary to condemn 'revisionist tendencies' in the party, and to strengthen socialist principles – especially in the countryside.

In May 1963, the Central Committee issued a resolution, known as the 'First Ten Points', which set down the campaign's objectives and methods. However, two revised versions – by Deng Xiaoping and Liu Shaoqi – came out in September 1963 and September 1964 respectively. These tried to limit the scope of the campaign. Consequently, Mao became concerned that the campaign was no longer being carried out in a truly revolutionary way.

> ### SOURCE C
>
> This is a struggle that calls for the reeducation of man. This is a struggle for reorganizing the revolutionary class army for a confrontation with the forces of feudalism and capitalism which are now feverishly attacking us. We must nip their counterrevolution in the bud … With cadres and masses joining hand in hand in production labor and scientific experiments, our Party will take another stride forward in becoming a more glorious, greater, and more correct Party …
>
> Extracts from the 'First Ten Points'. Translated in Baum, R. and Teiwes, F. C. 1968. *Ssu-Ch'ing: The Socialist Education Movement of 1962–1966.* Berkeley, USA. University of California Press. pp. 62–71.

7 China and the struggle for power after 1976

School students reading Chairman Mao's Little Red Book in Beijing; the book's influence spread quickly from the People's Liberation Army

Mao was supported by **Lin Biao**, the minister of defence. In May 1964, Lin got the Political Department of the People's Liberation Army (PLA) to publish the pocket-sized book, *Quotations from Chairman Mao* – later known as the 'Little Red Book'. This was made required reading for all military personnel, who were expected to be able to memorise the quotes. As a result, the PLA became a stronghold of Maoist thought – and support for Mao. This was the starting point for the creation of a cult of personality around Mao.

SOURCE D

Giant portraits of him now hung in the streets, busts were in every chamber, his books and photographs were everywhere on display to the exclusion of all others … It gave me … [an] uneasy recollection of similar extravaganzas of worship of Joseph Stalin seen during wartime years in Russia … The one-man cult was not yet universal, but the trend was unmistakable.

Snow, E. 1971. *The Long Revolution*. New York, USA. Random House. pp. 68–69.

Lin Biao (1907–71) Lin Biao's real name was Lin Yurong, and he was an important Red Army leader during the civil war that ended in victory for the communists in 1949. He rose to prominence during the Cultural Revolution. After Liu had been purged, Lin Biao was named at a party conference as Mao's second-in-command, and described as 'closest comrade-in-arms and successor to Mao Zedong'. However, in 1971 he died under mysterious circumstances, after the '571 Affair' (see page 152).

Fact
In all, nearly a billion copies of *Quotations from Chairman Mao* were printed, along with 150 million copies of Mao's *Selected Works*. By 1965, the Mao cult had spread across China and he became known as 'the Great Helmsman'. Mao had previously said that personality cults had valuable political uses – he attributed Khrushchev's overthrow in the Soviet Union in 1964 to the fact that he had not developed a cult of personality. When Edgar Snow, an American journalist partly sympathetic to Communist China, visited China in the winter of 1964–65, he was puzzled by the 'immoderate glorification' of Mao.

Communism in Crisis

Fact
Wu Han's play was just one of several anti-Maoist satires written during the 'Bitter Years' that followed the collapse of the Great Leap Forward. Such satires rapidly declined, once the Socialist Education Movement had begun in September 1962. However, these writers and intellectuals had been supported by both Liu and Deng.

Fact
The Chinese traditionally prefer to achieve consensus wherever possible, and tend to be uneasy with concepts such as factions and dissent. Instead, they prefer to see these as 'differences' within the leadership. Groups based on these differences have, at different times, been given various 'labels'. Those wanting to preserve Maoism have been identified as leftists, ultra-leftists, conservatives or revolutionaries. Meanwhile, those favouring fundamental reform of Maoism have been labelled as rightists, capitalist roaders, revisionists, reactionaries, counter-revolutionaries or moderates.

Cultural Revolution Generally taken as lasting from May 1966 to April 1969, its official name was the 'Great Proletarian Cultural Revolution'. However, those who took power after Mao's death – many of whom were its victims – state that it lasted until October 1976, when the Gang of Four were overthrown and arrested. It has thus been described as a decade-long 'catastrophe', which resulted in the 'heaviest losses' suffered by the party, state and the people of China since 1949. The Cultural Revolution was partly based on the *Quotations from Chairman Mao*. However, the destructive aspects of the Cultural Revolution were not apparently anticipated by Mao.

Intellectuals and 'revolutionary successors'

In February 1964, Mao called for intellectuals to be sent from the cities to the countryside, to 'learn from the peasants'. Mao had long distrusted intellectuals, and the cities they lived in. He regarded cities as breeding grounds of ideological corruption and revisionism. In June 1964, he called for a 'rectification' campaign (similar to the Anti-Rightist campaign of late 1957) to be conducted against intellectuals.

By 1964, Mao and his supporters were becoming increasingly concerned about the need to train 'revolutionary successors' amongst the youth of China. He therefore proposed that the period of formal education be reduced. Instead, Mao wanted education to be combined with productive labour – in order to stop the 'corruption' of China's youth. This led to growing unease amongst intellectuals in the party.

Mao's concerns about the existence of 'capitalist roaders' within the CCP leadership were voiced in January 1965. This led to the 'Twenty-three Articles', which warned that the struggle between socialism and capitalism was also taking place within the party at its highest levels.

However, those in the party who opposed Mao's statements, and who wanted a more flexible interpretation of Marxism, looked for an opportunity to undermine Mao. An earlier veiled criticism had been made in 1960 by allowing the publication of a play by Wu Han (a professor of history, a playwright and deputy mayor of Beijing). Although set in the Ming period, the play had clear parallels with the dismissal of the PLA general Peng Dehuai in 1959, which Mao had pushed for.

This led Mao to take more serious action. In January 1965, at a Politburo meeting, he identified as the principal enemy of socialism 'those people in authority within the Party who are taking the capitalist road'. He then demanded that Wu Han's play be criticised by the party, as part of a cultural revolution. This was delayed repeatedly. Urged on by his wife, Mao then had a critical review of the play published in Shanghai in November 1965. Most of Mao's supporters later saw this as the start of the **Cultural Revolution**.

Liuists versus Maoists

By the spring of 1966, the party was divided into two factions: the 'Liuists' who dominated the party and state apparatus; and the minority 'Maoists', supported by the PLA. In early May 1966, the PLA's newspaper, the *Liberation Army Daily*, began to call for a purge of anti-socialist elements in cultural circles – and also of 'anti-socialist elements' in the party itself. As a first step, the heads of newspapers and cultural and propaganda departments in Beijing were purged. A new 'Central Cultural Revolutionary Committee' was set up, headed by Mao's wife Jiang Qing.

The Cultural Revolution

In 1966, Mao launched the Cultural Revolution. This was Mao's attempt to eradicate old anti-revolutionary ideas, especially 'capitalist' and 'bourgeois' ideas. It was also directed against those holding such ideas – and was part of Mao's bid to restore his power and influence, which had been reduced as a result of the Great Leap Forward. To carry it out, Mao relied on the PLA and the youth of China. Thus, the Cultural Revolution was a deliberate attempt to turn the young against the old, and so secure the revolutionary future.

The Cultural Revolution had much to do with political rivalries amongst the leadership, but it was also based on real ideological differences. These included dealing with issues such as growing social inequalities, the fading of socialist idealism and commitment, and the emergence of new bureaucratic élites divorced from the people. The Maoists believed that all these problems had increased as a result of the economic policies adopted by the Liuists.

Mao used the Cultural Revolution to purge the party of his opponents and rivals. He also wanted to persuade Chinese youth (who only knew from books how bad things had been under the emperors, the warlords and the nationalists) to support the continuation of a 'revolutionary road' for China in the future. However, the Cultural Revolution became increasingly violent and destructive. It also split the party, and turned young against old. Mao and Jiang Qing moulded the young so they could be the vanguard of this revolutionary campaign and become the 'revolutionary successors' of the pre-1949 generation.

The campaign was officially launched in August 1966, when Mao returned to active politics. He got the Central Committee to issue a directive calling for a great 'cultural revolution' to attack all remnants of the old society so that a new, truly revolutionary one could be built.

SOURCE E

The Great Proletarian Cultural Revolution now unfolding is a great revolution that touches people to their very souls and constitutes a new stage in the development of the socialist revolution in our country ... Although the bourgeoisie has been overthrown, it is still trying to use the old ideas, culture, customs and habits of the exploiting classes to corrupt the masses, capture their minds and endeavor to stage a comeback ...

Since the Cultural Revolution is a revolution, it inevitably meets with resistance. This resistance comes chiefly from those persons in power taking the capitalist road who have wormed their way into the Party ... Don't be afraid of disturbances. Chairman Mao has often told us that revolution cannot always be so very refined, so gentle ... Make the fullest use of big-character posters and great debates to ... criticize the wrong views and ... draw a clear line between ourselves and the enemy.

Extracts from The 16-Point Directive on the Cultural Revolution, 8 August 1966. Quoted in Milton, D., Milton, N. and Schurmann F. 1974. The China Reader: People's China. New York, USA. Random House. pp. 272–83.

Mao called for the 'Four Olds' to be destroyed. By the 'Four Olds', he meant bourgeois (capitalist) tendencies still existing in old ideas, old culture, old customs, and old habits. His call to destroy these bourgeois tendencies was taken up enthusiastically by many of the younger generation. These young people were instructed to form revolutionary groups known as Red Guards.

Questions
What is meant by the phrase 'taking the capitalist road'? Which members of the communist leadership do you think were being referred to?

Fact
The Red Guards were named after the armed workers and soldiers who had secured the victory of Lenin's Bolshevik Revolution in November 1917. The first to respond to Mao's calls to rebel against established authority were university and middle-school students. By early June, there was much turmoil in the universities. In an attempt to turn the attentions of the Red Guards away from Communist Party bodies and leaders, Liu Shaoqi sent party 'work teams' to get students to attack 'bourgeois authorities' instead, meaning individual intellectuals, teachers and professors. It was thus not the Maoists but official party-organised groups sent by the Liuists that first began the violent persecution of individual intellectuals.

Communism in Crisis

Red Guards mock people they see as enemies of the Cultural Revolution, by parading them through the streets of Beijing in dunces' caps

There was a mass rally of a million young people in Tiananmen Square in Beijing on 18 August 1966. The Red Guards (who had male and female members of equal status) then went back to their areas to carry out attacks on traditional Chinese culture. Soon, they began to publicly criticise party leaders, teachers and professors they thought were 'Rightists', who were not carrying out Mao's ideas sufficiently.

As the Red Guards carried out their campaigns across China, Mao moved against his political opponents in Beijing. These included Liu Shaoqi, who was accused of being a Rightist. He was dismissed from office and sent to prison, where he later died. Another of those purged during the Cultural Revolution was Deng Xiaoping. He was accused in 1967 of being the 'number one capitalist roader', and of trying to destroy the revolution from within by keeping Mao out of power after 1958. In 1969, Deng was **'sent down to the countryside'**.

During 1968, the Cultural Revolution became increasingly violent. It has been calculated that up to 400,000 died as a result of torture, beatings and forced suicides. Thousands more were brutalised by the physical punishments, while many suffered psychological damage from the public humiliations that were carried out.

Question
What does this photograph tell us about the nature of some aspects of the Cultural Revolution?

'sent down to the countryside'
This phrase essentially meant that such people needed to be 're-educated' by learning from the peasants and commune industrial workers. Deng was forced to work in a tractor factory in Jiangxi. Conditions were quite hard, but it seems that Zhou Enlai used his influence to lessen the effects of the punishment.

The situation began to get out of control, with different groups of Red Guards fighting each other. As early as 1967, Mao and Lin felt the excesses needed to be curbed; in April 1969, Mao decided that the Cultural Revolution had achieved its main objectives. On 5 September, the PLA was told to restore order, and young people were commanded to return home and go back to school. There was then a harsh crackdown on those wanting to continue their revolutionary campaign. Meanwhile, others were sent to work on the communes or in industry. Gradually, order returned to China.

Mao judged the Cultural Revolution to be a success, partly because he was once again the most powerful person in China. Many Rightist leaders in the provinces had been purged, and replaced by those loyal to Mao's more radical plans. To prevent any future return to bureaucratic rule, and the taking of 'the capitalist road', he called for a shake-up of government structures. 'Revolutionary Committees', which included workers, party members and members of the PLA, were set up to run the government, communes and industries.

However, China had suffered economically during this upheaval. The majority of the campaigns were in urban areas. This meant that industrial production suffered, as workers were involved in political campaigns and meetings, which left them little time for work. Agricultural production also declined. Thus, Mao's hopes for an economically and militarily strong China suffered another setback as a direct result of his campaign during 1966–69. At the same time, many people had become used to repeating 'politically correct' slogans, rather than saying what they really felt. This resulted in growing cynicism about Mao and the CCP.

Question
Why did Mao think the Cultural Revolution had been a success?

With power firmly in his hands, Mao began to introduce relatively egalitarian socio-economic policies during the late 1960s and early 1970s, in an attempt to reverse the Liuist economic policies. But the violence of the years 1966–69 left a legacy of considerable animosity and bitterness, which later created the setting for what happened after Mao died.

7 China and the struggle for power after 1976

Activities

1. Carry out some research on the results of the Great Leap Forward and the Cultural Revolution. Then, for each event, make an assessment of: (a) Mao's position and (b) the relative positions of the Liuists and the Maoists.
2. Write a couple of paragraphs about the importance of Lin Biao in the events of 1964–69.
3. Find out what life was like during the Cultural Revolution for: (a) the Red Guards and (b) their victims.
4. Begin to make a record of the political ups and downs of Deng Xiaoping. At this stage, just cover the years up to 1970.

Why was there another power struggle after the Cultural Revolution?

Mao's position in 1969 seemed politically very secure. Most of the 'moderates' had been expelled from the party and the government, and his supporters held all the top positions. In fact, this proved not to be quite the case. Nonetheless, in April 1969, the 9th Congress of the CCP hailed the Cultural Revolution a success and described itself as a congress of 'unity and victory'.

Soon, however, new struggles broke out. These were partly connected to foreign policy. During the Cultural Revolution, Mao – and China – had taken little interest in what was happening outside China. At this time, when the US was massively escalating the war in Vietnam, it was Liu (not Mao) who issued the strongest warnings concerning US actions in Vietnam. In fact, in 1970, Mao told Edgar Snow that one of the reasons for purging Liu was that Liu wanted to revive the old Sino–Soviet alliance (which had broken down in the early 1960s) in order to limit US aggression in Vietnam. Mao felt this would hinder the progress of the Cultural Revolution.

During the April 1969 Congress, Lin Biao's main report attacked Soviet and US imperialism equally strongly. In August of the previous year, the USSR had led the Warsaw Pact invasion of Czechoslovakia. There had also been clashes on the Sino–Soviet border in northern Manchuria. Zhou and Mao came to the conclusion that the USSR was the main threat. Zhou therefore felt it was necessary to reach some understanding with the US to counter this Soviet threat. Nonetheless, the US was still generally seen as the 'most ferocious enemy of the peoples of the world'. Lin believed this suggested accommodation with US imperialism was a betrayal of 'proletarian internationalism'.

The other issue that caused a rift between Lin and Mao was the decision to restore party control. During the Cultural Revolution, power had passed to the army. Mao accepted Zhou's conclusion that restoration of party authority was essential – and that to do this, many of those purged during the Cultural Revolution should be allowed to return to China. The return of these leaders would seriously undermine Lin's influence once Mao was dead. Consequently, Lin proposed that the Cultural Revolution Committee should continue – even though he disagreed with it on many issues. Nonetheless, it was abolished in December 1969.

In August 1970, at the Second Plenum of the 9th CC in Lushan, the rift between the two widened. With no prior notification to Mao, Lin Biao suddenly launched an attack on Zhou's foreign and domestic policies. Lin was criticised, and the CC endorsed the foreign policy of 'peaceful coexistence'.

Theory of knowledge

History, bias and ways of knowing

Since Mao's death and the overthrow of the Gang of Four, those people in China who have been free to talk about the impact of the Cultural Revolution have largely been its victims. Historian Harry Harding says that we need to bear this in mind, and be sceptical about their accounts of what happened. If not, we risk repeating the mistakes some observers made in the late 1960s, when the official explanations of what the Cultural Revolution was about were taken at face value. Maurice Meisner says it will be decades before the full history of the Gang of Four can be written with any reasonable degree of accuracy. Is it therefore almost impossible for historians to establish what happened in the past?

Discussion point

How important do you think ideals and principles should be in politics? Should Lin Biao have taken the pragmatic (practical) approach over foreign policy in the period 1969–71? Or is it sometimes necessary to defend certain values, regardless of the consequences for you or other people?

Fact

In the early 1960s, Mao condemned Khrushchev and the Soviet Union as 'revisionist' for advocating the policy of peaceful coexistence between countries with different social systems. He claimed this meant they were moving away from 'orthodox' Marxism and proletarian solidarity.

Communism in Crisis

The four key figures in the power struggle: Zhou Enlai (far left), Lin Biao (second left), Mao Zedong (centre) and Mao's wife Jiang Qing (right) in April 1967

SOURCE F

To Lin Biao [the new diplomacy] seemed, if not necessarily so much a betrayal of principle, then certainly a politically damaging repudiation of the vision of a worldwide 'people's war' with which he had been so intimately identified. On the question of China's foreign policy, particularly the policy of rapprochement with the United States, one of the battle lines between Mao and his designated 'successor' was drawn. Another battle line was drawn on a second and closely related question: the pace and manner that Mao and Zhou proposed for rebuilding the Communist Party and re-establishing its authority … No matter how much proletarian virtue the PLA might possess, the situation gave rise to Bonapartist fears, and Mao began to criticize the rule of the military commanders as 'arrogant.'

Meisner, M. 1999. Mao's China and After: A History of the People's Republic. New York, USA. The Free Press. p. 379.

Fact
The official Chinese account (finally given in July 1972) was that Lin had plotted, with the Soviet Union's approval, to blow Mao up. When the plot was discovered, Lin had tried to flee China and reach the USSR by plane. He was apparently killed when his plane had crashed (a later version said it had been shot down) somewhere over Mongolia. However, several historians, including Maurice Meisner, wonder if it was actually Mao who decided to eliminate Lin, rather than the other way round. This led Lin to draw up plans for a counter-coup, known as 'Project 571'.

The '571 Affair'

Lin Biao was defence minister and head of the PLA, and had supported Mao throughout the Cultural Revolution. However, Lin now began to have doubts about the direction Mao was taking. By 1970, both men had come to distrust each other. Mao felt Lin might not wait until he had died to take up his posts; Lin believed that Mao had become power-hungry and would not share control.

Aware of Lin's power as head of the army, Mao began to undermine his position by removing political and military leaders who were loyal to him. Mao also ordered Lin's troops to leave Beijing and go to Manchuria. Both these moves were seen as preparing for Lin's removal from power. Meanwhile, Mao pushed ahead with the policies Lin had opposed. In December 1970, Mao let it be known that US president Richard Nixon would be a welcome visitor. In July 1971, US adviser Henry Kissinger came to China to prepare for Nixon's official visit.

During September 1971, in what later became known as the '571 Affair', Lin vanished from public view. There was also a wholesale purge of the upper levels of military and civilian administrations, including 21 people being removed from the Politburo.

Rightists versus Leftists

The 'discovery' of Lin's plot (see page 152) undermined faith in Mao, as he had clearly made a mistake in favouring Lin. Briefly united over the Lin Biao Affair in 1971, Liuists and Maoists soon begun taking different positions. As early as 1973, there was another political clash looming – between the older leaders who had been attacked during the Cultural Revolution, and the younger ones who had risen during it.

In 1973, again with help from Zhou Enlai, Deng was allowed to return to Beijing. By this time, Mao's health was rapidly worsening, and the struggle for power between Rightists and Leftists intensified. Several Rightists who had been demoted or expelled during the Cultural Revolution were quietly rehabilitated and restored to power.

The Rightists were initially led by Zhou Enlai, the prime minister, and Deng Xiaoping. Zhou wanted to focus on economic development and saw Deng, who was appointed a vice-premier of the Council of State, as a useful ally. This was partly because Deng was prepared to consider things from a pragmatic point of view, rather than trying to ensure that revolutionary ideology was maintained at all costs. The Leftists were led by Mao's wife, **Jiang Qing**, and three radical party members from Shanghai. They later became collectively known as the **Gang of Four**. They were supported by the trade unions, by the Communist Youth League and by the militias of the big cities.

The new economic and foreign policy initiatives were endorsed by the 10th National Congress of the CCP in August 1973. In elections to the Politburo, the return of the old pre-Cultural Revolution 'capitalist roaders' was confirmed, with Deng being re-elected to the CC and the Politburo. In this clear split between right-wing moderates and left-wing radicals, the Rightists increasingly had a greater say than the younger leaders, who had been promoted between 1966 and 1969. At this time, it was assumed that Mao still favoured the Leftist emphasis on correct ideology as the way to achieve economic development.

The Gang of Four

During the Cultural Revolution, in November 1966, the 17-strong Central Cultural Revolutionary Committee was headed up by Jiang as first vice-chairwoman. The committee included several of her closest Shanghai political associates: Yao Wenyuan (Mao's chief propagandist); Wang Hongwen (a trade union leader); and Zhang Chunqiao (deputy secretary of Shanghai's Municipal Committee). They were Mao's strongest supporters during the Cultural Revolution – though whether they were controlled by him, or whether they were increasingly imposing their views on him, remains unclear. These four leading members of this Committee later became known as the Gang of Four – and they favoured an even more revolutionary approach to politics and the economy.

Although Jiang's position gave the Gang of Four an advantage over their opponents, they were not very strong, as their power base was mainly within the cultural and media organisations. They had little support in the party as a whole, or in the People's Liberation Army (PLA). Although their excesses were eventually quelled by the PLA in 1969, Jiang retained her influence.

Jiang Qing (1914–91) Jiang Qing was an actress. In 1938, she became Mao's fourth wife (or third, if Mao's first unconsummated marriage is ignored). During the 1950s, she worked with the Ministry of Culture, where she promoted plays and operas that expressed revolutionary sentiments. In the 1960s, she increasingly took control of the national media to ensure that it followed a 'correct' cultural line. This allowed her to become increasingly politically important. Several leading communists became worried about her influence – especially during the Cultural Revolution.

Gang of Four This term was allegedly first coined by Mao. The Gang of Four were amongst the highest-ranking leaders of the CCP. All four were members of the Politburo, and two of them (Zhang and Wang) were members of its Standing Committee. Both these bodies were more or less equally divided between Rightists and Leftists.

Communism in Crisis

Fact
During the Cultural Revolution, the Central Cultural Revolutionary Committee tried to promote the thoughts of Chairman Mao, and to eliminate all traces of the 'Four Olds'. It was very active in campaigns against the Rightists, such as Liu and Deng; and it encouraged the Red Guards to hold mass protest rallies. The Committee used quotations from Mao's 'Little Red Book' to support their accusations and actions. This made it difficult for people to oppose them – as they risked being seen as disagreeing with Mao himself.

Fact
As well as the proposed 'normalisation' of Sino–American relations covered by the Shanghai Communiqué, agreements to trade with other non-communist countries were also signed. This was a shock for Leftists. They believed China to be the true defender of communism, and they knew the USSR had been strongly criticised by China in the past as a 'revisionist' state that had made deals with the US.

Four Modernisations This plan sought to modernise China's agriculture, industry, science and technology, and national defence. It had first been proposed by Zhou at the 3rd National People's Congress in 1964. In 1973, Deng had made similar proposals and the plan was presented at the 11th Congress of the CCP in 1977.

Question
What were the 'Four Modernisations'?

The turn to the US

After 1971, political tensions were heightened by China's developing relationship with the USA, which had always been depicted as an evil imperialist power. Apart from the wider issues of foreign policy, the arguments centred over whether political principles were more or less important than practical economic considerations. In February 1972, US president Nixon made an official visit to China. The meeting between Mao and Nixon resulted in the Shanghai Communiqué, which called for the 'normalisation' of Sino–American relations – though this was not completed until 1979. However, shortly after the visit, Mao became increasingly ill.

The two factions disagreed about almost everything. Their fundamental differences centred around whether politics or the economy was more important. They also disagreed on whether to use capitalist techniques to modernise the economy. The Rightists wanted an end to the political arguments and upheaval that had dominated China since the start of the Cultural Revolution in 1966. Instead, they wanted to build a strong and wealthy China.

The Leftists, on the other hand, wanted to continue the political struggle to ensure that China followed a 'correct' revolutionary line. This meant removing from power all those 'moderates' (or 'reactionaries') who favoured introducing capitalist mechanisms. Instead, they wanted to involve the majority of the Chinese people in decision-making. In particular, they believed that decisions should be based on what was good for the revolution – even if they did not make the greatest economic sense. The Leftists also believed that everyone should do some manual labour, so they could keep in touch with the people.

The Four Modernisations

Between 1974 and 1976, this political and ideological split was particularly focused on a plan known as the **Four Modernisations**. This plan was favoured by the Rightists, and was put forward by a dying Zhou in January 1975, at the 4th National People's Congress. Afterwards, Deng (who was appointed as chief of staff of the Armed Forces) often stood in for Zhou at State Council meetings. Once restored to some influence, Deng began attempts to move the CCP away from the more revolutionary, and disruptive, influences of the Gang of Four. Deng favoured the use of capitalist methods. He was supported by Zhou, who had disliked the disorder of the Cultural Revolution.

Jiang and her group continued to argue in favour of continuing the Cultural Revolution. They also criticised those in the party whom they saw as promoting Western thoughts and values. At first, Mao seemed to support his wife but then he began to distance himself from her, and to criticise some of the activities of her supporters. However, he also used them to keep control of other members of the Politburo. In February, the Leftists stepped up their campaigns against 'bourgeois' and outdated ideas in the arts and in education. Although they also attacked Zhou's ideas, their campaign was really directed at Deng. Deng fell from favour again in 1975, but Zhou continued to back him.

As he became weaker, Mao increasingly came to rely on his nephew, Mao Yuanxin. His nephew was sympathetic to the Leftists, who, from 1975, were his main means of liaising with the Politburo. This gave the Gang of Four an advantage over their rivals. However, Mao's bodyguards, led by General Wang Dongxing, were opposed to them and worked with some members of the Politburo against them.

Activities

1. See what extra information you can find out about the '571 Affair'. Why do you think it is difficult for historians to find out about what happened in China's recent past?
2. Draw up a table to summarise the main events of the power struggle between 1969 and 1976. Then write a paragraph assessing the strength of the Gang of Four by 1976.
3. Imagine that you are a journalist who has been asked to interview Jiang Qing about her political beliefs. Then write a newspaper article, setting out what you think she would have said about the political and economic situation in China in the mid 1970s.
4. Continue adding information to your record of Deng's political career – this time for the years 1971–75.

What were the main stages of the power struggle between 1976 and 1981?

In January 1976, Zhou died. This was a big setback for the Rightists. A few months later, Zhu De (Mao's long-time military commander) also died. Meanwhile, Mao himself had increasing health problems (he would die in September the same year). Mao and Zhou had dominated China's communist state for almost 30 years. Thus, Zhou's death and Mao's illness created a vacuum and a struggle for power. Although the Cultural Revolution had ended in 1969, the Gang of Four still seemed powerful, and it remained difficult to criticise them. However, once Mao's health took a serious turn for the worse, the struggle for power became more intense.

The nature of the struggle

This power struggle was similar to the one that began in the Soviet Union following Lenin's first stroke in 1921. In both cases, the contest was essentially ideological, rather than simply a case of individuals wanting to obtain power for its own sake. In China, it demonstrated a fundamental split between the two main factions of the Chinese Communist Party: the Leftist, radical Gang of Four; and the Rightist, more **'reformist' elements** of the CCP.

Essentially, the Gang of Four were Maoist revolutionaries who felt that Chinese communism had lost its way since the 1950s. Their response was to push for the re-introduction of greater radicalism. Their leader, Jiang, was growing increasingly influential during Mao's illness. Opposed to the Gang of Four were those, led by Deng, who argued that China needed to adopt aspects of market capitalism and Western technology in order to modernise the Chinese economy.

Thus, the struggle was between economic 'modernisers' (portrayed by the Leftists as the 'bourgeois right') and those who were more concerned about reducing social and economic inequalities than just focusing on increased production and efficiency. In addition, the Leftists favoured more authoritarian control, to prevent capitalist restoration. Meanwhile, the Rightists seemed prepared to loosen controls to an extent. Again, as in the USSR in the 1920s, there were those in the middle of the two factions. These people favoured a compromise between the two positions. This, more moderate, Maoist centrist group was led by **Hua Guofeng**, who had been named as a possible successor to Mao after Lin's death in 1971.

'reformist' elements In the context of Chinese politics in 1976, this term meant those who favoured almost outright capitalism. Under Mao, such people were called 'revisionists' (who wanted to 'revise' Marxism almost out of existence), and even 'capitalist roaders'.

Hua Guofeng (1921–2008)
Hua's real name was Su Zhu, and he started out as a relatively unknown top security official from Hunan, Mao's home province. His rapid rise to prominence in the party led to his nickname, 'the Helicopter'. While he was a moderate Leftist, he did not particularly like the Gang. He actively tried to broaden his support base and had some backing from Deng's supporters. It was rumoured that he was Mao's son. He certainly tried to look like him, adopting Mao's hairstyle and mannerisms.

Communism in Crisis

The rise of Hua Guofeng

After Zhou's death in January 1976, many waited to see who Mao would favour as successor. His choice would be likely to determine the future direction that China would take. The Gang tried to get Zhang appointed as premier, in order to ensure a more left-wing and radical set of policies. However, Zhou favoured Deng, who wanted to introduce market mechanisms into China's centrally planned economy. In the end, Mao surprised many by opting for Hua, who became the new premier.

As Hua had a centrist position, there were no serious objections from either of the two opposed factions. Mao seemed to trust him more than Deng. Indeed, Mao is supposed to have said in 1976 – in what some sources claim were his last coherent words – 'With you in charge, I am at ease.'

The Qingming Festival, 1976

This festival took place in Beijing during early April 1976, following Zhou's death in January 1976. It was an important traditional Chinese festival, in which people visited the graves of their ancestors to pay their respects. It was seen by the CCP as 'superstitious', 'bourgeois' and an outmoded feudal hangover, and they had tried to stamp it out. The mourning period for Zhou was cut short because the Gang did not want the funeral of a Rightist to last too long. Crowds of people then decided to use the festival as a way of showing their respect for Zhou, who had been a popular leader. Thousands went to Tiananmen Square over a four-day period, to lay wreaths and white paper chrysanthemums in his memory.

> **Fact**
> A protest took place in April 1976, which later became known as the April 5th Movement. This was an important development in popular protest and resistance against the authoritarian Chinese government. It became a powerful political symbol over the following years.

Some of the crowd wrote poems on the ground around the Monument to the People's Heroes, which showed support for Zhou, and for Deng and the Rightists. A few of the poems even criticised Mao himself, not just Jiang and the Gang of Four. This apparently spontaneous protest worried the party leadership. Hua advised Mao to have the wreaths quietly removed by the police at the end of the festival, hoping this would end the criticisms. However, when news spread about their removal on 5 April, masses of demonstrators marched to the square to protest. Over 10,000 placed more wreaths in the square, and wrote even stronger criticisms of Mao. Hua asked for Mao's opinion on what to do. Mao and the Politburo decided this was counter-revolution, and the Beijing authorities used force to disperse the protesters. Riots broke out and many were beaten and arrested.

The wreaths for Zhou Enlai in Tiananmen Square, Beijing, April 1976, photographed shortly before they were removed by police, triggering serious rioting

Meanwhile, there were accusations (mainly from the Left) that Deng had encouraged and even organised these demonstrations. He was thought to have done this in order to strengthen his position by weakening the Gang of Four. Consequently, he was once again removed from his positions of power – though not from the party – and was told he would be investigated for 'political mistakes'.

Deng immediately fled to Canton, where he sought the protection of General Ye Jianying (who later played an important part in the overthrow of the Gang of Four), remaining there until Mao's death.

Mao's death

As Mao's health deteriorated during 1976, Hua took greater control of affairs. However, when Mao died on 9 September 1976, the two factions tried to secure their positions. No longer having Mao as a supporter, the Gang made a bid for power, using their influence over the media, the urban militia and the universities. However, they underestimated Hua's determination – and the support he had amongst Deng's supporters in the Politburo and the military.

Jiang's first move was to try to make it look as if she was Mao's choice as successor. It was later apparently discovered that she even altered some of Mao's writings to give this impression. She certainly ordered that all his personal papers be given to her, and had the media publish articles showing the successful rule of women in China.

However, Hua fought back. In his speech at Mao's memorial ceremony, he praised Mao. Then he referred to one of Mao's speeches in which he had attacked the Gang of Four for factionalism. In the Politburo, Jiang then accused Hua of incompetence, and proposed that she should become the chair of the Central Committee. Backed by Deng's supporters, who included the defence minister, Ye Jianying, Hua insisted that the procedures should be followed. He said the vice-chair should take over until the next session of the Central Committee.

Surprised at Hua's determination, and realising their power was slipping, the Gang allegedly tried to organise a coup on 6 October. It was later revealed that Mao's nephew, Mao Yuanxin, who was political commissar of the Shenyang Military Region, would have provided military support for the coup by marching on Beijing. The Gang apparently also had plans to assassinate several Politburo members – including Hua and Ye.

Military support for the Gang was not strong, and it was rumoured that Jiang attempted to gain more supporters within the Politburo. Those she approached allegedly included Generals Chen Xilian and Su Zhenua – but they apparently immediately informed Hua. However, it is unlikely that the Gang actually did this, as they had little support among either party officials or the PLA. It is more likely that Hua and the Rightists decided that the best way to deal with the potential threat from the Gang was to strike first.

The defeat of the Gang of Four

Hua held a meeting in the PLA's headquarters with several of Deng's political and military supporters. At this meeting, they agreed to launch a 'pre-emptive' coup by protecting Beijing and arresting the Gang. On 5 October, Hua called an emergency meeting of the Politburo for midnight. When Zhang and Wang arrived, they were immediately arrested. Yao and Jiang, who had not arrived for the meeting, were arrested later. Any support the Gang had melted away, and the leaders were expelled from the party, while plans for their trial were made.

Hua and his supporters then began to portray Jiang – now called 'Madame Mao' – and the Gang as mere power-hungry plotters, deliberately downplaying any ideological motives. Posters appeared, with slogans such as 'Cut Jiang Qing in Ten Thousand Pieces' and 'Deep-Fry the Gang of Four in Oil'.

> **Question**
> Why were the Gang of Four angered by the events that took place at the Qingming festival?

> **Fact**
> Jiang was presented as someone who had manipulated Mao when he was ill and dying, and who tried to use his death to secure her 'lust for power'. The press, the radio and wall posters also portrayed her as a 'luxury-loving pornographer'. Photographs and posters where she appeared with Mao were altered in very obvious ways, to show the public that she had fallen from power.

Communism in Crisis

A propaganda poster after the fall of the Gang of Four, showing (left to right) Yao, Wang, Zhang and Jiang, with human heads and animal bodies, on a skewer

While Jiang was increasingly vilified by the regime, Mao's reputation and image remained untarnished. When news that the Gang had been arrested reached Chinese citizens, there were celebrations across China – though they were not necessarily spontaneous. The Gang's actions during the Cultural Revolution had made them deeply unpopular in many quarters, and many were pleased at this change in the party leadership.

Though the Gang had been arrested in October 1976, their trials were delayed until November 1980, and did not finish until 1981. This gave time for the Rightists to consolidate their hold on power, and for the public to forget the Gang. When the trials began, Jiang and the others were charged with 48 offences, mainly connected to violence during the Cultural Revolution. They were also accused of plotting to assassinate Mao. Although the trials were widely publicised and televised, the actual records of the trials have not been released. (The difficulty in obtaining reliable source material is a general problem for historians studying such a closed society as modern China.) Unlike the others, Jiang defended herself by arguing throughout that she had simply been following Mao's instructions. One statement she made was: 'I was Chairman Mao's dog. Whomever he told me to bite, I bit.' However, this refusal to admit she had made mistakes, or to confess her guilt, angered many people, and made her even more unpopular.

Question
In what ways were the trials of the Gang of Four similar to the show trials of Stalin's opponents during the 1930s in the Soviet Union?

Jiang was found guilty and sentenced to death, although this was later reduced to life imprisonment. When she was diagnosed with throat cancer, she was transferred to a hospital and, in 1991, she committed suicide. The other members of the Gang suffered similar fates. Zhang also had a death sentence reduced to life imprisonment. In 2002 he became ill, and he died of cancer in 2005. Wang was sentenced to life imprisonment, and died in hospital in 1992. Finally, Yo received a sentence of 20 years. Released in 1996, he died in 2005.

SOURCE G

She argued that she had done everything during the Cultural Revolution 'on behalf of Chairman Mao Zedong' or 'according to his instructions'. Again and again, she repeated these assertions of hers: 'Arresting me and bringing me to trial is a defamation of Chairman Mao Zedong.' 'Defaming Mao through defaming me.' 'I have implemented and defended Chairman Mao's proletarian revolutionary line.' She shrilled, 'During the war I was the only woman comrade who stayed beside Chairman Mao at the front: where were you hiding yourselves then?'

Extracts from an official summary from 1981 of the statement given by Jiang Qing at her trial in 1980. Quoted in A Great Trial in Chinese History. *Beijing, China. New World Press.*

Question
What are the limitations and value of Source G for a historian who is trying to discover what happened at the trials of the Gang of Four? Remember to look at the information provided about the source, as well as its content.

The rise of Deng Xiaoping

Although the trials of the Gang did not take place until 1980–81, the purge of the Gang and their supporters in the party was completed by the end of 1976. Hua was appointed in place of Mao as chairman of the party Several members of the Politburo thought this was unconstitutional, as the party had not initially chosen him. However, in the interests of unity, he was confirmed in that position. The Politburo gave Hua three tasks: to replace Mao; to rehabilitate Deng; and to carry out modernisation. Soon, wall posters began to appear, saying 'Bring Back Deng'.

Deng was supported by the army, and he also had strong support in the party, which cleared him of responsibility for the Tiananmen Square events of 1976. Once he admitted to some political mistakes, Deng was therefore quickly re-appointed to the Politburo.

At the Third Plenum of the 10th Central Committee in July 1977, three important decisions were made that were to shape the Politburo: the Gang were condemned for their views and actions; Hua was made chairman of the party and Military Commission, as well as continuing as premier (prime minister); and Deng was restored to the Standing Committee of the Politburo, and to his positions as vice-chairperson of the Central Committee, vice-premier of the State Council, vice-chairman of the Military Commission, and chief of the general staff of the People's Liberation Army.

Hua then decided that China once again needed to focus its efforts on industrialisation – but this time using very different methods from those used in the past. Significantly, Deng was put in charge of the Four Modernisations (see page 154). This gave him considerable economic and political power. At the same time, the Politburo was reorganised, and three factions emerged – nine supported Hua, nine supported Deng, and three supported Ye. Ye held the balance of power. Thus, where decision-making was unclear, he was often the one who helped make the final decision. Nonetheless, the 11th Congress of the CCP in August 1977, which confirmed the earlier CC decisions, called for 'unity, stability and co-operation' in party affairs.

Demystifying Mao

Hua also had the problem of how to preserve links to Mao, yet also 'remould' some of Mao's statements and policies. This would prepare the way for the significant changes in economic policy demanded by the Rightists. The 'demystification of Mao' was a delicate issue, as too much criticism would risk undermining the whole legacy of the Communist Revolution in China.

Hua began this process by making an official declaration announcing the end of the Cultural Revolution. The next step was completed by January 1981, when the trial of the Gang of Four ended. By 1981, Mao's reputation was being examined critically. The official judgement came in June 1981, at the Sixth Plenum of the 11th CC. Here, a resolution – drafted by Deng – was passed, which judged that Mao had made 'gross mistakes' during the Cultural Revolution. Overall, though, it stated that his mistakes were outweighed by his positive contributions. He was thus judged as being '70% right and 30% wrong'.

Hua and the 'Whateverists'

In 1977, Hua and his supporters had adopted a policy known as the 'Two Whatevers', in response to previous Gang of Four statements and their trial. The 'Two Whatevers' referred to their decision to uphold *whatever* policy decisions Mao had made and to follow *whatever* instructions he had given. This was a tactical mistake, as many in the party now believed that it was necessary to move on from Maoist-type policies and instead adopt more Western-style approaches. At the same time, because Hua had been in power during some of the worst excesses of the Gang, he was increasingly implicated in their activities as their trials took place.

Fact
The 'demystification of Mao' was not as thorough-going as Khrushchev's de-Stalinisation process in the USSR. It was easier for Khrushchev, because it could be demonstrated that Stalin was not a true follower of Lenin. Thus, Khrushchev could claim to be acting in line with Lenin, the founder of the Bolshevik state in 1917. In contrast, Mao represented all that had happened in China since 1949.

Communism in Crisis

> **Question**
>
> Why were Hua and his supporters known as the 'Whateverists'?

> **Fact**
>
> Hua's treatment after his fall indicated China's desire to move away from the usual brutal treatment of those who had lost power struggles in the 1960s. (There was a similar desire to avoid severe punishments in the USSR, following Stalin's death in 1953.) After admitting he had made mistakes, he was allowed to remain as vice-chairman until the post was abolished in 1982. Hua remained a member of the CC until 2002, when he wasten years older than the stated retirement age of 70. He later visited the Party Congress in 2007 as a special delegate.

> **Historical debate**
>
> Since Mao's death, various assessments of his legacy have been made. While many in China still see him as China's greatest 20th-century leader, Western historians have a much more negative view. Even the kindest ones (such as Jonathan Spence and Ross Terrill) tend to dismiss most of what he did after 1949. Yet others, such as Benson, while noting the millions of deaths resulting from some of his policies, point to the fact that much was still achieved. For example, life expectancy increased, from 36 in 1949 to 65 by 1976. Both industry and agriculture expanded under Mao from very low bases. And, as a result of new laws, women achieved equality in education and employment. Despite the upheavals resulting from political campaigns such as the Cultural Revolution, education and literacy also improved a great deal.

Deng and his supporters used all this to undermine Hua's position. In fact, Hua only had limited support because he had never represented either of the two main factions. He had risen to power mainly because he was Mao's preferred successor and also because he did not at first encounter much strong opposition, as he was not aligned with one side or the other.

Deng and the Rightists then began their moves. From 1977, with Deng restored to all his former party positions, Hua was quietly pushed into the background. Deng got his own supporters elected to the CC and the Politburo. Although Hua retained his posts, his real power was increasingly being reduced.

In December 1978, at the Third Plenum of the 11th Central Committee, Deng challenged the 'Whateverist' approach. He made a speech in which he stated that although revolutionary ideology was important in theory, evidence from practice was more important in deciding policies. This new practical approach was necessary if China was to improve living standards for both peasants and industrial workers, find extra resources for improving agriculture and consumer goods, and achieve economic progress.

Deng criticised both Lin Biao and the Gang for trying to establish ideological taboos. The meeting then decided to reappraise Mao and his revolutionary principles. Because this was based on Mao's idea that 'practice is the sole criterion for judging truth', it was an easy step to move on to criticise those who followed the 'Two Whatevers'.

In September 1980, Hua was pressured into resigning as premier, in favour of Zhao Ziyang (who Deng had got into the Politburo in January). In April 1981, Hu Yaobang – another of Deng's close supporters – became general-secretary of the CCP. In June 1981, Hua resigned as party chairman and chair of the Military Commission, and he was later removed from the Politburo. The 12th Congress of the CCP, in September 1982, confirmed these changes. Deng was now clearly China's 'paramount leader', though he mainly operated through his protégés.

These developments marked the close of the Maoist era. Almost all the veteran Chinese communist revolutionaries, who had begun their political struggles with the May 4th Movement in 1919, were now dead. Despite their various, sometimes bitter differences, they had all wanted to make China both modern and socialist. The younger generation of bureaucrats were certainly committed to making China modern, both economically and politically. However, whether they remained committed to the Marxist ideals of socialism leading to communism is a matter of speculation. This will be discussed in the following two chapters.

Activities

1. Write a report for Mao, summarising the strengths and weaknesses of his likely successors, and recommending whom he should support as China's next leader.

2. Carry out further research on how the Gang of Four were brought down. Then write a couple of paragraphs to assess whether their weaknesses, or the strengths of their opponents, played the most important part in their defeat.

3. Write two newspaper reports on the trial of the Gang of Four – one written by a Leftist journalist, and one by a Rightist.

4. Continue with your record of Deng's political career. This time, add information for the years 1976–81.

7 China and the struggle for power after 1976

End of chapter activities

Summary

You should now have a good understanding of developments in China after 1958, and how they led to the rise of opposing factions within the CCP.

You should also be able to explain how Deng Xiaoping and the Rightists were eventually able to defeat the Leftists in the power struggles that took place after 1971.

Summary activity

Copy this diagram. Then, using the information in this chapter and from any other available sources, make brief notes under the headings and sub-headings shown. Remember to include information on historical debate/interpretations – including names of historians.

China 1958–81

1 Mao's policies 1958–70
- The Great Leap Forward
- The Socialist Education Movement
- The Cultural Revolution

2 Power Struggles 1971–75
- Lin Biao
- The Gang of Four

3 Power Struggles 1976–81
- Mao's death
- Defeat of the Gang of Four
- Rise of Deng Xiaoping

Paper 1 exam practice

Question

According to Source A below, what sections of the CCP did the Gang of Four consist of and represent? [2 marks]

Skill

Comprehension of a source

SOURCE A

What the Four did represent was a sector of the post-Cultural Revolution bureaucracy, especially the millions of younger and lower-level cadres who had been admitted to the Party or had risen in rank by virtue of the Cultural Revolution. These were not the genuine radicals of the Cultural Revolution era, all of whom had now vanished in the continuing purge of the ultra-left that had begun in 1967, but rather more the careerists and the opportunists who (like the Four to whom they looked for leadership) had wound their way upward in the political hierarchy by faithfully following all the twists and turns of the Maoist line.

Meisner, M. 1999. *Mao's China and After: A History of the People's Republic*. New York, USA. The Free Press. p. 399.

Before you start

Comprehension questions are the most straightforward questions that you will face in Paper 1. They simply require you to understand a source *and* extract two or three relevant points that relate to the particular question. Before you attempt this question, you should refer to page 215 for advice on how to tackle comprehension questions and a simplified markscheme.

Student answer

According to Source A, the Gang of Four stood for those younger members who had joined the CCP during the Cultural Revolution, and then been promoted to various positions.

Examiner comments

The candidate has selected one relevant and explicit piece of information from the source that clearly and correctly identifies one aspect of the Gang of Four and its supporters. This is enough to gain 1 mark. However, there are other aspects mentioned in the source that have not been discussed in the answer. This candidate therefore fails to get the other mark available.

Activity

Look again at the source, and the student answer above. Now try to identify one other piece of information from the source, and try to make an overall comment about what the source says – this will allow you to obtain the other mark available for this question.

Paper 2 practice questions

1 Examine the ways in which events after 1958 contributed to the development of factions in the Chinese Communist Party in the period before 1971.

2 Analyse the successes and failures of the economic and political policies pursued by Mao in the period 1958–69.

3 'When Mao died in 1976, he left behind a Communist Party which was broadly united on what economic policies to follow.' To what extent do you agree with this assertion?

4 How, and with what results, did the Gang of Four attempt to secure power after Mao's health deteriorated in 1973?

8 The Chinese economy under Deng Xiaoping

Introduction

Within two years of Mao's death, Deng was re-established in the leadership of the CCP. He now became the dominant force in both party and government. As his economic policies were rolled out, it became increasingly clear that many of the aspects known as 'Maoism' were being replaced by what had previously been condemned as the 'capitalist road'. By the time of his death in 1997, Deng had overseen a tremendous restructuring of the Chinese economy, in both agriculture and industry. He had also laid the foundations for China to become a modern country that would be able to successfully compete with advanced Western economies in the world market.

However, there remains a question as to the exact nature of the state that resulted from his policies. Was it still 'communist'? (Some would argue that it never had been truly communist.) Was it 'state capitalist' or did it follow a policy of bureaucratic capitalism? Or was it moving rapidly towards a fully fledged 'red in tooth and claw' brand of authoritarian capitalism? Many assume that capitalism and democracy automatically go hand-in-hand. But regimes such as Nazi Germany, fascist Italy, and several other more recent ones, suggest that capitalism and authoritarianism can go together just as easily.

The debate about what kind of China Deng was creating also raises the question of just how socialist Maoist China had been. Private ownership in the industrial and agricultural economy had effectively ended as early as 1956. Unlike Stalin or Lenin, Mao believed that something more than industrial development was needed to create a socialist and then communist society. This explains his attempts to create the right attitudes amongst the people, in order to prepare them for socialism.

Contradictions developed between modernisation and socialism. In particular, there was a contrast between a powerful, bureaucratised central state, and the workers' self-rule that Marxists thought would result from the 'withering away of the state'. This lack of 'socialist democracy' in Mao's China (though it nevertheless kept alive a socialist vision of the future) indicated that the country had not succeeded in creating the political pre-conditions for socialism. Thus, many historians have preferred to describe China under Mao as 'post-capitalist' rather than socialist. Some have argued that, as China had not become socialist under Mao, Deng was not so much moving China from socialism as moving it even further away – arguably back to capitalism.

Timeline

1977 Aug: Deng's speech for the 'Four Modernisations'

Oct: 28th anniversary of the Chinese Communist Revolution; Hua Guofeng's first economic reforms

1978 Feb: Hua's Ten-Year Plan

Aug: Principles of the Ten-Year Plan and the Four Modernisations incorporated into Party constitution

Dec: Third Plenum of CC/'Open Door' policy announced

1979 Jun: Ten-Year Plan 'modified'

1980 Jun: CC accepts the Household Responsibility System for agriculture

Aug: National People's Congress accepts establishment of first Special Economic Zones

Sep: Hua replaced by Zhao Ziyang as premier; official start of 'one child' policy

1981 Apr: Hu Yaobang appointed general-secretary of CCP

Jun: Sixth Plenum of 11th CC sees start of critical review of Mao's record; Hua resigns as CCP chairman

1982 Sep: 12th Congress of CCP approves Deng's economic plans for Phase 2

1984 Jun: Deng's 'Socialism with Chinese Characteristics' speech

Oct: start of Phase 2 economic reforms

1986 Mar: official announcement of 7th Five-Year Plan

Communism in Crisis

A map showing China's administrative regions and Special Economic Zones, as well as Hong Kong, Macau and Taiwan

Key questions

- What economic policies were followed by Hua in the period from 1976 to 1978?
- What were the main features of Deng's 'Revolution' between 1979 and 1989?
- How successful have Deng's economic reforms been?

Overview

- For most of 1977 and 1978, it seemed that Hua was in control, but Deng was rapidly re-establishing his authority. Most of the economic policies announced by Hua during this period were in fact heavily influenced by Deng and his support for the Four Modernisations.
- In early 1978, Hua announced an ambitious Ten-Year Plan to massively increase both agricultural and industrial production. To a large extent, this was based on the aims of the Four Modernisations.
- In December, the Third Plenum of the Central Committee (CC) saw Deng become dominant; the plenum also approved the 'Open Door' policy on trade with capitalist states. Problems with aspects of Hua's Ten-Year Plan led to it being officially dropped in 1979.

- In 1980, Hua and his main supporters were replaced by those close to Deng. In that year, Deng pushed forward economic reforms such as the Household Responsibility System (HRS) in agriculture, and the establishment of Special Economic Zones.
- In 1982, Deng's policies were approved by the 12th Congress of the CCP. He then began planning for Phase 2, and this began officially in 1984.
- In 1986, a new Five-Year Plan was officially launched by Deng.
- Deng's reforms in agriculture and industry during the period 1978–89 led to significant increases in production, and to increased trade. However, they also resulted in national indebtedness and poverty for many in rural and especially urban areas.

What economic policies were followed by Hua in the period from 1976 to 1978?

According to Maurice Meisner, the Maoist economic record, though flawed, compared favourably with similar stages in the industrialisation of Germany, Japan and Russia, which had previously been seen as the most successful examples of late modernisation. This was an especially notable achievement, as it was largely the result of China's own efforts, with little or no outside assistance. (China did not even receive help from the Soviet Union, due to Sino–Soviet tensions in the early 1960s.)

The Four Modernisations

After the overthrow of the Gang of Four, Deng (in theory under Hua's direction) began to implement the economic policies associated with the Four Modernisations. These were intended to overcome some of the problems resulting from the Great Leap Forward and the Cultural Revolution, and to make the Chinese economy more efficient and productive. It was hoped that successful reform would result in renewed support for the party.

The Four Modernisations focused on four areas of the economy: agriculture, industry, science and technology, and the military. One essential difference between these policies and those that had often been implemented before 1976 was that they were based more on pragmatism than ideology.

As well as affecting domestic economic policy, this approach also involved the linked issue of foreign trade and relations with Western capitalist states. The relationship with the West had been an important factor in the struggle between Leftists and Rightists during the late 1960s and early 1970s, and had resulted in the fall of Lin Biao.

China's economy in 1976

Despite some real economic gains under Mao, by 1976 the Chinese economy faced many of the same problems as the Soviet Union and the Eastern European states. All these regimes suffered from inefficiency, technological backwardness, waste, low productivity, overstaffing and bureaucratic stagnation. While the political struggle (between Hua and the 'Whateverists', and Deng and the Rightists) was taking place in the period 1976–81, both factions attempted to address some of China's economic problems. There was some agreement between both groups on the general economic policies that were needed. Essentially, the intention was to implement the Four Modernisations by adopting more pragmatic economic policies.

Fact
The Four Modernisations were first put forward in the 1960s by Deng, and more recently by Zhou in 1975 (see Chapter 7). Deng then issued three documents setting out more specific ways in which to achieve Zhou's aims. The Gang of Four attacked Deng and his documents as deviationist, renaming them the 'Three Poisonous Weeds'. Once the Gang had been overthrown, Deng and his pragmatic supporters began to re-introduce these ideas.

Fact
In 1976, China's problems included 20 million unemployed, 100 million undernourished, and a 6.5 billion *yuan* deficit. In addition, science, technology and the military were all old-fashioned, compared to the advanced countries. All this had led to significant disenchantment amongst many Chinese citizens.

Fact
The general post-Maoist view of those like Deng was that Mao had sacrificed 'modernisation' to 'ideological purity', and that he had sidelined economic development in the rush to build a socialist utopia. However, according to historians such as Maurice Meisner, this idea is misguided. Deng's criticisms of Mao dwelt on the deficiencies rather than what was achieved. During Mao's rule, the value of gross industrial output grew 38-fold, and heavy industry 90-fold. Between 1952 and 1977, the output of Chinese industry increased at an average annual rate of 11.3%. This was as rapid a pace of industrialisation as has ever been achieved by any country during a comparable period in modern world history.

Communism in Crisis

early Maoism This type of Maoism pre-dated the Great Leap Forward. So, for instance, in culture and education (in something similar to the 'Hundred Flowers' campaign) Hua permitted previously banned films, operas and plays to be shown again. He also allowed the reappearance of certain literary and scholarly journals, and permitted the publication of short stories by young writers (known as the 'wounded generation') that described their experiences during the Cultural Revolution.

Fact
Under Hua, agricultural productivity increased by 8.9% in 1978, and by 8.6% in 1979. This was *before* Deng's Household Responsibility System (HRS) policy had been introduced (see page 171). Deng's system was not widely adopted until the early 1980s.

Hua's approach was based on the acceptance of Zhou's comments in 1975 that revolutionary principles, if applied too rigorously, could cause economic growth to slow down or even cease altogether. Thus, while publicly expressing continued support for Maoism, Hua quietly abandoned several aspects of late Maoism. Instead, he reverted to a modified 1950s form of **early Maoism**.

Unfortunately for Hua, this more relaxed approach allowed the emergence of an increasingly influential pro-Deng and anti-Maoist (and thus anti-Hua) body of opinion. While this weakened Hua, it strengthened Deng. This helped Deng in the mostly behind-the-scenes struggle between his 'Practice' faction and the Hua 'Whateverist' faction.

Hua's economic policies

Initially, Hua decided to concentrate on agriculture, and several conferences were held in 1977 to decide what to do. Peasant family plots were restored and increased, and subsidies increased, to boost agricultural production.

In industry, wage differentials and greater specialisation were introduced for the same purpose. There was also a 10% wage increase for all, announced on 1 October 1977, at the 28th anniversary of the Communist Revolution.

SOURCE A

Extracts from an Open Letter, dated 1 October 1977, by Neil Burton, a Canadian working in China, to Charles Bettelheim, a French economics professor, on the likely course of events in China following the defeat of the Gang of Four. Both Burton and Bettelheim were supporters of Mao, but came to differ over what Deng's intentions were. Bettelheim had resigned as president of the Franco–Chinese Friendship Association because of his concerns about the policies of the new leadership of the CCP.

And let's not be too quick to label those [leaders of the CCP] who do not quite measure up ... as 'revisionists,' 'capitalist roaders,' or what have you ... the present leadership ... is at this very moment implementing new regulations to alleviate the economic insecurity of city-dwellers in the lowest income categories through a re-adjustment of wage scales.

In your letter you raise the specter of the advances of the Cultural Revolution being wiped away. Some of its products will indeed be dropped, others modified – some for the right reasons, some not. And since classes and class struggle are going to be with us for some time to come, it's even conceivable that a revisionist line – a real revisionist line – might gain the upper hand for a time ... But could the really important gains of the Cultural Revolution ever be submerged for long? Not a chance! ... They infuse Chairman Hua Kuo-feng's speeches.

Quoted in Bettelheim, C. and Burton, N. 1978. *China Since Mao*. New York, USA. Monthly Review Press. pp. 34–35.

Question
Given the origin and possible purpose of this source, what are its value and limitations for historians trying to study Deng's intentions in the period 1976–78?

Question
Can you identify the 'capitalist roaders' referred to in Source A?

Even at this stage, Hua's economic policies were largely based on policy documents that Deng had drawn up in the autumn of 1975, before his temporary fall in 1976. These policies included a big increase in the amount of modern technology that China purchased abroad, from foreign suppliers. But Hua also claimed to be continuing Mao's legacy. In early 1977, he proclaimed his 'Whateverist' position. This, too, eventually played a part in Hua's downfall.

The Ten-Year Plan

When Deng fell from favour in 1976, as a result of the Qingming Festival (see page 156), the introduction of further and deeper reform was put on hold. However, by 1977 (when Deng was again restored to his positions), there were already some changes in direction. These in turn led to further political changes. Under Hua, at the 11th Party Congress in August 1977, Deng made a speech reiterating the importance of the Four Modernisations.

> **Fact**
> Linking himself to Mao proved to be a mistake on Hua's part, as most senior people in the party, government and army had been unhappy about the Cultural Revolution. They increasingly supported Deng, who wanted to give some justice to its victims. Yet Hua's main support base was precisely those in the lower levels who had risen during the Cultural Revolution. At first, Hua and Deng were united in bringing down the Gang of Four. However, once this had been accomplished in 1976, there was little to keep them together, and Deng's supporters were stronger and more numerous than Hua's.

Chinese leaders at the 11th Party Congress (from left to right): Hua Guofeng, Yeh Chien-ying, Deng Xiaoping, Li Hsien-nien and Wanf Tung-hsing

In February 1978, Hua announced an ambitious new Ten-Year Plan, to cover the period 1976–85. This was designed to implement the 'Four Modernisations', and its basic principles were incorporated into the party constitution in August 1978. This economic plan was largely based on a document drafted for the State Council by Deng in 1975. It focused on specific sectors of China's economy, especially heavy industry, in which state control would retain socialist principles. Meanwhile, there would be a relaxation of such principles in smaller enterprises.

The intention was to create 120 massive industrial projects. Targets were set for the period 1978–85, with the aim of greatly increasing production. For example, steel production had fallen significantly as a result of the Great Leap Forward. It had been 21 million tons in 1973, but was to increase to 60 million tons by 1985, and to 180 million tons by 1999. High targets were also set for oil, petroleum, coal and non-ferrous metals, electricity, railways and water transportation. It would require massive public works to provide the necessary infrastructure to meet these ambitious targets.

Communism in Crisis

Fact
Stalin had also realised that modernisation of agriculture was vital in the USSR during the late 1920s.

Improving irrigation and mechanisation would make agriculture more efficient, which would release workers for industry. According to Hua, China's industry would catch up with the world's most advanced nations by 2000.

Significantly, Deng was put in charge of carrying out these reforms, and he soon announced that 100,000 construction projects would be implemented, at a cost of 54 billion *yuan*. However, the targets were too ambitious and the costs too high. Hua had not developed any plan to raise the massive sums needed to invest in this expansion. The first year alone had cost 37% of GDP – and this was too high a figure for the government to sustain. Consequently, the Ten-Year Plan soon proved unworkable. Its problems played a significant role in Hua's downfall and the rise of Deng – even though Deng had been closely associated with the plan.

The end of the Ten-Year Plan

The Third Plenum of the CC in December 1978 was a turning point, as Deng was appointed chairman of the People's Political Consultative Conference. As well as confirming his return to top-level politics, this post was crucial as it carried the main responsibility for implementing conomic reform. The meeting also saw a significant number of Deng's supporters elected to the CC and the Politburo. This gave Deng effective control of both these bodies and thus of the party as a whole.

Question
Why was Deng's appointment as chairman of the People's Political Consultative Conference so important?

Most of Hua's supporters at first remained in post, but they lost many of their main economic and political responsibilities. The Third Plenum of December 1978 also accepted Deng's own plan to implement the Four Modernisations, which stepped up and then replaced Hua's economic policies. Thus, Deng's economic reform programme effectively began in 1979. The most dramatic indication of Deng's supremacy in economics came in June 1979, when the Ten-Year Plan was dropped.

SOURCE B

The Third Plenum of the Central Committee of the CCP … proved to be a landmark in China's post-Mao reformation. The decisions reached at the plenum meant a new departure for the People's Republic of China … [The] resolutions of the Third Plenum clearly meant that the Cultural Revolution had been abandoned. Deng Xiaoping's personal success at the plenum, in obtaining the full support of the CCP for his proposals, also showed that he was now the outstanding figure in Chinese politics. This was soon recognised by the CCP by its conferring on him the honorary title of 'paramount leader'. This had no specific functions attached to it but was all the more powerful because of that. He feigned humility by declining to accept formal positions while knowing that he had the influence and connections to remain in control of developments. He was now in a position to begin what was to become known as the Deng revolution.

Lynch, M. 2008. *The People's Republic of China, 1949–76*. London, UK. Hodder Education. pp. 156–57.

Activities

1. Carry out some further research on Hua's economic policies, and those favoured by Deng. Then draw up a table to summarise the differences and similarities.

2. Write a short report that: (a) explains what the Four Modernisations were; and (b) presents arguments showing why China needed to adopt them in 1976.

3. With a partner, carry out some further research, and then produce two posters: one arguing that Mao's emphasis on attitudes was the best way of achieving socialism; the other showing that economic development and increased efficiency were the most important aspects.

4. Produce a spider diagram to summarise the main economic policies and developments in China from 1976 to 1979.

8 The Chinese economy under Deng Xiaoping

What were the main features of Deng's 'Revolution' between 1979 and 1989?

Deng's main approach to economics was pragmatic, and several slogans were associated with the period of his influence, which lasted until 1992. These included: 'It doesn't matter if a cat is black or white, as long as it catches mice'; 'To get rich is glorious'; and 'Not introducing reforms will take us down a blind alley'. The evidence suggests that a *democratic socialist* alternative to the centralised command economy was never seriously considered. Instead, there were various schemes for economic decentralisation, and the introduction – to a greater or lesser extent – of **'market' mechanisms**.

Deng's economic approach

In June 1979, Deng persuaded the government to announce a three-year period in which some aspects of the Ten-Year Plan would be 'modified'. However, the main aspects of the Four Modernisations would be retained.

> **'market' mechanisms** According to Meisner, Deng's aim was not to restore capitalism, but to decentralise the inefficient command economy in order to gradually create the conditions for socialism. Many of Deng's supporters were encouraged by the reform communists in Hungary and Yugoslavia, who had adopted 'socialist market' models. These regimes had apparently introduced market mechanisms without weakening party control of the 'commanding heights' of the economy. As previous chapters have shown, though, this approach soon led to a weakening of political control over their citizens.

SOURCE C

Major problems faced the new Deng administration: the government now had a 6.5 billion yuan deficit; 20 million Chinese were unemployed; and an estimated 100 million were undernourished. The military was woefully out of date, as was China's own technology and scientific research. Thousands of CCP members and wide segments of the population questioned the decisions of the Party leadership … If the legacy of the [Maoist] revolutionaries was to mean anything, new approaches to China's many problems were imperative … Deng and his supporters realized that without economic advances, the future position of the CCP would be untenable.

Benson, L. 2002. *China Since 1949*. Harlow, UK. Longman. p. 46.

SOURCE D

Thus, in the discussions among Communist leaders and intellectuals in the politically victorious Deng camp around the time of the Third Plenum, a genuinely socialist alternative to the command economy was never seriously considered. Only reformist measures which could be accommodated within the existing political system were discussed. These included various schemes for economic decentralization and the introduction of market mechanisms …

The decentralization of economic administration and decision making … posed no threat to general Communist rule … Nor was the market the mortal threat to the Communist political system that it was assumed to be by many foreign observers …

That a market economy inevitably breeds capitalist social relationships, and all the inequitable consequences of capitalism, was well known to China's Communist leaders in the late 1970s. But Deng Xiaoping and his reformist associates did not envision a capitalist future for China … most did not champion a market economy or a capitalist regime because of their intrinsic virtues. Rather, they saw the mechanism of the market as a means to eventual socialist ends, as the most efficient way to break down the stifling system of centralized state planning and to speed up the development of modern productive forces, thereby creating the essential material foundations for a future socialist society.

Meisner, M. 1991. *Mao's China and After: A History of the People's Republic*. New York, USA. The Free Press. pp. 451–52.

Communism in Crisis

> **Historical debate**
>
> There continues to be considerable debate about the ultimate aims of Deng and his supporters. Some historians, such as Carl Riskin, stress the number of Deng's supporters who seemed captivated by the 'wonders of the market'. Meanwhile, Charles Bettelheim argues that Deng was intent on moving back to capitalism. However, others (such as Meisner) argue strongly that, while Deng had no intention of building socialist democracy in China, he also had no desire to restore capitalism.

This time, however, Deng wanted to concentrate on agriculture, light industry and consumer goods, rather than heavy industry. In particular, he believed that encouraging farmers and factory workers to become rich, and allowing them more freedom and initiative, would ensure that they worked harder. This would in turn help increase production and efficiency. Like Andropov and later Gorbachev (his Soviet counterparts), Deng also believed that for these economic reform plans to work, it would be necessary to reduce the central bureaucracy's power over some aspects of the planning system. The aim was to make the state bureaucracy the servant, rather than the master, of the economy.

Implementing the Four Modernisations

To put his long-held ideas for economic reform into practice, Deng readjusted the Ten-Year Plan's goals: 348 heavy industry projects, and 4800 smaller ones, were put on hold, though many of the core ideas were retained. In particular, he decided to concentrate on short-term projects that could earn foreign capital, which would then be used to finance other projects. This approach was facilitated by Zhou and Mao's decision, in the early 1970s, to open up relations with the US and the West. It thus became possible for China to export goods to non-communist countries, and to receive some foreign investment capital for its own projects. This generated extra capital to make more improvements, though there were still problems with energy and transportation.

These changes were accompanied by various techniques, which began to raise the question of whether or not the new leaders of China were still communists at all. (For further discussion of how Deng's policies related to the principles of communism or capitalism, see page 175.)

These techniques included allowing incentives and bonuses; permitting peasant farmers to grow crops on small leased commune plots, and to sell any surplus produce for profit to the state; and also allowing more scope for individual initiatives in the industrial and scientific sectors. By 1996, China's State Statistical Bureau reported that 29% of enterprises (25 million businesses in total) were privately owned and operated; and that 1 in 12 Chinese workers were employed in these enterprises, which produced China's first multi-millionaires (up to 5% of private owners had incomes over 10 million yuan). The following sections will focus on the two Modernisations that relate to the economy: agriculture and industry.

Agriculture

After the initial setbacks involving the industrial aspects of the Ten-Year Plan, the leadership decided that agriculture was the economic sector most in need of modernisation. This area became Deng's main concern during the period 1978–84. Although China's population had increased rapidly between 1955 and 1977, and thus so too had total grain production, the per capita figure for grain was still at the same level. In addition, 80% of China's people were still based in the countryside, making China still a largely agricultural economy.

A more efficient and productive form of agriculture would release people to work in the factories. The leadership therefore wanted peasants to move away from traditional methods (based on extensive manual labour), and instead to adopt mechanised farming. To assist these moves, incentives, and plans for diversification, were approved.

8 The Chinese economy under Deng Xiaoping

The first steps were taken in December 1978, when the vast communes (set up in 1958 by the Great Leap Forward) were broken up into smaller production units. The policy of collectivisation was maintained. This had been a core element of the 1949 Revolution and, although not very efficient, could not easily be abandoned. However, Deng began to persuade the bureaucrats that the production units should be allowed more freedom to make decisions. He also substantially raised the subsidies and prices paid to farmers for their agricultural products.

Central planning continued, with the government setting targets and quotas and issuing directives on how to achieve greater productivity. The plan was to increase agricultural production by 4–5% per year, and to increase food production to 400 million tons by 1985. The plan also aimed to mechanise 85% of farming, promote a greater use of chemical fertilisers, and to improve irrigation of fields. In addition, the government wanted to improve the distribution of food products – so 12 commodity and food base areas were created.

Household Responsibility System (HRS)

In 1979, the government resurrected a plan from the 1950s, which had been stopped by Mao. This, the Household Responsibility System (HRS), was officially adopted by the June 1980 CC meeting – and has been seen as the first attempt to introduce capitalism into the countryside. Deng ensured that one of his closest supporters, Wan Li, was put in charge of the new plan. At first, Wan applied it to the Anhui province. After it proved successful there, it was applied to the whole country.

Though there was still no private ownership of land, by means of the HRS each farming family would be able to rent a plot of commune land they could use – to an extent – as they wanted. In late 1982, a new state constitution transferred the administrative functions of communes to township or county governments, as new units of central state administration. These were called *xiang*.

Families signed an annual contract with their local *xiang* to provide a certain amount of work, and to plant a specified amount and type of crops. A fixed quota would then go back to the commune, in return for being able to lease the land. In 1984, the lease was increased to 15 years. Families would control their own labour any way they wished, and were free to keep or sell any surplus produce, either to the commune or in the local market.

In 1980, the government decided to set aside 15% of agricultural land for this scheme of family plots, instead of the previous 5%. This effectively resulted in the virtual dismantling of the communes established by the Great Leap Forward, with farmers gaining more and more control over the land they farmed. Although it began as a voluntary scheme, it soon became compulsory.

By 1983, over 90% of farming households were involved in the scheme, and it was official policy 'to make the peasants rich'. (This was similar to the USSR where, under the NEP in the 1920s, peasants were told to 'enrich yourselves'.) These changes led to a significant rise in living standards for the rural population, although there were regional variations. In 1983, the government allowed families to rent out 'their' lease – and also allowed farmers and workshop owners to hire wage labourers. Thus, new classes of sub-tenants and wage labourers reappeared in rural China, after having been abolished under Mao.

xiang These bodies effectively replaced the communes. Each *xiang* still had to meet state food production quotas, but this was now to be done by individuals and their families, who contributed their share of the local quota. Once they had met this, and paid their taxes, they were free to sell any surplus produce for private profit.

Question

What were the main characteristics of the Household Responsibility System?

Communism in Crisis

> **Fact**
> In practice, 'improving the attitudes' of the workers meant getting them to give up their relatively privileged position regarding job security, wages and subsidies.

> **Zhao Ziyang (1919–2005)**
> Zhao was one of the younger generation of communists who joined the party during the Second World War. He rose rapidly and was appointed to the province of Sichuan, which had suffered badly during the Cultural Revolution. In 1975, he began to implement successful reforms aimed at increasing food supplies. These reforms were known as the 'contract responsibility system', based on leasing commune land to individual families. He came to favour privatising state enterprises. Zhao's support for the students protesting in Tiananmen Square in 1989 led to his dismissal. He was then effectively placed under house arrest.

A 'free market', where families could sell their own farm produce, in Kashi, a city in Xinjiang, western China

Industry

Deng hoped that the Ten-Year Plan would result in a vastly improved infrastructure. The aim was also to reach a level of industrialisation that at least equalled the industrialisation that had taken place in China in the decades after 1949. In addition, the leadership wanted to catch up with, and even exceed, the industrial development of the advanced capitalist states in the West. However, industry proved more difficult to reform than agriculture. This was partly because the industrial workers had been the main beneficiaries of the 1949 Communist Revolution. Each worker was hired as part of a *danwei* (work unit), and could ensure that his children would be employed when they were old enough. This led to high job security, reasonable wages, and social wage benefits such as subsidised housing, medical care, pensions and other benefits.

Deng's economic reforms in industry involved two phases: Phase 1, 1978–84, and Phase 2, which began in October 1984.

Phase 1, 1978–84

This set of reforms was partly intended to 'improve the attitudes' of industrial workers, and involved moving away from detailed central planning to less restrictive guidelines. The process was overseen by **Zhao Ziyang**, another strong supporter of Deng. He had been party secretary in Sichuan province, where he had applied a 'responsibility' system similar to the one that Wan Li was introducing in agriculture. According to this system, once they had met their quotas, individual families could sell their surplus at newly established 'free markets'. This became known as the 'Sichuan Experiment'.

Zhao's success in Sichuan led him to be appointed to the State Council in 1980. In September 1980, he became premier in place of Hua Guofeng, who slipped into the background. Zhao's methods were then applied to industry. Over 400,000 factories were given more 'responsibility' (i.e. more freedom and independence) to set wages and prices, and produce goods, which the state would then buy. Any surplus above the set quota could be sold for a profit. This policy was later applied to China as a whole.

Similar to the Household Responsibility System in agriculture, the Industrial Responsibility System created by the government was based on creating a supervisory body for each State-Owned Enterprise (SOE). Each SOE had a contractual agreement, under which part of the production and/or profits would go to the state, with the surplus being kept by the SOE. This created an incentive to improve productivity. Later, contracts were used to try to address the issue of quality as well. By 1980, 6600 reformed SOEs had been created. However, workers were dubious about the reforms, as the previous system had provided them with job security, along with many social benefits such as housing and medical care. Even factory managers were not keen on the idea of a market-based system – especially those in heavy industry.

The 'open door' policy

It soon became obvious that China's economy alone could not generate all the capital investment funds needed to fulfil the ambitious goals of the Ten-Year Plan. The earlier re-establishment of cordial relations with the US, resulting from Nixon's visit in 1972, was therefore very helpful.

President Nixon and Mao greeting each other in Beijing in 1972

When the UN formally recognised the People's Republic of China in October 1971 (as the US no longer vetoed it), China's isolation ended. Moves were now made to open China up even further to Western countries. It is this area of trade that really supports the argument that China was gradually becoming capitalist. Between 1971 and 1974, China's foreign trade increased by more than 300% – most of it with non-communist countries. Foreign trade increased even further under Hua's rule. From 1978 to 1988, under Deng's supervision, it increased by over 400%. It then rose by a further 400% from 1988 to 1994.

In December 1978, the party adopted the 'open door' policy, to open China up to the world even more. By engaging in trade with the West, China could earn cash from exports. It could also develop and/or import science, technology, capital and managerial skills. Deng and his supporters decided to diversify exports, raise the quality of goods, devalue the yuan, and build up currency reserves. Later, in 1980, China secured its first loans from the International Monetary Fund and the World Bank. This provided money to upgrade industrial machinery and set up new enterprises.

Many other nations quickly saw the advantages of moving into the massive new Chinese market – first Japan and Taiwan, soon followed by West Germany and the US. Hong Kong, with its special status and connections to both China and the West, was able to take advantage of this new policy.

China's leaders still felt that more foreign capital was needed for the country's economy to be fully modernised and expanded. While trying to maintain state ownership of the 'commanding heights' of the economy, they therefore tried various ways to encourage Western firms to invest in China. However, it was decided that all joint ventures with foreign firms had to be at least 50% Chinese-owned. This would allow China to retain control over its economy.

Fact
Hong Kong Island had been a British colony since the First Opium War (1839–42). In 1860, following the Second Opium War, Britain also took control of the Kowloon Peninsula. In 1898, Britain took a lease on the New Territories to the north. These three regions together made up the British colony of Hong Kong. The 99-year lease eventually expired in 1997. At this point, China regained sovereignty, under a policy of 'one country, two systems'. Hong Kong became one of two Special Administrative Regions (SARs) in China – the other being Macau. Foreign joint venture companies in Hong Kong and Macau were encouraged to set up factories in mainland China. By adopting capitalist-friendly policies, Deng hoped Taiwan (which had been ruled by the Nationalists since 1949, and which also had a thriving market economy) might eventually be returned to China.

Question
Why was the 'open door' policy seen as being important for China's rapid economic development?

Special Economic Zones

In 1979, the government also created Special Economic Zones (SEZs) in coastal areas in the south of China. Here, economic policies were more 'liberal' (in other words, more friendly to capitalist economic mechanisms) than in the rest of the country. This included special tax concessions: 15% tax was waived for the first two years of profitability, and there were 50% exemptions for years three and four; and no import duties were applied to production materials or equipment. These zones were almost like 'states within a state', as they were given regional autonomy. Non-residents needed special permission and an internal passport to travel to them. This was because Deng was aware that the SEZs would become more and more like capitalist Hong Kong, and that workers there would come into contact with Western ideas. He wanted to ensure that 'bad influences' (such as democracy) would not spread to the rest of the country.

Inside the SEZs, the government built roads, railways and port facilities to help attract foreign companies. These foreign organisations liked the idea of a large pool of disciplined, educated and relatively cheap workers, and the promise of profit-friendly regulations and policies.

The aim of these zones was to increase the chances of direct foreign investment and expand the importation of advanced modern technology. The zones also gave China access to important world export markets. In addition, it was hoped that local Chinese managers (including those who had studied abroad) would learn the latest management methods from these foreign firms. Meanwhile, workers would learn how to use the latest technology and machinery.

The first four SEZs were established in 1979, in the Guangdong and Fujian provinces. They were in Shenzhen (just across the border with Hong Kong) and Zhuhai (near Macau) in the south; and in Shantou and Xaimen (across from Taiwan) in the north. These were approved by the National People's Congress in August 1980. In the 1980s, a fifth zone was established on Hainan Island, off the southern coast.

Criticism and Deng's response

These policy directions led to a resurgence of concerns about 'taking the capitalist road' in the party. Several leaders feared that they would lead to the restoration of capitalism. Others feared that foreign domination of China would soon reappear. (The ending of foreign domination had been one of the main achievements of the 1949 Chinese Communist Revolution.)

In 1980, Deng responded to this growing criticism by resigning his formal positions of power, officially on account of his age, thereby forcing potential opponents to do the same. In this way, he was able to remove from power those who opposed his economic policies. Their places were taken by younger, more pragmatically minded leaders (see Chapter 9). However, Deng remained incredibly powerful, as the behind-the-scenes 'paramount leader'.

Deng's approach seems to have been based on the Marxist view that capitalism provides the base for the construction of socialism. In fact, as early as September 1956, at the 8th Party Congress, Deng argued that class divisions (and thus class struggle) had been virtually eliminated. He claimed that all that was left to deal with was China's backward productive forces in order to be able to move on to advanced socialism.

Fact
During the 19th century, under the emperors, China had come under increasing domination by Western powers such as Britain, Japan, France and the US. Nationalist concerns had led to the 'Double Tenth' Revolution, which had overthrown the last emperor. However, under the nationalists, foreign influence had continued. To some, the Special Economic Zones seemed very like the old treaty ports. These were Chinese ports that had been forced to open up to Western trade under very unfavourable conditions, for instance after the Opium Wars. Such problems had led to the May 4th Movement, after China had been further weakened by the peace treaties that had ended the First World War.

8 The Chinese economy under Deng Xiaoping

Indeed Deng's power was consolidated by the events of 1981, which included the ending of the trial of the Gang of Four. The passing of the resolution that Mao was '70% right and 30% wrong' made it possible to move forward and away from Maoism; and Deng's power was further strengthened by Hua's resignation as party chairman (see Chapter 9). By 1982, when Deng had secured full control of both party and government, he was able to push ahead with the policies he favoured. These were intended to make China wealthier and so enable the country to advance to full socialism.

Communism or capitalism?

To achieve his aims, Deng favoured introducing aspects of a 'free' market economy, which would enable China to compete with the West in production and economic efficiency. He therefore pushed for Western-style, capitalist industrial policies.

However, this does not necessarily mean that Deng and his supporters were capitalists, even though they were accused of this by the Maoists and Leftists in the period before 1976. In many ways, the policies adopted by China's leaders after 1976 were similar to those of Lenin's NEP, or Stalin's 'Stakhanovite' movement. Both these Soviet policies had used incentives and bonuses to increase productivity. Indeed Marx (and until Lenin's death in 1924, Soviet communist leaders) had always said that socialism could only emerge in developed capitalist economies.

Deng's approach was based on the concept of 'economics in control', rather than the Maoist idea of 'politics in control'. In other words, economic pragmatism was more important than political dogma (or 'Practice' versus 'Whatever'). In September 1982, the 12th Congress of the CCP approved Deng's economic plans, as well as various personnel changes. He was then in a position to introduce the second phase of his plans for industry.

Industry Phase 2, 1984–89

In October 1984, the 'Resolution on the Reform of the Economic System' began Phase 2. This further reduced state control over enterprises, though they remained under public ownership. Deng also made it clear that unprofitable enterprises would be closed down. To make profits easier, the state tax on enterprise revenues was reduced from 55% to 33% in 1983–84.

This emphasised that ownership and management were two separate aspects, and that managers could be given some freedom in selecting ways to improve production. In particular, it allowed private groups to lease small and medium-sized enterprises, though the largest ones remained under direct government control. The government also introduced a legal framework that protected private investment. This meant that more people were prepared to put money into enterprises. As the incomes of many people increased during this early period, there was an increased demand for more consumer goods, which provided a stimulus for small family-based enterprises.

Fact
Deng's reforms were similar to those of the reform communists in the USSR and Eastern Europe, who also tried to modernise the socialist system in their countries. Deng's argument was that China still had a legacy from its feudal past. However, there is an ongoing debate as to whether China has now become a capitalist country in all but name.

Hu Yaobang and Zhao Ziyang (chief architect of China's reforms), in Beijing, 9 September 1982

Discussion point
Does the use of market mechanisms, and allowing the existence of privately owned enterprises, automatically mean that China's economy has become a fully developed capitalist state, or will soon become one? To answer this, you will need to do some research on key terminology and definitions.

The 7th Five-Year Plan

In June 1984, Deng made a speech at a meeting with a Japanese delegation, in which he said that China was 'building socialism with a specifically Chinese character'.

In 1985, Deng drew up a 7th Five-Year Plan, to cover the period 1986–90, with slightly different goals from those in the 1984 Resolution. This plan was officially announced in March 1986. In particular, he said he had three main aims:

1. to give more autonomy to state enterprises, and place more emphasis on making a profit
2. to 'smash the **iron rice bowl**', and so increase workers' productivity by introducing the fear of unemployment
3. to allow prices of goods (especially food and consumer goods) to be determined by 'market forces'.

The plan was based on the idea of removing state subsidies. This would force state enterprises to become competitive and profitable, which would in turn make them cut costs and increase productivity. However, this would be at the cost of workers' wages and jobs. To underline the need for competition between state enterprises, new short-term state contracts replaced the longer-term ones.

Deng's approach was based on observing that when younger and reform-minded party officials had been given greater freedom to try new approaches, the results had been mostly spectacular. This was especially true in the provinces of Sichuan and Guangdong.

His main aims, as set out in the new plan, were to:

- increase gross agricultural and industrial output by 38% over the five-year period of the plan – at an average growth rate of 6.7% per year (4% for agriculture and 7.5% for industry)
- increase gross national output by 44%, at a yearly average of 7.5%
- increase import and export volumes by 35% by 1990
- expand both foreign investment and the import of advanced technology
- increase consumption for China's population by 5% a year
- spread the nine-year compulsory education system, in order to train 5 million professionals – twice the level of the previous plan.

However, as Gorbachev discovered in the USSR, having ambitious plans does not mean that they can be implemented. Nor, if they are implemented, does it necessarily mean that they will be successful.

Activities

1. Complete your record of Deng's career, by covering the period 1981–89.
2. Carry out some further research on the main economic policies that China followed in the 1980s. Then draw up a table to summarise the main points under these three headings: Agriculture | Industry | Foreign trade and investment.
3. Split into two groups. One group should develop arguments to support, and the other to oppose, the following statement:

---

iron rice bowl This phrase meant job and wage security for industrial workers. The word 'iron' meant 'long-lasting', and the 'rice bowl' referred to living standards. Along with the idea of a social wage and subsidised prices for food, electricity and rent, full employment had always been one of the main principles of communism. It had also been part of Mao's Great Leap Forward. As discussed in previous chapters, it became an important issue in the USSR and Eastern Europe, when reform communists tried to introduce various market mechanisms into their economies.

'Deng's speech to Japanese businessmen in June 1984 shows that he was still a communist, and that capitalism would not be restored in China.'

4 Carry out further research on the SEZs. In particular, see what you can find out about wages and working conditions in these areas, and compare your findings with the situation in the rest of China.

How successful have Deng's economic reforms been?

According to official government figures, Deng's reforms have been highly successful. While this seems to be largely true, the overall results have been mixed. Government statistics claim an average annual growth rate of 11% for agriculture and industry. In 1985, China's GNP was 778 billion *yuan*. In certain sectors of the economy, the growth rates were even higher – especially in the heavy industry areas of steel, coal, oil and electricity. By 1985, government investment in publicly owned enterprises had reached 530 billion *yuan*.

Agriculture

Deng had argued that any significant reform of the Chinese economy would have to start with agriculture. Under him, the family came to replace the commune as the economic unit of production. Farmers were now rewarded by how hard they worked for themselves and their families, rather than for the community as a whole.

According to official statistics, agricultural productivity increased by 15%, above the targets set by the Ten-Year Plan; and 5% of that increase was due to the HRS policy. Production increased by an average of 6.7% each year, and grain output rose to 500 billion kilograms in 1996. This made China the largest agricultural producer in the world – based on the world's largest smallholder farming system. In view of the successes of the HRS, it has continued in this way to the present.

SOURCE E

China's agricultural statistics, 1978–89

Year	Grain production (millions of tonnes)	Meat production (millions of tonnes)	Index of gross output compared to base of 100 in 1952
1978	304.8	8.6	229.6
1979	332.1	10.6	249.4
1980	320.6	12.1	259.1
1981	325.0	12.6	276.2
1982	354.5	13.5	306.8
1983	387.3	14.0	330.7
1984	407.3	15.4	373.1
1985	379.1	17.6	385.7
1986	391.5	19.2	398.9
1987	404.7	19.9	422.0
1988	394.1	21.9	438.5
1989	407.8	23.3	452.0

From Lynch, M. 2008. *The People's Republic of China 1949–76*. London, UK. Hodder Education. p. 160. Reproduced by permission.

Township and Village Enterprises (TVEs)

These results allowed more farmers to leave their family plots. However, they mostly stayed local, becoming involved in developing local factories or reviving local crafts. These are known as Township and Village Enterprises (TVEs).

By 1989, these new small-scale industries accounted for 58% of the total value of rural output. Over 25% of TVEs were run by rural women, allowing them to make a huge contribution to family incomes. Overall, by 1984, official figures claimed that 4 million people were employed or self-employed in these industries, with more than 32 million in urban collective enterprises.

It was through these, rather than through standard farming, that rural living standards initially improved. Yet most of these TVEs are in fact owned by and/or managed by private capitalists and local governments, all operating on a capitalist basis in both the national and international markets.

De-collectivisation

Agricultural land use in China had clearly been privatised. However, land *ownership* – in theory – has not, as land remains in state hands. Once leases expire, the land reverts to the state. For this reason, many people were reluctant to put much effort into improving their land, or to invest in long-term projects to give better yields. As a result, many farmers stuck to traditional methods, rather than embracing the modern equipment and techniques the government wanted them to use. Consequently, leases were increased from one year to 15 years, then to 30 years and, after 1984, to 50 years. Farmers who did not want to farm their plots were allowed to rent them out to other farmers. More controversially, Deng allowed land-lease contracts to be passed on to farmers' children. This created almost a free market, with land being dealt with as virtually private property that could be 'inherited'.

Stagnation

After 1984–85, growth in grain production actually declined, as farmers found it more profitable to grow those crops receiving higher subsidies, such as rice. Meanwhile, others were still reluctant to put massive effort into land that they did not actually own. This led to food shortages, and wide fluctuations in price, and in turn to much anger in some rural areas, as living standards began to fall.

Agricultural production then virtually stagnated. The changes in the countryside gave rise to problems for the official 'one-child policy', as the ability to 'pass' land on to children down the years led rural families to want more children, especially sons. This led to a rise in abortions and the infanticide of girl babies.

There were also some severe implications for the environment, which included deforestation and subsequent flooding. These problems were worsened by the rapid industrial growth examined in the next section. Later, these issues would feed into the growing demands from various political movements for more democracy.

Industry

As Source F shows, Deng's industrial policies and reforms had a significant impact on China's GDP and manufacturing output. However, because of continued reluctance, by 1990 over 50% of industry was still directly controlled by the state.

Fact

Adopted in 1980, in order to 'fight the enemy within the womb', the 'one-child policy' was an attempt to slow down China's rapidly growing population. It imposed penalties on women and families who had more than one child. Since 1985, the government has relaxed this policy – effectively allowing families two children each. This has undone the original plan to stabilise China's population at 1.2 billion by 2000. In March 2011, the government announced that the one-child policy would officially end in 2015.

SOURCE F

China's industrial performance, 1979–89

Year	GDP (in billions of yuan)	Annual GDP growth rate (%)	Annual inflation rate (%)	Annual manufacturing output growth rate (%)
1979	732.6	7.6	6.1	8.6
1980	790.5	7.9	−1.5	11.9
1981	826.1	4.5	7.0	1.6
1982	896.3	8.5	11.5	5.5
1983	987.7	10.2	8.3	9.2
1984	1130.9	14.5	12.9	14.5
1985	1276.8	12.9	1.8	18.1
1986	1385.4	8.5	3.3	8.3
1987	1539.1	11.1	4.7	12.7
1988	1713.1	11.3	2.5	15.8
1989	1786.7	4.3	3.1	4.9

From Lynch, M. 2008. *The People's Republic of China 1949–76*. London, UK. Hodder Education. p. 162. Reproduced by permission.

Losing the 'iron rice bowl'

It took time for entrepreneurs to find opportunities to make profits, but soon small workshops and businesses emerged. These small businesses then hired workers and operated in what was essentially a market economy framework. However, many workers were reluctant to lose their 'iron rice bowl', which was seen as a positive gain from the Communist Revolution of 1949. Consequently, there was often obstruction and lack of co-operation, which meant that it took longer to implement the reforms. It was not until 1986 that the government was able to put in place a labour-contract scheme that linked wages to effort and productivity. Even then, it only applied to new employees – not those already employed. The government also provided unemployment insurance to encourage acceptance. However, even as late as 1992, only 20% of the 80 million employees in SOEs were covered by the new contract.

These problems also contributed to the student-led democracy demonstrations that occurred in China in 1989. As in Poland and Czechoslovakia, these demonstrations were increasingly supported by disgruntled workers.

The impact of the SEZs

The SEZs caused various problems – including the sometimes savage exploitation of Chinese workers and reduction of trade union rights. However, initially, they led to a significant increase in direct foreign investment in China. At first, funds came mostly from Hong Kong and Taiwan, and China also received considerable aid from abroad. The success of the SEZs (especially the one at Shenzhen) led the government to authorise 14 other coastal towns to offer special privileges to foreign investors. Soon, almost the entire Chinese coast had been opened up in this way, along with some inland regions.

In fact, the SEZs have had a much bigger impact on China's industrial economy than Deng's domestic reforms. At first, the main type of work carried out in them was basic manufacturing, with foreign firms using Chinese workers as cheap labour for unskilled work. Also, most of the goods were then sold in China, rather than being exported (which had been Deng's original plan). However, eventually, skill levels increased, along with the quality of goods and exports. Some party leaders who were initially sceptical of these developments soon became less critical. Instead, they made profitable connections with foreign joint venture partners. They also found jobs for their relatives in the SEZs, where wages – though low by international standards – were higher than in the rest of China.

The result of Deng's industrial reforms – especially the SEZs – was a dramatic increase in China's international trade. Between 1978 and 1989, exports grew by over 500% and foreign investment increased by 400%. However, young specialists, often trained abroad, found it difficult to apply their new knowledge to the more old-fashioned equipment used in China. Meanwhile, older workers (many of whom had received little education during the Cultural Revolution) were resentful of these younger workers, who got promotion. There was now greater consumer choice and better-quality goods were available. But the impact of inflation on the real value of wages reduced the workers' spending power, which led to resentment.

The 'open door' policy necessarily favoured coastal towns and areas. This led to many wanting to move from rural areas to the coast. In addition, the rapid economic growth put increasing pressures on China's infrastructure.

SOURCE G

China's foreign trade, 1978–89

Year	Imports	Exports
1978	10.9	9.8
1979	15.7	13.7
1980	20.0	18.1
1981	22.0	22.0
1982	19.3	22.3
1983	21.4	22.2
1984	27.4	26.1
1985	42.3	27.4
1986	42.9	30.9
1987	43.2	39.4
1988	55.3	47.5
1989	59.1	52.5

From Lynch, M. 2008. The People's Republic of China 1949–76. London, UK. Hodder Education. p. 161. Reproduced by permission.

Communism in Crisis

> **Question**
>
> What negative impacts have the industrial reforms of the 1980s had on the urban workforce, both inside and outside the SEZs?

For instance, there were problems with transporting large quantities of raw materials to the factories, which hampered manufacturing. The impact of high unemployment and inflation led to declining living standards for many, and an increase in worker discontent and even unrest. In the SEZs, workers were often employed on short-term contracts, to avoid giving them the same benefits as full-time workers. If any of them objected to the working conditions, there were plenty of poor unemployed migrant workers ready to take their place.

Also, the huge concentration on economic growth and increased production led to a deterioration of the environment, with industrial pollution becoming a major problem. Soon, environmental issues started to become important to many younger Chinese people.

Unemployment and poverty

Inflation became a serious problem. From late 1988, rising inflation forced the government to slow down economic growth. This led to high unemployment (officially said to be 20% in the cities) and reduced living standards.

One result of this was a widening of the gap between rich and poor – especially in rural areas. The de-collectivisation of agriculture showed that about half the 400 million who worked on the land were surplus to requirements. About 100 million eventually found work in the TEVs. There, they usually failed to win the benefits enjoyed by those in state enterprises such as medical care and retirement pensions, and they also received lower wages and working longer hours. The remaining 100 million have either become under-employed casual wage labourers getting irregular work, or they have joined the mass migrant labour force. These labourers move to the cities, live in shanty towns and work for very low wages – or end up being involved in prostitution or criminal activities.

A slum area in Shanghai, 1980s

Many of China's cities have also seen the re-emergence of stark contrasts (typical of capitalist states in the West) between rich and poor. For instance, many of those working for private concerns are paid subsistence wages, while begging and prostitution – virtually eradicated under Mao – have reappeared.

SOURCE A

Premier Zhao Ziyang's 'coastal strategy,' which loosened central financial controls over local governments after 1985 and encouraged regionalism, vastly expanded opportunities for official profiteering and the growth of bureaucratic capitalism, especially along the southern coast and in the Yangzi delta. A new urban bourgeoisie thus began to take shape in the mid-1980s, a class which in addition to bureaucratic capitalists included the rapidly growing number of large and small private entrepreneurs ... they are socially and economically distinct from the great majority of the urban population ... their distinctiveness as a class in Chinese society expresses itself in a taste for luxury – and the means to satisfy those tastes in expensive restaurants and nightclubs, in new and spacious apartments, and in exclusive boutiques ... And the contrast between wealth and poverty in Chinese cities today is probably as great, and certainly as glaring, as it is in the metropolitan areas of most Western and Third World capitalist countries. The Dengist prediction that 'some must get rich first' has come to pass with a vengeance.

Meisner, M. 1991. Mao's China and After: A History of the People's Republic. New York, USA. The Free Press. p. 477.

China's debt

Deng's reforms at first led to increased borrowing. By 1989, China's external debt was almost $45,000 million. This was a major transformation, as China had been a debt-free nation before the 'open door' policy. By world standards, its debt was relatively modest. However, it does mean that China is now increasingly dependent on fluctuations in the (capitalist) world market. It is also subject to economic pressure from international (US-controlled) lending organisations such as the IMF and the World Bank. These organisations are not renowned for favouring the establishment of socialist societies.

Corruption

The various economic developments – and even the problems associated with the one-child policy – resulted in growing corruption amongst party and government officials. As well as often flouting the one-child policy, they also began to benefit from links with Western businesses. As the party élites became more bureaucratised and less revolutionary, many began to award themselves various perks that enabled them to live privileged lives. For instance, their children automatically got into universities, and were exempted from military service. Also, local and national officials took commissions and bribes from foreign firms for arranging deals in the SEZs.

This corruption and profiteering became so common that it gave rise to a new term, *guan dao* ('official profiteers'). In 1985, the governor of Hainan Island, who got round the regulations for importing motor vehicles, was dismissed.

Theory of knowledge

History and ethics
'Property is theft' – this famous quotation is from Pierre-Joseph Proudhon (1809–65), who first raised the question of whether the concept of private property is ethical. Do the economic policies enforced by a society (such as whether property should be privately or socially owned) affect the morality of that society? Consider, for example, human rights, justice, social responsibility, equality and freedom. Is it possible to argue that one economic system is, in principle, more just than another?

Communism in Crisis

There have since been several prosecutions of high-ranking officials for corruption. The children of leading party members (even those of Deng and Zhao) have sometimes been involved. While some of the money ended up in private Swiss bank accounts, a lot was invested in private enterprises in China itself by these budding Chinese capitalists. The emergence of these 'crown princes and princesses' led to growing anger.

> ### SOURCE I
>
> Instituting the responsibility system, increasing the role of the market in determining economic activity, 'opening to the world', and other changes have pushed growth of the gross national product to an overheated 13 percent by 1984, the highest rate of any country in the world. But continued growth too rapid for the economy to support and assimilate without severe penalties has led to economic conditions often characterised today as 'chaos'.
>
> Over the nine years 1979–1987 China's state revenue and per capita income approximately doubled ... but there are numerous and serious economic imbalances within the overall situation ... In fact, China, with a GNP in 1987 of US$277.50 per capita, ranked in the bottom 20 percent of nations, and its peoples have not experienced the even greater growth of affluence found in some other Asian countries.
>
> Ethridge, J. M. 1990. *China's Unfinished Revolution: Problems and Prospects Since Mao. San Francisco, USA. China Books. p. 46.*

Despite the slower-than-planned progress and all the above-mentioned difficulties, China made significant progress in terms of modernisation and increasing efficiency. By 1989, as a result of these economic policies, it seemed that China was set to become a leading industrial nation by 2040.

However, in the late 1980s, as Deng continued pushing through his economic policies, the increasing discontent amongst workers combined with political discontent amongst students. The growing dissatisfaction culminated in the Democracy Movement and the 1989 protests in Tiananmen Square. These issues will be examined in the next chapter.

Activities

1. 'The system of leasing land from the communes has re-created capitalism in rural China.' Split into two groups – one to support the statement, and the other to argue against it.

2. Carry out further research on the 'one-child policy'. Why was it introduced? And should it be maintained?

3. Imagine you have moved from your family's farm and you are now a factory worker in one of the SEZs. Using the information in this book, and from other sources available to you, write a letter to your family describing what your new life is like.

4. Investigate further the reappearance of extremes of wealth and poverty in China, and the growing problem of corruption, after 1976. Does the extent of these problems mean that China is now a capitalist country?

8 The Chinese economy under Deng Xiaoping

End of chapter activities

Summary

You should now have a good understanding of the main agricultural and industrial aims and policies pursued in China in the period from 1976 to 1989.

You should be able to comment on how successful Deng's reforms have been – in terms of both production and increased efficiency. You should also be able to discuss the economic and social problems associated with his reforms.

Summary activity

Copy the chart below. Then, using the information in this chapter and from any other available sources, make brief notes under the headings shown. Include aims, main policies and successes/failures. Also, remember to include information on historical debates/interpretations – including names of historians – where relevant.

	Agriculture	Industry	Foreign trade and investment
1976–78			
1979–85			
1986–89			

Paper 1 exam practice

Question

With reference to their origin and purpose, assess the value and limitations of Source A (right) and Source B (page 184) for historians studying Deng's economic aims during the 1980s.
[6 marks]

Skill

Value and limitations (utility/reliability) of sources

SOURCE A

Extracts from Charles Bettelheim's response, *The Great Leap Backward*, dated 3 March 1978, to Neil Burton's Open Letter on the likely course of events in China, following the defeat of the Gang of Four. Both Bettelheim and Burton were supporters of Mao before 1976.

The political changes which have taken place in China since October 1976 … have become clearer than they were: in particular, it is more obvious what policy has triumphed as a result of the elimination of the Four, namely a bourgeois [capitalist] policy and not a proletarian one …

Secondly, alongside the announcement that the Cultural Revolution is over, the measures which have been taken since more than a year ago, and the themes expounded in official speeches and in the press, constitute a de facto negation of the Cultural Revolution. There has been a veritable leap backward. These two aspects of the present situation are obviously not accidental. They are the product of profound tendencies, the result of a certain relation of forces between classes and also of a political line which forms part of this relation of forces and reacts upon it.

Quoted in Bettelheim, C. and Burton, N. 1978. *China Since Mao*. New York, USA. Monthly Review Press. pp. 38–39.

Communism in Crisis

SOURCE B

What is socialism and what is Marxism? We were not quite clear about this in the past. Marxism attaches utmost importance to developing the productive forces … Therefore, the fundamental task for the socialist stage is to develop the productive forces … Socialism means eliminating poverty. Pauperism is not socialism, still less communism …

Capitalism can only enrich less than 10 per cent of the Chinese population; it can never enrich the remaining more than 90 per cent …

Our political line is to focus on the modernization programme and on continued development of the productive forces … The minimum target of our modernization programme is to achieve a comparatively comfortable standard of living by the end of the century … To do this, we have to invigorate the domestic economy and open to the outside world …

We therefore began by invigorating the economy and adopting an open policy … We adopted this policy at the end of 1978, and after a few years it has produced the desired results. Now the recent Second Session of the Sixth National People's Congress has decided to shift the focus of reform from the countryside to the cities …

We have opened 14 large and medium-sized coastal cities. We welcome foreign investment and advanced techniques. In general, we believe that the course we have chosen, which we call building socialism with Chinese characteristics, is the right one.

Extracts from Deng's speech, 'Build socialism with Chinese characteristics', 30 June 1984, to the Japanese businessmen's delegation at the second session of the Council of Sino–Japanese Non-Governmental Persons. From: http://english.peopledaily.com.cn/dengxp/vol3/text/c1220.html

Before you start

Value and limitations (utility/reliability) questions require you to assess two sources over a range of possible issues – and to comment on their value to historians studying a particular event or period of history. You need to consider both the origin and purpose and also the value and limitations of the sources. You should link these in your answer, showing how origin/purpose relate to value/limitations.

Before you attempt this question, refer to pages 216–17 for advice on how to tackle these questions and a simplified markscheme.

Student answer

Source B, which is an extract from a speech, has a useful origin, as it was made by Deng himself to Japanese businessmen in 1984. However, this means it has both value and limitations for finding out about Deng's economic aims in the 1980s. As he was talking to capitalist businessmen – and not the Chinese people – he could have said he wanted to turn China capitalist in order to get more foreign investment. Yet he is strongly saying he wants to build socialism, so we could assume that socialism – not capitalism – is his real aim. Yet, as it is a public speech, as opposed to a private diary entry, its value is limited – even though it is from Deng himself. For instance, the phrase 'with Chinese characteristics' could be cover, so that his opponents in the CCP do not suspect him of wanting to return China to capitalism.

Examiner comments

There is reasonable assessment of Source B, referring clearly to both origin and possible purpose and to value and limitations. These comments are also clearly linked to the question – these are not just general comments about a source. The candidate has thus done enough to get into Band 2, and so be awarded 3 or 4 marks. However, as there are no comments about Source A, this answer fails to get into Band 1.

Activity

Look again at the two sources, the simplified markscheme, and the student answer above. Now try to write a paragraph or two to push the answer up into Band 1, and so obtain the full 6 marks, by assessing Source A.

Paper 2 practice questions

1 Analyse the political and economic reasons why Hua Guofeng was gradually forced out of power by Deng and his supporters.

2 How, and with what results, was agriculture in China reformed in the period 1976–89?

3 Examine the ways in which Deng attempted to reform China's industrial economy in the period 1979–89.

4 'The decisions to adopt an "open door" policy towards the West, and to create Special Economic Zones, showed that Deng and his supporters were intent on restoring capitalism in China.' To what extent do you agree with this assertion?

9 Political developments in China under Deng

Timeline

1978 Nov: start of Democracy Wall

Dec: Wei Jingsheng's 'Fifth Modernisation'

1979 Mar: arrest of Wei; Deng's 'Four Cardinal Principles'

Oct: Wei's show trial

Dec: Democracy Wall closed down

1980 Feb: 'Four Big Rights' abolished

Aug: Third Plenum, 5th National People's Congress

1982 Sep: 12th National Party Congress: older leaders 'retired'

1984 Apr: President Reagan's visit to China

1985 Sep: National Conference of Party Delegates; more 'retirements' of older members

1986 Nov: National People's Congress: electoral reforms for local congresses

Dec: student demonstrations

1987 Jan: fall of Hu

1989 Jan: Fang Lizhi's Open Letter

Apr: death of Hu; student demonstrations and protests in Tiananmen Square; start of Democracy Movement

May: Zhao says student demands are reasonable; protests increase; start of hunger strike; Gorbachev's visit; martial law declared

Jun: military used to crush protests in Tiananmen Square; arrests and executions of ringleaders; Zhao dismissed and replaced by Jiang Zemin

Introduction

From Mao's death in September 1976 until 1978, the power struggle between Leftists and Rightists continued, with various factions amongst the top party and government leaders manoeuvring for overall control. By 1978, it was clear that Deng and his supporters were winning, although it was not until 1980–81 that their position was fully consolidated.

As noted in Chapter 8, one reason for Deng's economic reforms was to secure the power of the CCP. It was felt that the party's power had been damaged by the events of the Cultural Revolution and the policies of the Gang of Four. The period after 1976 would show that, although Deng's political policies seemed to fluctuate from liberal to authoritarian, there was in fact a consistent desire to uphold the one-party system.

The first signs of Deng's new approach to politics appeared during the campaign against the Gang of Four, and the use of 'big character' posters on what became known as Democracy Wall. However, this approach did not reflect his *underlying* political style. He is in fact likely to be remembered as a leader who was repressive rather than liberal. This is best illustrated by his forceful suppression of the Democracy Movement's protests in Tiananmen Square on 4 June 1989.

Key questions

- What was Deng's political approach in the period from 1976 to 1979?
- Why did political unrest re-emerge in the period from 1980 to 1988?
- What led to the Tiananmen Square Massacre of June 1989?

Overview

- Once the Gang of Four had been overthrown in 1976, and Deng had been rehabilitated again, it seemed that he favoured a more liberal political approach.
- At first, a Democracy Wall in Beijing was tolerated. But when students moved from attacking the Gang of Four to criticising Deng and demanding democracy, his attitude began to change. In December 1979, Democracy Wall was closed down.

- During the 1980s, Deng's political approach varied from some limited liberalisation to campaigns against 'bourgeois liberalisation'. While he carried out some reforms to the party (including replacing older leaders with younger ones), he made it clear that he would maintain the CCP's monopoly on political power.
- However, his implementation of liberal economic policies resulted in growing demands from intellectuals and students for a similar liberalisation of politics. Meanwhile, from 1985 onwards, the effects of his economic policies, and growing signs of corruption, were creating distress and dissatisfaction amongst many workers and peasants.
- From late 1986, student protests again began to spread, with many calling for democracy. These Democracy Movement protests tailed off in early 1987. However, because of his support for pro-democracy intellectuals, Hu Yaobang was dismissed as general-secretary of the CCP.
- Some protests occurred again in 1988. In January 1989, Fang Lizhi, a leading intellectual, issued an Open Letter calling for the release of political prisoners.
- This, and the death of Hu in April 1989, began a rapidly increasing number of student protests. The most famous one took place in Tiananmen Square in Beijing. By May, these protests were sometimes a million strong, and were increasingly supported by workers.
- After much debate and hesitation, Deng's government declared martial law. The PLA was sent in to suppress the protests and clear Tiananmen Square – with significant loss of life.
- Afterwards, there were many arrests of ringleaders, and executions of workers who had joined the protests. Deng made it clear that he had no intention of adopting a more democratic political system.

This cartoon, by Nicholas Garland, was published in the Independent, *a British newspaper, on 16 June 1989; the man standing in front of the tank (see page 6 photo) represents Deng Xiaoping trying to prevent the truth being told about the massacre in Beijing*

Communism in Crisis

What was Deng's political approach in the period from 1976 to 1979?

After the rise of Hua Guofeng and the fall of the Gang of Four, there was at first a political relaxation or 'loosening', and a more open approach. Many of those who had either been imprisoned or 'sent down to the countryside' (see page 150) during the Cultural Revolution were released or allowed to return home. Several important leaders – including Deng – were rehabilitated.

Democracy Wall, 1976–80

One sign of this political relaxation was that students in several universities began to put up 'big character' posters (known as *dazibao*, and easily read when pasted on walls), calling for rapid moves towards political liberalisation. These included a large number of posters attacking Jiang in the period between the fall of the Gang of Four and the conclusion of their trials. China's new government was happy at first to allow people to have their say about recent events. In November 1978, in the centre of Beijing, on a wall in Xidan Street near the Forbidden City and Tiananmen Square, students (and later workers) put up 'big character' posters, letters and poems. This soon became known as 'Democracy Wall'.

Following the line of the new government, which was to 'seek truth from facts', people used the wall to express their views – about what had happened in China in the period since 1967, and also about a whole range of other things. Such people included former Red Guards and those who had missed out on formal education during the 'Ten Wasted Years'. However, during that turmoil they had learned how to organise political action, and they used this to spread their ideas and form networks.

Fact
The 'Ten Wasted Years' was a phrase used to refer to the period from the start of the Cultural Revolution in 1966 to Mao's death in 1976.

Fact
The April 5th Movement referred to the Qingming Festival protests in Tiananmen Square, following the death of Zhou Enlai. Deng had been blamed by the Gang of Four for encouraging and even organising these protests, and they had led to him being briefly removed from power.

At first, most of their posters criticised the Gang of Four – and even Mao – so the government tolerated them. In fact, Deng even encouraged them, as it helped him in his struggle against his opponents in the party (especially the Leftists who were reluctant to adopt new economic policies). Many of these posters supported his return to power and the Four Modernisations, while some began to criticise Hua. Deng was thus happy for the Wall to remain. He also approved of the posters that demanded a reappraisal of the April 5th Movement of 1976. Some of these posters now called for the protests to be termed 'revolutionary', rather than 'counter-revolutionary'.

At first, this only really affected people living in Beijing, but news of Democracy Wall spread to other parts of China, and foreign journalists reported what the posters said. Especially important was the BBC World Service, which was listened to by many Chinese people.

In December 1978, when some posters began to criticise Deng, the government still took no action. What later became known as the Democracy Movement is generally regarded as having begun at this time. The protests widened, with a number of pro-democracy activists publishing pamphlets and even underground magazines. Some magazines (such as *Beijing Spring*) sold 100,000 copies to Chinese people. These increasingly called for more far-reaching changes, and some even began to criticise the government, the party as a whole and the socialist system itself. Their main calls were for freedom, political self-determination and human rights. These pro-democracy activists even made appeals to Western leaders and countries (such as US president Jimmy Carter), asking them to condemn human rights abuses in China.

9 ► Political developments in China under Deng

In December 1978, posters criticising Deng appeared on Democracy Wall

This was a step too far for Deng, as he did not support increased democracy. In addition, large numbers of people began to arrive in Beijing from rural areas. These country people wanted to call attention to abuses of power and corruption by party officials, and to present petitions asking the government for redress. When they were refused permission to hand in their petitions, they began to gather in Tiananmen Square and organise demonstrations. Unlike the earlier phase of the protest, which had been directed against abuses in the period before 1976, they were now criticising the very recent past and the present. Deng's various economic polices (especially opening up to the West), implemented as part of the Four Modernisations, soon led to open political dissent. There was now a growing demand for the 'Fifth Modernisation' – political democracy. Many students and intellectuals, in particular, believed that the economic reforms should be accompanied by political reforms leading to greater democracy.

'The Fifth Modernisation'

The most famous of all the pro-democracy pamphlets published during this period was 'The Fifth Modernisation', by **Wei Jingsheng**. In this pamphlet, he agued that, for full modernisation to succeed in China, there needed to be a Fifth Modernisation – democracy – to ensure that the economic changes worked. Intellectuals like Wei saw the economic reforms as an opportunity to change the political system as well. Wei openly criticised Deng and his policies in a series of articles. He even accused Deng of becoming a fascist dictator, and said that his power should therefore be restricted. On 5 December 1978, Wei put up a big character poster on Democracy Wall calling for this 'Fifth Modernisation'.

Consequently, on 29 March 1979, Wei was arrested. At his brief show trial in October, he was found guilty of treason and sentenced to 15 years' imprisonment in solitary confinement. He is considered the first martyr of the 'Democracy Movement'.

Wei Jingsheng (b. 1950)
Wei was a worker, and had been a Red Guard. Imprisoned in 1979, he was released in 1993. He then resumed his criticisms, and was sentenced to another 14 years in 1995 – this time for 'conspiracy to subvert the government'. ('Counter-revolution' had been removed as an offence.) He was released in 1997, and went into exile.

Communism in Crisis

SOURCE A

After the arrest of the Gang of Four, people eagerly hoped that Vice-Chairman Deng, the so-called "restorer of capitalism," would once again appear as a great towering banner ... However, to the people's regret, the hated old political system has not changed, and even any talk about the much hoped for democracy and freedom is forbidden ...

Why Democracy? ... Others have conducted careful analyses and indicated on the Democracy Wall how much better is democracy than autocracy ...

People should have democracy ... Do the people have democracy now? No. Do they want to be masters of their own destiny? Definitely yes ... Freedom and happiness are our sole objectives in accomplishing modernization. Without this fifth modernization all others are merely another promise ...

Today ... the people have ... a clear orientation, and they have a real leader. This leader is the democratic banner, which is [sic] now taken on a new significance. Xidan Democracy Wall has become the first battlefield in the people's fight against reactionaries ... Let us unite under this great and real banner and march toward modernization for the sake of the people's peace, happiness, rights and freedom!

Extracts from Wei Jingsheng's 'The Fifth Modernisation'. From: http://www.rjgeib.com/thoughts/china/jingshen.html

SOURCE B

To achieve the four modernizations and make China a powerful socialist country before the end of this century will be a gigantic task ...

The Central Committee maintains that, to carry out China's four modernizations, we must uphold the Four Cardinal Principles ideologically and politically ...

As we all know, far from being new, these Four Cardinal Principles have long been upheld by our Party. The Central Committee has been adhering to these principles in all its guidelines and policies adopted since the smashing of the Gang of Four, and especially since the Third Plenary Session of the Eleventh Central Committee ...

To sum up, in order to achieve the four modernizations we must keep to the socialist road, uphold the dictatorship of the proletariat, uphold the leadership of the Communist Party, and uphold Marxism–Leninism and Mao Zedong Thought ... The Central Committee considers that we must now repeatedly emphasize the necessity of upholding these four cardinal principles, because certain people (even if only a handful) are attempting to undermine them. In no way can such attempts be tolerated ... To undermine any of the four cardinal principles is to undermine the whole cause of socialism in China, the whole cause of modernization.

Extracts from Deng's speech, 30 March 1979. From: english.peopledaily.com.cn/dengxp/vol2/text/b1290.html

Deng decided to make it clear that, despite economic reforms, demands for democracy were an example of 'bourgeois liberalism', from which the Chinese people needed protection. On 30 March 1979, he therefore made a speech setting out the **'Four Cardinal Principles'** that the party needed to uphold, as the Four Modernisations were implemented. This, he stated, was because China was aiming for socialist modernisation, rather than other types of modernisation. He saw bourgeois liberalisation as leading China to capitalism. This was why he felt the need to uphold the Four Cardinal Principles, and carry out a lengthy struggle against bourgeois liberalisation.

These principles, he said, were the basis of the Chinese state, could not be debated, and would not be abandoned. This was partly an attempt to claim that the party leadership was still following the 'old revolutionary road'. Although, he implied that other political issues *could* be debated and discussed, events soon showed that, despite the various reforms, the party was determined to maintain its monopoly on political power.

By the end of 1979, Deng no longer needed to use the posters on Democracy Wall in his struggle against his opponents. In December, he ordered the closure of the wall, which was moved to a more remote part of Beijing. The government then quietly began quietly to arrest and detain, or 'send down to the countryside', the most important activists of the Democracy Movement – possibly as many as 100,000. Those from outside the main cities had their residents' permits to live in those cities revoked, in an obvious attempt to prevent urban organisation and resistance. The **'Four Big Rights'** dated back to the Cultural Revolution, and had been incorporated into the 1978 constitution. Nevertheless, in February 1980, these rights were abolished and it was made illegal to put up any more wall posters. These actions were a clear warning to intellectuals and journalists that post-Maoist China would not allow unlimited criticism of the party and government.

Although this policy forced the pro-democracy groups and reform communists underground, they managed to stay in contact with each other. Occasionally, limited protests continued to emerge.

Activities

1 Complete your record of Deng's career, by covering political events in the period 1980–89.

2 Carry out some further research on the way Democracy Wall was used in the period 1976–79. Then, individually (without consulting any of your classmates), draw up some 'big character' posters/poems/letters of your own, protesting about or commenting on any national/international issues you feel strongly about. When you have done this, display them on the walls in your classroom. Are there more differences than similarities?

3 Split into two groups. One group should develop arguments to support, and the other to oppose, the following statement:

'Political rights (such as free speech, freedom of association, a multi-party system) are more important than social rights (such as the right to a job, free education, free healthcare).'

4 See what more you can find out about Wei Jingsheng. Why did he call his demand for democracy the 'Fifth Modernisation'?

'Four Cardinal Principles'
These were sometimes also referred to as the Four Basic or Fundamental Principles. They were:
1 The Socialist Road
2 The Dictatorship of the Proletariat
3 The Leadership of the Communist Party
4 Marxism–Leninism and Mao Zedong Thought.

Question
Why did Deng place such importance on the Four Cardinal Principles?

'Four Big Rights' These were the rights of: *daming* (to speak out freely); *dafang* (to air views fully); *dabianlun* (to hold great debates); and *dazibao* (to write big character posters).

Communism in Crisis

Why did political unrest re-emerge in the period from 1980 to 1988?

The 1980s in China were, politically, rather confusing. At times, intellectuals were encouraged to speak out in a limited form of political liberalisation. Yet it was stated that no 'bourgeois' values were to be re-introduced. By the end of the decade, Deng's regime would face its most serious challenge – from national protest movements of students and workers.

Reform of the CCP

The only real political reform Deng favoured was reform of the CCP. He realised that the party's standing had been damaged by the various developments since 1967. It was now necessary to make some changes to restore its credibility – but not by abandoning the idea of a single-party system.

However, Deng also wanted it made clear that there would be no automatic harassment of party members with different ideas. In other words, it would not be like during the Cultural Revolution, when people were targeted for being 'revisionists' and 'capitalist roaders'. As long as the authority of the party was accepted, and no more demands for greater political freedom were made, then Chinese citizens could confidently live in peace.

In the struggle between pragmatists such as himself, and those Leftists who did not want government policies to deviate too much from communist ideology, Deng saw the advantage of loosening the very close links between party and government. But this did not mean he was not still a communist. Deng (and his younger supporters) wanted to reform the system to make it more efficient and productive. While he advocated economic policies with Western capitalist features, he had no intention of adopting a democratic political system similar to those existing in the major capitalist states. Indeed he preferred the regimes in lesser capitalist states, such as Malaysia, which were often ruled by authoritarian regimes.

Deng's reorganisation of the party along these lines was approved in August–September 1980 by the Third Plenum of the 5th National People's Congress. At the top of the party, Deng was keen to make it clear that the adoption of capitalist-style mechanisms and technologies was all part of a Chinese-style socialism. Any open renunciation of socialism would undermine the party leadership and the party itself – and thus the whole political power structure in Communist China.

He was, however, aware that the party had become isolated from the mass of the Chinese people. Many party members and officials were poorly educated and not very efficient. Yet they remained in their posts, even at the highest levels, because they were politically 'reliable'. In the upper reaches of the party, in the Politburo and the Central Committee, a small number of old men – including Deng himself – monopolised power.

Consequently, in 1982 (building on his previous actions in 1980), Deng began another campaign to 'encourage' senior members of the party to retire. At the 12th National Party Congress, in September, older leading members were 'promoted' to the Central Advisory Commission, headed by Deng. Their official positions were taken by younger members. In September 1985, the National Conference of Party Delegates oversaw further retirements, so that younger and better-educated members could take the places of older ones. Similar changes were encouraged at the lower levels, too. By 1986, a total of 1.8 million had gone.

Fact
It is important to remember that the single-party communist system was a Stalinist, not a Marxist, belief. The 1921 Bolshevik ban on all other parties (and factions in their own party), was intended as an extraordinary and temporary pragmatic departure from the norms of socialist democracy. This later allowed Gorbachev to claim that his more democratic style of politics was simply a return to Leninist practice. The Chinese Communist Party, despite Mao's disagreements with Stalin, was mainly organised along Stalinist lines. Although Deng broke away from Mao on economic policies, he remained a Stalinist in terms of opposing socialist democracy.

Fact
This plenum also approved Deng's policies to modernise China. At the same time, it condemned, as liberal bourgeois views, the idea that people have the 'right to speak out freely' or 'hold great debates'.

9 Political developments in China under Deng

Deng and his fellow party leaders were getting older but their images remained strong and vigorous on billboards like this one, which read 'Uphold the party's fundamental line – we will not waver in a hundred years'

Deng also supervised a 'cleansing' purge. Between 1983 and 1987, the CCP expelled over 150,000 cadres (officials) for various offences, including abuse of power, and bribery and corruption. At the same time, he took steps to improve the overall educational level of cadres. As a result, over 60% of the party membership below the Politburo soon consisted of younger men and women with college qualifications. This purge also allowed Deng to remove those who were less than enthusiastic about his economic reforms. However, underlying all these reforms of the party, Deng's commitment to his version of communism remained.

Inner-party divisions

By 1982, Deng had full control over both the government and the party. He never formally held any high political post himself, such as premier, or chairman or general-secretary of the CCP. Instead, he chaired important economic committees, preferring to put his supporters into the top positions – in particular **Hu Yaobang** and Zhao Ziyang. By then, in fact, it seemed fairly clear that Deng would eventually be replaced either by Zhao, the premier, or by Hu, the general-secretary of the CCP.

Hu, in particular, favoured a more democratic approach to dissent. He tried to protect intellectuals when Deng occasionally launched attacks on 'bourgeois liberalisation' – especially during 1983–84. For example, in 1980, Hu made speeches in which he announced the rehabilitation of intellectuals. (They had been known as the 'stinking ninth' – one of the groups previously singled out as 'revisionists', 'bourgeois' and 'capitalist roaders'.) His reforms of the education system emphasised improving the quality of specialist schools and of higher education, thus reversing some aspects of the Cultural Revolution.

Fact
Mao had worried that the children of important party officials were getting an advantage in schools and universities, and would thus become a new middle class at the expense of workers and peasants. Hence, under Mao, students had to have a good work record and the support of their work team before acceptance at a university. He also placed more emphasis on a good basic education for all, rather than spending a lot of money on the education of those who were more able.

Hu Yaobang (1915–89)
Hu joined the Red Army in 1930, when he was only 15, and served under Deng in his Second Field Army. After 1949, his fortunes fluctuated along with Deng's. In 1980, when Hua Guofeng was forced to relinquish his positions, Hu became general-secretary of the CCP. He was on the libertarian wing of Marxism and the CCP, favouring democratic procedures. He supported Deng's desire to 'rehabilitate' those purged in the period before 1976.

Communism in Crisis

> **Fact**
> Corruption had been a growing problem for some time. In the late 1970s, a case of corruption and embezzlement of state funds had come to light in Heilongjiang province. This resulted in the trial and execution of the main guilty parties, all of whom had been leading members of the local CCP.

> **Question**
> Why did corruption become such a problem in China during the 1980s?

> **Fact**
> 'Li-Yi-Zhe' were Li Zhengtian, Chen Yiyang and Wang Xizhe. They first became known nationally in November 1974, when their pamphlet 'On Socialist Democracy and the Legal System' was put on a wall in Canton. It covered around 100 metres of the wall.

> **Wang Ruoshui (1926–2002)**
> Wang studied philosophy in the late 1940s, became a Marxist philosopher and joined the CCP before its victory in 1949. He became the theory editor on the *People's Daily* newspaper. Wang was originally a Maoist, but later became an exponent of Marxist humanism and liberalism. His beliefs and his journalism led to him losing his editorial job. He was then expelled from the CCP in 1987, in one of Deng's campaigns against 'bourgeois liberalism'.

Hu also backed the official party newspaper, the *People's Daily*, in the early 1980s, when it promoted democratic reform and exposed official corruption. Indeed, Deng's government initially relaxed controls on newspapers, allowing them to report on certain negative aspects of life in China. In particular, several important middle-ranking party leaders criticised the increasing prevalence of corruption.

Zhao also supported greater political freedom. Having lost his position during the Cultural Revolution, Zhao was restored by Mao in 1972, and was then put in charge of Guangdong province as party secretary. There he had quietly supported young democratic activists known by the acronym 'Li-Yi-Zhe'.

However, it was not Zhao's support of democratic activists that gained him Deng's support, but his introduction of market-reform economic policies. This had resulted in his election to the Politburo and becoming premier in 1980. As premier, he enthusiastically supported Deng's economic reforms and especially the 'open door' policy.

Though Deng promoted Hu and Zhao, he did not share their approach to greater political democracy. On the contrary, Deng's political approach was closely linked to his economic policies. Essentially, he was as conservative politically as he was progressive economically. As he saw it, if China's economy was going to be modernised successfully, the country needed internal political stability. Like many others, he believed that the chaos of the Cultural Revolution had impeded both economic and educational progress. He wanted China to turn its back on political debates, and instead get on with economic transformation. He believed that politics was less important than turning China into a modern and powerful country, and so should be subordinated to that task.

Renewal of student activism, 1986–87

During a visit to China in April 1984, US president Ronald Reagan made two speeches, which included references to 'freedom' and 'trust in the people'. Despite government attempts to censor these, uncensored translations of the speeches began to circulate in China.

These translations, as well as the earlier anti-corruption newspaper articles, helped resurrect the pro-democracy groups. In 1985, there was a 17,000-strong student demonstration at the élite China University of Science and Technology (CUST) in Hefei, in Anhui province. The students, most of them the children of high-ranking officials and prominent intellectuals, called for greater reform 'especially political reform'.

In May 1986 (on the 30th anniversary of Mao's launch of the 'Hundred Flowers' campaign), Deng ended another more repressive period – by launching a period of political relaxation, which encouraged ideological flexibility and stressed the need for 'political reform'. **Wang Ruoshui**, a democratic Marxist, had previously been dismissed in 1983 as managing editor of the *People's Daily* but he continued to work as a journalist. In the summer of 1986, Wang had his treatise 'On the Marxist Philosophy of Man' published in a Shanghai newspaper; in it, he stressed the democratic and humanitarian strands of Marxist philosophy and politics.

In November 1986, the National People's Congress introduced some changes to the election of candidates to local congresses. Further student demonstrations were held, apparently to encourage more students to get involved in local government. However, they soon moved on to demanding better living standards and greater freedom. At first, the government concentrated on simply dispersing the demonstrations, without arresting the organisers.

The students were supported by Professor **Fang Lizhi** and, more circumspectly, by intellectuals associated with Hu Yaobang. In a speech delivered on 18 November, Fang made the point that China would only be able to develop towards modernity if the people were allowed to think freely. He also said socialism had failed, and that, for modernisation to work, it would be necessary to adopt Westernisation as well.

SOURCE C

I have to judge this era [since 1949] a failure. This is not my opinion only … many of our leaders are also admitting as much, saying that socialism is in trouble everywhere. Since the end of World War II, socialist countries have by and large not been successful … Are the things done in the name of socialism actually socialist? We have to take a fresh look at these questions and the first step in that process is to free our minds from the narrow confines of orthodox Marxism.

We've talked about the need for modernization and reform, so now let's consider democracy … the word 'democracy' is quite clear, and it is poles apart from 'loosening up'. If you want to understand democracy, look at how people understand it in the developed countries … In democratic countries, democracy begins with the individual. I am the master, and the government is responsible to me … If you want reform – and there are more reforms needed in our political institutions than I have time to talk about – the most crucial thing of all is to have a democratic mentality and a democratic spirit.

Extracts from Fang Lizhi's speech of 18 November 1986. Quoted in Fang, L. 1990. (trans. Williams, J. H.) Bringing Down the Great Wall: Writings on Science, Culture and Democracy in China. New York, USA. W. W. Norton. pp. 157–88.

During December 1986, in the leading universities of Hefei, Shanghai and Wuhan, students called for even greater changes to the electoral system. In Hefei, on 5 December, about 3000 CUST students demonstrated, demanding further reforms. On 20 December 1986, over 50,000 demonstrated in Shanghai. This time, there were minor clashes with the police. Deng and his supporters were particularly worried by the fact that, in Shanghai and one or two other places, the student demonstrations attracted the support of some workers. These student pro-democracy protests then spread to Beijing.

Many students were concerned about the relatively slow expansion of job opportunities for the growing number of graduates as the Chinese economy began to slow down in the mid 1980s. In the late 1970s, along with the removal of the need to perform manual labour to get into university, there had been a rapid expansion of university places. Now, however, graduates were finding it difficult to get jobs.

Fang Lizhi (b. 1936) Fang was a popular astrophysics professor and vice-president at CUST in Hefei. He was also an outspoken campaigner for democratic reform. As a result of his support of the student protests in 1986–87, he was expelled from the CCP. On 5 June, the day after the Tiananmen Square Massacre, he sought asylum in the US embassy in Beijing.

Question
Why would Deng and his supporters have been against Fang's speech?

Discussion point
Chinese intellectuals, such as Fang, had an idea of what democracy was like in the West. Looking at the way democracy functioned in some Western countries at the time, how often did it fall short of their idealised version? Try to identify some specific examples to make your points.

Fact
Student discontent has often been a critical factor in pre-revolutionary and revolutionary situations – as in China in 1919. Other examples include the French Revolution and the Russian Revolution – and even the 17th-century English Revolution. Hope and idealism tend to be more of a feature of youth than of middle age. Young people, especially those who continue their education, are therefore often attracted to revolutionary movements. This is particularly true if they live in a society that tends to ignore or exclude the young, and where power is in the hands of middle-aged or older people.

Communism in Crisis

Deng condemned these protests in January 1987, dismissing them as the work of a small number of 'anti-socials'. The government then dismissed Fang, giving him a new post in Beijing, where the authorities could monitor him more effectively. However, he continued to speak out. Some saw him as a Chinese equivalent of Andrei Sakharov in the USSR (see page 52). Other prominent dissidents were the journalists Lin Binyan and Wang Ruoshui. Both of them had continued to investigate cases of corruption amongst government and party officials, even after Wang's removal from his editorial position; and both were expelled from the CCP and their posts. However, despite these government actions, intellectuals continued to speak out in favour of democracy. They were encouraged in part by some sympathetic comments made by Hu, the general-secretary of the CCP.

As exams began in January, the 1986 pro-democracy student movement mostly faded away. The main ringleaders were arrested, but were soon released. However, the regime was tougher on the workers who had joined them. Many of these workers were given prison sentences for 'counter-revolution'. Deng's government then launched a new campaign against 'bourgeois liberalisation' in 1987. This was his third 'witch hunt' (the other two were in 1980 and 1983).

The fall of Hu

Deng decided that these protests required a new purge – and the most prominent victim was Hu Yaobang. In January 1987, Hu – who had criticised the slow pace of political reform and had supported some of the students' demands for political liberalisation – was dismissed as general-secretary, though he remained on the Politburo. In fact, it seems that Deng actually decided on this move in late 1986. At that point, Hu's exposure of corruption amongst the children of senior party leaders, and his close ties to democratic intellectuals, had angered several senior party leaders. He had also criticised the new educational rules.

Deng had originally planned to remove Hu at the 13th Party Congress, scheduled for autumn 1987. However, events during the winter of 1986–87 made him decide to act earlier. In the event, Hu was dismissed at an informal meeting between Deng and a group of the most senior party 'elders' (who soon became known as the 'Gang of Old'). At this meeting, Hu was forced to admit that he had made 'serious mistakes'. Officially, it was announced that the Politburo had dismissed him.

Hu was replaced by Zhao Ziyang and Zhao's place as premier was taken by the more conservative Li Peng. These changes of leadership were later formally approved by the 13th Party Congress in late October 1987. At this congress, Deng retired from the Standing Committee of the Politburo, forcing other elderly members to resign as well. As well as removing possible opponents, this action also reduced the average age of committee members from 77 to 63. Of the older ones, only Zhao remained.

However, Deng remained chair of the Military Affairs Commission, as well as 'paramount leader'. He also retained some power through the establishment of the 'retired' senior party elders as a 'Gang of Old'. Deng and this group continued to exert great influence, behind the scenes. Deng reiterated that Western-style democracy was not a feature of the modernisation programme – partly because of China's vast size and its mixed population, and the lack of education of the majority. Thus the leadership of the Communist Party was still essential. Without that, he believed there could be 'no building of socialism'.

Fact
Government reforms to higher education included some new educational rules. According to these rules, students had to undertake two years of assigned labour before they could start work. In addition, 30% of each graduating class had to accept jobs assigned to them by the government. These measures were clearly attempts to limit student access to dissident intellectuals and lecturers, and thus to limit the spread of protest.

Fact
Hu had also suggested the previous year, 1986, that Deng was too old and should therefore resign. This was perhaps due to an over-eagerness to replace Deng himself. He was accused of 'saying many things he should not have said'. His dismissal made him a hero to many students, who became very active in the Democracy Movement in the late 1980s.

Continuing unrest

These developments in 1987 gave a clear signal about the government's attitude to the student demonstrations. Though fewer, these demonstrations continued. The students protested not only against the new reforms of higher education, but also about student grants (or stipends), which were low, and poor living conditions. In 1988, student organisers circulated a petition calling for greater reform. Encouraged and inspired by intellectuals such as Fang, and some radical student leaders, these demands soon included calls for democracy. Another wave of student demonstrations broke out in the summer of 1988 in cities across China. But they were not joined by workers or peasants this time, and the numbers involved declined as exam time approached. However, unrest in the universities continued in the new academic year, 1988–89.

These protests worried Deng, who seems to have feared another power struggle between his pragmatist faction and the more hardline Maoists in the party. He managed to get several more of these hardliners to retire on age grounds (though Deng himself, at 83, had no intention of stepping down). Essentially, as described by Immanuel C.Y. Hsu, Deng was an odd mixture of an economic progressive and a political conservative. He saw market mechanisms and Western technology as a means to strengthen the Chinese economy and communist rule. Michael Lynch, too, sees him as a reformer but only in the economic sphere. In politics, he was a CCP hardliner. An eventual show-down between Deng and the democracy activists was therefore almost inevitable.

The departure of older committee members was depicted in 'The Long March', a cartoon by Kevin Kallaugher, published in the Observer *newspaper, 22 September 1985; the original Long March took place in 1934, when the early communists marched and fought more than 12,000 km across southern China to escape Jiang Jieshi's attempts to crush them*

Impact of Deng's economic reforms

What helped make the protests of 1988–89 so serious, compared to the 1986 protests, was the larger number of workers who joined the students. This was largely because of the impact of Deng's economic policies on living standards.

As discussed in Chapter 8, one of the results of Deng's moves towards greater freedom for enterprises was less state involvement in guaranteeing basic necessities for Chinese peasants and industrial workers. By the mid 1980s, the commune system had been virtually dismantled. In 1985, grain production actually dropped, as peasants decided to grow more, higher-paying crops. In the state industrial sector, greater freedom for the SOEs meant attempts to smash the 'iron rice bowl' (see page 176). As well as rising unemployment, industrial workers lost their food coupons, free heath care and free education. In addition, there was the pressure of inflation, leading to rising food prices. In early 1985, the prices of basic necessities increased by 30%. All these factors reduced the real value of wages, especially for factory workers and lower-level government employees.

As a result, the government adopted austerity measures. Many factories closed down and unemployment rose higher; large numbers of people were forced into the cities in search of work. This often paid low wages with no benefits, so, once again, beggars and prostitutes became a familiar sight on the streets of some Chinese cities.

Communism in Crisis

Fact

At first, Deng tried to avoid any direct confrontations with those voicing political or economic criticisms. He had been observing events in Poland, where the rise of Solidarity in 1980 had led to the introduction of martial law. This was something he wished to avoid in China.

Question

How did Deng's economic reforms contribute to the outbreak of political unrest in 1988–89?

One result of all this was a change in public attitudes to Deng's reforms. By 1985, there was a growing feeling that things were going wrong. And by 1989, Deng's popularity was much lower than it had been in the late 1970s and early 1980s. It also began to produce divisions within the CCP – especially between Deng and Chen Yun, an old-style economic planner who felt that market mechanisms should only play a supplementary role. However, despite his 'Polish fear' (the fear that China might see similar events to those that occurred in Poland in 1980), Deng had no intention of reversing his economic policies.

Nonetheless, as these economic policies were pushed through, their social impact increased. By early autumn 1988, inflation in the main cities had reached 30% a year, the economy was out of control, and the government imposed further austerity measures. These hit the TVEs particularly hard. By late 1988, living standards for many dropped dramatically. This led to an increasing number of workers' strikes and 'slow-downs' in factories. Meanwhile, in rural areas, farmers found it increasingly difficult to buy expensive fertilisers. Rural industrial jobs were lost, and there were clashes with local officials. Renewed student activism saw protests spread into the city streets, and illegal 'big character' posters began to appear in the winter of 1988–89.

Neo-authoritarianism

One response by the authorities was to send Chinese police abroad to learn the latest crowd-control and anti-riot techniques. Another was to work out some ideological backing for the practical results of Deng's programme – combining a capitalist market economy with the continued political dictatorship of the CCP. The intellectuals who developed the 'new politics' became known as the 'new authoritarians' and they pointed to places such as Taiwan and Singapore. Using these examples, they argued that, in order to achieve rapid modern economic development, it was necessary to have governments that were strong enough to 'tame the masses' and 'discipline the working population'.

This political debate revealed how the situation had changed since 1978, when Deng's re-emergence was seen by many intellectuals as ushering in 'socialist democracy'. Both sides of the debate now accepted the market economy. The difference was over whether the regime should be democratic or authoritarian. Deng's supporters had come to accept the idea of a capitalist autocracy.

SOURCE D

China could not afford democracy, which would bring the chaos of Party politics and disruptive protests by the victims of the transition to a market economy, thus delaying China's modernization. Political democracy was not ruled out entirely, but the neo-authoritarians said it presupposed a highly developed economy and a viable capitalist class. This did not yet exist, and thus democracy was put off until an indefinite time in the future …

Neo-authoritarian doctrines, tacitly endorsed by Party General Secretary Zhao Ziyang and based on the ideas of Deng Xiaoping, or so its proponents claimed, brought criticism from democratic Marxist intellectuals. Many democratic Marxists, such as Su Shaozhi, had been associated with ousted Party head Hu Yaobang, and thus now found themselves in political limbo, increasingly in opposition to both Deng Xiaoping and Zhao Ziyang.

Meisner, M. 1999. Mao's China and After: A History of the People's Republic. *New York, USA. The Free Press. p. 494.*

Activities

1. Find out the names of those who belonged to the inner party group known as the 'Gang of Old'. Why might students have seen Deng's moves in 1987, which maintained the influence of senior party members, as a significant obstacle to demands for increased democracy in China?

2. Draw a spider diagram to summarise the main political developments in the period 1980–88. Try to link these political issues to the impact of Deng's economic policies on aspects of daily life, such as living standards, employment prospects and corruption.

3. Find out more about the similarities between Fang Lizhi and the Soviet dissident Andrei Sakharov. Which one do you think had more of an impact on their society?

4. Carry out further research on Hu Yaobang and Zhao Ziyang and their connections to intellectuals associated with the Democracy Movement. Then write a brief summary explaining why, before 1989, Hu was more of a hero to pro-democracy students than Zhao was.

What led to the Tiananmen Square Massacre of June 1989?

Developments in the second half of 1988 rapidly developed into the infamous confrontation in Tiananmen Square in June 1989.

Democracy salons

During the summer and autumn of 1988, democratic Marxists and intellectuals who had been dismissed or sidelined following the disturbances of 1986–87, held informal lectures at Beijing University and elsewhere. The most famous of these 'democracy salons' (named after those who had contributed to the start of the French Revolution of 1789) was organised by Wang Dan, a history student at Beijing University.

In December 1988, Su Shaozhi, a prominent Marxist theoretician (who had been sacked as head of the Marx-Lenin-Mao Institute after the fall of Hu), attacked the new official ideology of Deng's regime. Su called for an open debate about the various strands of Western libertarian Marxism, which had always been banned in Communist China.

Then, on 6 January 1989, Fang Lizhi wrote an Open Letter to Deng, calling for the release of Wei Jingsheng and other political prisoners. In his letter, he said this would be a good way to celebrate the 40th anniversary of the foundation of the People's Republic, the 70th anniversary of the May 4th Movement (see page 201), and the bicentennial of the French Revolution (which had proclaimed 'liberty, equality and fraternity'). This inspired an unprecedented number of intellectuals to issue similar appeals for a general amnesty for all political prisoners.

By early 1989, the democracy salons of 1988 had turned into regular democracy discussion groups in Beijing University. At the same time, secret political groups in Beijing and other universities were planning their own unofficial demonstrations to mark the May 4th Movement anniversary.

The death of Hu

In the end, things moved faster because of the unexpected death of Hu Yaobang. His death, on 15 April 1989, was rumoured to be the result of his removal from office and subsequent undergoing of 'self-criticism' instigated by 'anti-reformers' in the party. It became the catalyst for the dramatic events in Tiananmen Square in June 1989.

Hu's death provided an opportunity for renewed dissent, as part of the tradition of 'mourning the dead to criticise the living'. There were several marches and rallies, especially in Beijing (10,000 strong in Beijing's Tiananmen Square on 16 April) and Shanghai (1000 strong), at which people spoke in favour of change. Their speeches covered a range of issues, including freedom of information and a free press. As the days went by, the marches and demonstrations grew larger.

Communism in Crisis

Some students staged a sit-in at the Great Hall of the People, demanding that representatives of the National People's Congress receive their petitions. These petitions called for democratic rights such as free organisation and freedom of the press, and condemned corruption and nepotism. Other students – joined by some workers – tried to break into the old Forbidden City, where top CCP leaders had their homes. However, they were met by police, and clashes took place. Meanwhile, the numbers in Tiananmen Square grew as students were joined by workers and other member of the public.

The Politburo decided not to give in to the students' demands, and fixed 22 April as the official day of mourning. As Li Peng and other government officials tried to go into the official ceremony, three students attempted to give Li a petition demanding political liberalisation. However, the government officials refused to accept the petition. By then, over 100,000 demonstrators were standing in the square, silently protesting against Deng's regime; and more than 1 million lined the streets to watch the funeral procession.

Soldiers keep student demonstrators away from the official memorial for Hu Yaobang at the Great Hall of the People, where the service is being held

The government issued a ban on demonstrations and called for them to end. Zhao, who might have argued against this, was away in North Korea on an official visit. The pro-democracy activists ignored the ban. After their mass memorial service on 22 April, the activists began a number of sit-ins and boycotts of university classes. These started on 24 April – and they were soon joined by many non-students, including significant numbers of workers. The protests, which continued throughout April, called for greater democracy and an end to corruption amongst officials.

The *People's Daily* editorial, 26 April

Student leaders then announced the formation of an 'Autonomous Federation' to co-ordinate student activities. In particular, they declared a student strike, while some students began to make speeches on street corners appealing to ordinary citizens to support their calls for democracy and denunciations of corruption.

Deng was getting increasingly annoyed. He wrote an editorial in the *People's Daily* on 26 April condemning the protesters. He said they were a small handful of plotters, who were aiming to cause chaos and undo the leadership of the CCP and the socialist system, and they must be crushed. Even though the editorial had forbidden the students to associate with workers and peasants, transport workers showed solidarity with the students by not collecting fares as they travelled to Beijing from over 40 universities across China. The students (especially those who had made great efforts to show their loyalty to the CCP and socialism) were angered by the editorial, and became more united and determined. However, they were also concerned that they might be repressed at any time, so they called for dialogue with top government and party leaders.

'Beijing Spring' This term was used for events that were similar to the Prague Spring in Czechoslovakia in 1968 (see Chapter 6). Many other Chinese cities, such as Shanghai, Wuhan, Guangzhou and Xian, were also the scenes of demonstrations and protests. Several student activists travelled to Beijing to record the speeches for democracy – along with music by China's main rock bands – and then returned to play them to protesters in their areas. Workers increasingly joined the students in mass demonstrations. Like the ones in the capital, these protests all called for greater political reform.

The 'Beijing Spring'

The next day, 27 April, over 100,000 students from the various campuses in Beijing pushed through the cordons intended to keep them from leaving. Others marched through the streets of Beijing for over 12 hours, to the approval of many local residents. About 500,000 onlookers gave their support in the form of food and money, and even by joining them. The protesters then went to Tiananmen Square. This was the largest demonstration since the death of Zhou in April 1976. The Democracy Movement's actions on 27 April were seen as the start of the **'Beijing Spring'**, and the beginning of a new era of democracy for China.

Splits in the CCP

The actions of the students began to lead to a split in the CCP leadership, with several party leaders now wanting to back down from Deng's uncompromising attitude. These divisions widened on 30 April, when Zhao returned from North Korea. Evidence suggests that the relationship between Deng and Zhao had been deteriorating since the start of the year, with Deng becoming increasingly suspicious of Zhao's links with pro-democracy intellectuals.

Zhao was already unpopular because he had been pushing the new economic policies, and because his two sons had been involved in corruption. For these reasons, Zhao seems to have calculated that he was about to be dropped. He therefore decided to support those CCP leaders who sought compromise with the students. This put him on an unavoidable collision course with Deng.

While this struggle over how to handle the protests went on for much of May, the Democracy Movement continued to spread and grow. The protesters now started to organise a demonstration in Tiananmen Square, outside the CCP headquarters.

Tiananmen Square, May–June 1989

On his return, Zhao tried to appease the protesters, and suggested opening a dialogue with the student leaders. He also suggested that the *People's Daily* had gone too far in attacking the protesters. But he was very much in a minority in the Politburo. His attitude, similar to that of Hu in 1986–87, led to a growing conflict with Premier **Li Peng**.

On the anniversary of the **May 4th Movement**, Zhao characterised the students' demands as 'reasonable'. He urged that they should be implemented in democratic fashion and by legal means.

However, the majority of student leaders were no longer prepared to co-operate with sympathetic government leaders like Zhao. Instead they increased their protests, holding another mass demonstration of over 60,000 in the capital, which the police were unable to control. This was shortly followed by another, 300,000-strong, rally in Tiananmen Square. This protest involved students from all over China, as well as several non-student groups – older intellectuals, journalists and workers.

Though Zhao made no contact with the student leaders, he did support their demand for a retraction of the 26 April editorial, and he called for democratic negotiations with the students. But Deng – and the 'Gang of Old' (most of whom, like Deng, had been victims of the Cultural Revolution) – still refused to consider any compromise. Crucially, they managed to get the support of most of the PLA generals.

The hunger strike

By 13 May, the students had filled Tiananmen Square with makeshift camps. However, by then, splits in the student ranks had helped Deng win the upper hand within the party leadership. On 14 May, a group of about 300 to 500 students marched into the square. Surrounded by thousands of supporters, they began a hunger strike. Their morale was boosted by visits from China's rock stars, who often performed impromptu rock concerts. This merely increased the numbers of those in the square. For the first time, government leaders made contact with student leaders, urging them to end the hunger strike – as Gorbachev was due to arrive the next day.

Li Peng (b. 1928) Li was a hardliner, who was totally opposed to making concessions to the Democracy Movement. This led to growing conflict between him and Zhao. In particular, Li disapproved of Zhao's idea of including trade unions and student organisations in discussions about economic and political reform. Instead, Li supported Deng's continuing belief that the CCP needed to retain an authoritarian political system in order to keep control of the economic reforms.

May 4th Movement
This movement began as a student protest in May 1919, against the terms of the treaties that followed the First World War. These treaties allowed Japan to take over German concessions in China. Many of the people who later went on to form the CCP in 1921 were involved in these earlier student protests.

Fact
There was a split between the older graduate students (who had started the Democracy Movement, and who wanted to work with leaders such as Zhao), and younger, more radical ones (who wanted nothing to do with the existing leadership, which they distrusted). These more radical students were led by Wang Dan and Wuer Kaixi amongst others. It was this latter group that called for a hunger strike.

Communism in Crisis

Gorbachev's impact

Just as Gorbachev's policies and statements since 1985 had encouraged reform communists and others in Eastern Europe (leading to a reduction of communist influence and power), so too were many Chinese influenced by his ideas of *perestroika* – and especially of *glasnost* and *demokratizatsiya* (see page 67). In the spring of 1989, it seemed that several Eastern European satellite states were moving towards ending single-party rule. This encouraged optimism and hope amongst Chinese pro-democracy activists.

> **Fact**
> Gorbachev's visit to China was the first Sino–Soviet summit since 1959, since the start of the split between Mao and Khrushchev over 30 years before. It was planned for 15–19 May, and the visit was seen as very important by the Chinese government leaders.

The students had no intention of calling off their protests. On the contrary, they were emboldened by the presence of international TV crews and journalists, who had arrived early to cover Gorbachev's visit to China. Consequently, their protests were becoming known worldwide, turning a national problem into an international embarrassment for the CCP leaders. The students also believed that the imminent arrival of the Soviet leader would tie the government's hands, and that it would therefore not carry out any repression during Gorbachev's visit.

When the Soviet leader arrived on 15 May, the students ignored orders to disperse, and were joined by 500,000 people. By 17 May, there were 1 million protesters in the square (now including members of the CCP, government office workers, policemen and even PLA cadets), calling for democratic reforms and Deng's resignation.

The protests were so huge that Deng was forced to abandon part of the official schedule. The official reception was moved to Beijing Airport, and Gorbachev's tour of the Forbidden City and a wreath-laying ceremony in Tiananmen Square were cancelled. Gorbachev was kept in indoor meetings until his departure for Shanghai on 18 May. All this was hugely embarrassing for the government, and it strengthened the case of the hardliners who called for firm measures to end the protests.

On 18 May, Li Peng agreed to a televised interview with student leaders such as Wang Dan and Wuer Kaixi – including some of the hunger strikers. The students continued to raise the issues of greater democracy, and the need for the government and party to listen to the people about what should happen next in China. However, the Politburo had already decided that there would be no real dialogue and that no concessions would be made. Instead, that day, the Politburo decided to declare martial law. Though some other members were apparently reluctant, they did not want to oppose the 'paramount leader', so only Zhao voted against this decision.

Zhao's speech

On 19 May, at 4.50 am, on the day Gorbachev was due to leave China, Zhao visited the demonstrators in the square to call on them to end their hunger strike. He also apologised – tearfully – for the actions of the Politburo, and admitted that mistakes had been made and that the students' criticisms were justified.

Zhao (centre, holding the megaphone) talks to students in Tiananmen Square, 19 May 1989

Martial law

On the evening of 19 May, Li Peng broadcast a speech announcing that the government was declaring martial law, in order to deal with the 'rioting' students. PLA units were ordered to take up positions in Beijing, but did not enforce martial law. The students reacted by resuming the hunger strike, which they had only just suspended. In Beijing, local people were able to disarm these PLA units, as many soldiers were sympathetic and unwilling to use force against the protesters.

On Sunday, 21 May, over 1 million people protested. Then, on 23 May, an equally large number of protesters gathered, and many workers and citizens helped construct barricades and roadblocks across streets to prevent military action. Factory workers went on strike, and transport in Beijing was severely disrupted. Workers and students plastered walls with posters, leaflets were produced and distributed, and speeches were made on street corners.

At the same time, the Democracy Movement spread to even more towns and cities – including Hong Kong. The Standing Committee of National People's Congress declared its support for the students, and called for martial law to be repealed. Meanwhile, several retired PLA generals issued an Open Letter to Deng, pointing out that the PLA belonged to the people and could not 'stand in opposition to the people'.

By then, some protesters wanted to end the demonstrations altogether and disperse, as suggested by several sympathetic professors who wished to avoid a bloody confrontation. After some discussion, the students decided to end the hunger strike, but to continue occupying the square.

These developments led to serious continuing divisions over what to do, and so delayed immediate government orders to disperse the protesters from the square. Deng himself was uncertain at first as to how to deal with the students and their demands. However, the students were then joined by workers and ordinary citizens, who blocked the roads leading to the square. This prevented the first wave of PLA troops from reaching the square, and Deng's concerns increased.

Many soldiers were confused about how to react to the mass popular resistance. After discussions with student leaders, the commanders ordered their troops to withdraw to the outskirts of Beijing. Some of the soldiers had started fraternising with the demonstrators, and responded to invitations to join the protesters in singing revolutionary songs. At the same time, the protesters made increasing references to the corruption of party leaders and officials.

SOURCE E

Students, we came too late. Sorry, students. Whatever you say and criticise about us is deserved. My purpose here now is not to ask for your forgiveness … You have been on a hunger strike for six days, and it's now the seventh day. You cannot go on like this … Now what is most important is to end this hunger strike. I know, you are doing this in the hope that the Party and the government will give a most satisfactory answer for what you are asking for. I feel, our channel for dialogue is open, and some problems need to be resolved through a process …

You are still young and have much time ahead of you. You should live healthily to see the day that the Four Modernisations … of China are realised … Now the situation is very dire as you all know, the Party and nation are very anxious, the whole society is worried … You mean well, and have the interests of our country at heart, but if this goes on, it will go out of control and will have various adverse effects … If you stop the hunger strike, the government will not close the door on dialogue, definitely not! What you have proposed, we can continue to discuss. It is slow, but some issues are being broached … All the vigour that you have as young people, we understand as we too were young once, we too protested and we too laid on the tracks without considering the consequences.

Finally I ask again sincerely that you calmly think about what happens from now on. A lot of things can be resolved. I hope that you will end the hunger strike soon and I thank you.

Extracts from Zhao's speech, taken from: http://www.theasiamag.com/cheat-sheet/zhao-ziyangs-tiananmen-square-speech

Activity

Visit http://www.youtube.com/watch?v=JRshth1Nyb4 to see footage of Zhao making this speech.

Communism in Crisis

This photograph, entitled 'Goddess of Democracy versus Chairman Mao', was taken by an anonymous photographer and posted online in June 1989

Between 27 and 30 May, art students built the 'Goddess of Democracy and the Spirit of Liberty' as a symbol of their hopes and aims. After the unveiling of this statue, the numbers in the square itself stood at over 300,000. As the protest continued, more and more people began to side with the pro-democracy protesters.

Repression

Deng and Li at last decided to take strong action. On 29 May, many trade union and workers leaders who had supported the protests were arrested. By the end of May, more politically reliable troops, numbering 200,000, began to move to Beijing. These soldiers came from outside the capital and were led by commanders specially appointed by the government. Under this kind of pressure, the Democracy Movement began to crumble. The large-scale marches and demonstrations ceased, and many students returned to their colleges. Soon, the number remaining in the square had dropped to 5000 – mostly from outside Beijing.

As the student activists dispersed, the protests moved to workers' districts, which had been suffering from the market-based economic reforms. Yet there was no real alliance between the workers and the intellectuals. The latter had never shown much interest in the workers' grievances. In fact, in the early days, students had actively sought to exclude workers, who they felt might be undisciplined and so give the authorities an excuse to take repressive action. The 'Polish fear', which so worried the CCP leadership, was therefore less of a problem than they first thought.

By 2 June, new troops surrounded the square, and controlled the routes leading to and from it. The clashes began in the evening of 3 June, with the first shots being fired at 10 pm. Workers, students and others – using sticks, bricks and Molotov cocktails (home-made explosive devices) – did what they could to prevent the troops reaching the square. It was in the side streets, out of sight of the cameras, that most of the casualties were suffered, as workers in residential areas tried to prevent the tanks reaching the square. At midnight on 3–4 June, Deng finally ordered the army to 'take all necessary measures' to take control of the square and arrest the activists.

In full view of TV cameras, troops and tanks went into action to clear the square and end the demonstrations. Some of the protesters tried to fight back, but most did not. However, all those who tried to remain in the square were fired upon, and hundreds were killed (some put the death toll at about 1500, while others go as high as 7000, with up to 10,000 injured). Towards the end, last-minute discussions between the army officers and rock star Hou Dejian, and literary critic Liu Xiaobo, allowed a group of protesters at the south end of the square to leave. They did so, singing the *Internationale*, the anthem of the international communist movement. Consequently, there were fewer casualties in the square itself. By midday on 4 June, the six-week occupation was over. Riots and resistance were also reported in 80 other cities. Nevertheless, the government was able to quickly suppress all the uprisings and protests.

According to the first official accounts, no civilians had been killed in the square, but 23 students had been killed in fighting that took place in the surrounding streets. The government also that claimed 150 soldiers had been killed and 5000 wounded. Angry members of the crowd did attack and beat some soldiers to death; but there were also unconfirmed reports that some troops who were against the repression had fired on those shooting the protesters. Later official accounts said that fewer than 300 had been killed.

Questions

What is the message of this statue? Why would it have angered many of the CCP leaders?

Fact

The 'Goddess of Democracy and the Spirit of Liberty' was similar to the Statue of Liberty in New York. Many commentators saw this as showing that students were asking for Western or capitalist-style liberal parliamentary democracy. However, many students were calling for socialist democracy, and they saw the statue as having closer links with the French Revolution's demands for 'liberty, equality and fraternity' (the last two not generally being seen as aspects of capitalism). Their statue was erected opposite the official painting of Mao over the central gate, at the north end of the square.

The government imposed a news blackout about the events in the square. Deng sent out an official message, on 9 June, saying that the army had suppressed a 'counter-revolutionary rebellion' that had been planned to spark a coup by 'misguided party leaders'. Deng and the party leadership condemned the student protests, and reaffirmed that the economic reforms would continue. It has been argued that the government used live ammunition (rather than tear gas and water cannons) in order to make it clear to China's people that attempts to press for political democracy would not be tolerated.

During June and July, some estimate that 40,000 people were arrested, with several hundred executed (all workers), and thousands (mostly workers) given long prison sentences. Other estimates give much lower figures. These conflicting statistics illustrate the confusion that followed the events of 4 June. Students – many of whom had relatives in high places – were treated with leniency.

Many leaders of the protests, such as Fang Lizhi, Wang Dan, Wuer Kaixi and **Chai Ling**, managed to avoid arrest. This was despite being on a 'most wanted' list of 21 sought by the authorities. They were eventually able to escape abroad, where they continued the Democracy Movement's struggle.

World reaction

After some initial shock and condemnation, most democratic Western states made very little reference to the violence in the square and the repression and human rights abuses that followed. As the West was keen to get involved in the rapidly expanding Chinese economy, it was very much 'business as usual'. Foreign investment was briefly halted, and cultural exchanges were suspended, but these were resumed relatively quickly. However, organisations such as Amnesty International did take up the cause of pro-democracy activists imprisoned by Deng's regime, and those sent to labour camps for *laogai* (reform through labour).

Why did the Democracy Movement fail?

Part of the reason for the failure of the movement was that the organisers were not united in their aims. Beyond wanting more freedoms, and reform of the party, there was little to bring them together. This made it difficult for sympathetic members of the party and government to negotiate with them. In addition, there were groups amongst the protesters who wanted a violent confrontation with the authorities, and therefore had no wish to compromise. The lack of unity and an agreed list of demands made it easier for Deng to claim that his policy of repression was necessary to prevent China descending into chaos.

The aftermath of the 'Beijing Spring'

One early result was the dismissal, on 24 June, of Zhao (like Hu before him) as general-secretary of the CCP. He was replaced by one of Deng's loyal supporters – Jiang Zemin.

However, the events in Tiananmen Square also saw increased criticism of Deng and his reforms within the CCP leadership. Those who had been unhappy at the move away from Maoism now criticised his privatisation policies. They were even able to block further investment in the SEZs – for a time. Later that year, Deng resigned as chair of the Central Military Commission. However, he continued to exert huge influence over Chinese politics behind the scenes until his death in 1997, aged 92. By 1994, he had made something of a comeback. He successfully challenged his 'conservative' opponents, and his economic policies were soon restored.

Activity

For a live report (by the BBC journalist, Kate Adie) on the suppression, go to: http://www.youtube.com/watch?v=0rVZZQCiEXU There are also videos on youtube of Kate Adie's update and interviews with pro-democracy dissidents in 2009, 20 years after the events of 1989.

Chai Ling (b. 1966) Chai was one of the main women leaders of the demonstrations in Tiananmen Square, and she helped organise the hunger strikes towards the end of the demonstrations. Her parents were both members of the CCP, as she was. However, in 1987, she began to get involved in the demonstrations calling for greater democracy. Known as the 'general commander', she became one of the top 21 dissidents sought by the Chinese government after the Tiananmen Square massacre. She later became a Christian.

Theory of knowledge

History, ethics and utilitarianism

When Edward Hallett Carr came to the end of writing his massive history of the early years of the Russian Revolution, he concluded by saying: 'the danger is not that we shall draw a veil over the enormous blots on the record of the Revolution, over its cost in human suffering, over the crimes committed in its name. The danger is that we shall be tempted to forget altogether, and to pass over in silence, its immense achievement.' How far should utilitarian ethics be applied to what happened in China under Deng in the period 1976–89 – and to what Mao achieved in China in the period 1949–76?

Communism in Crisis

> **Fact**
> It has been estimated that almost 5000 people were arrested immediately after the events of 4 June. Many more were arrested in the weeks that followed. By 17 July, 29 had been given quick trials and executed. Many of these were trade union activists who had tried to link workers' economic demands to the political demands for greater democracy. Deng wanted to make sure that no Solidarity-type movement would emerge in China that might stall his economic reforms. Many others were given long prison sentences. Members of the CCP, known to be sympathetic to some of the demands, were purged. As late as 2007, some activists remained in prison.

At first, in the period immediately following Mao's death, it had not been clear in what direction China was likely to go. But, by 1989, the signs were pretty clear. Under Deng, there would be economic modernisation and liberalisation. However, it was also clear that there would be no 'Fifth Modernisation' – in other words, no political democratisation or liberalisation. Instead, the Chinese Communist Party (unlike almost all of those in Eastern Europe) was determined to retain control. Thus, Chinese political and intellectual life after 1989 was markedly more repressive than it had been during most of the 1980s.

Persecution of dissidents was harsher, and the activities of the secret police were stepped up. Prison sentences for protest became more common, and there was much more censorship of newspapers, books, journals and films.

Activities

1. Carry out further research on the 'democracy salons' that took place in 1988–89. Why did people hold these types of meetings?
2. Produce a spider diagram to summarise the influence of CCP individuals such as Hu Yaobang and Zhao Ziyang on the emerging Democracy Movement during 1988–89.
3. Investigate the different student groups involved in the Tiananmen Square protest. Then draw a chart that briefly indicates their various aims and demands.
4. 'Non-violent protest, against a state prepared to use its armed forces, is always doomed to failure.' To what extent does your study of the crisis of communism – in both China and Eastern Europe – support this statement?

Conclusion

The collapse of the USSR in 1991 left the USA as the only remaining superpower. However, China remains a nuclear power controlled by a communist regime. It has a large population and a rapidly expanding economy, which has made it the second-largest economy in the world (predicted to overtake the USA in 2017). China clearly has the potential to become a rival superpower in the very near future. This is especially true because (unlike the USSR) it has been able to modernise its economy without making any fundamental changes to its political structures.

> **Discussion point**
> Several historians have noted that revolutions do not usually result in balanced appraisals. It usually takes several generations before the bitterness of ideological battles and disappointments has faded enough to allow the historical record to be looked at dispassionately. When Zhou Enlai was asked his assessment of the French Revolution of 1789, he relied: 'It is too early to tell.' Do you think it's possible to properly assess the contributions of Mao and Deng to China's development?

Although this progress has had much to do with Deng's policies, the achievements under Mao should not be forgotten. Certainly the biggest blots on Mao's record – the Great Leap Forward and the Cultural Revolution – should not take away from the fact that the Maoist period was one of the greatest modernising periods in world history. It brought great social and human benefits to the Chinese people. However, it could be argued that Mao did significantly less to create a socialist society than he did to create an industrially modern economy. What do you think the long-term verdict on Deng's reforms will be?

ial developments in China under Deng

End of chapter activities

Summary

You should now have a good understanding of the main political developments in China in the period 1976–89. You should also be able to comment on the reasons for the emergence of the Democracy Movement, and for its suppression in June 1989.

Summary activity

Copy the spider diagram below. Then, using the information in this chapter and from any other available sources, make brief notes under the headings and sub-headings shown. Remember to include information on historical debate/interpretations, including names of historians.

Paper 1 exam practice

Question

Compare and contrast the descriptions of the events in Tiananmen Square on 4 June 1989, as given in Sources A and B below.
[6 marks]

Skill

Cross-referencing

Politics in China 1976–89

1 Political relaxation, 1976–79
- Democracy Wall
- The Fifth Modernisation
- The closure of Democracy Wall

2 Political developments, 1980–88
- Reform of the CCP
- Role of intellectuals
- Renewed student unrest, 1986–87
- Fall of Hu and renewed opposition

3 Road to Tiananmen Square, 1988–89
- Democracy salons and intellectuals
- Tiananmen Square, April–June 1989
- The aftermath

SOURCE A

A shocking counter-revolutionary rebellion took place in the capital of Beijing on the 3rd. and 4th. of June following more than a month of turmoil ... In the early morning hours of June 4, a group of rioters at a junction on Dongan Road attacked fighters [PLA troops] with bottles, bricks and bicycles. The faces of the [soldiers] were covered with blood. At Fuxing Gate a vehicle was intercepted. All 12 [soldiers] ... were beaten soundly. Many of them were seriously wounded ... After dawn, the beating and killing of PLA fighters reached a degree that made one's blood boil ...

At 0430, the notice of the Martial Law Command was broadcast in the square ... Upon hearing the notice, the several thousand young students remaining in the square immediately assembled and deployed pickets who linked their hands ... The martial law troops left a wide opening in the southern entrance of the eastern side of the square, thereby ensuring the swift, smooth, and safe withdrawal of the students ... During the entire course of evacuation ... not a single one of the sit-in students in the square ... died. The claim that 'blood has formed a stream in Tiananmen' is sheer nonsense.

Extracts from the 9 June broadcast by China's official Xinhua News Agency, on the events in Tiananmen Square; translated in Foreign Broadcast Information Service (FBIS-CHI-89-111), 12 June 1989, pp. 62–66.

Communism in Crisis

SOURCE B

The crackdown continued through the night, and by early morning June 4, as this cable reports, the PLA was in control of Tiananmen Square ... Based on eyewitness accounts of the violence, this ... is the Embassy's initial effort to provide some detail on the final PLA assault on the approximately 3,000 demonstrators who had not yet left the square. 'Some 10,000 troops' ... formed a ring around the square, and 'a column of about 50 APC [armoured personnel carriers], tanks, and trucks entered Tiananmen Square from the east.' ... 'PLA troops in Tiananmen Square opened a barrage of rifle and machine gun fire.' Another column of military vehicles entered soon thereafter, and more gunfire ensued, 'causing a large number of casualties.' [There were] ... also ... violent PLA clashes with demonstrators on Changan Boulevard, the main thoroughfare in the Tiananmen area, and in other parts of Beijing. Embassy officials also report conversations with angry citizens, some 'claiming more than 10,000 people had been killed at Tiananmen.'

Extracts from a cable sent by the US Embassy, Beijing, to the Department of State, Washington DC, about the events of 4 June 1989. Quoted in Tiananmen Square, 1989. The Declassified History. A National Security Archive, Electronic Briefing Book No. 16. George Washington University.

Examiner's tips, common mistakes and a simplified markscheme for cross-referencing questions can be found on page 216.

Student answer

Sources A and B give quite different descriptions of what happened in Tiananmen Square. This is not surprising as Source A is from an official Chinese government source. According to this, no students were killed in the square – instead, it concentrates on giving information about attacks on PLA soldiers, including the 'killing of PLA fighters', by the demonstrators.

However, in Source B – which is an official US government document, based on information provided by 'eyewitnesses' – there is no mention of students attacking PLA troops, or even of resisting them. According to this source, the PLA fired at the demonstrators – apparently without any of the provocation mentioned in Source A. According to Source B, ' ...more than 10,000 people had been killed at Tiananmen'; this is in complete contrast to Source A which states quite clearly that accounts of bloodshed in the square are 'sheer nonsense'.

Examiner's comments

There are several clear/precise references to both the sources, and several **differences/contrasts** are identified. Also, the sources are clearly linked in the second paragraph, rather than being dealt with separately. The candidate has thus done enough to get into Band 2, and so be awarded 4 or 5 marks. However, as no similarities/comparisons are made, this answer fails to get into Band 1.

Activity

Look again at the two sources, the simplified markscheme, and the student answer above. Now try to write a paragraph or two to push the answer up into Band 1, and so obtain the full 6 marks, by commenting on any similarities. There are one or two – including the dates both sources give.

Paper 2 practice questions

1 How, and with what results, did Deng promote a 'loosening' of political controls in the period 1976–79?

2 Analyse the reasons why political unrest affected China for large parts of the 1980s.

3 'The main reason why the Democracy Movement was defeated by the end of 1989 was because it was divided into several different factions.' To what extent do you agree with this assertion?

4 Examine the ways in which Deng attempted to retain the CCP's political monopoly in the period 1980–89.

10 Conclusion: Communism – from crisis to collapse

Introduction

By 2000, it seemed fair to argue that communism – in the USSR, Eastern Europe and China – had conspicuously failed. During the period 1989–91, the Soviet Union and all the communist regimes in Eastern Europe had collapsed, following unsuccessful attempts to cope with their various economic and political crises. In addition, Russia (the most significant republic in the former Soviet Union) rapidly moved to full-blooded capitalism after 1991.

In contrast, the communist regime in China seemed to have overcome similar crises *and* managed to maintain its authoritarian one-party rule. However, many observers have argued that the ruling party and government were communist in name only. China appeared to have successfully solved the economic problems of stagnation and low productivity that had greatly contributed to the collapse of communism in Europe. But it seemed the government had only been able to do so by rapidly turning China into a capitalist economy. Thus, many have suggested that communism had actually ended in China, too.

After 1991, communism remained the official ideology of only a handful of states. Apart from China (which was quickly applying capitalist economic policies), the only states to remain communist were North Korea, Cuba and Vietnam. Of these, the latter two also started moving towards market-based economic reforms, once aid from the Soviet Union ceased. By 2000, therefore, the verdict of history on communism (as a general political theory and practice) seemed mixed, to say the least.

What caused the collapse of communism?

Since the collapse of communism in Eastern Europe and the USSR between 1988 and 1991 (and its increasing abandonment in China since 1976), historians have been debating the causes of these events. In seeking to explain this relatively rapid and largely unexpected collapse, many historians have focused on the internal contradictions and weaknesses of these regimes. Others have also attempted to assess external factors: in particular, the role of the US.

Internal weaknesses

There were clearly many long-standing economic and political weaknesses within the Eastern European regimes, and the Soviet Union itself, that played a big part in the eventual downfall of communism in Europe. These included bureaucratic control of the economy, which resulted in much inefficiency and waste, and in rates of productivity significantly lower than those achieved in the West. In addition, from the late 1980s, the Eastern European regimes and the USSR became increasingly drawn into the global capitalist economy.

Fact
After the break-up of the Soviet Union in December 1991, Yeltsin was president of the Russian Federation until 1999. He decided to establish a 'free' market economy, based on price rises and a massive privatisation programme. This resulted in a small group of oligarchs getting possession of former state property – and becoming billionaires in the process. But for many Russians, the result was high unemployment, unpaid wages and pensions, and poverty.

Fact
During the 1930s, the USSR under Stalin remained largely isolated from world capitalism, and achieved dramatic industrial growth at a time when the US and other Western economies experienced serious economic problems as a result of the Great Depression. The situation in the late 1980s was very different – by then the USSR and Eastern Europe had developed much closer links with the global capitalist economy.

Furthermore, the undemocratic political systems existing in these communist-ruled states alienated large sections of their populations. Gorbachev-style reforms arguably came too late to save the system. However, it does seem that earlier US policies (especially maintaining and escalating the nuclear arms race) also contributed to the ultimate collapse of Soviet economic and political structures. These external pressures also made it harder for the USSR to continue supporting the regimes in Eastern Europe.

The role of the USA

In 1992, George Kennan (a leading architect of US foreign policy in the early years of the Cold War) claimed that the US did not have the power to bring about changes within the USSR. This was a surprising claim for him to make, as he had helped formulate the policy of containment of communism, implemented immediately after the Second World War. This policy was originally based on the belief that containment would not just counter Soviet influence in the world and stop it spreading, but would also help *undermine* the Soviet system.

In addition to economic barriers and sanctions, imposed at various times, US agents actively sought to provoke and assist unrest both within the USSR and in various other communist regimes. For example, as noted in Chapter 6, during the 1980s the CIA channelled funds to Solidarity, the unofficial trade union in Poland. Also important were the increasingly expensive developments in nuclear weapons throughout the Cold War. These placed a much bigger burden on the relatively weaker Soviet economy, and diverted resources from producing consumer goods. The USA's refusal to abandon its SDI project presented real problems for Gorbachev and other Soviet leaders, who realised that the Soviet economy would crack if they attempted to maintain parity.

US officials knew about the Soviet economic weakness and they used this knowledge at the Malta Summit in December 1989, between Gorbachev and US president George Bush. At the same summit, the end of the Cold War was officially announced. Gorbachev agreed to a loosening of Soviet ties with the Eastern European states, although he had not yet accepted that they would end completely. In return, the US agreed to provide much-needed economic aid and investment for the Soviet Union – but with some conditions. These included promising to move towards a capitalist market economy, as well as introducing political reforms. In fact, many of these US funds were held back during 1990–91 – for example, to put pressure on Gorbachev to agree to the reunification of Germany. Back in 1947, these possible consequences were precisely the reasons why Stalin had rejected participation in the USA's Marshall Plan.

The end of history?

The collapse of the Eastern European regimes during 1989, and the clearly serious crisis facing Soviet communism, had significant global implications beyond the **Iron Curtain**. In particular, it led to the end of the Cold War. By the end of 1991, the communist-dominated regimes of Eastern Europe, and the Soviet Union itself, had collapsed. Along with them, the Eastern bloc's Cold War military and economic organisations – the Warsaw Pact and the Council for Mutual Economic Assistance (Comecon) – had also gone. Meanwhile, the Western versions (NATO and the European Union) still existed. The Cold War was clearly at an end; after the collapse of the Soviet Union in December 1991, only one of the two superpowers remained.

Iron Curtain This refers to the at-first imaginary border dividing the capitalist states of Western Europe from the Eastern European states under Soviet domination. As the Cold War developed, this border became physical.

Communism in Crisis

This left the USA with supreme global power after decades of struggle. Some historians, such as Richard Crockatt, have seen 1991 as the end of what has been described as 'the Fifty Years' War' between the US and the USSR – a war that had clearly been won by the US, with its greater economic, technological and military strength.

This cartoon about the end of the Cold War appeared in the Guardian, *a British newspaper, in June 1988*

> **AN EPIPHANY.**
> LOOK AT THE FACTS, SIR. THE SOVIETS ARE IN THE THROES OF PERESTROIKA, THE CHINESE ARE RESTRUCTURING **THEIR** ECONOMY...
>
> FROM POLAND TO VIETNAM, DISCREDITED COMMUNIST ECONOMIC AND POLITICAL MODELS ARE BEING CHALLENGED, WHILE CAPITALIST VALUES ARE EMBRACED!
> WHAT ARE YOU SAYING HERE, HOWARD?
>
> I'M SAYING THE COLD WAR IS **OVER**, SIR! IT'S OVER, AND WE **WON**!
> WE WON?
>
> **WITHIN HOURS, TIMES SQUARE ERUPTED.**
> U.S.A.! WE'RE NUMBER ONE!
> VICTORY! WEST K.O.'S EAST! COLD WAR OVER!

Other commentators have argued that the collapse of the Soviet Union heralded not just the end of the Cold War, but also something of even wider significance. They believe it showed that the 'Great Contest' between capitalism and communism, which began with the Bolshevik Revolution in Russia in 1917 and lasted for almost 75 years, was finally over. Thus Francis Fukuyama, a US official at the time, announced that the 'end of history' had arrived. By this, he meant the final victory of 'liberal' capitalism over Marxism and communist (or other radical) movements based on this political philosophy.

10 Conclusion: Communism – from crisis to collapse

The idea of communism

However, in view of the ecological crises and the 2008 financial crash, Fukuyama's claims that capitalism was secure and that Marxism had been permanently consigned to the 'dustbin of history' might prove to be premature. Communism has certainly experienced crises, including the collapse of the communist states of Europe during 1988–91, and the developments in China after 1976. Nevertheless, some historians argue that these events do not necessarily mark the end of Marxism, communism and the 'Great Contest'.

In particular, these historians point out that Marxist theory and communist practice arose from conditions of poverty, the destruction of war, and a strong desire for liberty, fairness and equality. While it could be argued that most people in the developed world enjoy these freedoms and conditions, this is hardly true of the majority of the world's population. With the collapse of the USSR and its satellite regimes in Eastern Europe, and the continuing authoritarian rule of the CCP in China, commentators have suggested that a newer, more liberal and libertarian, version of communism might emerge. This could challenge the global economic interests of the US and Western capitalism, and of Chinese 'capitalism'. It could also challenge the Stalinist version of Marxism and communism, which has historically marked the political forms of rule associated with these 'communist' states.

In fact, the original version of Marxism can be seen as a logical extension of the more radical socialist interpretation first given by François-Noël Babeuf (1760–97) to the French Revolution's ideals of 'liberty, equality and fraternity'. Significantly perhaps, 200 years later, the demand for the full implementation of these ideals formed the core demands of the crowds in Eastern European cities and in Tiananmen Square, Beijing. Thus, it may be rather too early for historians to proclaim the death and funeral of communism.

In this cartoon, Gorbachev leads a funeral procession, burying communism, as Lenin, Stalin and Marx look down from communist paradise above

'I CAN'T BELIEVE MY EYES!'

Question

What is the message of this cartoon? How does the cartoonist get their message across?

SOURCE A

We have to take the long view of the historical process ... For as long as contemporary capitalism, a system based on exploitation and inequality and recurring crises, not to mention its impact on the fragile economy of the planet, continues to exist, the possibility of anti-capitalist movements taking power cannot be ruled out ... The duels between the possessors and the dispossessed continue, taking new forms.

Ali, T. 2009. *The Idea of Communism.* London, UK. Seagull Books. pp. 112–14.

11 Exam practice

Introduction

You have now completed your study of the main aspects and events of Communism in Crisis – both in the USSR and Eastern Europe, and in China – during the period 1976–89. In the previous chapters, you have had practice at answering some of the types of source-based questions you will have to deal with in Paper 1. In this chapter, you will gain experience of dealing with:

- the longer Paper 1 question, which requires you to use both sources and your own knowledge to write a mini-essay
- the essay questions you will meet in Paper 2.

Exam skills needed for IB History

This book is designed primarily to prepare both Standard and Higher Level students for the Paper 1 Communism in Crisis topic (Prescribed Subject 3), by providing the necessary historical knowledge and understanding, as well as an awareness of the key historical debates. However it will also help you prepare for Paper 2, by giving you the chance to practise writing essays. The skills you need for answering both Paper 1 and Paper 2 exam questions are explained in the following pages.

Paper 1 skills

This section of the book will give you the skills and understanding to tackle Paper 1 questions. These are based on the comprehension, critical analysis and evaluation of different types of historical sources as evidence, along with the use of appropriate historical contextual knowledge.

For example, you will need to test sources for value and limitations (i.e. their reliability and utility, especially in view of their origins and purpose) – an essential skill for historians. A range of sources has been provided, including extracts from official documents, tables of statistics, memoirs and speeches, as well as visual sources such as photographs and cartoons.

In order to analyse and evaluate sources as historical evidence, you will need to ask the following **'W' questions** of historical sources:

- **Who** produced it? Were they in a position to know?
- **What** type of source is it? What is its nature – is it a primary or secondary source?
- **Where** and **when** was it produced? What was happening at the time?
- **Why** was it produced? Was its purpose to inform or to persuade? Is it an accurate attempt to record facts, or is it an example of propaganda?
- **Who** was the intended audience – was it aimed at decision-makers, or the general public?

11 Exam practice

You should then consider how the answers to these questions affect a source's value. The example (right) shows you how to find the information related to the 'W' questions. You will need this information in order to evaluate sources for their value and limitations. This approach will help you become familiar with interpreting, understanding, analysing and evaluating different types of historical sources. It will also aid you in synthesising critical analysis of sources with historical knowledge when constructing an explanation or analysis of some aspect of the past. Remember – for Paper 1, as for Paper 2, you need to acquire, select and use relevant historical knowledge to explain causes, consequences, continuity and change. You also need to develop and show (where relevant) an awareness of historical debates and different interpretations

Paper 1 contains four types of question:
1 Comprehension/understanding of a source (2 or 3 marks)
2 Cross-referencing/comparing or contrasting two sources (6 marks)
3 Assessing the value and limitations of two sources (6 marks)
4 Using and evaluating sources to reach a judgement (8 marks)

Comprehension/understanding of a source

Comprehension questions require you to understand a source and extract two or three relevant points that relate to the particular question.

Examiner's tips

Step 1 – Read the source and highlight/underline key points.

Step 2 – Write a concise answer. Just a couple of brief sentences are needed, giving the information necessary to show that you have understood the message of the source – but make sure you make three clear points for a 3-mark question and two clear points for a 2-mark question. If relevant, also try to make some brief overall comment about the source. Make it as easy as possible for the examiner to give you the marks by clearly distinguishing between the points.

Common mistakes

- Make sure you don't comment on the wrong source! Mistakes like this are made every year. Remember – every mark is important for your final grade.
- Don't just copy the source. Summarise the key points in your own words.

Simplified markscheme

For **each item of relevant/correct information** identified, award 1 mark – up to a **maximum of 2 or 3 marks.**

SOURCE A

We must make a special effort to explain the question of democracy clearly to the people, and to our youth in particular. The socialist road, the dictatorship of the proletariat, the leadership of the Communist Party and Marxism–Leninism and Mao Zedong Thought – all these are tied up with democracy. What kind of democracy do the Chinese people need today? It can only be socialist democracy, people's democracy, and not bourgeois democracy, individualist democracy.

Extract from a *speech* made by Deng Xiaoping on 30 March 1979, setting out his views to 'Democracy Wall' students about democracy and the Four Cardinal Principles, following the arrest of Wei Jingsheng, the author of 'The Fifth Modernisation'.

---

speech WHAT? (type of source)
Deng Xiaoping WHO? (produced it)
30 March 1979 WHEN? (date/time of production)
setting out his views WHY? (possible purpose)
'Democracy Wall' students WHO? (intended audience)

Timing: For a 3-mark question you should spend no more than about 7 minutes, and for a 2-mark question no more than about 5 minutes. Don't spend too long on these questions, or you will run out of time!

Examples of a comprehension question can be found at the end of Chapter 2 (see page 40) and Chapter 7 (see page 161).

Communism in Crisis

Cross-referencing/comparing or contrasting two sources

Cross-referencing questions require you to compare **and** contrast the information/content/nature of **two** sources, relating to a particular issue.

Examiner's tips

For cross-referencing questions, you need to provide an integrated comparison, rather than dealing with each source separately.

Step 1 – Read the sources and highlight/underline key points.

Step 2 – Draw a rough chart or diagram to show the **similarities** and the **differences** between the two sources. That way, you should ensure you address both elements of the question.

Step 3 – Write your answer, ensuring that you write an integrated comparison. For example, you should comment on how the two sources deal with one aspect, then compare and contrast the sources on another aspect. Avoid simply describing/paraphrasing each source in turn – you need to make **clear and explicit** comparisons and contrasts, using precise details from the sources.

Common mistakes

- Don't just comment on **one** of the sources! Such an oversight happens every year – and will lose you 4 of the 6 marks available.
- Make sure you comment on the sources identified in the question – don't select one (or two) incorrect sources!
- Be careful to make **explicit** comparisons – do not fall into the trap of writing about the two sources separately and leaving the similarities/differences implicit.

Simplified markscheme

Band		Marks
1	**Both** sources **linked**, with **detailed references** to the two sources, identifying **both** similarities **and** differences.	6
2	**Both** sources **linked**, with **detailed references** to the two sources, identifying **either** similarities **or** differences.	4–5
3	Comments on both sources, **but** treating each one **separately**.	3
4	Discusses/comments on just **one** source.	0–2

> Examples of a cross-referencing question can be found at the end of Chapter 4 (see page 87), Chapter 5 (see page 111) and Chapter 9 (page 207).

Assessing the value and limitations of two sources

Value and limitations (utility/reliability) questions require you to assess **two** sources over a range of possible issues/aspects – and to comment on their value to historians studying a particular event or period of history.

Examiner's tips

The main areas you need to consider in relation to the sources and the information/view they provide are:

- **origin** and **purpose**
- value and limitations.

These areas need to be linked in your answer, showing how the value and limitations of each source to historians relate to the source's origin and purpose.

For example, a source might be useful because it is primary – the event depicted was witnessed by the person producing it. But was the person in a position to know? Is the view an untypical view of the event? What is its nature? Is it a private diary entry, and therefore possibly more likely to be true? Or is it a speech or piece of propaganda intended to persuade? The value of a source may be limited by some aspects, but that doesn't mean it has no value at all. For example, it may be valuable as evidence of the types of propaganda produced at the time. Similarly, a secondary (or even a tertiary source) can have more value than some primary sources – for instance, because the author might have been writing at a time when new evidence has become available.

For these questions it is best to deal with each source separately, as you are not being asked to decide which source is more important/useful.

Step 1 – Read the sources and highlight/underline key points.

Step 2 – For **each source**, draw a rough chart or spider diagram to show the origin/purpose of the source, and how it links to that source's value/limitation.

Step 3 – Write your answer, remembering to deal with **all** the aspects required: **origins, purpose, value and limitations**. To do this, you will need to make **explicit** links between a source's origins/purpose **and** its value/limitations to a historian.

Common mistakes

- Don't just comment on **one** of the two sources! As with cross-referencing questions, every year a few students make this mistake and lose up to 4 of the 6 marks available.
- Don't just comment on content and ignore the nature, origins and purpose of the sources.
- Don't say 'a source is/isn't useful because it's primary/secondary'.

Band		Marks
1	**Both** sources assessed, with **explicit consideration** of BOTH origins and purpose AND value and limitations.	5–6
2	**Both** sources assessed, but without consideration of BOTH origins and purpose AND value and limitations. OR **explicit consideration** of BOTH origins and purpose AND value and limitations – BUT only for **one** source.	3–4
3	**Limited** consideration/comments on origins and purpose OR value and limitations. Possibly only one/the wrong source(s) addressed.	0–2

origins The 'who, what, when and where?' questions

purpose This means 'reasons, what the writer/creator was trying to achieve, who the intended audience was'.

Remember – a source doesn't have to be primary to be useful. Remember, too, that content isn't the only aspect to have possible value. The context, the person who produced it, and so on, can be important in offering an insight.

Examples of a value and limitations question can be found at the end of Chapter 3 (see page 65), Chapter 6 (see page 140) and Chapter 8 (see page 183).

Communism in Crisis

Using and evaluating sources and knowledge to reach a judgement

The fourth type of Paper 1 is a judgement question. Judgement questions are a *synthesis of source evaluation and own knowledge*.

Examiner's tips

- This fourth type of Paper 1 question requires you to produce a mini-essay, with a clear/relevant argument, to address the question/statement given in the question. You should try to develop and present an argument and/or come to a balanced judgement by analysing and using these **five** sources **and** your own knowledge.

- Before you write your answer to this kind of question, you may find it useful to draw a rough chart to note what the sources show in relation to the question. This will also ensure that you refer to all or at least most of the sources. Note, however, that some sources may hint at more than one factor/result. When using your own knowledge, make sure it is relevant to the question.

- Look carefully at the simplified markscheme below. This will help you focus on what you need to do to reach the top bands and so score the higher marks.

Common mistake

- Don't just deal with sources or your own knowledge! Every year, some candidates (even good ones) do this, and so limit themselves to – at best – only 5 out of the 8 marks available.

Simplified markscheme

Band		Marks
1	**Developed and balanced** analysis and comments using **BOTH** sources **AND** own knowledge. References to sources are precise; sources and detailed own knowledge are used together; where relevant, a judgement is made.	8
2	**Developed** analysis/comments using **BOTH** sources **AND** some detailed own knowledge; some clear references to sources. But sources and own knowledge not always **combined**.	6–7
3	**Some developed** analysis/comments, using the sources **OR** some relevant own knowledge.	4–5
4	**Limited/general** comments using sources **OR** own knowledge.	0–3

Student answers

The student answers below have brief examiner's comments in the margins, as well as a longer overall comment at the end. Those parts of the answers that make use of the sources are **highlighted in green**. Those parts that use relevant own knowledge are **highlighted in red**. In this way, you should find it easier to understand why particular bands and marks were – or were not – awarded.

11 Exam practice

Question 1

Using Sources A, B, C, D and E on pages 219–20, **and** your own knowledge, analyse the reasons for the political stagnation in the Soviet Union that developed under Brezhnev.

[8 marks]

SOURCE A

Leonid Brezhnev … became increasingly the central element in the political leadership … Originally, in 1964, a 'collective leadership', it had become a leadership 'headed by comrade L. I. Brezhnev' by the early 1970s. The Politburo had been listed in alphabetical order after 1964 to emphasise its collective character, but in 1973, after the KGB chairman Yuri Andropov had joined it, Brezhnev's name continued to be listed first although this was a violation of strictly alphabetical principles … At the 26th Party Congress in 1981 … Brezhnev's son, Yuri, a first deputy minister of foreign trade … became a candidate member of the Central Committee … and so too did his son-in-law Yuri Churbanov, a first deputy minister of internal affairs.

White, S. 1993. *After Gorbachev.* Cambridge, UK. Cambridge University Press. p. 2.

SOURCE B

Brezhnev being helped to his seat after giving a speech; by 1979, his health was already visibly declining

SOURCE C

Underlying the stagnation – but also constituting its main symptom – was a deadlocked Politburo around a brain-dead Brezhnev … The other aspect of the picture, which was blatant enough to be widely known throughout Russia, was the spread of a tentacular corruption. Members of Brezhnev's family were ostentatiously involved in it – a subject poor Leonid did not like to hear spoken about. Mushrooming mafia networks, with which many highly placed party officials were associated, were something else the country (if not certain leaders) was aware of. Nothing on such a scale had been known before.

Lewin, M. 2005. *The Soviet Century.* London, UK. Verso. p. 261. *Lewin is a professor of history at the University of Pennsylvania, USA.*

Communism in Crisis

SOURCE D

1. Principles of the Social Structure and Policy of the USSR
Chapter 1
The Political System

Article 1. The Union of Soviet Socialist Republics is a socialist state of the whole people, expressing the will and interests of the workers, peasants, and intelligentsia, the working people of all the nations and nationalities of the country.

Article 2. All power in the USSR belongs to the people. The people exercise state power through Soviets of People's Deputies, which constitute the political foundation of the USSR.
All other state bodies are under the control of, and accountable to, the Soviets of People's Deputies.

Article 4. The state and all its bodies function on the basis of socialist law, ensure the maintenance of law and order, and safeguard the interests of society and the rights and freedoms of citizens.
State organizations, public organizations and officials shall observe the Constitution of the USSR and Soviet laws.

Article 6. The leading and guiding force of Soviet society and the nucleus of its political system, of all state and public organizations, is the Communist Party of the Soviet Union. The CPSU exists for the people and serves the people.

Extracts from the Constitution (Fundamental Law) of the USSR, 1977. *Quoted in Lane, D. 1985.* State and Politics in the USSR. *Oxford, UK. Wiley-Blackwell. p. 348.*

SOURCE E

This photograph of the Troizkoje Psychiatric Clinic was taken without official permission, and was then smuggled out of Russia, to be published abroad by supporters of dissidents

Student answer

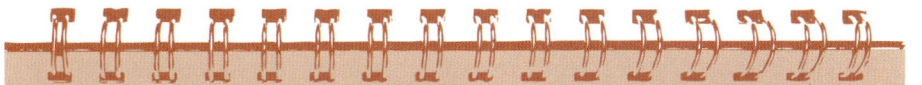

There are a number of reasons why political stagnation happened under Brezhnev's leadership. One reason is shown by Source B, which shows an ageing and ill Brezhnev, having to be helped down after giving a speech. This is also one of the points made by Source C, which refers to him as 'brain-dead'. Yet Brezhnev went on as the dominant leader until 1982, thus wasting valuable years when reforms could have been introduced.

Brezhnev came into power in 1964, following the overthrow of Khrushchev, who had attempted to carry out some significant political and economic reforms. Several of the CPSU leaders were against real change and, although at first, it was supposed to be a 'collective leadership' – as stated by Source A – Brezhnev soon made himself strong enough to sideline reformers such as Kosygin, who wanted to make some economic reforms which were similar to those later implemented by Gorbachev after 1985.

Examiner's comment
This is a good, well-focused, start, with a clear argument – Sources A, B and C are referred to and used, along with a little own knowledge.

Sources A and C also refer to another problem linked to Brezhnev's long period of control – this was the problem of nepotism and corruption. Source A mentions that both Brezhnev's son and his son-in-law were given important government jobs. However, more important than giving jobs to family members was the corruption, which became so extensive under Brezhnev, that Source C refers to it as 'tentacular', and clearly states that 'Nothing on such a scale had been known before'. More worryingly, Source C refers to 'mafia networks'. This not only involved top leaders, such as his daughter and son-in-law (in the Sokolov case, the director of Moscow's leading food store), but even Brezhnev himself. His successor, Andropov, tried to stamp it out, before he died in February 1984, but had limited success. An example came to light later in 1984, when long-lived corruption in the cotton industry in the Central Asian Republics was discovered. However, there were no prosecutions, as the main leader was the top party leader in Uzbekistan – so these problems continued as those at the top had a vested interest in keeping things as they were, thus helping to maintain political stagnation.

Examiner's comment
Sources A and C are again clearly referred to and used, showing good understanding, and there is some own knowledge about corruption, which is explicitly linked to political stagnation.

Communism in Crisis

Finally, Sources D and E relate to another reason – the lack of freedom and democracy. Source D, which includes extracts from the new 1977 'Brezhnev' Constitution, states that 'All power in the USSR belongs to the people', and that 'The CPSU exists for the people and serves the people'. However, this was not the case, as the CPSU had a monopoly of political power, as the only legal party in the one-party system which, in many ways, had not altered much from the days of Stalin. As a result, there was an increase in dissidence under Brezhnev, by intellectuals (such as Sakharov, Sinyavsky and Daniel) who were increasingly prepared to challenge the government – for instance, on civil and human rights issues (especially after the Helsinki Accords of 1975). Source E shows one way in which Brezhnev tried to cope with dissidents – the use of psychiatric clinics. Many young people were also turning to alternative lifestyles – but, under Brezhnev, dissatisfaction with political stagnation did not really affect the workers.

Examiner's comment
As before, two more sources (D and E) are clearly used and linked. There is also some relevant own knowledge. However, the student does not make it very clear or explicit how these are reasons (as opposed to symptoms) of stagnation.

So, in conclusion, these five sources touch on all the main reasons why there was political stagnation under Brezhnev. The Cold War had begun by 1949. Overall, the main reason was probably the one shown in Sources A, B and C – Brezhnev's old age, his reluctance to support reform, and the corruption which meant most leaders were happy to let things continue in the old way.

Overall examiner's comments

There is a clear argument, and good use of the sources, with clear references to them. However, although there is a mixture of some precise and general own knowledge, which is mainly integrated with comments on the sources, there are some omissions. For instance, own knowledge could have been used to give other reasons not touched on by the sources – such as the presence of other ageing members of the Politburo and the Central Committee; the fact that the USSR was improving its military defences (thus militating against changing a political system which seemed to be delivering 'the goods'); the fear that greater freedom might lead to developments such as those in Czechoslovakia in 1968; and the lack of a free press. Also, the student could have pointed out that, for most people, Brezhnev's rule coincided with improved living standards. Many ordinary people were therefore not interested in the demands of dissidents for political reform. Hence, this answer fails to get into Band 1 – but this is a reasonably sound Band 2 answer and so probably scores 6 marks out of the 8 available.

11 ▶ Exam practice

Activity

Look again at all the sources, the simplified markscheme, and the student answer above. Now try to write a few paragraphs to push the answer up into Band 1, and so obtain the full 8 marks. As well as using all/most of the sources, and some precise own knowledge, try to integrate the sources with your own knowledge, rather than dealing with sources and own knowledge separately. And don't lose sight of the need to use the sources and your own knowledge to explain *why* political stagnation developed under Brezhnev.

Question 2

Using the sources *and* your own knowledge, explain how successful Deng Xiaoping was in achieving his aims for economic reform.
[8 marks]

SOURCE A

Major problems faced the new Deng administration: the government now had a 6.5 billion yuan deficit; 20 million Chinese were unemployed; and an estimated 100 million were undernourished. The military was woefully out of date, as was China's own technology and scientific research. Thousands of CCP members and wide segments of the population questioned the decisions of the Party leadership … If the legacy of the [Maoist] revolutionaries was to mean anything, new approaches to China's many problems were imperative … Deng and his supporters realized that without economic advances, the future position of the CCP would be untenable.

Benson, L. 2002. *China Since 1949*. Harlow, UK. Longman. p. 46.
Benson is a professor of history at Oakland University, Michigan, USA.

SOURCE B

What is socialism and what is Marxism? We were not quite clear about this in the past. Marxism attaches utmost importance to developing the productive forces … Therefore, the fundamental task for the socialist stage is to develop the productive forces … Socialism means eliminating poverty. Pauperism is not socialism, still less communism …

Capitalism can only enrich less than 10 per cent of the Chinese population; it can never enrich the remaining more than 90 per cent …

Our political line is to focus on the modernization programme and on continued development of the productive forces … The minimum target of our modernization programme is to achieve a comparatively comfortable standard of living by the end of the century … To do this, we have to invigorate the domestic economy and open to the outside world …

Extracts from Deng's speech, 'Build socialism with Chinese characteristics', 30 June 1984, to the Japanese businessmen's delegation at the second session of the Council of Sino–Japanese Non-Governmental Persons. From http://english.peopledaily.com.cn/dengxp/vol3/text/c1220.html

Communism in Crisis

SOURCE C

China's industrial performance, 1979–89

Year	GDP (in billions of yuan)	Annual GDP growth rate (%)	Annual inflation rate (%)	Annual manufacturing output growth rate (%)
1979	732.6	7.6	6.1	8.6
1980	790.5	7.9	−1.5	11.9
1981	826.1	4.5	7.0	1.6
1982	896.3	8.5	11.5	5.5
1983	987.7	10.2	8.3	9.2
1984	1130.9	14.5	12.9	14.5
1985	1276.8	12.9	1.8	18.1
1986	1385.4	8.5	3.3	8.3
1987	1539.1	11.1	4.7	12.7
1988	1713.1	11.3	2.5	15.8
1989	1786.7	4.3	3.1	4.9

SOURCE D

Not surprisingly, the modernisation schemes met strong resistance from the SOEs. No matter how much the reformers emphasised the virtues of the new proposals, the workers were unwilling to put their 'iron rice bowls' at risk and were slow to co-operate. This meant that the intended reforms took far longer to implement than had been planned ... The government offered further concessions in the form of unemployment insurance, but 6 years later the scheme covered barely one-fifth of the 80 million employees in the SOEs.

Such resistance to new ideas did not prevent progress towards industrial modernisation, but it did slow it down.

Lynch, M. 2008. *The People's Republic of China, 1949–76.* London, UK. Hodder Education. p. 162. Lynch is a senior history lecturer at the University of Leicester, England.

SOURCE E

But this material progress, while real enough and certainly heartily welcomed by the Chinese people, was accompanied by social and psychic developments of epic proportions. The boom-and-bust cycles (officially known as 'overheating' and 'retrenchment') came quickly and sharply, bringing hardship and insecurity to much of the urban working population. Adding to the hardships, especially in the 'boom' phases of the cycles, were bursts of inflation, which became chronic after the partial implementation of 'price reform' in 1985 ... A working population buffeted by unruly market forces was shocked by the growth of obvious and grotesque inequalities in economic and social life. Between a monied elite of entrepreneurs and bureaucrats who profited lavishly from the 'free market' (and who were increasingly uninhibited in ostentatious displays of their new wealth in cities that were hastily spawning luxury boutiques and nightclubs), and a pauperized lumpenproletariat of migrant day laborers who lived in shanty towns, there was opened as wide a gulf between rich and poor as existed in any of the great cities of the capitalist world.

Meisner, M. 1991. *Mao's China and After: a History of the People's Republic.* New York, USA. The Free Press. pp. 473–74. Meisner is a professor of history at the University of Wisconsin-Madison, Canada.

11 Exam practice

Student answer

These sources give a mixed overview of how successful Deng was in achieving what he wanted from his economic reforms – which related to both agriculture and industry, and also involved greater trade with Western capitalist countries. In a way, any answer to this question depends not just on identifying his aims, but also on deciding what is meant by 'success'.

Examiner's comment
This is a brief and good introduction, showing a clear understanding of the topic and the question.

Source A, which identifies some of the many problems facing China and Deng's new government is the best place to start. In particular, it makes it clear that the aim was 'economic advances'. This is supported by Source B, which is from Deng himself – this is very useful as he sets out his aims. These were to 'focus on the modernization programme' and to 'develop the productive forces'. The main way this was to be done was via the 'Four Modernisations'. These were put forward by both Deng and Zhou Enlai in the 1970s – most recently by Zhou in 1975. An attempt had been made under Hua Guofeng, in his Ten-Year Plan, but this had run into problems. It had then been 'revised' by Deng in 1979, who then pushed the 'Four Modernisations' forward in both agriculture and industry.

Examiner's comment
There is good use of Sources A and B, and the use of some precise own knowledge, which is integrated in the answer.

Source C, which is a table of industrial production statistics for the period 1979–89, gives evidence that he had been successful in his aims – the growth rate of manufacturing output increased from 8.6% in 1979, to 18.1% in 1985. To this extent, then, it is possible to claim he was successful. These improved growth rates were achieved by a variety of policies, especially the setting up of Special Economic Zones on the coast, and by increasing trade with – and investments from – Western states. This is what he meant in Source B by 'opening up to the outside world'. Much of this was overseen by Zhao Ziyang, who had implemented such reforms in the province of Sichuan (where he was party secretary). As a result, Zhao was made premier by Deng, once Hau had been displaced.

225

Communism in Crisis

There were similar improvements in agriculture – especially once the Household Responsibility System was introduced as a way of 'de-collectivising' agriculture. This reform – which involved letting peasants have leases on commune land, in return for them agreeing to meet certain quotas – was undertaken mainly by Wan Li, one of Deng's closest supporters. Over the years, the length of leases was increased from 5 to 30 years. As a result, grain production rose from just over 300 million tonnes in 1978 to just over 400 million tonnes in 1989. At the same time, there was a great increase in small-scale industrial production in rural areas – mainly undertaken by 'Township and Village Enterprises' (TVEs), which were greatly expanded in the 1980s. Their output during this period increased by 35% a year, and they soon employed over 100 million people.

Examiner's comment
There is good understanding and clear use of Source C, which is linked to Source B. There is also plenty of sound and relevant own knowledge, which is integrated with assessment of the sources.

However, the overall picture is not one of total success. In Source C, it is clear that the rapid improvements in industry were not constant. From about 1984–85, production begins to decline – by 1989, it was almost half the figure for 1979. This is something that is mentioned in Source E, which talks about 'boom-and-bust' cycles, which seem to have begun in about 1985 – when, according to Source C, things began to slow down. Source D explains the problems as resulting from resistance to the reforms of SOEs on the part of the workers, who did not want to see their 'iron rice bowls' removed. These were the job security, and various other benefits (such as subsidised food prices and housing, and free health care), which industrial workers had been given in the past. Thus, as Source D notes, 'the intended reforms took far longer to implement than had been planned'. One example of this was that it was not until 1986 that the government was able to get a modified labour-contract scheme accepted – and even then, it only applied to new SOE workers.

In addition, another possible example of lack of success is the appearance of poverty and inequality mentioned in Source E. This source – apart from showing how inflation hit living standards – mentions 'grotesque inequalities' and refers to the creation of 'a pauperized lumpenproletariat of migrant day laborers' living in 'shantytowns'. This has to be seen as a failure – even according to Deng's aims: in Source B, Deng had said that socialism was meant to 'eliminate poverty', and that he wanted to achieve a 'comparatively comfortable standard of living by the end of the century'.

According to Source E, this seems a long way off – certainly, the gap between rich and poor has widened, with many people either having no job, or only low-paid insecure temporary employment. *As a result, there has been an increase in crime – and prostitution, which had been almost completely ended under Mao,* became a feature of Deng's new China.

Examiner's comment
Once again, there is a good synthesis of sources and some precise own knowledge, to produce a balanced assessment of the degree of success achieved by Deng's economic reforms.

Consequently, the answer to how successful Deng's economic reforms have been is a mixed one. If production figures are seen as the main indicator of success, then Deng's reforms have been mainly successful. Despite some slowdown in the mid 1980s, *China is now the second biggest economy in the world, and is predicted to become number one in about 2017.* However, if social aspects are taken into consideration then clearly many Chinese people have seen their living standards and quality of life decline. This has to be seen as a lack of success, as we have seen that Deng had said his reforms would remove poverty.

Overall examiner's comments

There is good and clear use of sources throughout, and constant integration of precise own knowledge to both explain and add to the sources. The overall result is a sound analytical explanation, focused clearly on the question. The candidate has done more than enough to be awarded Band 1 and the full 8 marks.

Activity

Look again at all the sources, the simplified markscheme, and the student answer above. Now try to write your own answer to this question – and see if you can make different points with the sources, and use different/additional own knowledge, to produce an answer that offers an alternative view.

Question 3

Using the sources *and* your own knowledge, analyse the reasons for the collapse of the Soviet Union in 1991. [8 marks]

SOURCE A

We are obviously not going to change the system of Soviet power or its fundamental principles … [but] we attach priority to political measures, broad and genuine democratization, the resolute struggle against red tape and violations of the law, and the active involvement of the masses in managing the country's affairs. All of this is directly linked to the main question of any revolution, the question of power … The perestroika drive started on the Communist Party's initiative, and the Party leads it … Hence we must – if we want perestroika to succeed – gear all our work to the political tasks and the methods of the exercise of power …When the command-economy system of management was propelled into existence, the soviets were somehow pushed back … This lessened the prestige of the soviets. From that moment the development of socialist democracy began to slow down. Signs appeared that the working people were being alienated from their constitutional right to have a direct involvement in the affairs of state.

Gorbachev, M. 1987. Perestroika: New Thinking for Our Country and the World. London, UK. HarperCollins. pp. 54–55 and p. 111.

SOURCE B

There were, in fact, considerable limitations upon the powers of the new President, extensive though they undoubtedly were. He could be impeached by a two-thirds vote of the Congress of People's Deputies; his ministerial nominations required the approval of the Supreme Soviet, which could force the resignation of the Cabinet as a whole if it voted accordingly; and he had himself to report annually to the Congress of People's Deputies upon the exercise of his responsibilities. Explaining his position to a gathering of miners in April 1991, Gorbachev pointed out that he had voluntarily surrendered the extraordinary powers of the General Secretary of the CPSU, powers which at that time were greater than those of any other world leader. Would he have done so if he had been seeking unlimited personal authority?

White, S. 1993. After Gorbachev. Cambridge, UK. Cambridge University Press. p. 67. White is a professor of politics at Glasgow University, Scotland.

SOURCE C

This cartoon from *Punch* magazine shows an indecisive Gorbachev as Humpty Dumpty, sitting on a crumbling wall

11 Exam practice

SOURCE D

Militant nationalism and republican separatism contributed enormously to the mounting chaos ... More importantly, it was nationalism and republican separatism that brought about the final dissolution of the Soviet Union and Gorbachev's removal from power at the end of 1991 ... We can now see that the Soviet federal system generated the potential for enormous conflict, first of all because its internal structure was extremely complex. And, secondly, because it was in the federal system that the old contradictions and tensions of the Soviet system were most precariously balanced ... As long as the central party-state authorities retained their coercive control over society it proved possible to prevent these contradictions and tensions from becoming unmanageable. However, once the reform process began to undermine the authority of central institutions, federal relations required much more careful and imaginative management than they actually received.

Unfortunately, Gorbachev's extraordinary complacency about, and insensitivity to, the 'nationality question', meant that he not only managed it very badly, he actually failed to manage it at all.

Walker, R. 1993. Six Years That Shook the World: Perestroika – The Impossible Project. Manchester, UK. Manchester University Press. pp. 164–67. Walker was a lecturer in Soviet and Russian Studies at the University of Essex, England.

SOURCE E

Yeltsin (standing, with raised fist) in Moscow in August 1991, opposing the attempted coup, with the Russian 'White House' in the background

Communism in Crisis

Student answer

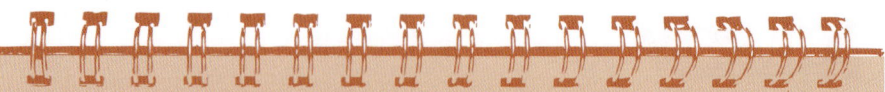

There were several reasons behind the collapse of the Soviet Union in 1991 – these include the impact of Gorbachev's various attempts at reform (such as perestroika, glasnost and demokratizatsiya), the problems of the Soviet economy (many of them long-standing), the rise of nationalism in the various Soviet republics, the role of individuals such as Yeltsin, the refusal of old-style communists to support or implement his reforms, and the mounting problems caused by attempting to achieve national security by trying to follow each new nuclear weaponry development by the US. The sources mention some, but not all, of these.

Examiner's comment
There is a clear understanding of the topic, and a good grasp of the factors involved in this introduction.

The most important reason for the collapse of the USSR was the weakness and relative backwardness of the Soviet economy compared to that of the USA – especially in relation to productivity and developments in computer technology. Furthermore, in industry, production of coal, gas and oil was declining. In addition, in agriculture – always the weakest sector of the Soviet economy – although production had increased since the 1970s, it was not enough, and the USSR had to import grain from the US and other capitalist countries. Under Khrushchev, GNP had risen by about 5% each year – but, by the time Gorbachev took over in 1985, the rate had declined to about 2% a year. It was clear that the Soviet economy was stagnating.

Examiner's comment
There is good use of relevant own knowledge, which is mostly precise, and focused on the question. However, so far, there has been **no reference to, or use of, any of the sources**.

Another important reason for the collapse of the USSR was that Gorbachev didn't always push his reforms hard enough (Source C). In part, this was because he met with a lot of opposition from hardline communists who wanted to retain the Stalinist system. Such people included Ligachev who, originally, had been a supporter of Gorbachev but who quickly became one of the conservatives opposed to his reforms. It was Yeltsin's attack on Ligachev in 1987 – in part for opposing the full implementation of the perestroika and glasnost policies (Source B) – that led to Gorbachev dismissing Yeltsin. This was a mistake, as it made Yeltsin into an enemy and rival. Many historians, such as Colton, argue that it was Yeltsin who, in the end, did much to break up the USSR once he became president of Russia in June 1991. It was some of these conservative hardliners who, in August 1991, tried unsuccessfully to overthrow Gorbachev in a coup – this allowed Yeltsin to increase his authority (Source E).

Examiner's comment
There is some more good use of relevant own knowledge, which is mostly precise, and focused on the question. However, so far, only three sources have been (briefly) referred to – and **none of them have been used**. In other words, the student has not used what the sources say/show to illustrate an argument or support a point.

11 Exam practice

Also important was the issue of nationalism (Source A). This played a crucial role – especially in the closing stages of the Soviet Union's existence. Especially important were the Baltic republics of Estonia, Latvia and Lithuania. These had always continued to resent their incorporation into the USSR in 1939, and were among the first to begin moves to secede from the Soviet Union. Along with this, Yeltsin began to push Russia's national interests. This made the other republics, who had resented Russian dominance for many years, decide to break away themselves. Significantly, it was Yeltsin who was the main architect of the Commonwealth of Independent States (with Ukraine and Belorussia), which replaced the USSR in December 1991. He even informed the US of his plans before telling Gorbachev.

Examiner's comment
There is, unfortunately, the same approach as before: some good use of relevant own knowledge, which is mostly precise, and focused on the question, but only the briefest mention of one source.

One of the reasons was the long economic war the USA (along with other capitalist nations) had waged against the USSR. This was part of what the historian Deutscher called the 'Great Contest', which had been going on since the Bolshevik Revolution of 1917. As the Russian economy was much weaker and smaller than the USA's, any expenditure on costly military equipment had a much more negative impact on the USSR than on the US. For instance, with a GNP about half of that of the USA's, the USSR had to spend double the proportion of its GNP just to match US developments. This is why the end of détente, and the start of a Second Cold War in 1979, was so significant – especially Reagan's 'Star Wars' project. In the end, Gorbachev came too late to prevent the nuclear arms race (almost always begun by the US) from 'busting' the Soviet economy.

Overall examiner's comments

There is good use of plenty of relevant own knowledge, which is mostly precise, and focused on the question. However, there are only a few – very brief – references to the sources, **and no use of sources**. Hence, as Paper 1 is mainly a source-based exam, this answer fails to get beyond Band 3.

Activity

Look again at the all sources, the simplified markscheme, and the student answer above. Now try to write a few paragraphs to push the answer up into Band 1, and so obtain the full 8 marks. As well as using all/most of the sources, and some precise own knowledge, try to integrate the sources with your own knowledge, rather than dealing with sources and own knowledge separately.

Paper 2 exam practice

Paper 2 skills and questions

For Paper 2, you have to answer two essay questions from two of the five different topics offered. Very often, you will be asked to comment on two states from two *different* IB regions of the world. Although each question has a specific markscheme, you can get a good general idea of what examiners are looking for in order to be able to put answers into the higher bands from the 'generic' markscheme opposite. In particular, you will need to acquire reasonably precise historical knowledge in order to address issues such as cause and effect, or change and continuity, and to learn how to explain historical developments in a clear, coherent, well-supported and relevant way. You will also need to understand and be able to refer to aspects relating to historical debates and interpretations.

Make sure you read the questions carefully, and select your questions wisely. It is important to produce a rough essay plan for each of your essays before you start to write an answer, and you may find it helpful to plan both your essays **before** you begin to write. That way, you will soon know whether you have enough own knowledge to answer them adequately.

Remember, too, to keep your answers relevant and focused on the question. For example, don't go outside the dates mentioned in the question, or answer on different individuals/states from the ones identified in the question. Don't just describe the events or developments – sometimes, students just focus on one key word or individual, and then write down all they know about it. Instead, select your own knowledge carefully, and pin the relevant information to the key features raised by the question. Also, if the question asks for 'reasons' and 'results', or two different countries/leaders, make sure you deal with **all** the parts of the question. Otherwise, you will limit yourself to half marks at best.

Examiner's tips

For Paper 2 answers, examiners are looking for clear/precise analysis, and a balanced argument, linked to the question, with the use of good, precise and relevant own knowledge. In order to obtain the highest marks, you should be able to refer, where appropriate, to historical debate and/or different historical interpretations or historians' knowledge, making sure it is relevant to the question.

Common mistakes

- When answering Paper 2 questions, try to avoid simply describing what happened. A detailed narrative, with no explicit attempts to link the knowledge to the question, will only get you half marks at most.
- If the question asks you to select examples from **two** different regions, make sure you don't chose two states from the **same** region. Every year, some candidates do this, and so limit themselves to – at best – only 12 out of the 20 marks available.

11 Exam practice

Simplified markscheme

Band		Marks
1	Clear analysis/argument, with very specific and relevant own knowledge, consistently and explicitly linked to the question. A balanced answer, with references to historical debate/historians, where appropriate.	17–20
2	Relevant analysis/argument, mainly clearly focused on the question, and with relevant supporting own knowledge. Factors identified and explained, but not all aspects of the question fully developed or addressed.	11–16
3	**EITHER** shows reasonable relevant own knowledge, identifying some factors, with limited focus/explanation – but **mainly narrative** in approach, with question only implicitly addressed **OR** coherent analysis/argument, but limited relevant/precise supporting own.	8–10
4	**Some limited/relevant** own knowledge, but **not linked effectively** to the question.	6–7
5	**Short/general** answer, but with very **little accurate/relevant knowledge and limited understanding** of the question.	0–5

Student answers

Those parts of the student answer that follow will have brief examiner's comments in the margins, as well as a longer overall comment at the end. Those parts that are particularly strong and well-focused will be highlighted in red. Errors/confusions/loss of focus will be highlighted in blue. This should help you understand why marks were – or were not – awarded.

Question

For what reasons, and with what results, did Deng Xiaoping oppose the demands of the Democracy Movement in the period 1976–89?
[20 marks]

Skill

Analysis/argument/assessment

Examiner's tip

Look carefully at the wording of this question, which asks for a **range** of reasons and results to be considered in relation to the Democracy Movement in China. Just focusing on one reason will not allow you to score the highest marks.

Student answer

While Deng was in favour of modernising the Chinese economy through his Four Modernisations policies, he was not in favour of introducing political democracy. Instead, he wanted to maintain a one-party state, with the CCP remaining in total control. He followed this policy throughout this period – eventually using the PLA to violently suppress protesting students in Tiananmen Square.

Examiner's comment
This is a brief introduction, with a little supporting own knowledge, which is connected to the topic – though, as yet, nothing explicit has been said about reasons or results.

Communism in Crisis

The pro-democracy movement in China really began in April 1976, with protests against the Gang of Four at the Qingming Festival, following the death of Zhou Enlai. Though Deng was initially blamed for these protests, and so lost influence again, he was soon back in power once the Gang of Four had been arrested. He allowed students to put up posters attacking the Gang (whose trials didn't begin until 1980) and, in 1978, allowed the creation of what became known as Democracy Wall. They were allowed to put up political 'big character' posters until an activist put up a poster which attacked Deng and called for the 'Fifth Modernisation' – democracy. Deng had the man arrested, and Democracy Wall was first moved, and then closed down at the end of 1979.

At this time, Deng was involved in removing Hua Guofeng and his supporters from positions of power. This was because Hua's Ten-Year Plan was running into problems, and Deng wanted to put his Four Modernisations into operation a different way. By 1980, Deng had managed to get his own supporters into position – such as Hu Yaobang and Zhao Ziyang.

Examiner's comment
There is some relevant supporting own knowledge about the beginnings of the Democracy Movement – but it is rather narrative-based. In addition, there is a section at the end of the paragraph that is not really relevant.

Things quietened down after 1979, but students and intellectuals began to raise demands for democracy again in the mid 1980s. This was partly because US president Reagan had made a speech in China in 1984, which had spoken about democracy – this had been unofficially translated and circulated amongst students. In 1986, the protests began to grow and were backed by dissident intellectuals such as Fang Jingsheng, who wrote an Open Letter demanding the release of political prisoners. The student demonstrations in university towns increased during early 1987 – and this time, they were joined by some workers. The workers were unhappy at this time because by 1985, the early success of Deng's economic policies had begun to fade – instead, many workers were facing falling living standards because of inflation, and many were becoming unemployed as their 'iron rice bowls' were being broken by Deng's economic reforms.

These intellectuals and student demonstrations had also been given some limited support by Hu Yaobang – as a result, he was dismissed as general-secretary, and replaced by Zhao Ziyang.

Examiner's comment
Again, there is some relevant and accurate own knowledge (but note the mistake over the intellectual who supported the student demonstrations in 1986–87 – he was Fang *Lizhi*; Wei Jingsheng was the author of 'The Fifth Modernisation'). However, there is also some more, largely irrelevant information on why some workers were prepared to join the protests – though it could have been made relevant by pointing out that Deng would have opposed this, because he feared dissatisfied workers allying with students, as was to happen on a much bigger scale in 1989. More worryingly, the approach is still essentially narrative-based. There are no explicit explanations of Deng's **reasons** for opposing demands for democracy. Some of the **results** are *described*, but they are not explicitly flagged up as results. Remember – always pay **close** attention to the wording of the question.

These protests of 1986–87 faded away after Hu's fall from power. However, in April 1989, Hu died unexpectedly – and this led to large demonstrations in support of him in Tiananmen Square. Intellectuals once again supported the students, who began to occupy the square. During April and May, these grew in size, with many calling for democracy. Demonstrations continued in Beijing – and elsewhere – and were not called off when Gorbachev came on an important official visit to China in mid-May. This was very embarrassing for Deng and the other Chinese leaders. Later that month, the students built a statue of freedom and liberty.

This led to a split in the CCP leadership, with most supporting Deng, who wanted to suppress them – especially as their protests were getting world coverage. However, Zhao – who at first had not been that much in favour of democracy – made comments sympathetic to the students' demands. Nonetheless, martial law was declared and, after first attempts by Beijing's troops to disperse the protesters failed, Deng brought in special troops from outside the capital. On 4 June, they fired on the students, killing an unknown number – this ended the Democracy Movement's protests.

Examiner's comment
This answer has continued along the same lines – relevant own knowledge (some of it quite precise), but still essentially an account of what happened.

After 4 June, many students and workers were arrested. While most of the students were released after a time, several of the workers who had joined their protests were executed. One reason for the failure of the Democracy Movement's protests was because they were themselves divided. So Deng was able to avoid having to introduce democratic political reforms, and he could continue with his economic policies.

Overall examiner's comments

This answer makes no real attempt to explicitly address either reasons or results – but there is plenty of precise/correct own knowledge. However, because the approach is almost entirely narrative, this supporting information has not been 'pinned' to the question. Consequently, the answer is not good enough to go higher than Band 3 – probably getting about 9 marks. To reach the higher bands, some **explicit focus on both reasons and results** is needed. Frustratingly, much of the information needed to do this well is already in the answer.

Also, for Band 1, you need to have some **mention of relevant specific historians/ historical interpretations** – there are several to choose from on this topic.

Activity

Look again at the simplified markscheme on page 233, and the student answer above. Now try to write a few extra paragraphs to push the answer up into Band 1, and so obtain the full 20 marks. As well as making sure you explicitly address **both** aspects of the question, try to integrate some references to relevant historians/historical interpretations.

Further information

Soviet Union and Eastern Europe

Ali, Tariq. 1988. *Revolution From Above*. London, UK. Hutchinson.
Brown, Archie. 1997. *The Gorbachev Factor*. Oxford, UK. Oxford University Press.
Deutscher, Isaac. 1985. *The Unfinished Revolution*. Oxford, UK. Oxford University Press.
Garton Ash, Timothy. 1993. *The Magic Lantern*. New York, USA. Vintage.
Gorbachev, Mikhail. 1987. *Perestroika*. London, UK. HarperCollins.
Halliday, Fred. 1986. *The Making of the Second Cold War*. London, UK. Verso
Hawkes, Nigel. (ed.) 1990. *Tearing Down the Curtain*. London, UK. Hodder & Stoughton.
Hosking, Geoffrey. 1992. *A History of the Soviet Union 1917–1991*. London, UK. Fontana.
Lane, David. 1985. *Soviet Economy and Society*. Oxford, UK. Basil Blackwell.
Lane, David. 1985. *State and Politics in the USSR*. Oxford, UK. Basil Blackwell.
Lane, David. 1992. *Soviet Society Under Perestroika*. London, UK. Routledge.
Laver, John. 1997. *Stagnation and Reform*. London, UK. Hodder & Stoughton.
Lewin, Moshe. 2005. *The Soviet Century*. London, UK. Verso.
Mandel, Ernest. 1989. *Beyond Perestroika*. London, UK. Verso.
McCauley, Martin. 1996. *The Soviet Union 1917–1991*. Harlow, UK. Longman.
Nove, Alec. 1993. *An Economic History of the USSR 1917–91*. Harmondsworth, UK. Penguin.
Service, Robert. 1997. *A History of Twentieth-Century Russia*. London, UK. Allen Lane/Penguin.
Stokes, Gale. 1993. *The Walls Came Tumbling Down*. New York, USA. Oxford University Press.
Tompson, William. 2003. *The Soviet Union Under Brezhnev*. Harlow, UK. Longman.
Trotsky, Leon. 1972. *The Revolution Betrayed*. New York, USA. Pathfinder Press.
Trotsky, Leon (ed.) Allen, Naomi and Saunders, George. 1980. *The Challenge of the Left Opposition (1926–27)*. New York, USA. Pathfinder Press.
Walker, Rachel. 1993. *Six Years That Shook the World*. Manchester, UK. Manchester University Press.
White, Stephen. 1993. *After Gorbachev*. Cambridge, UK. Cambridge University Press.

China

Benson, Linda. 2002. *China Since 1949*. Harlow, UK. Longman.
Bettelheim, Charles and Burton, Neil. 1978. *China Since Mao*. New York, USA. Monthly Review Press.
Ethridge, James 1990. *China's Unfinished Revolution*. San Francisco, USA. China Books & Periodicals.
Evans, Richard. 1997. *Deng Xiaoping and the Making of Modern China*. New York, UK. Penguin.
Gittings, John. 2006. *The Changing Face of China*. Oxford, UK. Oxford University Press.
Goodman, David. 1994. *Deng Xiaoping and the Chinese Revolution*. London, UK. Routledge.
Hsu, Immanuel. 1990. *China Without Mao*. Oxford, UK. Oxford University Press.
Lawrance, Alan. 2004. *China Since 1919*. London, UK. Routledge.
Lynch, Michael. 1998. *The People's Republic of China Since 1949*. London, UK. Hodder & Stoughton.
Meisner, Maurice. 1999. *Mao's China and After*. New York, USA. The Free Press.
Spence, Jonathan. 1999. *The Search for Modern China*. New York, USA. W. W. Norton.

Index

'571 Affair' 152

Abalkin Programme 84
absenteeism from work, USSR 34, 75
Afghanistan 38, 53, 57–61, 63, 118
Aganbegyan, Abel (b. 1932) 71, 73
agriculture
    in China 145, 150, 166, 168, 170–1, 177–8
    in the USSR 21, 23, 24, 28–9, 75, 77–8, 80
Albania 124
alcoholism 32, 34, 52, 75
All-Union government 84, 99
America *see* United States
American Prospect, The (journal) 85
Amnesty International 205
Andropov, Yuri (1914–84)
    the economy under 33–6
    historians on 63
    political developments 62–3
anti-Semitism 102, 104
anti-war demonstrations 61
April 5th Movement, China 156, 188
April Theses 93
Armenia 105
autarchy 20

Babeuf, François-Noël 213
Baikal-Amur Mainline (BAM) railway 27
Baruch, Bernard 11
Baryshnikov, Mikhail 94
'Beijing Spring' 200
Beijing Spring (magazine) 188
Berlin Wall 127, 128
'big character' posters 188
Biryukova, Alexandra 97
'black economy' 74
black market, USSR 76, 78
Bolsheviks, the 9
Brandt, Willi 54
Brezhnev, Leonid (1906–82) 20
    the Brezhnev Constitution 49–50
    'Brezhnev Doctrine' 12, 56, 119
    cult of personality 47
    the economy under 21–33
    historians on 47, 219
    invasion of Czechoslovakia 12
    political developments under 44–61
Britain
    and Hong Kong 173
    and Solidarity in Poland 124
    unemployment 82
Brown, Archie 110
Brzezinski, Zbigniew 38, 60
Bulgaria 129–30
Bush, President George 109, 110, 211

capitalism 11
Carter, President Jimmy (b. 1924) 38, 56, 60
CCP (Chinese Communist Party) 13, 14, 16–17, 144, 192–4, 201
Ceaușescu, Nicolae (1918–89) 130
censorship
    in China 166
    in the USSR 50–3, 96
Central Committee (CC), USSR 13
Central Intelligence Agency (CIA) 38, 53, 56, 211
central planning, USSR 78–80
CESC (Conference on European Security and Co-operation) 53
Chai Ling (b. 1966) 205
Charter 77, Czechoslovakia 132, 133
Chen Yun 198
Chernenko, Konstantin (1911–85) 33, 36–7
    political developments under 63–4

Chernobyl disaster 94
'Chicago School' 85
China University of Science and Technology (CUST) 194, 195
Chinese Communist Party (CCP) 13, 14, 16–17, 144, 192–4, 201
Christian Democrats, USSR 102
CIA (Central Intelligence Agency) 38, 53, 56, 211
CIS (Commonwealth of Independent States) 109
civil rights *see also* demonstrations
    censorship 50–3, 96, 166
    in China 188, 191
    freedom of speech 188, 191
    in the USSR 49–50, 107
civil war, in China 13–14
client states 12
coal production, USSR 29, 77
Cohen, Stephen 96
Cold War, the 11–12, 37–9
    Second Cold War 55–6, 117
collective farms 24, 28
    in China 171
    in the USSR 80
Comecon 56, 84, 211
Commission of Security and Co-operation in Europe (CSCE) 129
Commonwealth of Independent States (CIS) 109
communes, China 145
communism, definition of 14
Communist Party of the Soviet Union (CPSU) 12–13, 21, 44, 47, 49–50, 76, 92–3, 96, 97–103
Conference on European Security and Co-operation (CESC) 53
Congress of People's Deputies, USSR 99–102
Congress of Soviets 13
consumer goods
    in China 170, 175
    in the USSR 30–1, 75, 83
corruption
    in China 181–2, 189, 194
    in the USSR 47, 62, 63, 75
CPSU (Communist Party of the Soviet Union) 12–13, 21, 44, 47, 49–50, 76, 92–3, 96, 97–103
Crockatt, Richard 212
CSCE (Commission of Security and Co-operation in Europe) 129
cult of personality 47, 147
Cultural Revolution 148–50, 154
CUST (China University of Science and Technology) 194, 195
Czechoslovakia 12, 49, 54, 81, 131–7

Daniel, Yuri 52
Daniels, Robert 96
Darzhavna Sigurnost (DS) 129
de-collectivisation, China 178, 180
de-nationalisation, USSR 84
death penalty, USSR 51
Democracy Movement, China 188, 189, 200, 201, 203, 204, 205
'democracy salons', China 199
'Democracy Wall', China 188–9, 191
democratic centralism 15
Democratic Party, USSR 102
Democratic Reform Movement, USSR 102
Democratic Russia Election Bloc 101, 102
demokratizatsiya 91, 96–7, 121
demonstrations
    in Bulgaria 129
    in China 150, 156, 179, 189, 194–6, 197, 199–205
    in Czechoslovakia 134–7
    in East Germany 128
    in Hungary 125
    in Romania 130

Deng Xiaoping 14
    becomes vice-premier of the Council of State 153
    the economy under 165–82
    and the 'First Ten Points' 146
    political developments under 186–206
    purging of 150
    the Qingming Festival, 1976 156–7
    the rise of 158–9
    speech on democracy 215
    and the 'Whateverists' 160
détente 11, 12, 54–5
Deutscher, Isaac 11
'developed socialism' 48–9
'dictatorship of the proletariat' 48
dissidents
    in China 193, 195–6, 199–205
    in Eastern Europe 122, 129, 132
    in the USSR 50–3, 62–3, 95–6
divorce rates 32
Doctor Zhivago (Pasternak) 52
'Double Tenth' Revolution 174
Drach, Professor Marcel 81
DS (Darzhavna Sigurnost) 129
Dubček, Alexander 12, 56, 131, 134, 136

early Maoism 166
East Germany 25, 81, 126–8
Ecoglasnost 129
economic 'shock therapy' 85
economy
    in China 150, 163–82
    in the USSR 18–39, 67–86, 119
education
    in China 193, 196
    in the USSR 45, 52
elderly, the, pensions in the USSR 83
elections
    in China 153
    in the USSR 47, 91, 97, 98, 100, 104
embargoes 25
employment
    absenteeism 34, 75
    migrant labour force 180
    pensions 172, 180
    skilled labour shortages 28
    strikes 83, 124, 136, 198, 203
Engels, Friedrich (1820–95) 15
entropy 22
environmental impacts, China 178
Estonia 53, 78, 105
executive presidency, USSR 101–2

factory 'associations', USSR 30
famines *see* food shortages
Fang Lizhi (b. 1936) 195, 196, 199, 205
farming *see* agriculture
Federation of Democratic Youth (FIDESZ), Hungary 125–6
Federation of Socialist Clubs, Moscow 101
FIDESZ (Federation of Democratic Youth), Hungary 125–6
'Fifth Modernisation, The' 189–91
First Opium War (1839–42) 173
'First Ten Points' 146
Five-Year Plans
    in China 176
    in the USSR 20, 21, 22, 24, 27, 29, 75
food, subsidised prices 28
food shortages 9
    in China 165, 178
    in Poland 56
    in the USSR 32, 83
'Four Big Rights' 191
'Four Cardinal Principles' 191
Four Modernisations 154, 165, 167, 170–4, 190
'Four Olds,' the 149

Index

'free' market economy 175
freedom of speech, China 188, 191
Friedman, Milton 85
Fukuyama, Francis 212, 213

Galbraith, J. K. 85
Gang of Four, the 153, 154, 155, 157–8, 188
Gates, Robert 56
GDP (Gross Domestic Product)
    in China 168, 178
    in the USSR 37, 38
Geneva Conference (1988) 118
Georgia 104, 105
German Democratic Republic *see* East Germany
Germany, reunification of 123, 128
glasnost 91, 92, 94, 121
GNP (Gross National Product)
    in China 177
    in the USSR 37, 70, 77
'Goddess of Democracy and the Spirit of Liberty' 204
gold production, USSR 27
Gorbachev, Mikhail (b. 1931) 228
    Afghanistan 118
    attempted coup against 108–9
    and the 'Brezhnev Doctrine' 12
    Eastern Europe 118–39
    economy 68–86
    historians on 82, 110, 112, 120
    Malta Summit (1989) 211
    nationalist protests 53
    perestroika 76–82
    political developments 90–110
    rise to power 34, 36–7
    the Second Cold War 117
    visit to China 202
Gorbachevism 72–3
Gosagroprom (State Committee for the Agro-Industrial Complex) 79
Gosplan 20, 21, 35
'Great Contest' 11
Great Leap Forward, the (GLF) 145–8
Grishin, Victor 73, 100
Gromyko, Andrei 73
Gross Domestic Product (GDP)
    in China 168, 178
    in the USSR 37, 38
Gross National Product (GNP)
    in China 177
    in the USSR 37, 70, 77
Grósz, Károly 125, 126
guan dao ('official profiteers') 181
Gulag Archipelago, The (Solzhenitsyn) 52

Halliday, Fred 59
Havel, Václav (b. 1936) 132
Hayek, Friedrich 85
HDF (Hungarian Democratic Forum) 125
health care
    in China 172, 180, 197
    in the USSR 45, 52
Helsinki Accord 53, 126
Helsinki Act (1973) 55
Helsinki Final Act on Human Rights 129
Hobsbawm, Eric 138
Honecker, Erich (1912–94) 126, 127
Hong Kong Island 173
Hou Dejian 204
Hough, Jerry 96
Household Responsibility System (HRS) 166, 171
housing
    in China 172
    in the USSR 32, 52
HRS (Household Responsibility System) 166, 171

HSWP (Hungarian Socialist Workers' Party) 126
Hu Yaobang (1915–89) 100, 193, 196
Hua Guofeng (1921–2008) 155, 156, 157–60, 165–8
human rights *see* civil rights
Hundred Flowers campaign 144
Hungarian Democratic Forum (HDF) 125
Hungarian Socialist Workers' Party (HSWP) 126
Hungary 12, 57, 81, 125–6
    Hungarian Rising (1956) 33
hunger strike, China 201, 203
Husák, Gustáv (1913–91) 12, 131, 132, 133, 136

Iliescu, Ion 130
Independent Society for Human Rights (ISHR), Bulgaria 129
Independent Song Club, USSR 50
Industrial Responsibility System 172
industry
    in China 150, 165, 166–7, 172–4, 175–6, 178–80
    in the USSR 21, 22–3, 24, 27, 29–31, 34, 74, 75, 77, 78–80
infanticide, China 178
intellectuals
    in China 148
    in the USSR 50
Intermediate Nuclear Forces (INF) Treaty 117
International Students' Day rally, Czechoslovakia 134
Iron Curtain, the 211
'iron rice bowl' 176, 179
ISHR (Independent Society for Human Rights), Bulgaria 129
Izvestia (newspaper) 78

Jakeš, Miloš (b. 1922) 133
Jarulzelski, Wojciech (b. 1923) 57
Jews 53, 102, 104
Jiang Jieshi (1887–1975) 13
Jiang Qing (1914–91) 149, 153, 155, 157–8
Jiang Zemin 205
jihad (holy war) 58
Judaism *see* Jews

Kádár, János (1912–89) 12, 33, 125, 126
Kagarlitsky, Boris (b. 1958) 101
Karmal, Babrak 58, 59
Kennan, George 211
KGB (*Komitet gosudarstvennoy bezopasnosti*) 13, 33, 47, 62, 97
Khrushchev, Nikita (1894–1971)
    de-Stalinisation 17
    and 'developed socialism' 48–9
    economic reforms 21
    and nuclear arms 54
    overthrowing of 97
Kissinger, Henry 152
kolkhozy 24, 28
Komitet gosudarstvennoy bezopasnosti (KGB) 13, 33, 47, 62, 97
Kosygin, Alexei (1904–80) 21, 22, 23, 46, 54
Krenz, Egon (b. 1937) 128
Kryuchkov, Vladimir 108

labour shortages 28
land-lease contracts, China 178
Latvia 53, 105
Law on Individual Labour Activity (1986) 78
Law on Joint Enterprises (1986) 79
Lenin, Vladimir Ilyich (1870–1924) 9
    April Theses 93
    democratic centralism 15, 16
    on lack of culture 50
    and nationalism 10, 104–5

New Economic Policy 16, 77, 79
Leninism, definition of 15–16
Leninist practices 116
Lewin, Moshe 62
Li Peng (b. 1928) 196, 200, 201, 202, 204
'Li-Yi-Zhe' 194
Liberal Democratic Party, USSR 102
Ligachev, Yegor (b. 1920) 74, 97
Lin Biao (1907–71) 147, 151–3
Lin Binyan 196
Lippmann, Walter 11
Lithuania 105
'Little Red Book', the 147
Liu Shaoqi 145, 146, 150, 151
Liu Xiaobo 204
living standards
    in China 171, 198
    in the USSR 31, 52, 82–3

Macau 164, 173, 174
Malta Summit (1989) 211
Mandel, Ernest 109
Mao Yuanxin 154
Mao Zedong (1893–1976) 13, 14, 17, 144
    condemns the USSR 151
    Cultural Revolution 148–50, 154
    death of 155, 157
    and the death of Zhou 156
    demystification of 159
    on education 193
    and the Four Modernisations 154
    the Great Leap Forward (GLF) 145–8
    rift with Lin Biao 151–3
    Socialist Education Movement 145–7
    and the US 154
Maoism, definition of 16–17
Maples, David 110
'market' economies 84, 92
'market' mechanisms 169
martial law
    in China 202, 203–4
    in Poland 57
Marx, Karl (1818–83) 15, 50
Marxism 213
    definition of 15
Marxism–Leninism, definition of 16
May 4th Movement, China 174, 201
Mazowiecki, Tadeusz 124
media, in the USSR 94, 107
Medvedev, Roy (b. 1925) 62
Meisner, Maurice 165, 169, 181, 198
mental illness rates, USSR 32
migrant labour force, China 180
military expenditure, USSR 33, 39
MIRV (Multiple Independently Targeted Re-entry Vehicles) 55
Mladenov, Petar (1936–2000) 129, 130
modernisation, USSR 74
Moldavia 105
Moscow People's Front 101
Mujahideen 58, 60, 118

Nabokov, Vladimir 94
Nagy, Imre 12, 126
National People's Congress, China 174
nationalism, USSR 53, 106
NATO (North Atlantic Treaty Organisation) 13
Nazi–Soviet Pact (1939) 104
neo-authoritarianism 198
NEP (New Economic Policy) 79, 80
nepotism
    in China 179, 181, 193
    in the USSR 47
New Democratic Movement, USSR 106
New Economic Policy (NEP) 16, 79, 80
New March Front, Hungary 125
Nixon, President Richard 152, 154

Index

nomenklatura system 44–6, 73, 96
'normalisation' 131
North Atlantic Treaty Organisation (NATO) 13
novostroika 85
Novy Mir (magazine) 52
nuclear arms race 12, 37–8, 54, 55, 63, 116, 117
nuclear power disasters 94

Observer (newspaper) 71
'official profiteers' (*guan dao*) 181
oil crisis, USSR (1973) 24–6
oligarchs, Russian 85
'one-child policy', China 178, 181
'open door' policy, China 173, 179
Opposition Round Table, Hungary 126
Orlov, Yuri 53

Paris Commune 15
Party of Labour, USSR 101
Pasternak, Boris 52, 94
PDPA (People's Democratic Party of Afghanistan) 58–9, 118
Peng Dehuai 145
pensions, in China 172, 180
'People's Control' inspectorate, USSR 34
People's Daily (newspaper) 194, 200, 201
People's Democratic Party of Afghanistan (PDPA) 58–9, 118
People's Liberation Army (PLA) 14, 147, 203
perestroika 76–82, 93, 94, 121
PLA (People's Liberation Army) 14, 147, 203
Plastic People of the Universe 132
Podgorny, Nilokai (1903–83) 44, 45
Poland 30, 56–7, 124, 211
Politburo
  in China 14, 148, 159, 168, 194, 200, 202
  in the USSR 13, 30, 31, 34, 45, 74, 103
political developments
  in China 186–206
  in the USSR 42–64, 90–110, 116–39
political revolutions 122
Popov, Gavril 83
Pozsgay, Imre (b. 1933) 125, 126
'Prague Spring' 12, 49, 131
Pravda (newspaper) 34
Presidium, the, USSR 44
privileges, Soviet bureaucracy 45
protests *see* demonstrations
puppet states 12
purges
  in China 149, 151, 193, 196
  in the USSR 16

Qingming Festival, China 156

Reagan, President Ronald 12, 55, 63, 116, 117, 118, 194
Red Guards 149, 150
'reformist' elements, China 155
religious persecution *see* Jews
reunification, Germany 123, 128
'revisionist' 17
Romania 57, 130
Romanov, Grigori 73, 74
Roosevelt, President Franklin D. 73
RSDLP (Russian Social Democratic Labour Party) 9
RSFSR (Russian Socialist Federal Soviet Republic) 9–10
'Russian New Left' 62
Russian Orthodox Constitutional Monarchists 106
Russian Social Democratic Labour Party (RSDLP) 9
Russian Socialist Federal Soviet Republic (RSFSR) 9–10

Ryzhkov, Nikolai (b. 1929) 74, 77, 84

Sakharov, Dr Andrei (1921–89) 52, 53, 62, 95
SALT 1 talks 55
SARs (Special Administration Regions), China 173
satellite states 12
SDI ('Star Wars') 12, 63, 116
Second Cold War 55–6, 117
secret police force
  in Bulgaria 129
  in the USSR 13, 33, 47, 62, 97
SED (Socialist Unity Party of Germany) 126
Service, Robert 110
SEZs (Special Economic Zones), China 174, 179–80, 205
Shatalin Plan, the 84
Shelepin, Alexander 45
Shevardnadze, Eduard (b. 1928) 74, 106, 119
'Sichuan Experiment' 172
Sinyavsky, Andrei 52
skilled labour shortages, USSR 28
Slabakov, Petar 129
Snow, Edgar 151
social developments
  in China 171, 172, 180–1, 197
  in the USSR 31, 82–3
social wage 31
socialism 11
socialism in one country 16
'socialism with a human face' 56
socialist democracy 16, 17, 49
Socialist Education Movement, China 145–7
Socialist Party of Russia 101
Socialist Unity Party of Germany (SED) 126
SOE (State Owned Enterprise) 172, 176
Solidarity, Poland 30, 56–7, 124, 211
Solzhenitsyn, Alexander (1918–2008) 52
Soviet Communist Party of Bolsheviks 101
sovkhozy 24
Soyuz 106
space programme 12, 63, 116
Special Administration Regions (SARs), China 173
Special Economic Zones (SEZs), China 174, 179–80, 205
'stagnation' 22
Stalin, Joseph (1880–1953) 16
  ban on alternative political parties 9
  and China 14
  the Cold War 12
  collective farms 24
  and the Communist Party 13
  the economy under 20–1
  industrialisation 10
  Russification 104
Stalinism 49, 192
  definition of 16
Star Wars programme 12, 63, 116
'State Emergency Committee', USSR 108
State Owned Enterprise (SOE) 172, 176
steel production, China 167
'stinking ninth' the 193
Strategic Arms Limitation Treaty (START) 117
strikes
  in Britain 124
  in China 198, 203
  in Czechoslovakia 136
  in Poland 124
  in the USSR 83
Su Shaozhi 199
suicide rates, USSR 32
Supreme Soviet 13, 85
Supreme Soviet of the Russian Federation 106

Taiwan 173

Taliban, the 118
taxes
  in China 175
  in the USSR 80
'Ten Wasted Years', the 188
Ten-Year Plan, China 167–8
Thatcher, Margaret 124
'Thaw, the' 11
'Three Bitter Years,' China 145
Tiananmen Square demonstrations 150, 188, 189, 199–205
Township and Village Enterprises (TVEs), China 177–8
trade unions
  in China 179, 204, 206
  in Hungary 125
  in Poland 30, 56–7, 124, 211
  in the USSR 31, 83
Trotsky, Leon (1879–1940) 72, 87
  democratic centralism 15–16
  and Stalin's Russification 104
  warns of a revolution 93
Truman, President Harry S. 12
TVEs (Township and Village Enterprises), China 177–8
'Twenty-three Articles', the 148
'Two Whatevers', the 159–60

Ulbricht, Walter (1893–1973) 127
UN (United Nations) 173
unemployment
  in China 165, 180–1, 195, 197
  in the USSR 82
Union Treaty 105–6, 108
unions *see* trade unions
United Nations (UN) 173
United States
  and China 33, 154
  nuclear arms race 55
  role in the collapse of communism 211
  SDI ('Star Wars') 12, 63, 116
  and the USSR invasion of Afghanistan 60
  the Vietnam War 151
uskorenie 75

Velvet Revolution, Czechoslovakia 131–7
Vietnam War 151
Volkogonov, Dmitri 85, 110
VONS (Committee for the Defence of the Unjustly Prosecuted), Czechoslovakia 132

Wang Dan 201, 202, 205
Wang Hongwen 153, 157–8
Wang Ruoshui (1926–2002) 194, 196
Warsaw Pact 12, 13, 52, 121, 124, 138, 211
Wałęsa, Lech (b. 1943) 56–7
Wei Jingsheng (b. 1950) 189, 199
West Germany 54
work *see* employment
Wu Han 148
Wuer Kaixi 201, 202, 205

xiang 171

Yakovlev, Alexander (1923–2005) 74, 94, 106, 116
Yao Wenyuan 153, 157–8
Yeltsin, Boris (1931–2007) 84, 100, 105, 106, 108–9, 210
Yom Kippur War (1973) 25

Zaslavskaya, Tatiana (b. 1927) 73, 75
Zhang Chunqiao 153, 157–8
Zhao Ziyang (1919–2005) 160, 172, 193, 194, 196, 200, 201, 202, 203, 205
Zhivkov, Todor (1911–98) 129
Zhou Enlai (1898–1976) 144, 151, 153, 154, 155, 156

Acknowledgements

The volume editor and publishers acknowledge the following sources of copyright material and are grateful for the permissions granted. While every effort has been made, it has not always been possible to identify the sources of all the material used, or to trace all copyright holders. If any omissions are brought to our notice we will be happy to include the appropriate acknowledgement on reprinting.

Cold War International History Project (CWIHP), www.cwihp.org by permission of the Woodrow Wilson International Centre for Scholars: p. 59 (Source G) 'Minutes of the Meeting of the CPSU CC Plenum on the situation in Afghanistan, 23 June 1980,' RGANI, op. 14, d. 40, 11. 30, telegraphic copy, C; p. 124 (Source E) Memorandum by Lech Wałęsa, 'On Starting the Roundtable Talks,' 4 September 1988, Andrzej Stelmachowski Papers, translated by Jan Chowaniec.

Picture Credits

Cover Peter Turnley/Corbis; p. 5 Reuters/Corbis; p. 6 Topfoto/AP; p. 9 (t) Thinkstock/Getty Images; p. 9 (b) Library of Congress; pp. 10/11 Popperfoto/Getty Images; p. 13 (t) Matthew Trommer/Dreamstime; p. 13 (b) Wikipedia; p. 14 Pictorial Press Ltd/Alamy; p. 20 National Archives and Record Administration; p. 21 (t) National Archives and Record Administration; p. 21 (b) Yoichi R. Okamoto/LBJ Photo Library; p. 22 ITAR-TASS Photo Agency/Alamy; p. 25 © 2006 Topfoto.co.uk; p. 29 © 2005 Topfoto.co.uk/AP; p. 34 RIA Novosti archive, image #850809/Vladimir Vyatkin/CC-BY-SA 3.0; p. 38 (t) Shoe Cartoons; p. 38 (b) National Archives and Record Administration; p. 46 Popperfoto/Getty Images; p. 51 © Stern; p. 52 (t) RIA Novosti archive, image #25981/Vladimir Fedorenko/CC-BY-SA 3.0; p. 52 (b) Wikimedia Commons (Xpucmo); p. 55 RIA Novosti/Topfoto; p. 57 (l) Popperfoto/Getty Images; p. 57 (tr) David Fowler/Shutterstock; p. 57 (br) Wikimedia Commons; p. 60 Time & Life Pictures/Getty Images; p. 65 Topfoto.co.uk; p. 68 Gamma-Keystone via Getty Images; p. 72 Time & Life Pictures/Getty Images; p. 74 (t) Dmitry Rozhkov; p. 74 (b) Nick Parfjonov; p. 75 Robert D. Ward/US Department of Defense Media; p. 76 © TopFoto.co.uk; p. 81 © RIA Novosti/Topfoto.co.uk; p. 85 © David Horsey; p. 92 Kanstantsin Khatsyanouski; p. 95 Gamma-Rapho via Getty Images; p. 100 (l) www.kremlin.ru; p. 100 (r) AFP/Getty Images; p. 101 Jenya Demina; p. 109 AFP/Getty Images; p. 115 Peter Turnley/Corbis; p. 117 Popperfoto/Getty Images; p. 125 (t) Romanian National Archives; p. 125 (b) Vadas Róbert; p. 126 Bundesarchiv, Bild 183-R0518-182/CC-BY-SA; p. 127 Time & Life Pictures/Getty Images; p. 128 © Jeff Koterba/Omaha World-Herald; p. 129 Romanian National Archives; p. 132 (t) Haak78/Shutterstock; p. 132 (b) Yonas Media/The Plastic People; p. 135 AFP/Getty Images; p. 137 © Camera Press/B. Gysemburgh; p. 141 © Roger Hutchings; p. 144 (l) Wikimedia Commons; p. 144 (r) Getty Images; p. 147 (l) Camera Press/photographer?; p. 147 (r) Wikimedia Commons; p. 150 Popperfoto/Getty Images; p. 152 AFP/Getty Images; p. 153 Wikimedia Commons; p. 156 © Camera Press/GIP Photograph by Globe Photos, Camera Press London; p. 158 Henri Bureau/Sygma/Corbis; p. 167 AFP/Getty Images; p. 172 Topfoto.co.uk; p. 173 AFP/Getty Images; p. 175 AFP/Getty Images; p. 180 © Hans Reinhard/Corbis; p. 187 © Nicholas Garland; p. 189 AFP/Getty Images; p. 193 (t) © Julia Waterlow/Eye Ubiquitous/Corbis; p. 193 (b) Wikimedia Commons; p. 197 © Kevin Kallaugher; p. 200 © Peter Turnley/Corbis; p. 202 AFP/Getty Images; p. 204 AFP/Getty Images; p. 212 Doonesbury © 1988 G. B. Trudeau. Reprinted by permission of Universal Uclick. All rights reserved; p. 213 Library of Congress/Edmund Valtman; p. 219 Popperfoto/Getty Images; p. 220 © Stern; p. 228 Punch Limited; p. 229 AFP/Getty Images.

Produced for Cambridge University Press by

White-Thomson Publishing
+44 (0)843 208 7460
www.wtpub.co.uk

Series editor: Allan Todd
Development editor: Margaret Haynes
Reviewer: Neil Tetley
Project editor: Kelly Davis
Lead editor: Sonya Newland
Designer: Clare Nicholas
Picture researcher: Alice Harman
Illustrator: Stefan Chabluk